New Perspectives on Mixed Languages

Language Contact and Bilingualism

Editor
Yaron Matras

Volume 18

New Perspectives on Mixed Languages

From Core to Fringe

Edited by
Maria Mazzoli
Eeva Sippola

ISBN 978-1-5015-2094-5
e-ISBN (PDF) 978-1-5015-1125-7
e-ISBN (EPUB) 978-1-5015-1114-1
ISSN 2190-698X

Library of Congress Control Number: 2021935983

Bibliographic information published by the Deutsche Nationalbibliothek
The Deutsche Nationalbibliothek lists this publication in the Deutsche Nationalbibliografie;
detailed bibliographic data are available on the Internet at http://dnb.dnb.de.

© 2022 Walter de Gruyter Inc., Boston/Berlin
This volume is text- and page-identical with the hardback published in 2021.
Cover image: Anette Linnea Rasmus/Fotolia
Typesetting: Integra Software Services Pvt. Ltd.
Printing and binding: CPI books GmbH, Leck

www.degruyter.com

In memory of Pieter Muysken (1950–2021)

Contents

Maria Mazzoli and Eeva Sippola
Mixed languages: From core to fringe —— 1

Peter Bakker
Noun-Verb mixed languages: Similarities and differences —— 27

Jesse Stewart and Felicity Meakins
Advances in mixed language phonology: An overview of three case studies —— 57

Evangelia Adamou
How sentence processing sheds light on mixed language creation —— 93

Maria Mazzoli, Peter Bakker and Verna DeMontigny
Michif mixed verbs: Typologically unusual word-internal mixing —— 121

Isabel Deibel
VO vs. OV: What conditions word order variation in Media Lengua? —— 157

Katja Hannß
Linguistic manipulations in Kallawaya —— 189

J. Clancy Clements, Patrícia Amaral and Jordan Garrett
Social identity and the formation and development of Barranquenho —— 225

Eeva Sippola
Ilokano-Spanish: Borrowing, code-switching or a mixed language? —— 253

Elizabeth Herring Dudek and J. Clancy Clements
Jopara as a case of a variable mixed language —— 277

Nantke Pecht
Pronominal usage in *Cité Duits*, a Dutch-German-Limburgish contact variety —— 299

Erika Sandman
Wutun as a mixed language —— 325

Yaron Matras
Repertoire management and the performative origin of Mixed Languages —— 361

Subject Index —— 405

Language Index —— 407

Maria Mazzoli and Eeva Sippola
Mixed languages: From core to fringe

1 Introduction

Mixed languages present an intriguing type of language contact. They arise in bilingual settings, often as markers of identity or as secret languages, and they combine parts from different language families or branches, showing unique splits that challenge theories of genetic classification and contact-induced change. Thomason and Kaufman (1988) identified mixed languages as a type of contact language in its own right, and since then, research on mixed languages has grown into a subfield of contact linguistics (Bakker and Mous 1994; Matras and Bakker 2003). So far, around forty languages from diverse backgrounds have been identified as "mixed" (Meakins 2013: 161–164). However, the status of many varieties is unclear. This volume examines the current state of the theoretical and empirical debate on mixed languages and presents new descriptive advances from a diverse set of mixed language varieties. These cover well-known mixed languages, such as Media Lengua, Michif, and Kallawaya, and varieties whose classification is still debated, such as Barranquenho, Cité Duits, Jopara, and Wutun.

Split ancestry, change by deliberation, bilingualism, stability as a language and the degree of mixing have been proposed as defining factors for mixed languages. However, the debate on the existence of the category of "mixed languages" still continues today and centers around two questions (Auer 2014; Versteegh 2017). Should mixed languages be seen as a distinct category of unmixed languages with types of mixing that differ from ordinary cases of borrowing? Or are they extreme cases on a continuum where mixed languages are at one end and ordinary borrowing is at the other? The distinctiveness take on these issues sees mixed languages as a distinct category with structural mixing patterns and social contexts that differ from code-switching or ordinary borrowing (Bakker 1997, 2003: 142). The continuum view (e.g. Auer 1999, 2014; Croft 2003; Myers-Scotton 2003; Meakins 2011) posits no clear boundary between mixed languages and other languages and sees the question of distinctiveness as an issue of gradience and conventionalization of code-switching patterns. Cases where the path from code-mixing to a stable mixed language has been

Maria Mazzoli, University of Groningen, m.mazzoli@rug.nl
Eeva Sippola, University of Helsinki, eeva.sippola@helsinki.fi

documented are Gurindji Kriol (McConvell and Meakins 2005) and Light Warlpiri (O'Shannessy 2011).

A motivation for maintaining mixed languages as a typological category is that it captures some exceptional features of these languages, and therefore is of functional value for theories of language contact. Matras (2000, 2003) defined this exceptional character as the tendency for the new variety to acquire wholesale lexical items pertaining to a specific category (e.g. all stems, all nouns), and consequently, as the ability to borrow grammatical features otherwise highly resistant to borrowing, while Bakker (2003) places the emphasis on the quantity of borrowed items.

In this introduction, we want to clarify how to classify mixed languages within their category based on sociohistorical and typological definitions. We also want to explore how established cases differ from borderline cases, and how these differences inform the debate on gradience vs. distinctiveness. To answer these questions, we will offer an integrated typology of mixed languages based on sociohistorical and structural factors and present the issues that the chapters in this volume shed further light on. These include both structural and social factors conditioning mixing and cases at the fringe of the category of mixed languages, special cases of borrowing, and the mixing of closely related varieties.

2 Classification of mixed languages: Towards an integrated typology

2.1 Sociohistorical classification

Mixed languages are born in different sociohistorical circumstances. They are a product of the social situations of their speakers, and there is a general consensus that a severe social upheaval is an important factor in their formation. They typically emerge in situations of community bilingualism, for in-group communication and in relation to the expression of identity, reflecting either a new social category or an ancestral group membership, often as a conscious linguistic operation led by a group of speakers. Children of mixed marriages (Bakker 1997, 2017; Croft 2000) are a special case where a new cultural and linguistic identity is born. In these cases, men from one linguistic and cultural group and women from another come together, and their children form their own distinct identity in the mixed language. A well-known case is that of Michif (Bakker 1997) where children of Canadian French-speaking men and Algonquian women stabilized the mixed code. Another typical social situation is that of nomadic populations, where mixed languages are used to express a group feeling or an ethnic identity in special situations (Matras et al. 2007; Bakker 2017). In these cases, the mixed language rarely has full functional use, but is tightly connected to the language of the wider community. Recognized cases are those of the Para-Romani varieties.

Since information on the sociohistorical background of mixed languages has become more widely available, it became clear that there are two distinct groups of mixed languages. The first group is a result of (completed or interrupted) community *language shift* to a non-ancestral language,[1] as in the case of Angloromani, Ma'á, Oschideutsch, Mednyj Aleut, Gurindji Kriol, Old Helsinki Slang, and Light Warlpiri. In all these cases, the defining and diagnostic feature is that the language that the populations shifted to is the language providing the backbone structure, the matrix for the language mixing (Myers-Scotton 2002), also defined by Matras (2003) as the language providing the finite verbal inflection (INFL-language or predication grammar). In this group, the greater part of the lexicon, especially nominal, is provided by the heritage language of the community, or of a subgroup of the community. In these cases, the borrowing is happening from the ancestral language into the newly adopted language, although this may seem counterintuitive in some cases.

The second group includes languages that are the result of the *introduction of a non-ancestral language* into the repertoire of a community, but without a shift taking place, namely without the introduced language becoming the matrix language for the mixed variety. This is the case of Media Lengua, Michif, Bilingual Navajo, Okrika Igbo, and Kallawaya. In all these cases, the defining and diagnostic feature is that the language that provides the backbone structure is the ancestral language, while the bulk of the lexicon, especially nominal, comes from the introduced language. These cases where a non-ancestral language is introduced are similar to heavy borrowing. Clearly, languages with heavy borrowing are not the result of language shift, but rather of a contact situation where shift did not take place. For instance, in the case of Chamorro, the speakers borrowed elements of a colonial language into their Chamorro, and thus the language's structural profile has remained Austronesian while the Spanish (and today English) elements mostly concern items that have a prominent pragmatic role (e.g. Stolz 2003).

---

[1] There are different possible ways of defining the languages involved. These might highlight chronological differentiation (ancestral vs. introduced), identity aspects of the community or place (ethnic vs. non-ethnic; local vs. non-local), or language dominance at an individual or community level (L1 vs. L2).

These two sociohistorical profiles ("shift" and "massive introduction") correspond to two different directionalities of the borrowing process with respect to the ancestral and non-ancestral languages. Also, when discussing different types of language shift, it is important to clarify that we are dealing with a continuum where the shift away from the ancestral language does not necessarily take place in the whole community. In fact, at a certain point in time, the community shift may take the form of frequent and increasingly conventionalized practices of code-switching. Taking another perspective, the shift can be seen as the introduction of a non-ancestral language from a synchronic, situated perspective (cf. Adamou, this volume). However, in reconstructing the sociohistorical background of an autonomous mixed language or for the purpose of interpreting the mixing processes that shaped its synchronic make-up, it should always be possible to determine whether or not a shift took place in the community, or at least what language the community adopted as a matrix for the mixed variety. It should also be possible to connect this piece of sociohistorical information with the observed structures of the mixed variety.

2.2 Structural classification

From the structural point of view, the languages that have been traditionally labeled as mixed present a typological variation that cannot be predicted from the sociohistorical contexts in which they emerged or continue to be spoken (Matras 2000). The structural classifications proposed by Bakker (2003, 2017) and Muysken (2008: 211–226) show as well that languages from both sociohistorical profiles conform to one general structural typology (cf. also Meakins and Stewart forthcoming). The structural typology differentiates two groups, (a) languages presenting a Grammar-Lexicon (G-L) split, also called a lexical/functional split or "intertwined" (Bakker 1994); and (b) mixed lexicon (with mixed structure) languages that present a variation of Noun-Verb (N-V) splits. We will now present the structural and sociohistorical profiles of four languages that serve as prototypical examples in our classification.

Mixed languages with a *G-L split* have grammatical morphemes and a general predication structure from one language, and stems or free lexical morphemes from a different language. Examples of this group include Ma'á and Angloromani pertaining to the socio-historical group of languages that have undergone shift, and Media Lengua and Bilingual Navajo from the group of massive introduction.

Ma'á is the language of the Ma'á or Mbugu people, in the Usambara mountains in Tanzania. Ma'á, also known as Inner Mbugu, is essentially a manipulated variety of Normal Mbugu, a Bantu language very similar to Pare. Mous (2003: 1) considers Normal and Inner Mbugu to be one language with two parallel lexicons. The Ma'á or Mbugu people are culturally and physically different from the other Bantu populations of the region, as they are the descendants of a Southern Cushitic-speaking group who migrated to the Usambara mountains and shifted to a Bantu language (probably Pare). Ma'á uses a lexical reservoir from the ancestral Cushitic language, developed in order to reverse language shift and resist assimilation to the Bantu language. The mixed variety shows a grammar using Bantu patterns and matter (in boldface), while the lexical roots are mainly Southern Cushitic, with elements from Pare and some from Maasai. The lexical manipulation found in Ma'á is similar to that found in Angloromani and to that of many urban youth languages and jargons (e.g. Old Helsinki Slang).

(1) *hé*-ló   *mw*-agirú   *é*-sé-*we*   *kimwéri* dilaó   *w-a*   (Ma'á)
    hé-na   *m*-zima   *é*-tang-*we*   *kimwéri* *m*-fumwa *w-a*   (Mbugu)
    16-have   1-elder   1-call-PST.PF   Kimweri   king   1-CON

    yá   *i*-dí   *l-á*   *lusótó*   (Ma'á)
    i-i   *i*-sanga   *l-á*   *lusótó*   (Mbugu)
    this   5-land   5-CON   Lushoto
    'There was an elder called Kimweri, king of this land Lushoto' (Mous 2003: 9)

Media Lengua is spoken in Highland Ecuador. It probably arose in relation to an expression of hybrid identity as Indigenous populations did not fully identify with either their ancestral language, Quichua, nor the introduced language, Spanish. It was formed quickly and deliberately by Quichua-Spanish bilinguals. Today, it is spoken by bilinguals alongside Quichua and/or Spanish. Media Lengua's make-up is rather unique: it reproduces the structure of the ancestral language and makes use of Quichua's bound functional morphemes (in boldface), over 90% of its lexical roots are from the introduced language Spanish.

(2) Mujer-*ka*   madera-*ta*   casa-*man*   lleva-*n*   (Media Lengua)
    Warmi-*ka*   kaspi-*ta*   wasi-*man*   apa-*n*   (Quichua)
    woman-TOP   wood-ACC   house-to   take-3SG
    La mujer lleva la madera a casa.   (Spanish)
    'The woman is carrying the wood home' (Deibel, this volume)

In comparison, languages with a mixed lexicon present a *N-V split* or other structural dichotomies. Examples include Mednyj Aleut and Gurindji Kriol (3) from the socio-historical group of languages that have undergone shift, and Okrika-Igbo and Michif (4) from the group of massive introduction.

Gurindji Kriol in northern Australia originated from contact between Aboriginal Gurindji people and new settlers. The mixed language represents an attempt to maintain an ancestral language under severe cultural pressure from Kriol, given that most Aboriginal groups in the region have completely shifted to Kriol. Gurindji Kriol arose from the crystallization of code-switching insertional practices of ancestral Gurindji noun phrases in a predication structure based on Kriol, the introduced language. One original feature of Gurindji Kriol is the productivity of both the Kriol-derived verbal morphology and the Gurindji-based nominal morphology. In (3), the Gurindji ergative marker -*tu* combines with an English noun, and TMA markers of Kriol origin combine with a lexical verb of Gurindji origin, which are both rather common possibilities in the language.

(3)   **man(-tu)**   i   bin   **jarrwaj**   (im)   dat   guana   **karnti-yawung**
       man-ERG   3SG   PST   spear   3SG   the   goanna   stick-PROP
       'the man speared the goanna with a stick' (Meakins and O'Shannessy 2010: 1697)

Michif is also a N-V mixed language with a mixed grammar. It has its roots in the mixed marriages between Indigenous women that were speakers of Algonquian languages and French-Canadian fur traders. Notwithstanding the European ancestry, the Metis communities identified as Indigenous. The mixed variety emerged as an affirmation of original identity and power, during the long political struggle between the Indigenous populations of the North American Plains and the British/Canadian settlers. Today Michif is spoken as an autonomous language, and most of its speakers are not fluent in either Metis French or Cree. The following example of Michif illustrates a prototypical N-V mixed language, where the complex noun phrases from the introduced language Metis French are inserted into the structure derived from the ancestral language Plains Cree (in boldface):

(4)   **Maaka**   li   darie   zhornii,   **anima**   la
       but   DEF.M.SG   last   day.M.INAN   that.INAN   DEF.F.SG
       maezooñ   **kaa-kii**-li-rent-ii-**yaan**,   ma   klee
       house.F.INAN   CNJ-PST-the-rent-AI-CNJ.1S   POSS   key.F.INAN
       gii-doo-meek-in   **kiihtwam**
       1.PST-go-give.AI-IND.1SG   again
       'But the last day, that house I rented, I went there again to give back my key' (Mazzoli 2019: 113)

2.3 An integrated typology

The combined sociohistorical and structural classification can be represented as a four-cell table (Table 1) that corresponds to the classification proposed by Muysken (2008: 212). The presence of prototypical cases defines poles in a continuum of mixing practices. Here, languages are described as non-prototypical if their splits are less clearly defined or because the sociohistorical background of shift or maintenance is less straightforward.

Table 1: An integrated typology of sociohistorical and structural features in mixed languages.

		Sociohistorical type	
		Shift	**Massive introduction**
Structural type	G-L	Ma'á	Media Lengua
		Angloromani, Caló Català, Kallawaya, Lekoudesch, Old Helsinki Slang, Oschideutsch, Shelta	Bilingual Navajo, Chindo, Javindo, Petjo
	N-V	Gurindji Kriol	Michif
		Light Warlpiri, Mednyj Aleut, Reo Rapa	New Tiwi, Okrika Igbo

The type "G-L shift" includes languages that have an entire matrix (i.e. form and function of both noun phrase [NP] and verb phrase [VP] inflection [INFL]) from the introduced language, as in Ma'á. They result from the wholesale manipulation of lexical roots taken from the ancestral language. Typical examples of this class are ex-nomadic varieties (e.g. Shelta), lexical reservoir registers of an ancestral language in the process of attrition (Angloromani, Caló Català, Oschideutsch), secret languages (Kallawaya) and urban jargons (Old Helsinki Slang). The great majority of the so-far known mixed languages can be classified under this class. Most of them are spoken as a register of their matrix source language. When this is the case, diachronically, G-L shift languages may emerge from a gradual corrosion of available functional elements and grammatically productive morphemes from the ancestral language (cf. Adiego 2012 for Caló Català; Matras et al. 2007: 14, 25 for Angloromani).

The type "N-V shift" includes languages that have VP INFL from the introduced language that the community has shifted to, like in Gurindji Kriol. The NP INFL is borrowed from the ancestral language. Typical examples are mixed varieties that emerged in situations of interrupted shift to an introduced language to avoid language loss (Mednyj Aleut, Reo Rapa), or emergence of new identities that do not match the introduced or the ancestral language (Light Warlpiri). In the prototypical scenario, the community has shifted to the introduced language and speak it alongside the mixed variety (Gurindji Kriol), but non-prototypical scenarios include non-concluded or interrupted shift to the introduced language (e.g. Light Warlpiri, O'Shannessy 2006). This class presents more diversity in terms of patterns of grammatical and lexical mixing, and the source of lexical verbs and nouns may or may not align to the source of the respective inflection. For example, Gurindji Kriol and Light Warlpiri differ in that verbs and verbal inflection are almost always derived from Aboriginal English/Kriol in Light Warlpiri, while VP-internal mixing is common in Gurindji Kriol (i.e. Gurindji stems and Kriol TMA marking, as in [3]). Furthermore, some languages in this class present less prototypical N-V INFL splits. For example, Reo Rapa resulted from an interrupted shift to Tahitian and has verbal inflection from both Tahitian and Old Rapa, based on the phonological shape of the stem (Walworth 2017). Moreover, although prototypically VP and NP INFL coincide with these aspects of the source languages in both form and function, some mixed languages depart from this picture. In Mednyj Aleut finite verbal morphology differs considerably from that of Russian as a result of a simplification of the verbal inflectional paradigm (Sekerina 1994: 27).

The type "G-L massive introduction" includes languages that have an entire matrix (i.e. form and function of both NP and VP INFL) from the ancestral language, like in Media Lengua. They are the mirror image of what found in the G-L shift type. They result from the wholesale manipulation of lexical roots taken from the introduced language. There are rather few attested examples of this class, and they probably have the most intriguing and unusual triggering factors at the sociolinguistic level, being in many cases fully deliberate creations. Bilingual Navajo can be included in this class, although it represents a less prototypical case, as not all the Navajo stems are replaced by the English ones. In addition, it seems that Ilokano-Spanish (Sippola, this volume) and the Indonesian varieties Petjo (Malay grammar with Dutch lexicon), Javindo (Javanese grammar with Dutch lexicon), Chindo or Peranakan Chinese (Javanese grammar with Malay lexicon) would fall within this class.

The type "N-V massive introduction" includes languages that have an VP INFL from the ancestral language, like in Michif. The NP INFL is borrowed from the introduced language. Typical examples of this type are mixed varieties related to the emergence of a new identity. Michif is prototypical in this class because introduced (Metis French) NP INFL is used with introduced noun roots, while ancestral (Plains Cree) VP INFL is used mostly with ancestral stems (although Mazzoli, Bakker and DeMontigny [this volume] analyze occurrences of verb stems from Metis French, the introduced language). Other languages in this class have less prototypical splits. For example, in New Tiwi, Tiwi-derived verb inflection is partly reduced and innovative with respect to Traditional Tiwi, and the majority of verb stems are from English (cf. Bakker, this volume). Okrika Igbo can also be seen as less-prototypical case in this class, despite some difficulties in establishing the sociohistorical background and the source of its nominal grammar. Finally, languages like Chamorro, Tetun Dili and other heavy borrowers could be classified within this class if they had borrowed more grammar from the introduced language.

One of the defining criteria for mixed languages is that they have an evident split in the source of their morphemes' form. Prototypical mixed languages are those which combine typologically distant varieties, where the split is immediately visible. Non-prototypical cases include languages with two closely related varieties as their source, like Barranquenho (Clements, Amaral, and Garrett, this volume) and Cité Duits (Pecht, this volume). In these cases, it is often difficult to distinguish the origin of many lexical roots and functional morphemes and to define a matrix from one specific source variety. Clements, Amaral, and Garrett (this volume) present data from Barranquenho spoken in a predominantly Portuguese-speaking area with mainly Portuguese lexicon and multiple Spanish-derived morphosyntactic features. This analysis would place Barranquenho among G-L mixed languages resulting from massive introduction (of Portuguese lexicon into a Spanish matrix). Moreover, the sociolinguistic factors determining the mixing support classifying Barranquenho as a mixed language: the motivation for retaining prominent morphosyntactic features from Spanish was not lack of access to Portuguese but rather a deliberate affirmation of hybrid identity.

"Converted languages" present a special case, where the "mixing occurs below the level of the form" (Meakins 2013: 216). Bakker (2017: 221) labels them Frame-Root (F-R) mixed languages because they adopt the typological frame (F) from one source language, but all the lexical and/or functional roots (R) from another source language (cf. the distinction between pattern and matter, Matras and Sakel 2007). In the attested cases, this is the result of a long-lasting process of convergence, called "metatypy" (Ross 1996), that is the restructuring of a language's typological configuration in intense, prolonged contact situations. Known examples of converted languages are Sri Lanka Malay, Sri Lanka Portuguese, Takia (Meakins 2013: 164; Bakker 2017: 222), and Wutun (Sandman, this volume). Sociohistorically, converted languages emerge when the ancestral language maintains its lexicon but its morphosyntax undergoes restructuring due to contact with an introduced language. They are not the product of language shift, but rather of gradual convergence and community bilingualism. It is unclear to what degree converted languages conform to the criteria used for defining mixed language creation. Their mixing occurs below the level of the form, and several sources can be identified for their structural make-up, but it is debatable whether they are conscious, deliberate creations. Sandman (this volume) offers important insights on Wutun from a mixed language perspective.

3 Lexical manipulation and phrase insertion

Mixing processes responsible for the formation of mixed languages can be divided into lexical manipulation and phrase insertion. Lexical manipulation creates mixed languages of the G-L structural type and phrase insertion (or insertional code-mixing) originates the N-V structural type.

Lexical manipulation plays a role in language mixing especially after shift to a new language. It does not require full bilingualism and can occur when knowledge of one of the languages is limited. In mixed language formation, it means the wholesale manipulation of content-full stems. Therefore, in cases involving lexical manipulation, the creation of G-L mixed language is indeed a matter of quantity in the number of the manipulated items. This is the typical case of most mixed languages, e.g. G-L split secret languages, such as Kallawaya, or G-L split due to retention of ethnic lexicon after shift, such as Para-Romani varieties, Oschideutsch, and Ma'á. Matras (2000) uses the term "lexical re-orientation" when the ancestral language anchors the predication and the introduced language is the source for the lexical manipulation, as in the case of Media Lengua and Bilingual Navajo, and the term "selective replication" to refer to cases where the socially dominant language anchors the predication and a parallel lexical reservoir from the ancestral language is used for the mixed variety, as in Angloromani or Ma'á.

Especially in the case of retention of an ethnic lexicon after shift, borrowed forms carrying inflection marking can trigger the borrowing of certain grammatical categories or morphemes, which become productive in the mixed variety either at the level of the language system (psychological availability of the grammatical morphemes), or even in production of new coinages. However, in many cases, the productivity of the alleged borrowed grammatical forms is uncertain (e.g. some Romani morphology in Angloromani or Caló Català), or unlikely due to the typology of the languages involved (e.g. Okrika Igbo, given the absence of segmentally-realized bound morphology in the Okrika noun phrase borrowed into the Igbo frame). This also opens to a continuum between lexical manipulation and phrase insertion.

Phrase insertion is conventionalized and stable intra-sentential code-switching. In mixed language formation, phrase insertion triggers the borrowing of grammatical features from the embedded language into the structural frame of the matrix language (e.g. the productive use of the feminine gender in coding borrowed English nouns in Michif, Sammons 2019: 231–234). In mixed language formation, as well as in less extreme contact situations, the borrowing of lexical or phrasal material from the non-matrix language concerns first of all contentfull items. In the case of a "massive introduction" from a non-matrix language without intention to shift, the borrowing of lexical items or phrases concerns primarily nouns, as in other borrowing situations (cf. section 5). Here the status of "mixed" depends on the degree of productivity, or on the amount of available, nominal grammar from the introduced language. Grammatical borrowing and the productive use of inflection from the non-matrix language determine a "matrix ambiguity" in the fused lect, which determines how structures are mixed. In the context of balanced bilingualism, mixed language creation by phrase insertion may involve "a transitional period of ambiguity in the default construction of the utterance" (Matras et al. 2007: 143). This ambiguity is a pivotal stage in the formation of mixed languages presenting a variation of the N-V split, and it has been connected to sociohistorical circumstances determining a matrix language turnover (Myers-Scotton 1998).

4 The matrix language

Different criteria can be used to identify a matrix language in a multilingual production. Matras (2000) identifies the matrix with the language that provides the finite verbal inflection. McConvell and Meakins (2005: 18–19), in their analysis of the code-switching practices in the formation of Gurindji Kriol, identify the matrix as the language that supplies a clause's TMA markers or inflection morphology, auxiliaries, and pronominal enclitics. However, Myers-Scotton (2002) attributes the inflection morphology marking agreement in both the verb and the noun phrases to the matrix language, as these phrases establish the relationship between an argument and a verb. In Myers-Scotton's model, pronouns also belong to the matrix, but other types of morphemes, such as plurals or nominal classification morphology, are often predicted to belong to the non-dominant, embedded language. Prolonged bilingualism brings about a deeper interaction between the matrix and the embedded language. Within the embedded noun phrase, this may lead to the extensive use of functional elements, such as articles, and outcomes not in line with the matrix in the case of feature clashes, as in the case of gender assignment (Fuller and Lehnert 2000).

In most mixed languages, it is possible to identify a coherent matrix language. It is straightforward for the G-L languages whether or not they result from a shift. On the other hand, identifying a matrix can be more difficult for the N-V languages, as they show a greater degree of structural mixing. Although this holds for the whole group of N-V languages, the degree of matrix ambiguity appears greater in those languages that resulted from shift and in conditions of more balanced bilingualism. This reflects an extraordinary tension between shift and maintenance, and/or specific identity claims. The following analysis explains the continuum of grammatical mixing among the known mixed languages presented by Meakins (2013: 179).

In mixed languages, a single matrix language seems to be the source of finite verb inflection, word order, and pronouns (cf. Tables 2–5 presenting linguistic aspects related to an ideal matrix language for 12 mixed languages). These features thus constitute a coherent definition and diagnostic for identifying a matrix language in mixed languages, even if information on the social history is not available. This holds true for the less structurally mixed languages (G-L), like Media Lengua (Quichua matrix), but also for more structurally mixed languages. Predictably, nominal inflections, demonstratives, and determiners often come from the embedded language, especially in N-V mixed languages after shift, like in Gurindji Kriol and Light Warlpiri. Mixed language formation often happens in situations of maintenance of an ancestral language after shift, and the social factors pushing in the direction of reclaiming an ancestral identity are often strong enough to motivate the retention of ancestral

Table 2: Grammar-Lexicon languages after massive introduction.

	Media Lengua	**Bilingual Navajo**
Verb inflection or TMA marking	Quichua	Navajo
Word order	Quichua (main source)	Navajo
Personal pronouns or markers	Spanish	Navajo
Negation	Quichua and Spanish	Navajo
Demonstratives	Spanish	–
Noun inflection	Quichua	Navajo
Articles and other determiners	Spanish	–
Phonology	Quichua	Navajo
source	(Deibel, this volume; Stewart 2011)	(Schaengold 2004)

Table 3: Grammar-Lexicon languages after shift.

	Angloromani	Ma'á	Old Helsinki Slang	Kallawaya
Verb inflection or TMA marking	English	Pare	Finnish	Quichua
Word order	English	Pare	Finnish (?)	Quichua
Personal pronouns or markers	English (replaced Romani ones)	Cushitic	Finnish	Quichua
Negation	Romani	Pare	Finnish	Opaque and Quichua
Demonstratives	Romani	Cushitic (vague resemblance)	Finnish	Opaque (but not Quichua)
Noun inflection	English and Romani	Pare	Finnish	Quichua
Articles and other determiners	English (replaced Romani determiners)	Cushitic (possessive)	Finnish	Quichua (Pukina)
Phonology	English (convergence is documented)	Pare	Finnish and Finland Swedish consonants and phonotactics, Finnish vowels	Quichua
source	(Matras et al. 2007)	(Mous 2003)	(Jarva 2008)	(K. Hannß p.c.)

Table 4: Noun-Verb languages after massive introduction.

	Michif	New Tiwi	Okrika Igbo
Verb inflection or TMA marking	Plains Cree	Tiwi	Igbo
Word order	Plains Cree	Innovative (restructured typology)	Igbo
Personal pronouns or markers	Plains Cree	Tiwi	Igbo

Table 4 (continued)

	Michif	New Tiwi	Okrika Igbo
Negation	Plains Cree	?	?
Demonstratives	Plains Cree	Tiwi	Igbo
Noun inflection	Metis French	?	Okrika (but mixed prepositional phrases)
Articles and other determiners	Metis French (but mixed possessive forms)	?	No articles as in Igbo
Phonology	Plains Cree	?	Mixed
source		(Lee 1987; McConvell 2008)	(Wakama 1999)

Table 5: Noun-Verb languages after shift.

	Gurindji Kriol	Light Warlpiri	Mednyj Aleut
Verb inflection or TMA marking	Kriol	Kriol	Russian (but simplified)
Word order	Kriol	Kriol	Innovative
Personal pronouns or markers	Kriol	Kriol and Warlpiri	Russian
Negation	Kriol	Kriol	Aleut and Russian
Demonstratives	Gurindji and Kriol	Warlpiri	Aleut and Russian
Noun inflection	Gurindji and Kriol	Warlpiri	Aleut
Articles and other determiners	Kriol	–	Aleut and Russian (mixed forms in possessives)
Phonology	Gurindji	Mixed?	Mixed (contradictory evidence on reciprocal assimilation)
source	(McConvell and Meakins 2005; Meakins and O'Shannessy 2010; Meakins 2011; Stewart and Meakins, this volume)	(O'Shannessy 2006, 2011)	(Golovko and Vakhtin 1990; Sekerina 1994)

grammar and for using it productively. Full bilingualism and access to the ancestral language permit the insertion of full phrases, but attrition in the ancestral language results in cases of lexical manipulation. Instead, when N-V mixed languages emerge by massive borrowing from an introduced language, like in Michif, the social factors that push mixing are often tied to the birth of a new identity. This factor is less common among the known mixed languages and apparently less likely to trigger productive grammatical borrowing from the introduced language.

On top of the triad of verb inflection, word order, and pronouns, other structural features and functional elements, such as discourse markers and conjunctions, contribute to determining a clear language matrix, even in extreme cases of language mixing. Alignment of negation and phonology with the matrix is contradictory (Table 2–5). Irrespective of the type of mixed language, negation can pattern against the matrix frame, as in Media Lengua, Angloromani and Mednyj Aleut, but also in Kumzari (Anonby 2014) and Javindo (Winford 2013: 377). Matras (2003: 156) notes that negators, as well as existentials, have high referential value and propositional saliency, which is why they pattern against the matrix, especially if the mixed code serves as a secret register. Many non-experimental accounts of the phonology of mixed languages argue for a mixed phonology, stratified according to the source languages of the lexemes (e.g. Wakama 1999: 42 for Okrika Igbo; Sekerina 1994 for Mednyj Aleut; Papen 2017 and van Gijn 2009 for Michif). Stewart and Meakins (this volume) present experimental evidence in support of the fact that the phonology of mixed languages is fundamentally based on that of the ancestral languages, irrespective of the source of the matrix. This applies to Michif (N-V massive introduction), Gurindji Kriol (N-V shift), and to Media Lengua (G-L massive introduction). In the case of Michif and Media Lengua, the phonology aligns with the matrix, but not in the case of Gurindji Kriol. Interestingly, known cases of G-L shift mixed languages like Angloromani have a phonology based on the introduced language, in alignment with the matrix (cf. Matras et al 2007: 20). Therefore, the mismatch between the matrix and the phonology in Gurindji Kriol may have to do with the level of access to the introduced language the community has shifted to. Further analysis of N-V mixed languages that emerged after shift may contribute to our understanding of social factors shaping mixed language formation, especially in relation to the mixed language phonology.

From superficial observation of linguistic evidence alone, it has been difficult to draw the line between an incomplete shift to a new language and a massive introduction of lexicon and structure from an introduced language By combining the sociolinguistic information available and the structural cues expected to point to a matrix language (source of verb inflection, TMA marking in the verb phrase, personal pronouns, and word order, cf. Matras 2000), we are able to reconstruct in what direction the borrowing took place.

5 Structural borrowing and mixed languages

In mixed languages, borrowing processes are often extreme: in addition to structural elements that come with lexical insertions and free functional elements, rare cases of borrowing are also attested (Matras 2003). In general, typological factors conditioning the mixing of specific language pairs are connected to the structural properties and the typological distance between the languages in question (McConvell and Meakins 2005; Winford 2010).

The borrowing of structural items is also known from heavy borrowing languages. However, both in mixed and other languages, the productivity of the alleged borrowed grammatical forms, such as inflectional affixes (Seifart 2015), and structural categories is often uncertain (cf. some Romani morphology in Angloromani or Caló Català; Romance items in Chamorro and Tetun Dili, Stolz 2003). In addition, the difference between heavy borrowing and mixed languages can be observed in that mixed languages also borrow grammatical (nominal) features, including contextual inflection, from the embedded language (cf. Gurindji case marking in Gurindji Kriol, French sex-based gender in Michif), exhibit structural features that are innovative with respect to both source languages (cf. Media Lengua negation strategies, Stewart 2011; Michif mixed possessive forms, Rosen and Souter 2009: 60), and/or exhibit features of wholesale manipulation of the content-full items (cf. Media Lengua, Kallawaya).

Structural borrowing is constrained by factors related to the degree of integration, abstract semantic value and transparency (Moravcsik 1978; van Hoot and Muysken 1994; Field 2002; Mithun 2012). In general, thus, nouns and other open-class items are more amenable to borrowing than closed-class items, derivational morphology is borrowed more easily than inflectional morphology (Singh 1982; Muysken 2000), and inherent inflection is borrowed more frequently than contextual, syntactically relevant inflection, e.g. agreement (Gardani 2008). For example, Bakker (this volume) and Mazzoli, Bakker and DeMontigny (this volume) show that the indivisibility of the verb or the noun have an effect on the structural outcome of some N-V mixed languages. If a functional item is tightly connected to its main root (e.g. indivisible morphology, cohesion as to tone and vowel harmony), and thus less available for separation and replacement, it can be retained even if the overall structural setup seems to point towards a different matrix language. Although these principles seem to apply for languages in general, some of the accommodation strategies are typologically rare, even when looking at other contact languages. It has also been proposed that speakers of head-marking verb-coding languages retain the verbal elements from their first language, while speakers of dependent-marking noun-coding languages retain the nominal elements (McConvell 2008: 200). Bakker (this volume) points out that these processes seem to include simplification as well, at least in the case of New Tiwi.

The borrowing of inflectional morphology is generally limited to cases of dialect contact and close typological fit between the languages involved (Winford 2010: 176; Thomason 2015: 42). In addition, complete inflectional paradigm borrowing has been viewed as a defining feature of mixed languages (Thomason and Kaufman 1988; Matras and Bakker 2003), e.g. in the case of the entire English inflectional paradigm in Angloromani, as well as the Bantu grammatical frame in Ma'á, or the Russian-derived finite verbal paradigm in Mednyj Aleut (e.g. Golovko and Vakhtin 1990). However, considering these cases as examples of "borrowing" is misleading, as in all cases the shift has already happened. Vakhtin (1998) argues that in Mednyj Aleut specific mixing has emerged once the mixed community, who had shifted to Russian, re-introduced Aleut after it was partially lost (cf. also Auer 2014: 302). Russian being the language of the predicate structure, Aleut items are borrowed into Russian, and Russian-derived finite inflection can no longer be said to be borrowed or copied into Mednyj Aleut. Similarly, in Ma'á, a shift to Pare, a Bantu language providing verbal and nominal inflection in Ma'á, had already happened (Mous 2003). Here, a process of lexical manipulation re-introducing Cushitic lexicon into a Bantu frame is done to re-affirm a partially lost ancestral identity. Again, the Bantu grammar in Ma'á is not borrowed. Likewise, in Angloromani and other Para-Romani varieties English inflection is proof of a completed shift to English. In this case, Romani lexicon and variably productive nominal inflection are retained in an effort to reconnect to the Romani ethnic identity (Matras 2015: 72). Notwithstanding this solid evidence, mixed languages continue to be cited as rare cases of complete paradigm borrowing, associated to the formation of G-L or N-V mixed languages (Pakendorf 2009; Meakins 2011: 63; Gardani 2012: 75; Seifart 2013; Gardani, Arkadiev and Amiridze 2015: 11).

Also, interesting evidence regarding borrowed inflection is emerging from mixed languages. Gurindji Kriol shows borrowing of contextual inflection, the most uncommon case of grammatical borrowing (Meakins 2011). Clements and Luís (2015) illustrate a case of exceptional morphological borrowing in Korlai Indo-Portuguese, which borrowed a Marathi non-finite verb form to create a new inflectional class, specifically for integrating loan verbs. The Korlai case appears to be surprisingly similar to Michif, where the French infinitive marker -*er* accommodates English loans to form animate intransitive Michif verbs

(Mazzoli, Bakker and DeMontigny, this volume). In addition, in Greek Thrace Romani (Adamou and Granqvist 2015; Adamou, this volume), Muslim Roma speakers regularly draw on Turkish verb inflection when using Turkish-derived lexical verbs. Unintegrated inflected Turkish verbs are inserted into a Romani dominant speech where Romani verbs and nouns inflect with Romani inflection and the word order is Romani. The split in verbal morphology shows evidence of a typologically rare case of borrowing. However, in these cases inflectional morphology is replicated along with lexical word forms from the same language and the diffusion of inflection into other lexicon is blocked (cf. compartmentalization by Matras 2015: 67; parallel system borrowing by Kossmann 2010; paradigm transfer by Adamou 2012). Matras (2015) proposes that the borrowing of inflection is dispreferred in contact situations, since inflection anchors the predication to a coherent language frame and grants it integrity and stability (see Thomason 2015 for a different view in reference to mixed languages). The overviewed cases in the use of verbal inflection are motivated by special social conditions of mixed language formation, where communities are "re-negotiating language boundaries, which in turn is part of a process of re-negotiating identity" (Matras 2015: 76).

6 Sociolinguistic motivations

Of the sociolinguistic motivations in mixed language formation, new identity marking, recuperation of an ancestral connection, and a need for camouflage and secrecy are often mentioned (Meakins 2013: 181; Bakker 2017: 244). An act of identity (LePage and Tabouret-Keller 1985) is a useful concept when explaining some cases, such as Barranquenho, Ilokano-Spanish, Michif, Romani varieties, Cité Duits, and Media Lengua. A mixed group uses the mixed variety to signal a new ethnic identity or to differentiate themselves from the speakers of the ancestral and/or introduced language (cf. Muysken 1981; Bakker 1997; Croft 2003). However, the application of this factor to mixed languages spoken by Aboriginal groups, such as Light Warlpiri and Gurindji Kriol, is problematic, as their identity remains aligned with the Aboriginal identity (Meakins 2008; Bakker, this volume). The same could be argued for Wutun, whose speakers align with the Tibetan community (Sandman, this volume). In some cases, the new identity is born out of mixed marriages and reflect a gendered division between the languages (Bakker 1997 for Michif; Sandman, this volume for Wutun; Dudek Herring and Clements, this volume for Jopara), but this is not always the case (e.g. Romani varieties, Barranquenho, Kallawaya). The recuperation of an ancestral connection (cf. the U-turn hypothesis, Sasse 1992; Boretzky and Igla 1994;

Vakhtin 1998) happens in cases of shift towards an introduced language where the group deliberately attempts to reclaim its ancestral identity (e.g. Angloromani, Ma'á). Secrecy is a way of excluding outsiders from understanding, used especially for in-group communication and ritual and secret languages. In general, consciousness and deliberation are central in signaling a distinct identity or for creating secrecy for a code. All in all, the diversity of situations presents no single, cohesive sociolinguistic motivation for mixed language formation beyond motivations related to in-group communication and deliberation (Meakins 2013: 181; Thomason 2003) and responses to shift.

The level of access to the languages involved includes different degrees of bilingualism in situations of shift a new language and in language loss and attrition. The roles of the different languages that participate in the formation of mixed languages are sociolinguistically diverse, ranging from limited presence in the community to full bilingualism, and from language shift to language maintenance situations. Bilingualism is thus tightly connected to variation, as is not necessarily equal for the whole community, as also shown in Dudek Herring and Clements (this volume). These are thus necessary conditions, but they alone do not explain the outcome (Versteegh 2017: 222; Bakker, this volume). An integrated typology, as proposed here, combining both structural and sociolinguistic factors is needed to explore processes and factors of mixed language formation.

7 Conventionalization

The analysis of multilingual contexts in which some kind of conventionalized mixing already plays a role is of great interest with regard to social and structural motivations for mixed language formation. For example, Dudek Herring and Clements (this volume) show that the degree of conventionalization in Jopara differs according to one's communities of practice and can be sensitive to factors of register and style. The same could be said about Tetun Dili, although the overall degree of Portuguese borrowings is lower despite the diglossic situation involving both Tetun (Dili) and Portuguese. Regarding structural motivations, if code-switching is a common practice in a community, it might lead to a preference for code-switching in a certain structure. This specific pattern, be it insertional or alternational, will conventionalize with time and may start functioning as a way of inserting specific utterances that become automated (Backus 2003: 255). Conventionalization is thus a mechanism that is needed for code-switching or borrowing patterns to stabilize.

Adamou (this volume) shows with the Romani-Turkish example that fused lects represent a dynamic stage in the continuum from language mixing to stable mixed languages where certain mixing patterns have become conventionalized. Turkish Romani is characterized as a fused lect stage in mixed language formation (cf. Auer 1999). Structural exceptionality is shown in the fact that Muslim Roma from Greek Thrace insert unintegrated inflected verbs into Romani dominant speech. Experimental studies on Romani-Turkish mixing show no difference as to the processing costs of sentences that reflect the established patterns in the community – the mixing has thus become conventionalized. The socially dominant language in the community is Turkish, although the shift to Turkish contrasts with strong tendencies of Romani language maintenance in the community.

Light Warlpiri has probably been formed through a similar process (Meakins and O'Shannessy 2010; O'Shannessy 2012). In the Australian case intergenerational transmission permitted the formation of a stable mixed language, after adults consistently engaged in a baby talk register which included code-switching into English using English verbal structures. McConvell and Meakins (2005) describe a comparable scenario for the formation of Gurindji Kriol from code-switching practices involving Gurindji and Kriol. It is not clear if this scenario also applies to the formation of New Tiwi (Lee 1987: 355; Bakker, this volume), as suggested by Meakins (2014: note 10).

Conventionalization is not necessarily uniform but happens in different degrees and phases for different levels and compartments of the language system, according to the sociolinguistically conditioned language use in the community. This is shown, for example, by the experiments on compartmentalized Turkish verbs and the stable pronoun paradigm of Cité Duits with conventionalized forms (Adamou, this volume; Pecht, this volume). Similarly, although varieties of Media Lengua or Jopara show differing degrees of structural features from Spanish, this is not the case for the conservative Imbabura variety (Deibel, this volume) or rural varieties of Jopara (Dudek Herring and Clements, this volume). Especially in cases of larger communities, defining a variety as a mixed language or a code-switching variety should be carefully established for subsections of the community (Dudek Herring and Clements, this volume). In addition, variation in mixing patterns and their degree of conventionalization across a community can make it challenging to establish a variety or a sample clearly on a continuum from borrowing to code-switching of a mixed language. Jopara being a case in point from a larger community, while an example of a historical text is studied in the Ilokano-Spanish case (Sippola, this volume). If the mechanisms and processes involved in mixed languages are indeed similar to other language contact situations, this is not surprising.

8 Core to fringe

This volume presents studies on prototypical and non-prototypical mixed languages in our integrated typology. Of the uncontroversial cases, Media Lengua is an example of G-L massive introduction, Michif of N-V massive introduction, and Gurindji Kriol of N-V language after shift. In addition, Kallawaya is an example of G-L shift language, although its use is confined to a secret code. Less prototypical languages in the classification include Turkish Romani from the G-L shift group, Light Warlpiri and Mednyj Aleut from the N-V shift group, Ilokano-Spanish and Barranquenho from the G-L massive introduction and New Tiwi and Okrika Igbo from the group of N-V massive introduction. However, the splits in these languages do not show a perfect match with the prototypical case or their sociohistorical background is more complex. Some other cases are more difficult to classify. Wutun, for example, shows a high degree of structural mixing of at least three languages, without a clear split between the grammatical subsystems or between the lexical and the grammatical domains. It is here classified as a converted language and placed outside the typology. Similarly, Barranquenho and Cité Duits are born out of contact of closely related varieties, and due to the structural (and sometimes lexical) proximity of the languages in contact at the time of formation of the new variety, it is difficult to ascertain the origins of certain structures. For heavy borrowers, such as Chamorro and Tetun Dili, the degree of mixing is not sufficient.

This selection of studies highlights existing trends in mixed languages and relative implicatures which shed light on the linguistic and social forces at play in the emergence and development of mixed languages. The first chapters of the volume focus on the characteristics of mixed languages and the processes involved in their formation. The following chapters include case studies on particular varieties and the motivations behind their use and formation. Non-prototypical cases and different types of linguistic mixtures are also discussed. The final chapter proposes a performative account of mixed language formation. These themes shed light on the nature and characteristics of mixed languages, the social, grammatical, and cognitive mechanisms behind language mixing, and the role of mixed languages in the larger theorizing about language contact.

Abbreviations

3	third person
ACC	accusative
AI	animate intransitive
CNJ	conjunct
CONN	connective
DEF	definite
ERG	ergative
F	feminine
INAN	inanimate
INFL	inflection
IND	indicative
M	masculine
NP	noun phrase
PF	perfective
PROP	proprietive
PST	past
SG	singular
TOP	topic
VP	verb phrase

References

Adamou, Evangelia. 2012. Verb morphologies in contact: Evidence from the Balkan area. In Martine Vanhove, Thomas Stolz, Aina Urdze & Hitomi Otsuka (Eds.), *Morphologies in contact*, 143–162. Berlin: De Gruyter.

Adamou, Evangelia & Kimmo Granqvist. 2015. Unevenly mixed Romani languages. *International Journal of Bilingualism* 19(5). 525–547.

Adiego, Ignasi-Xavier. 2012. Catalan Romani (caló català) in the work of Juli Vallmitjana: An initial appraisal. *Zeitschrift für Katalanistik* 25. 305–320.

Anonby, Christina van der Wal. 2014. Traces of Arabian in Kumzari. In Orhan Elmaz & Janet C.E. Watson (eds.), *Languages of southern Arabia*, 137–146. Oxford: Archaeopress.

Auer, Peter. 1999. From codeswitching via language mixing to fused lects: Toward a dynamic typology of bilingual speech. *International Journal of Bilingualism* 3(4). 309–332.

Auer, Peter. 2014. Language mixing and language fusion: When bilingual talk becomes monolingual. In Juliane Besters Dilger, Cynthia Dermarkar, Stefan Pfänder & Achim Rabus (eds.), *Congruence in contact-induced language change*, 294–336. Berlin: De Gruyter.

Backus, Ad. 2003. Can a mixed language be conventionalized alternational codeswitching? In Yaron Matras & Peter Bakker (eds.), *The mixed language debate: Theoretical and empirical advances*, 237–270. Berlin: Mouton de Gruyter.

Bakker, Peter. 1994. Michif, the Cree-French mixed language of the Métis buffalo hunters in Canada. In Peter Bakker & Maarten Mous (eds.), *Mixed languages: 15 case studies in*

language intertwining, 13–33. Amsterdam: Institute for Functional Research into Language and Language Use.
Bakker, Peter. 1997. *A language of our own: The genesis of Michif, the mixed Cree-French language of the Canadian Métis*. New York: Oxford University Press.
Bakker, Peter. 2003. Mixed languages as autonomous systems. In Yaron Matras & Peter Bakker (eds.), *The mixed language debate: Theoretical and empirical advances*, 107–150. Berlin: Mouton de Gruyter.
Bakker, Peter. 2017. Typology of mixed languages. In Alexandra Y. Aikhenvald & R.M.W. Dixon (eds.), *The Cambridge handbook of linguistic typology*, 217–253. Cambridge: Cambridge University Press.
Bakker, Peter & Maarten Mous (eds.). 1994. *Mixed languages: 15 case studies in language intertwining*. Amsterdam: Institute for Functional Research into Language and Language Use.
Boretzky, Norbert & Birgit Igla. 1994. Romani mixed dialects. In Peter Bakker & Maarten Mous (eds.), *Mixed languages: 15 case studies in language intertwining*, 35–68. Amsterdam: Institute for Functional Research into Language and Language Use.
Clements, Clancy J. & Ana R. Luís. 2015. Contact intensity and the borrowing of bound morphology in Korlai Indo-Portuguese. In Francesco Gardani, Peter Arkadiev & Nino Amiridze (eds.), *Borrowed morphology*, 219–240. Berlin: John Benjamins.
Croft, William. 2000. *Explaining language change: An evolutionary approach*. Harlow: Longman.
Croft, William. 2003. Mixed languages and acts of identity. An evolutionary approach. In Yaron Matras & Peter Bakker (eds.), *The mixed language debate: Theoretical and empirical advances*, 41–72. Berlin: Mouton de Gruyter.
Field, Fred W. 2002. *Linguistic borrowing in bilingual contexts*. Amsterdam: John Benjamins.
Fuller, Janet & Heike Lehnert. 2000. Noun phrase structure in German-English codeswitching: Variation in gender assignment and article use. *International Journal of Bilingualism* 4(3). 399–420.
Gardani, Francesco. 2008. *Borrowing of inflectional morphemes in language contact* (European University Studies XXI Linguistics 320). Frankfurt am Main: Peter Lang.
Gardani, Francesco. 2012. Plurals across inflection and derivation, fusion and agglutination. In Lars Johanson & Martine I. Robbeets (eds.), *Copies versus cognates in bound morphology*, 71–97. Leiden: Brill.
Gardani, Francesco, Peter Arkadiev & Nino Amiridze. 2015. Introduction. In Francesco Gardani, Peter Arkadiev & Nino Amiridze (eds.). *Borrowed morphology*, 1–23. Berlin: Mouton de Gruyter.
Golovko, Evgenij V. & Nikolai B. Vakhtin. 1990. Aleut in contact: The CIA enigma. *Acta Linguistica Hafniensia* 72. 97–125.
Jarva, Vesa. 2008. Old Helsinki Slang and language mixing. *Journal of Language Contact* 1(2). 52–80.
Kossmann, Maarten. 2010. Parallel system borrowing. Parallel morphological systems due to the borrowing of paradigms. *Diachronica* 27(3). 459–487.
Lee, Jennifer. 1987. *Tiwi today: A study of language change in a contact situation*. Canberra: Pacific Linguistics.
LePage, Robert B. & Andrée Tabouret-Keller. 1985. *Acts of identity: Creole-based approaches to language and ethnicity*. Cambridge: Cambridge University Press.
Matras, Yaron. 2000. Mixed languages: A functional-communicative approach. *Bilingualism· Language & Cognition* 3(2). 79–99.

Matras, Yaron. 2003. Mixed languages: Re-examining the structural prototype. In Yaron Matras & Peter Bakker (eds.), *The mixed language debate: Theoretical and empirical advances*, 151–175. Berlin: Mouton de Gruyter.

Matras, Yaron, 2015. Why is the borrowing of inflectional morphology dispreferred? In Francesco Gardani, Peter Arkadiev & Nino Amiridze (eds.), *Borrowed morphology*, 47–80. Berlin: De Gruyter.

Matras, Yaron, Hazel Gardner, Charlotte Jones & Veronica Schulman. 2007. Angloromani: A different kind of language? *Anthropological Linguistics* 49(2). 142–184.

Matras, Yaron & Jeanette Sakel. 2007. Introduction. In Yaron Matras & Jeanette Sakel (eds.), *Grammatical borrowing in cross-linguistic perspective*, 1–13. Berlin & New York: Mouton de Gruyter.

Matras, Yaron & Peter Bakker. 2003. *The mixed language debate: Theoretical and empirical advances*. Berlin: Mouton de Gruyter.

Mazzoli, Maria. 2019. Michif loss and resistance in four Metis communities (Kahkiyaaw mashchineenaan, "All of us are disappearing as in a plague"). *Zeitschrift für Kanada-Studien* 69. 96–117.

McConvell, Patrick. 2008. Mixed languages as outcomes of code-switching: Recent examples from Australia and their implications. *Journal of Language Contact* 2(1). 187–212.

McConvell, Patrick & Felicity Meakins. 2005. Gurindji Kriol: A mixed language emerges from code-switching. *Australian Journal of Linguistics* 25(1). 9–30.

Meakins, Felicity. 2008. Land, language and identity: The socio-political origins of Gurindji Kriol. In Miriam Meyerhoff & Naomi Nagy (eds.), *Social lives in language*, 69–94. Amsterdam: John Benjamins.

Meakins, Felicity. 2011. *Case marking in contact: The development and function of case morphology in Gurindji Kriol*. Amsterdam: John Benjamins.

Meakins, Felicity. 2013. Mixed languages. In Peter Bakker & Yaron Matras (eds.), *Contact languages: A comprehensive guide*, 159–228. Berlin: De Gruyter Mouton.

Meakins, Felicity. 2014. Language contact varieties. In Harold Koch & Rachel Nordlinger (eds.), *The languages and linguistics of Australia. A comprehensive guide*, 365–416. Berlin: De Gruyter.

Meakins, Felicity & Carmel O'Shannessy. 2010. Ordering arguments about: Word order and discourse motivations in the development and use of the ergative marker in two Australian mixed languages. *Lingua* 120(7). 1693–1713.

Meakins, Felicity & Jesse Stewart (forthcoming). Mixed languages. In Salikoko Mufwene & Ana María Escobar (eds.), *Cambridge handbook of language contact*. Cambridge: Cambridge University Press.

Mithun, Marianne. 2012. Morphologies in contact: Form, meaning and use in the grammar of reference. In Martine Vanhove, Thomas Stolz, Aina Urdze & Hitomi Otsuka (eds.), *Morphologies in contact*, 143–162. Berlin: De Gruyter.

Moravcsik, Edith. 1978. Universals of language contact. In Joseph H. Greenberg (ed.), *Universals of human language*, 94–122. Stanford: Stanford University Press.

Mous, Maarten. 2003. *The making of a mixed language: The case of Ma'á/Mbugu*. Amsterdam: John Benjamins.

Muysken, Pieter. 1981. Halfway between Quechua and Spanish: The case for relexification. In Arnold Highfield & Albert Valdman (eds.), *Historicity and variation in creole studies*, 52–78. Ann Arbor: Karoma.

Muysken, Pieter. 2000. *Bilingual speech. A typology of code-mixing*. Cambridge: Cambridge University Press.
Muysken, Pieter. 2008. *Functional categories*. Cambridge: Cambridge University Press.
Myers-Scotton, Carol. 1998. A way to dusty death: The matrix language turnover hypothesis. In Lenore and Whaley Lindsay (eds.), *Endangered languages: Language loss and community response*, 289–316. Cambridge: Cambridge University Press.
Myers-Scotton, Carol. 2002. *Contact linguistics: Bilingual encounters and grammatical outcomes*. Oxford: Oxford University Press.
Myers-Scotton, Carol. 2003. What lies beneath. Split (mixed) languages as contact phenomena. In Yaron Matras & Peter Bakker (eds.), *The mixed language debate: Theoretical and empirical advances*, 73–106. Berlin: Mouton de Gruyter.
O'Shannessy, Carmel. 2006. *Language contact and children's bilingual language acquisition: learning a mixed language and Warlpiri in Northern Australia*. Sydney: University of Sydney dissertation.
O'Shannessy, Carmel. 2011. Young children's social meaning-making in a new mixed language. In Ute Eickelkamp (ed.), *Growing up in central Australia: New anthropological studies of Aboriginal childhood and adolescence*, 131–155. New York: Berghahn.
O'Shannessy, Carmel. 2012. The role of codeswitched input to children in the origin of a new mixed language. *Linguistics* 50(2). 305–340.
Pakendorf, Brigitte. 2009. Intensive contact and the copying of paradigms: An Éven dialect in contact with Sakha (Yakut). *Journal of Language Contact* 2(2). 85–110.
Papen, Robert A. 2017. On confirming the split phonology hypothesis for Michif. Paper presented at the 49th Algonquian Conference, Université du Québec à Montréal, 27–29 October.
Rosen, Nicole and Heather Souter. 2009. *Piikishkweetak aañ Michif!* Winnipeg: Louis Riel Institute.
Ross, Malcolm D. 1996. Contact-induced change and the comparative method: Cases from Papua New Guinea. In Mark Durie and Malcolm D. Ross (eds.), *The comparative method reviewed: Regularity and irregularity in language change*, 180–217. New York: Oxford University Press.
Sammons, Olivia N. 2019. *Nominal classification in Michif*. Edmonton: University of Alberta dissertation.
Sasse, Hans Jürgen. 1992. Theory of language death. In Mathias Brenzinger (ed.), *Language death: Factual and theoretical explorations with special references to East Africa*, 7–30. Berlin: De Gruyter Mouton.
Schaengold, Charlotte. 2004. *Bilingual Navajo: Mixed codes, bilingualism, and language maintenance*. The Ohio State University dissertation.
Seifart, Frank. 2013. *AfBo: A world-wide survey of affix borrowing*. Leipzig: Max Planck Institute for Evolutionary Anthropology. http://hdl.handle.net/11858/00-001M-0000-0015-39C5-A
Seifart, Frank. 2015. Direct and indirect affix borrowing. *Language* 91(3). 511–531.
Sekerina, Irina A. 1994. Copper Island (Mednyj) Aleut (CIA): A mixed language. *Languages of the world* 8(1). 14–31.
Singh, Rajendra 1982. On some 'redundant compounds' in Modern Hindi. *Lingua* 56. 345–351.
Stewart, Jesse, 2011. *A brief descriptive grammar of Pijal Media Lengua and an acoustic vowel space analysis of Pijal Media Lengua and Imbabura Quichua*. Winnipeg: University of Manitoba MA thesis.

Stolz, Thomas. 2003. Not quite the right mixture: Chamorro and Malti as candidates for the status of mixed language. In Yaron Matras & Peter Bakker (eds.), *The mixed language debate: Theoretical and empirical advances*, 271–316. Berlin: Mouton de Gruyter.

Thomason, Sarah & Terrence Kaufman. 1988. *Language contact, creolization and genetic linguistics*. Berkeley: University of California Press.

Thomason, Sarah G. 2003. Social factors and linguistic processes in the emergence of stable mixed languages. In Yaron Matras & Peter Bakker (eds.), *The mixed language debate: Theoretical and empirical advances*, 21–39. Berlin: Mouton de Gruyter.

Thomason, Sarah G. 2015. When is the diffusion of inflectional morphology not dispreferred? In Francesco Gardani, Peter Arkadiev & Nino Amiridze (eds.), *Borrowed morphology*, 27–46. Berlin: De Gruyter.

Vakhtin, Nikolai. 1998. Endangered languages in Northeast Siberia: Siberian Yupik and other languages of Chukotka. In Erich Kasten (ed.), *Bicultural education in the North: Ways of preserving and enhancing Indigenous peoples' languages and traditional knowledge*, 159–173. Münster: Waxmann Verlag.

van Gijn, Rik. 2009. The phonology of mixed languages. *Journal of Pidgin and Creole Languages* 24(1). 93–119.

van Hout, Roeland & Pieter Muysken. 1994. Modelling lexical borrowability. *Language Variation and Change* 6. 39–62.

Versteegh, Kees. 2017. The myth of the mixed languages. In Benjamin Saade & Mauro Tosco (eds.), *Advances in Maltese linguistics*, 217–238. Berlin: Mouton de Gruyter.

Wakama, Carol Gloria. 1999. A mixed language in Okrika. Nigeria: University of Harcourt BA Thesis.

Walworth, Mary. 2017. Reo Rapa: A Polynesian contact language. *Journal of Language Contact* 10(1). 98–141.

Winford, Donald. 2010. Contact and borrowing. In Raymond Hickey (ed.), *The handbook of language contact*, 170–187. Malden: Wiley-Blackwell.

Winford, Donald. 2013. Social factors in contact languages. In Peter Bakker & Yaron Matras (eds.), *Contact languages: A comprehensive guide*, 363–416. Berlin: De Gruyter Mouton.

Peter Bakker
Noun-Verb mixed languages: Similarities and differences

1 Introduction

The current wave of studies on mixed languages owes much to the groundbreaking monograph on language contact by Thomason and Kaufman (1988). In their book, several languages are discussed that still figure prominently in the discussion of mixed languages (Michif, Copper Island Aleut, Ma'a/Mbugu, and to some extent Angloromani and Media Lengua, which are mentioned but not discussed in detail). Their seminal study continued and inspired research on these mixed languages, and a search for additional ones. Bakker's book on Michif (1997, going back to 1992) contained a brief comparative chapter on mixed languages and thoughts about how they had come about. It only mentioned a limited number of mixed languages.

However, in the light of new data, novel insights, and the ensuing debates, thanks to a small but lively community of people working on mixed languages, much progress has been made. It is time to consider new forms of taxonomies of mixed languages, as the set of known examples has increased, and formerly unknown connections can be established. Any typological study starts with a taxonomy, and the link between sociohistorical circumstances and language types on the ensuing languages is of utmost interest for an understanding of the phenomena. Here I specifically focus on the known languages with a noun-verb dichotomy (i.e. languages with nouns and verbs or their inflection originating in different languages), the most intriguing group of all.

In recent work by Muysken (2008), Meakins (2013a, 2018), Meakins and Stewart (in press) and myself (Bakker 2017), new classifications of mixed languages have been proposed. Those will be summarized in the next section (2). Languages with some form of noun-verb dichotomy yield the most serious challenges for the

---

Acknowledgements: I would like to thank Cathrin Schäfer for help with Hubner Mischsprache materials, Carmel O'Shannessy for help with Light Warlpiri, Finn Thiesen for his help with Persian, Françoise Rose for information exchange on genderlects and the Velux Foundation (2013–2015) for support for "Cognitive Creolistics", and the editors and reviewers for their valuable observations. Further I would like to thank audiences in Bremen, Leiden, Amsterdam and Aarhus for feedback on some of the ideas presented here.

Peter Bakker, Aarhus University, linpo@cc.au.dk

https://doi.org/10.1515/9781501511257-002

classifications, as they are most unusual, less common and more challenging, and they show considerable diversity, as we will see below. These are the topics of this paper. In section 3, eight cases are described, with more attention for those languages that so far have not received enough attention. Section 4 deals with differences and similarities, many of them quite intriguing, between the languages with respect to the nature of the mixture. In section 4, I will speculate about sociohistorical and typological factors that may have played a role. The paper ends with conclusions and an outlook in section 5.

2 Recent classifications of mixed languages

In the past decades, a number of new mixed languages came to the fore, which makes it possible to produce a better classification, hopefully also with a link to specific social circumstances of genesis.

The most common type of mixed language is the G-L mixed language, with lexicon from one language and a grammatical system (phonology, morphology, syntax) from another. As an example, I present a case that has not been discussed in the literature on mixed languages. It is a language spoken in Iran, with a Semitic (Hebrew, Aramaic) lexicon and a Farsi (Iranian) grammatical system. Yarshater (1977: 2) describes the language as follows: "Loterā'i is, like Yiddish, a mixed language. The pronouns, adjectives and the majority of nouns and verbal bases, as well as some prepositions, are Semitic, whereas verbal endings, modal prefixes, suffix pronouns, most of the particles, as well as sentence structure are Iranian." This is clearly a G-L mixed language (unlike Yiddish). In this example, Hebrew/Aramaic elements are in bold (Yarshater 1977: 2).

(1)   a.   **anni bāy**-un   b-**ez**-on   xiābān, š-on   vā-**ez**-on. (Loterā'i)
       b.   mon gun   be-š-on   xiābān, š-on   o   var-e-gard-on.
           1SG   want-1   PUNCT-go-1SG   street   go-1SG   and   side turn-1SG
                                                                                                  (Farsi dialect)
           I want to go out (lit. in the street); I shall go and return.
           (cf. Hebrew/Aramaic *anni* 'I', Aramaic *ba/ba'a* 'want', Aramaic *ez/zl* 'to go')

The first recent classification of mixed languages to be discussed here, was made by Muysken (2008). Muysken's classification is based partly on sociohistorical criteria (distinguishing an original community and newcomers), and partly on the nature of the mixture of the languages spoken by these groups. Thus, Muysken (2008: 211–226) proposed four types: the *classical type*, like Media Lengua (unlike Loterā'i), where morphosyntax and functional categories are from the original community language and the lexicon from the newcomers. Media Lengua has Quechua (an indigenous language of Ecuador) morphosyntax and Spanish lexicon. There are a fair number of other cases with a similar structure, such as Para-Romani varieties (Bakker 2020a), and to some extent Kallawaya (Hannß this volume) and Ma'a (Mous 2003). For overviews, see Bakker (2017) and Meakins (2018). The second type he calls *split type*, exemplified by Michif. This type, represented by only one language, is not clearly defined, except that grammatical traits hail from two languages. Perhaps it means more concretely that the verbal system is from what he calls the original language (Plains Cree in Michif), and the nouns (or small DPs) from the introduced language (French, as in Michif). The third type is the *split reverse type*, which is represented by Mednyj Aleut and Gurindji Kriol. Here the verbal system is not from the original community language, but the nouns are. Finally, there is the *reverse type*, represented by Angloromani, which shows a grammar-lexicon divide, but the lexicon is from the original community language (Romani), and the morphosyntax is introduced to form a new language (English). Structurally, the classical type and the reverse type are similar, in that there is a grammar-lexicon dichotomy in both, but the sociohistorical circumstances are different. Both split types on the other hand, have grammatical features from two languages. This classification is thus based on structural features (grammar-lexicon, verb-noun) as well as a historical dimension (original community language, second, adopted language).

Bakker (2017; see also Bakker 2013, 2020b) distinguishes the following types: *GL mixed languages, FR mixed languages, VN mixed languages, VNN mixed languages, L-INFL mixed languages* and *LL mixed languages*. GL mixed languages are most common, with grammar A and lexicon B, exemplified by Media Lengua, Para-Romani and Loterā'i. FR mixed languages (Frame-Roots) combine the frame from one language A and all grammatical and lexical roots from language B. These languages would be the result of metatypy, but as no language has been discovered that show metatypy both in the verbal and nominal domain, we must assume these do not exist (see Bakker 2017). VN mixed languages combine verbs from one language and nouns from another, exemplified by the well-known case of Michif. VNN mixed languages combine verbs from one language with nouns from two languages, one being the same as the language of the verbs, and the other a different language. These have thus far only been found in Northern Australia (to be discussed below). L-INFL mixed languages have verbal inflection from one language, but much of the lexicon is from another language. There are only two known cases, both with Slavic verbal inflection (discussed below). Finally, there are a few mixed languages where the basic lexicon is from two languages, LL mixed languages, often with no conceivable semantic or other motivation, hence more or less arbitrary. The only known cases are creoles like Berbice Creole (Ijo and Dutch), Saramaccan (Portuguese, English) and Chabacano (Spanish, Philippine languages). In addition, Bakker (2017) also lists a few languages that are potentially mixed languages, but that are not easy to fit into this classification.

Meakins (2018) distinguishes three types of mixed languages: *L(exicon)-G(rammar) languages*, *structural mixes* and *converted languages*. Meakins and Stewart (in press) have the same classification. They base their classification on 24 "languages which have been identified as mixed languages". (1) L(exicon)–G(rammar) Languages are exemplified by Angloromani and Media Lengua, corresponding to Bakker's GL languages, (2) Structural Mixes are exemplified by Michif and Gurindji-Kriol, and (3) Converted Languages, like Sri Lanka Malay, corresponding to Bakker's FR languages. Thus, they merge Bakker's VN mixed languages, VNN mixed languages and L-INFL mixed languages into one. Note that they do not deal with the languages with mixed basic lexicon.

Thus, the challenging group, or groups, are those called "structural mixes", or "split languages" subsumed in one group by Meakins and Stewart (in press), in two groups by Muysken (2008) and in three groups by Bakker (2017). These will be the focus of the next section.

3 The Noun-Verb (N-V, N-VV, L-INFL) mixed languages

It was only in the last decades that Gurindji-Kriol, Light Warlpiri, and the Okrika-Igbo mixed language of Nigeria came to the fore. The Mednyj Aleut mixed language was known at the time but not as well understood as today, and it defied classification. It now appears that a number of clear patterns can be discerned. We characterize them here and compare them in the next section. All eight languages discussed in this section have a basic dichotomy between nouns and verbs, as far as the origins of these categories are concerned. The precise distribution, however, appears quite different when considered in detail.

3.1 Hubner Mischsprache

Huben is the former German name of a village in Slovenia. It is now known by its Slovenian name Spodnje Danje, and the population in 2002 was 62. There are a few dozen houses in the village, and it is one of a number of villages in the Upper Carniola region of Slovenia, where a German dialect was, or is, spoken, alongside Slovenian, the national language, and/or a Slovenian dialect. Purportedly, Bavarian German-speaking farmers immigrated from Tyrol to the region around 1200. Thus, German speakers were already present in the region in the Middle Ages (Lessiak 1959: 22). The Bavarian settlers maintained a variety of German and also acquired Slovenian. Language mixture in the area is mentioned already in the 17th century (Lessiak 1959: 25–27). This could be interpreted as the presence of code-mixing at the time or indeed a mixed language of the type documented later for Spodnje Danje.

Not much is known about the Hubner Mischsprache. The published corpus consists of only 13 sentences, which have been presented in the only published primary source on Hubner Mischsprache (Lessiak 1959, data from 1944; see also Pohl 1995). These sentences were published in Hubner Mischsprache, alongside equivalents of these sentences in Modern High German, local German, local Slovenian, and standard Slovenian. Here is one example, with the dialectal Slovenian elements in bold:

(2) a. *Unsere/**naše** ek-n   **ša**   net   aso hoch **kokr***
       1PL.POSS   mountain-PL **be.3PL** NEG so   high **as**
       *da-ire, **naše ša**   heh-ar*   (Hubner)
       your-PL **1PL be.3PL** high-COMPAR
   b. *īnžr   de   pērg-e   žēnt   et   ažou dā-ere*
       1POSS.PL 3PL mountain-PL 3PL.be NEG so   2POSS-PL
       žēnt   hēəy-ar   (Local German)
       3PL.be   high-COMPAR
   c. *nāʃe   xribe   ja   nis   viʃe*   (OR *bəl veʃōke*)
       1POSS.PL mountain 3PL.be NEG   higher   more high
       vaʃe   ʃa   (Local Slovenian)
       2POSS.PL 3PL.be
   'Our mountains are not so high as yours, yours are much higher'

Note that this is not code-switching, as the mixed language is not a combination of the two, but it draws on different dialectal varieties of both languages, different from the varieties in the village. Also, for the speakers it constitutes a separate variety (Pohl 1995; Lessiak 1959). Finally, the categorical distributions between German and Slovenian elements are much more systematic than expected in cases of code-mixing.

There are phonological and grammatical differences between local Slovenian and local German with Hubner Mischsprache. Apparently, after crystallization, the three languages evolved independently of one another, and they were also different from the standard varieties, corroborating earlier claims that mixed languages can show developments that are independent of their source languages (Bakker 2003: 125–128), indicating again that they are not on-the-spot mixtures but autonomous creations.

How are Slovenian and German combined into one language? There are 92 morphemes (types) in the small corpus. There are 13 verbal roots, mostly from German. The verbal inflection is always Slovenian, both for Slovenian roots (2) and for German roots (11). The two Slovenian roots cover very basic meanings: 'to give, to come'. The copula is from both languages: Slovenian (2) and German (1). Both of the modal auxiliaries are also from Slovenian. Depending on one's definition, there are eight or nine adjectives, all of them German. All 21 nouns are German (including some that are also German loans in local Slovenian). Adverbs are predominantly German.

In the realm of function words, it appears that all numerals, prepositions and negative markers are German, but the conjunctions 'and, that, or', personal pronouns and deictic pronouns are all Slovenian – except one of the five conjunctions.

Thus, in the Hubner Mischsprache, all roots are German, except possessive pronouns, personal pronouns, and deictic elements (*here, there*). Nominal inflection is German, verbal inflection is Slovenian. As grammatical markers like verbal inflection and personal pronouns are usually considered to be unborrowable and hence indicative of the genealogical affiliation of a language, and as these hail from a different source language than the lexicon, the affiliation is ambiguous and the language should be considered mixed indeed. This language appears to be very similar to Mednyj Aleut in its mixture, which is usually characterized as Aleut with Russian verb inflection (finite), and personal pronouns.

3.2 Mednyj Aleut

There are several sources on Mednyj Aleut (e.g. Thomason 1996; Vakhtin 1998), of which Sekerina (1994) is the clearest and most systematic, though only based on other publications, not her fieldwork. In Mednyj Aleut or Copper Island Aleut, most of the language is Aleut, but much of the verbal inflectional morphology is from Russian. Derivational morphology is Aleut. Some of the personal pronouns are Russian as well. According to Thomason and Kaufman (1988), the dichotomy for the pronouns is between tenses (present tense Russian, past tense Aleut), and according to Sekerina it is between object (Aleut) and subject (Russian) pronouns. Pronominal possession is mostly indicated with Aleut suffixes, occasionally also with Russian possessive pronouns. Negation is in Russian, and modal verbs as well. Nouns and all nominal morphology are Aleut. Demonstratives seem to be Aleut, but presentation deixis Russian ('This is . . .'). Phonology is a compromise between Aleut and Russian. Here are some examples (Sekerina 1994: 24; Thomason 1996: 457, 458), Russian elements in bold.

(3) **ya   tibe**   cíbu-x   ukayla:ya:sa:-l   (Mednyj Aleut)
     1SG.SUBJ 2SG.OBJ   parcel-ABS   bring-**PAST**
     'I br**ought** you a parcel'

(4) híŋa tayágu-x sisaxta:-l   (Mednyj Aleut)
     this man-ABS lose-**PAST**
     'This man is lost'

(5) eta   moj   asxinu-ŋ   (Mednyj Aleut)
     this **1SG.POSS** daughter-1SG.POSS
     '**This** (is) **my** daughter' (Russ.: *eto moja*)

Two thirds of the function words, including several personal pronouns, are from Russian. "The Aleut pronouns are used as direct objects when they would be used as direct objects in ordinary Aleut; Russian pronouns (but never Aleut pronouns) are used as subjects in the past tense, where Russian lacks person marking" (Thomason 1996: 457).

Thus, the language is overwhelmingly Aleut, and the verbal inflection and most pronouns are from Russian. The language is spoken by a population called 'creoles', which in this context means descendants of native Aleut women and Russian men.

3.3 Gurindji-Kriol

Gurindji-Kriol is a V-NN mixed language in Bakker's classification, a split reverse type in Muysken's and a structural mix in Meakins' classification. The verb phrase is in Kriol, the noun phrase can be in both languages, but all case endings are from Gurindji, a Pama-Nyungan Aboriginal language. In (6), the second position auxiliary is from local Creole English (*im-in* < *him been*), as is *najawan* (< *another one*), and the rest is from the Gurindji. 64% of verbs and 67% of nouns are from Kriol (Meakins 2013b). In the example, Kriol/English elements are in bold.

(6) **najawan**-tu   **im-in**   jawurra karu   (Gurindji Kriol)
    another.one-ERG   him-been   steal   kid
    'Someone else, he has stolen a child' (McConvell and Meakins 2005: 24)

It is spoken in an Aboriginal community in Northern Australia, in their own territory, and it continues the local Gurindji language, which was affected by massive code-mixing with the local English-lexifier creole and Aboriginal English in previous generations (McConvell and Meakins 2005), and learned as such by children, and transmitted and developed further.

3.4 Light Warlpiri

Warlpiri is a Pama-Nyungan Australian Aboriginal language, and Light Warlpiri a mixed language that emerged in the past few decades. Light Warlpiri is spoken in the Warlpiri community by children and young adults.

O'Shannessy (2013: 328) characterized Light Warlpiri as follows: "The structure of Light Warlpiri overall is that of a mixed language, in that most verbs and some verbal morphology are drawn from English and/or Kriol, and most nominal morphology is from Warlpiri. Nouns are drawn from both Warlpiri-lexicon and English-lexicon sources. The restructuring of the auxiliary system draws selectively on elements from Warlpiri and several varieties and styles of English and/ or Kriol, combined in such a way as to produce novel constructions."

Thus, Light Warlpiri resembles Gurindji-Kriol in its mixture. Here is an example sentence (Meakins 2013a: 176; Kriol elements in bold):

(7) en   karnta-pawu **i-m**   **kam** **geit**-kirra   (Light Warlpiri)
    and girl-DIM   3SG.S-NFUT   come   gate-ALL
    'And the girl came to the gate.'

One noun is from Warlpiri and one from English. The verb and the auxiliary (from English *he been* or *him been*) are from Kriol. The source for this language is undoubtedly code-switching between Warlpiri and Kriol.

3.5 Michif

Michif combines Cree (Algonquian) verbs, with all their polysynthetic complexity, with French nouns, including French definite and indefinite articles (French elements bold).

(8) **lii gros dans** kii-ushihtaaw-ak, **enn gros gros silibraasyon**
the.PL big.F dance PAST-make-3PL a.F big.F big.F celebration
mihceet kii-nipah-eewak **lii vash, lii koshon, lii**
many PAST-kill-they.them the.PL cow the.PL pig the.PL
pul. (Michif)
chicken
"They organized big dances, a really big celebration. They slaughtered many cows, pigs and chickens" (Norman Fleury, speaker)

The language is spoken by some of the Métis (people of mixed Amerindian-French ancestry) in Canada and the Northern USA by people of mixed Cree-French descent. Roughly, the noun phrases, including definite and indefinite articles, but not the demonstratives, are from French, whereas the complex verbal morphology is as in Cree (see Bakker 1997, Rhodes 1977).

3.6 New Tiwi

New Tiwi is spoken on Bathurst and Melville Islands in northern Australia, described by Lee (1983), based on fieldwork in the 1980s. The traditional form of the Aboriginal language Tiwi is considered to be an isolate. Traditional Tiwi, only spoken by the older generations, is a polysynthetic language. The young people have developed a new form of Tiwi, in which Creole English and (Aboriginal) English are integrated. Lee (1983) discusses the existence of a kind of continuum in the community, but she does identify a certain style as Modern Tiwi, also called New Tiwi. Meakins (2014: note 10) suggested it could be code-switching, and if it had stabilized at all in Lee's days, it appears to differ from Tiwi as spoken by four-year-olds just after 2010 (Wilson, Hurst and Wigglesworth 2018). Lee describes New Tiwi as fairly systematic.

Here is an example sentence of Traditional Tiwi (9a) and its equivalent in the mixed language, called New Tiwi (Creole/English in bold) (9b), from Lee (1983:2):

(9) a. a-*mpi-ni-watu-wujingi-ma-jirrakirningi-yangurlimay-ami*
   she-NON.PAST-LOC-MORNING-DUR-with-light-walk-MOVEMENT
   (Litt: She is walking over there in the morning with a light)
   b. *japinari* {**wokapat/mup**} *a-mpi-jiki-mi* *kutawu*
   morning {**walk/move**} she-NON.PAST-DUR-do there
   layt with
   with light
   (Lit. She (the sun) is walking/moving over there in the morning with a light)
   'She (the sun) is shining over there in the morning'

We can observe a polysynthetic structure in (9a) as used by older people, and a much less morphologically complex structure in (9b). The English sentence is expressed in one word in Traditional Tiwi and in six words in New Tiwi. A DO-auxiliary with Tiwi roots is used for integrating the English Creole verb. The auxiliary contains person reference and tense-aspect marking. The content words are from Creole English or Tiwi. In many cases, both an English and a Tiwi word could be used.

McConvell (2008) linked New Tiwi with mixed languages, and compared the mixing with the code-mixing situation in the Gurindji community. Recently, Meakins and Stewart (in press) listed it among their 24 mixed languages. The mixture is characterized, according to them, by VPs from Tiwi, the ancestral language, and NPs from Aboriginal English/Kriol. That is indeed what we observe in (9). But there is also a lexical verb from English; the inflected light verb is from Tiwi.

Lee's book gives many examples, but the systematicity between what is English/Creole and what is Tiwi in what she calls Modern Tiwi is unclear in the text, as many elements can be expressed both in Creole and in Tiwi. In order to investigate the noun-verb dichotomy, I decided to count the first and last full pages of the English-Tiwi dictionary in Lee (1983), which includes, in separate columns, both Traditional Tiwi and New Tiwi. I only counted words given for New Tiwi.

In New Tiwi, the following 16 English meanings or concepts (Lee 1983: 368, 391) can be expressed in both Tiwi and English: 'about', 'above', 'after', 'afternoon', 'again', 'all', 'always', 'angel', 'angry', 'animal', 'another', 'water', 'wet', 'wind', 'with', 'woman'. Note that there are no verbs among them, only (from an English perspective) nouns, prepositions, adjectives and adverbs. The following 19 meanings can be expressed only in Tiwi: 'adult(s)', 'almost', 'alone', 'also', 'and', 'ant', 'upper arm', 'lower arm', 'armband', 'arrive', 'ashes', 'asleep', 'watch out!', 'salt water', 'we', question words ('what', 'when', 'where', 'which', 'who', 'why'), rel. pron., 'wife', 'woman'. These Tiwi-only words (again, from an English perspective) cover nine nouns, adverbs, one verb and some function words, notably question words. The following 11 meanings can be expressed only in English: 'angel', 'angry', 'ask', 'wash', 'watch', 'will', 'win', 'wipe', 'wood', 'write'. Here, verbs appear to dominate, but there is also an adjective and two nouns.

A characterization of New Tiwi as a language with (predominantly) English creole verb stems and nouns from both Tiwi and English seems accurate. But note that the inflections in (9b) are given as part of a Tiwi-derived light verb or auxiliary, which seems to be typical for New Tiwi. In this sample, 80% of the (English-meaning) verb stems are from English, and 20% are from Tiwi. 50% of the nouns can have both Tiwi and English forms, and 50% only Tiwi, and just two nouns are expressed only in an English-derived form. At the same time, the grammatical structure of Traditional Tiwi is significantly reduced. Prepositions and particles in New Tiwi replace a number of bound morphemes present in Traditional Tiwi verbs. Modal auxiliaries are based on erstwhile Tiwi particles.

As described by Lee, the most mixed register used in the Tiwi community, New Tiwi, could be characterized as a mixed language. Structurally, it appears to differ from all other known mixed languages. In the other two Northern Australian mixed languages, the auxiliary is Creole English, in New Tiwi, it is Tiwi-based. It has mostly English verb stems, a Tiwi light verb expressing person inflection and tense and aspect, and English and Tiwi nouns.

The dating and the process of genesis of this mixture are unclear and need careful study of the diachrony. There are a number of studies on the history and anthropology of the Tiwi (e.g. Hart and Pilling 1960; Goodale 1971). The Tiwi were virtually isolated from the rest of the world until around 1900, when a mission was established on the island. The priest ended the complex cultural practice in which each woman had to have a husband, usually an adult appointed at the birth of the child, which meant that, traditionally, young women would be married to old men, who were also polygamic. Instead after arrival, the priest raised hundreds of young women around the mission, until they reached a marriage age, whereafter they could choose their own partner of a similar age. The language around the mission was mostly pidgin/creole English, also spoken by men in the 1920s (Hart, Pilling and Goodale 1988: 150). One can speculate that this gender division was a factor in the emergence of the mixed language (cf. Bakker 2019).

3.7 Okrika-Igbo mixed language

The Okrika-Igbo mixed language is spoken in a number of former villages in Rivers State in Southern Nigeria that have become part of the agglomeration of the city of Port Harcourt (Wakama 1999). People in these villages speak the mixed language as their mother tongue, and this mixed language is spoken in the churches, on the marketplace, playgrounds and in the homes (Wakama 1999). The indigenous language of the area is Okrika, an Ijoid language, and Igbo is a lingua franca of the region. The two languages are not genealogically related (Dimmendaal 2011: 92, Bøegh, Daval-Markussen & Bakker 2016), or, if so, very distantly (Greenberg 1963). The Okrika and Igbo languages are the two component languages of the mixed language.

The speakers and Okrika people call the mixed language Kịrịkẹnì-Ìgbònàyé, a combination of Okrika and Igbo, with what seems to be a nominalizer -nàyé. We will call it Okrika-Igbo, which is a standardized form of the name used by the speakers (in English). The Igbo people refer to the mixed language as Igbo-Okrika, whereas the Kalabari and Bonny people (Ijo speakers) call the people Okrika Igbos, all highlighting the two component languages. Wakama (1999) is the only primary source about the language. In the mixed language, nouns are overwhelmingly from Okrika, and verbs are almost always from Igbo. Both languages are relatively analytic, tonal languages. The mixed language is grammatically much closer to Igbo than to Okrika. In the mixed example, Okrika elements are bold:

(10) a. kà   m´ gá kúrú **fúló** n' **ọ̀pọ̀chúkū** n´nē   m´   (Mixed)
     b. kà   m´ gá kúrú ófē   n' ùsekwū   n´nē   m´   (Igbo)
        HORT 1SG go dish soup   in kitchen   mother 1SG
     c. Yé   à   mù   fúlọ́ dū   ì   yèngì   má   árā
        HORT 1SG go   soup dish my   mother   FEM   her
        ọ́pọ́chúkū ḅìè   (Okrika)
        kitchen   inside
        'Let me go and dish some soup from my mother's kitchen.' (Wakama 1999: 36, S46)

It is clear that we witness an insertion of Okrika nouns in an Igbo grammatical frame. The nouns meaning "soup" and "kitchen" are from Okrika. The word for "mother" is an exception in that it is Igbo, with an Igbo possessive. Okrika and Igbo are quite different structurally. Okrika is an AOV language, Igbo AVO, and the mixed language follows Igbo grammatical patterns. Okrika has postpositions,

Igbo has prepositions, the mixed language follows Igbo. In Okrika, modifiers (possessive pronouns, demonstratives) precede the noun, in Igbo these modifiers follow the noun, and the mixed language follows the Igbo order. All verbal derivation is from Igbo, also when the verb is from Okrika. In the mixed language, verbs, constituent order (S and NP), prepositions, demonstratives, and personal pronouns are all from Igbo, whereas nouns and nominalized verbs are from Okrika. The phonological systems of Okrika and Igbo are quite similar. From the description (Wakama 1999), it seems that Okrika and Igbo morphemes preserve their own phonology in the mixed language.

There are a few structural innovations. In (11), we can see that the location "in(side)" is indicated twice, once before the noun with a preposition, and once behind the noun with a positional noun. Thus, this combines the Okrika positional noun with the Igbo preposition.

(11) a. ọ̀   dị   nà   **njùkùrù ḅíē**   (Igbo-Okrika)
         3SG is   in   room   inside
      b. ọ̀   dị   n'   ímē   ụ́lọ̀-ímē   (Igbo)
         3SG is   in   inside   room-inside
      c. ọ̀   jùkùrù ḅíē   ómí   (Okrika)
         3SG room   inside is
      'Is he in the bedroom?' (Wakama 1999: 34, Q16)

Further, the mixed language grammaticalized the Igbo verb *mé* 'to do' in ways that Igbos do not use it. In such constructions, the mixed language makes use of nominalized verbs, in an innovative way. These nominalized verbs are formed with a DO-auxiliary. In (12), Okrika and Igbo use a verb with a factive past ending, while the mixed language nominalizes the verb 'to ground' (note the tonal difference) which is preceded by an auxiliary with tense marking in. Example (13) shows a difference in words order triggered by the auxiliary.

(12) a. ụ́gbọ́ mé-né   **gbàná**   (Igbo-Okrika)
         boat do-PAST   grounding
      b. ụ́gbọ́ áchíá-lá   (Igbo)
         boat ground-PAST
      c. árụ̀   gbànă-sàm   (Okrika)
         Boat ground.V-PAST
      'The boat has grounded.' (Wakama 1999: 27, S5)

(13) a. *Hán mè-rè*   *ḿ*   **kpọ́tíí**   (Igbo-Okrika)
      3PL do-PAST   1SG   deriding
   b. *Há kpàrị̀-rị*   *ḿ*   (Igbo)
      3PL insult-PAST   1SG
   c. *Ìnì í*   *kpọ̀tíí*   *mệ*   (Okrika)
      3PL ?   deride 1SG
      "They insulted me" (Wakama 1999: 28, S19)

In such cases, it seems that an Okrika verb is inserted in a nominalized form with an Igbo DO-auxiliary, reminiscent of verb borrowing in a range of languages in the world. Note also that word order in the mixed language deviates sometimes from Igbo, when a nominalized verb 'do' is used.

The social circumstances that led to the emergence of the mixed language were as follows:

> According to some speakers of the mixed language in Okrika, the mixed language came into existence through inter-marriage. Their ancestral fathers of Okrika origin who learned Igbo through trade, brought Igbos (mostly women) to make up their families. These people who were brought, came and got settled in some of the Okrika villages.

> These Igbos were married into Okrika, both women and men. As they got children, these children grew up with parents who spoke Okrika and Igbo to them depending on who is from Okrika and who is from Igbo. Their parents were either an Okrika father and an Igbo mother, or less commonly an Igbo father and an Okrika mother. Since they were more close to their Igbo mothers in interaction they could not speak Okrika fluently, and in the course of making sure they had at least one language, they found themselves mixing the two languages.   (Wakama 1999: 43)

3.8 Other cases: Guarache (Guarani-Aché), Balkan and Finnish Romani

By lack of sufficient reliable information, we cannot use the Guarache language in our comparison. The youngest generations of the Aché people are reported to use verbs from Guarani and nouns from Aché, according to Eva-Maria Rössler who calls it Guaraché. For a study of verbal borrowings together with the inflection, see Adamou and Granqvist (2015), where Turkish and Finnish verbs in Romani are discussed. In these cases, only a few verbs are borrowed.

3.9 Comparison of the verb-noun mixed languages

The group of mixed languages with some kind of dichotomy between verbs and nouns appears quite diverse, as we have seen above. Focusing on the verb-noun dichotomy, we find a simplified overview in Table 1.

Table 1: Summarizing overview of the seven mixed languages.

	nouns	verbs	auxiliaries
Michif	European nouns	indigenous verbs	no innovated auxiliaries
Okrika-Igbo	Indigenous nouns	imported verbs	innovated auxiliaries
Tiwi	European and indigenous nouns	imported verbs	innovated indigenous auxiliaries
Gurindji-Kriol	European and indigenous nouns	indigenous or imported verbs	Creole auxiliaries
Light Warlpiri	European and indigenous nouns	European verbs	Creole and innovated auxiliaries
Mednyj Aleut	Indigenous nouns	European verbal inflection and pronouns	no innovated auxiliaries
Hubner	German nouns	Slovene verbal inflection, Slovene pronouns	no innovated auxiliaries

In Table 2, I compare a number of grammatical categories in the seven languages discussed. I indicate from which source languages those categories are adopted. Here as well, the results are enormously diverse. In the next section, I will focus on recurring patterns, as some languages appear to pair. Proposed explanations are discussed for the observed similarities and differences.

4 Similarities and differences between mixed languages with a verb-noun split

The obvious question to be asked is how to account for the similarities and differences between the seven languages. There are two overarching ways of explaining the differences. One is that different, special *socio-historical* circumstances can be

Table 2: Language sources for selected grammatical categories in the seven languages.

	Nouns	Grammatical Case	Locative case	Demonstrative	Personal Pronoun	Tense and aspect	Modal Particles	Verb stems	Verbal Inflection	"New" auxiliaries
Michif (Cree-French)	F	C	–	C	C	C	F (innov.) C	C	C	NONE
Okrika-Igbo	O	NONE	– (Prep: I)	–	–	–	Aux?	–	–	–
New Tiwi (Tiwi, Kriol/English)	T,K	NONE	NONE	T	T	T	T	K	T	T
Gurindji-Kriol	K 64%	G	G	G, K	K, G	K	K	K 67%	K	K
Light Warlpiri (Warlpiri, Kriol/English)	W, K	W	W	K	K	K	K	K, W	K	K
Hubner Mischsprache (German, Slovenian)	G	G	G	G	S	S	S	G	S	NONE
Mednyj Aleut (Aleut, Russian)	A	A	A	A	A, R	A (R)	R	A	R	NONE

responsible for the differences between the resulting mixed languages, and the other, that the *typological* properties of the languages involved played a major role in the nature of the mixture. A combination is also possible. We will discuss some subtypes first, before moving to social and typological considerations.

Researchers on mixed languages have pointed to the following social circumstances: men/women dichotomies (Bakker 1997; Thomason 2003), settled nomads (Bakker 1997), U-turn (Sasse 1992; Boretzky and Igla 1994), arrested matrix language turnover (Myers-Scotton 2002), local versus imported languages (Muysken 2008), and conscious acts of identity (Golovko 2003; Thomason 2003). Note that several of them may have played a role for the same language. As none of the mixed languages here are spoken by settled nomads, that type will not be discussed.

In Tables 3–5, I first show that there are three pairs of mixed languages that are remarkably similar to one another. Differences are indicated with shading.

Table 3: Comparison between Gurindji Kriol and Light Warlpiri.

Structural feature	Gurindji-Kriol	Light Warlpiri
Word order	Kriol	Kriol
TAM markers	Kriol	Kriol, Warlpiri & innovations
Bound verbal morphology	Kriol	Kriol
Verb lexicon	Kriol and Gurindji	Kriol
Case morphology	Gurindji	Warlpiri
Other nominal morphology	Gurindji	Warlpiri
Negation	Kriol	Kriol/English
Regular free pronouns	Kriol and Gurindji	Warlpiri
Emphatic pronouns	Gurindji	Warlpiri
Possessive pronouns	Gurindji	Warlpiri & Kriol/English
Interrogative pronouns	Kriol	?
Demonstratives 'this/that'	Gurindji	Warlpiri & Kriol
Determiners	Kriol	Kriol
Conjunctions, coordination, relative pronoun	Kriol	Kriol
Subordination	Gurindji	English
Interjections	Gurindji	Warlpiri & English
Directionals (cardinals, 'up'/'down')	Gurindji	Warlpiri

Table 4: Parallels between Michif and Okrika-Igbo in categorial distribution.

	Michif	Okrika-Igbo
Nouns	French	Okrika (82 %)
Demonstratives	Cree	Igbo
Verbs	Cree	Igbo (94 %)
Verbal TMA	Cree	Igbo
Verbal derivation	Cree	Igbo
Nominalized verb	Cree	Igbo
Adjectival verb	Cree and French?	Igbo and Okrika
Numerals	French (except 1)	(unknown)
Personal pronouns	Cree	Igbo
Interrogatives	Cree	Igbo and Okrika
Prepositions	Cree and French	Igbo
Positional nouns	(not present)	Okrika (postposed)
Modals	Cree and French	Igbo (Okrika has no modals)
Conjunctions	Cree and French	Igbo
Phonology	Cree words Cree, French words French	Igbo words Igbo, Okrika words Okrika

Light Warlpiri and Gurindji Kriol share many features. Table 3 is based on the list of structural properties listed in Meakins (2013a: 137). It is supplemented by Carmel O'Shannessy (p.c.) for Light Warlpiri. There seem to be only few, superficial differences between the two languages. The only systematic differences are of a type where one of the languages has a choice between two languages, and the other language leaves no choice. One such difference is that verbal roots can be from both languages in Gurindji-Kriol but from Kriol/English only in Light Warlpiri. Meakins and O'Shannessy (2012) argue that typological constraints on verb integration are responsible: Gurindji verbs in Gurindji-Kriol are originally coverbs which are free forms, whereas in Warlpiri coverbs (called preverbs) are bound to the inflecting verb. The only exception is subordination. As Warlpiri and Gurindji territories are adjacent, there could be influence from one community to the other. Alternatively, typological properties of these related and rather similar languages could have played a role.

Table 5: Parallels between Mednyj Aleut and Hubner Mischsprache in categorial distribution.

	Mednyj Aleut	Hubner Mischsprache
(Bulk of) lexicon	Aleut (verbs and nouns) Verb stems: 94 % Aleut Noun stems: 61,5 % Aleut	German (verbs and nouns)
Nominal inflection	Aleut	German
Adjectival inflection	(no adjectives)	German adjectival inflection
Demonstratives	Aleut	(unknown)
Verbal inflection	Russian	Slovenian
Modal auxiliaries	Russian	Slovenian
Personal pronouns	Russian	Slovenian
Conjunctions	Russian	Slovenian
Adverbs of time, degree and quality	many Russian	Some Slovenian adverbs of time and mostly place
Numerals	Lower ones: both, higher ones: Russian	German
Negative particle	Russian	German

There is also another pair of language that appears remarkably similar. The two languages, however, are spoken in different continents, so each areal influence must be excluded. The structural parallel between Michif and Okrika-Igbo is clear from Table 4. What is French in Michif, is Okrika in Okrika-Igbo, and what is Cree in Michif, is Igbo in Okrika-Igbo. Sometimes Michif has two source languages, and Okrika-Igbo only one. This could very well be because Michif is much better documented. The Okrika-Igbo corpus is limited to some 100 sentences, which display rather limited structural variety.

Next, there is a final clear parallel between two of the other languages: Mednyj Aleut and Hubner Mischsprache. The distribution of the categories and inflection is summarized in Table 5. Again, areal influence is excluded, as they are spoken in different continents.

Note that these areas pattern in parallel ways: where Mednyj Aleut has a Slavonic component, Hubner Mischsprache has likewise. The only area in which the two languages differ is negation. It seems counterintuitive to ascribe the parallel to the fact that both mixed languages have a Slavonic component. The sociohistorical circumstances differ considerably. In the Aleut case, the Russians were powerful intruders, and they intermarried with Aleut women. In the Slovenian case, German farmers were the intruders, not the Slovenes.

4.1 Socio-historical explanations

Despite the apparent chaos in Table 2, it was possible to identify three pairs of languages that show structural similarities. Here we explore socio-historical explanations for the distributions encountered in the seven languages.

Bakker (1997) proposed that, in mixed populations, women provide the grammatical system, and men the lexicon, if a mixed language emerges. Thus, there is a gender-connected *men-women dichotomy* (see also Bakker 2019 for a discussion of connections between genderlects and mixed languages). In the cases known at the time, all men were immigrants and the women locals. Alternatively, it could be, as already suggested in Bakker (1997), that not the gender of the women, but the *locality of the language* (in all previous cases the women were locals, the men immigrants) is the decisive factor in providing the grammar language. Thus, the local language provides the grammatical system, and the imported language the grammatical system. The following languages can be associated with a man-woman dichotomy: Michif, Mednyj Aleut, Okrika-Igbo and possibly Tiwi and Hubner Mischsprache.

Interestingly, we now have two cases where the women were the migrants, and not the men: Tiwi and Okrika-Igbo. Tiwi women were raised on the mission, outside the community, with English Creole rather than Tiwi, while the men were dominant in Tiwi (with some knowledge of Creole as well). In this case, the grammatical system would be provided by the men's local language, rather than the women's, hence by Tiwi – albeit in a reduced form. In Mednyj Aleut, and possibly also in the case of the Hubner Mischsprache (if only men travelled to Slovenia), the verb and some of the verbal inflection is from the language of the local women (across the board in Hubner, finite verbs in Mednyj Aleut). In Okrika-Igbo, the grammatical system is in the imported language, which is also the language of the women (who were allegedly brought by traders). Here again, it is not clear why the verb roots are not also from Okrika. There could be typological reasons, such as vowel harmony and tone processes.

The concept of *local and imported language*, as espoused by Muysken (2008), is problematic in some of the cases. In the case of Michif, both Cree and French were imported languages (it was spoken in Ojibwe territory, Bakker 1991, 1997; Rhodes 2008). For Hubner Mischsprache, local and imported does not make sense today, as the migration of the German speakers took place some seven centuries ago, so both German and Slovenian should be considered local languages.

Unless, of course, one assumes that the mixed language developed at initial contact in the Middle Ages. In Table 6 we take the "colonial" languages to be the imported language, and the other one as the local one, in order to make comparison easier.

Table 6: Verbs, nouns and inflection with the parameters "local" and "imported" (letters refer to language names).

	Verb	Verb inflection	Noun	Nominal inflection
Hubner Mischsprache	Local GE	Local S	Local GE	Local GE
Mednyj Aleut	Local A	Imported R	Local A	Local A
Gurindj-Kriol	Imported K	Imported K	Imported or local K, G	Local G
Light Warlpiri	Imported K	Imported K	Imported or local K, W	Local W
Michif	Imported C	Imported C	Imported F	Imported or local F (F nouns), C (C nouns; rare)
New Tiwi	Imported or local K, T	Local T	Imported or local K, T	Local T
Okrika-Igbo	Imported I	Imported I	Local O	Imported I

In Table 6, no system can be detected between the different grammatical categories and whether they are local or imported. Colored background indicate contradictions.

For most mixed languages, researchers have suggested that they were created consciously, hence as an *act of identity* (cf. LePage and Tabouret-Keller 1985). For the Hubner Mischsprache, we have insufficient sociohistorical data. The Michif, Okrika-Igbo speakers and the Mednyj Aleut speakers are all new ethnic groups, having come about as a consequence of an act of identity. This cannot be said, however, about the three Aboriginal cases, all of which are continuations of the Aboriginal groups and their identity as Tiwi, Warlpiri and Gurindji (Meakins 2008). Thus, such an act of identity is unlikely in the case of the three Aboriginal groups. Previous code-switching could have played a role here, contrasting with acts of identity where code-switching plays no role.

The *U-turn hypothesis* (Sasse 1992; Boretzky and Igla 1994) is based on the idea that speakers regretted an ongoing shift from one language to another, and therefore they inserted disappearing lexicon, which is more easily retrievable, into a frame of the new language. In the three Aboriginal cases, it seems obvious that a shift from the indigenous language to Kriol was ongoing, but in these cases, insertion of lost lexicon is not observable. In addition, these languages show many grammatical innovations, such as the development of new auxiliaries, which would not be expected from a comparative perspective. Furthermore, there is no easy way of explaining why some meanings can be expressed in both languages, and others only in one. For Michif, a U-turn is extremely unlikely because of the preservation of all complexities in both components. For Okrika-Igbo it makes no sense either. The creators must have been bilinguals, with no intention to shift. For Mednyj Aleut and Hubner Mischsprache, it is not possible to assess. My skepticism about these cases being a result of a U-turn, should not be taken as a rejection of the U-Turn Hypothesis. It just does not make sense for the seven languages under scrutiny here.

In cases where mixed languages emerge, Myers-Scotton (1998) has proposed a *matrix-language turnover*. This idea was completely hypothetical when it was proposed. The matrix language (ML) is the language of the verb inflection and the grammatical frame. For each sentence, it should be possible to identify a ML, and one would expect that sentence structure, the verb and inflection would indicate the ML, and that these three would align. The turnover involves a type of code-switching with one matrix language (i.e. the language that provides the grammatical frame of utterances, in which words, phrases or stretches from other languages can be inserted) at one point in time, but for social reasons, speakers replace the matrix language with the other language. When this turnover process is arrested half-ways, new mixed languages can crystallize. If a verb stem cannot be combined with derivation and/or inflection from the other language, an auxiliary could be innovated. In that case, the auxiliary would also mark the ML (see also below on the auxiliary).

I summarize the data on the languages in Table 7.

In Table 7, we can see that it is impossible to identify the matrix language, as sentence structure, verb and verb inflection almost always point in different directions, except in the case of Michif and Okrika-Igbo. If this contradiction in five cases can be interpreted as the result of a matrix language shift, then there is some evidence for that suggestion, but otherwise the MLT hypothesis does not seem to work as an explanatory factor. For two Australian languages, there is historical evidence for the shift from a Gurindji/Warlpiri dominant verbal inflection to a Kriol-dominant system (Meakins 2011), and if one takes verbal

Table 7: Verbs, auxiliaries and sentence structure. Local language indicated grey and underlined.

	Verb inflection	Verb stems	Sentence Structure	Auxiliary
Hubner Mischsprache	S	G	Mix, innovation	(no)
Mednyj Aleut	R, A	A	Mostly R	R
Gurindj-Kriol	K	G, K	K	K
Light Warlpiri	K	K	K	K
Michif	C	C	C	(no)
New Tiwi	T	T, K	Mix, innovation	T
Okrika-Igbo	I	I	I, little innovation	I

inflection as an indication of the matrix language, there was a shift. For the other ones, it is difficult to find evidence.

In short, no unified model for the structures of all seven Noun-Verb languages is possible on the basis of socio-historical criteria. In fact, none of the current sociohistorical explanations fares very well in a general comparison based on these languages.

4.2 Typological explanations

As for typological properties, researchers have pointed to special consequences for polysynthetic languages when one cannot isolate stems from affixes (Bakker 1997 for Michif), differences between head-marking and dependent marking (McConvell 2008), and a possible origin in, or parallel with, Parallel Systems Borrowing (Kossmann 2010), in which typological properties play a role.

The verb-noun dichotomy in Michif with verbs overwhelmingly from Cree and nouns overwhelmingly from French, upwards of ca. 90%, was explained in Bakker (1997) as a consequence of the polysynthetic nature of the Cree verb. In Okrika-Igbo, however, we find the same dichotomy, but in this language, the verbs are from Igbo and the nouns form Okrika, neither of which can be characterized as polysynthetic. As Igbo is not a polysynthetic language, the typological nature of this language cannot be taken as an explanation – for this type, at least. Alternatively, there may be other cohesive processes in Igbo, like vowel harmony and tone processes that make it more difficult for speakers to separate words into smaller units in Igbo. This is in line with Matras' (2015) idea of the integrity of the verb.

McConvell (2008) explained some of the structural differences between mixed languages by pointing to head and dependent marking. Head-marking languages are, roughly, languages with morphosyntactic marking reflecting syntactic relations on the heads of sentences (verbs) or on heads of noun phrases (nouns), whereas dependent-marking languages indicate such grammatical relations on non-heads (e.g. cases in sentences, and possessor in possessive constructions). Dependent marking noun-coding languages would retain nominal grammar from the "old" language and verbal grammar from the "new" language, which would account for Mednyj Aleut and Gurindji Kriol. Languages can also be double-marking and non-marking. Polysynthetic languages are typically head-marking, as are Cree and Tiwi, and Gurindji and Warlpiri are double-marking or dependent-marking. Head-marking languages, according to McConvell, would retain verbal grammar from the "old" language and nominal grammar from the "new" grammar, and that is why the verbal system with inflection is Tiwi-based in New Tiwi and Michif. Inflected verbs are Creole-based in Gurindji Kriol and Light Warlpiri. We have seen that "old" and "new" or "local" and "imported" are not useful concepts in mixed languages. It may be mentioned that head-marking Tiwi verbs were reduced to reasonably simple auxiliaries/light verbs, indicating that the verb is not immune for structural reduction.

An important concept is Parallel Systems Borrowing (Kossmann 2010). Kossmann (2010) introduced the concept of Parallel Systems Borrowing (PSB) for the phenomenon where borrowed words are borrowed with their morphological properties, as in English SG *alumnus*/ PL *alumni* from Latin. He lists several examples, from non-written and non-learned vocabulary, notably Arabic and Tuareg nominal loans into Berber varieties. He also provides examples of adjectives, e.g. Italian into Maltese, and verbs, e.g. Turkish verbs borrowed with their Turkish inflection into Romani varieties (Adamou 2010; Friedman 2013). His cases definitely do not refer to code-switching, as speakers often do not speak the language from which the inflected forms were borrowed. That is, for instance, the case with the Romani dialect of Ajia Varvara in Athens, with Turkish verbs, but the speakers have no knowledge of Turkish. Kossmann discusses also the potential interest for mixed languages, in that Michif could have started in this way, with nominal PSB from French, preserving French gender and number distinctions. Indeed, a few Cree nouns are used in Michif, and these do receive Cree plural markers, and preserve Cree phonology. However, the results of PSB cannot account for the other mixed languages.

The typological explanations fare better than the sociohistorical ones. For instance, the indivisibility of the verb (as in Cree) or the noun (as in Slavonic), with their complexities, seem to play a main role in all three pairs discussed. None of them, however, can account for all of the phenomena. An explanation combining typological and sociohistorical features, such as Matras (2000), may be the way forward. There he compartmentalizes the genesis of mixed languages into processes of lexical orientation, selective replication, convergence, and categorial fusion as relevant in the compartmentalization in the genesis of mixed languages. Matras (2015) adds the principle of the integrity of the predication as an important factor as well.

5 Conclusions and outlook

Are there socio-historical reasons for the differences (i.e. special social circumstances, such as mixed origins) or typological differences (e.g. effects of certain properties of morphological marking, e.g. polysynthesis) that lead to certain choices in the mixtures?

The group of languages with some form of noun-verb dichotomy appears too diverse and too small at the same time to allow a single explanation for their genesis, either sociohistorical or typological. Still, there are the intriguing close parallels between languages that emerged in different parts of the world in an almost identical fashion, for instance Hubner Mischsprache in Slovenia and Mednyj Aleut in Northeast Asia, or Michif in North America and Okrika-Igbo in Africa. Typological explanations make better predictions than the sociohistorical ones for the seven languages, but they are not sufficient.

Even though I have not been able to provide a unified explanation, I would like to point to a number of additional remarkable points. One is the connection between overt personal pronouns and verbal inflections, which is encountered in most of the mixed languages. Another point is the possible connection between locative deictic markers, demonstratives and personal pronouns. Matras (2009) has pointed out some of this before. I have mentioned the parallels between mixed languages and genderlects in these, and other respects, elsewhere (Bakker 2019).

Finally, we can remark that all of these mixed languages have some level of difference in the phonological systems. In a number of cases (such as the Australian ones), one or both of the languages has been influenced strongly by the other. Still, in general, there are phonological differences between the source languages, which are very rare to nonexistent in the G-L mixed languages (see Van Gijn 2009).

Abbreviations

ABS	absolutive
ALL	allative
COMPAR	comparative
DIM	diminutive
DOM	differential object marker
DUR	durative
ERG	ergative
EX	exclusive
F/FEM	feminine
FUT	future
HORT	hortative
LOC	locative
NEG	negation
NFUT	nonfuture
NPAST	nonpast
OBJ	object
PL	plural
POSS	possessive
PROSP	prospective
PUNCT	punctual
SG	singular
SUBJ	subject
V	verb

Abbreviations of language names

A	Aleut
C	Cree
E	English
F	French,
G	Gurindji
Ge	German
I	Ijo
K	Creole
O	Okrika
R	Russian
S	Slovene
T	Tiwi
W	Warlpiri

References

Adamou, Evangelia. 2010. Bilingual speech and language ecology in Greek Thrace: Romani and Pomak in contact with Turkish. *Language in Society* 39(2). 147–171.

Adamou, Evangelia & Kimmo Granqvist. 2015. Unevenly mixed Romani languages. *International Journal of Bilingualism* 19(5). 525–547.

Bakker, Peter. 1991. The Ojibwe element in Michif. In William Cowan (ed.), *Papers of the Twentysecond Algonquian Conference*, 11–20. Ottawa: Carleton University. https://ojs.library.carleton.ca/index.php/ALGQP/article/view/1043/926 (accessed 10 January 2020)

Bakker, Peter. 1997. *A language of our own: The genesis of Michif, the mixed Cree-French language of the Canadian Métis*. New York: Oxford University Press.

Bakker, Peter. 2003. Mixed languages as autonomous systems. In Yaron Matras & Peter Bakker (eds.), *The mixed language debate: Theoretical and empirical advances*, 107–150. Berlin: Mouton de Gruyter.

Bakker, Peter. 2013. Mixed languages. *Oxford Bibliographies online*. Oxford University Press. www.oxfordbibliographies.com.

Bakker, Peter. 2017. Typology of mixed languages. In Alexandra Y. Aikhenvald and R.M.W. Dixon (eds.), *The Cambridge handbook of linguistic typology*, 217–253. Cambridge: Cambridge University Press.

Bakker, Peter. 2019. Intentional language change and the connection between mixed languages and genderlects. *Language Dynamics and Change* 9. 135–161.

Bakker, Peter. 2020a. Para-Romani varieties. In Yaron Matras & Anton Tenser (eds.), *The Palgrave handbook of Romani language and linguistics*, 353–386. London: Palgrave Macmillan.

Bakker, Peter. 2020b. Contact and mixed languages. In Raymond Hickey (ed.), *Handbook of language contact*, 201–220. 2nd edn. New York: Wiley.

Bøegh, Kristoffer Friis, Aymeric Daval-Markussen & Peter Bakker. 2016. A phylogenetic analysis of stable structural features in West African languages. *Studies in African Linguistics* 45 (1&2). 61–94.

Boretzky, Norbert & Birgit Igla. 1994. Romani mixed dialects. In Peter Bakker & Maarten Mous (eds.), *Mixed languages: 15 case studies in language intertwining*, 35–68. Amsterdam: Institute for Functional Research into Language and Language Use.

Dimmendaal, Gerrit J. 2011. *Historical linguistics and the comparative study of African languages*. Amsterdam: John Benjamins.

Friedman, Viktor. 2013. Compartmentalized grammar: The variable (non)-integration of Turkish verbal conjugation in Romani dialects. *Romani Studies*, 23(1). 107–120.

Golovko, Evgeniy V. 2003. Language contact and group identity: The role of "folk" linguistic engineering. In Yaron Matras and Peter Bakker (eds.), *The mixed language debate: Theoretical and empirical advances*, 177–208. Berlin: Mouton de Gruyter.

Goodale, Jane. 1971. *Tiwi wives*. Seattle: University of Washington Press.

Greenberg, Joseph H. 1963. *The languages of Africa*. Bloomington: Indiana University Press.

Hart, Charles William Merton & Arnold R. Pilling. 1960. *The Tiwi of North Australia*. New York: Holt, Rinehart, Winston. (Third edition, with Jane Goodale, 1988)

Hart, Charles William Merton, Arnold R Pilling & Jane Goodale. 1988. *The Tiwi of North Australia*. New York: Holt, Rinehart, Winston.

Kossmann, Maarten. 2010. Parallel system borrowing. Parallel morphological systems due to the borrowing of paradigms. *Diachronica* 27(3). 459–487. doi 10.1075/dia.27.3.03kos

Lee, Jennifer R. 1983. *Tiwi today: a study of language change in a contact situation*. Canberra: Australian National University.

LePage, Robert B. & Andrée Tabouret-Keller. 1985. *Acts of identity: Creole-based approaches to language and ethnicity*. Cambridge: Cambridge University Press.

Lessiak, Primus. 1959. *Die deutsche Mundart von Zarz in Oberkrain. A. Grammatik*. Marburg: N.G. Elwet Verlag.

Matras, Yaron. 2000. Mixed Languages: A functional-communicative approach. *Bilingualism: Language and cognition* 3. 79–99.

Matras, Yaron. 2009. *Language contact*. Cambridge: Cambridge University Press.

Matras, Yaron. 2015. Why is the borrowing of inflectional morphology dispreferred? In Francesco Gardani, Peter Arkadiev & Nino Amiridze (eds.), *Borrowed morphology*, 47–80. Berlin: de Gruyter.

McConvell, Patrick. 2008. Mixed Languages as outcomes of code-switching: Recent examples from Australia and their implications. *Journal of Language Contact* 2(1).: 187–212.

McConvell, Patrick & Felicity Meakins. 2005. Gurindji Kriol: A mixed language emerges from code-switching. *Australian Journal of Linguistics* 25(1). 9–30.

Meakins, Felicity. 2008. Land, language and identity: The socio-political origins of Gurindji Kriol. In M. Meyerhoff & N. Nagy (eds.), *Social Lives in Language*, 69–94. Amsterdam: John Benjamins.

Meakins, Felicity. 2011. *Case marking in contact: The development and function of case morphology in Gurindji Kriol*. Amsterdam: John Benjamins.

Meakins, Felicity. 2013a. Mixed languages. In Yaron Matras & Peter Bakker (eds.), *Contact languages: A comprehensive guide*, 159–228. Berlin: De Gruyter Mouton.

Meakins, Felicity. 2013b. Gurindji Kriol. In Susanne Maria Michaelis, Philippe Maurer, Martin Haspelmath & Magnus Huber (eds.), *The survey of pidgin and creole languages. Volume 3: Contact languages based on languages from Africa, Asia, Australia, and the Americas*, 131–139. Oxford: Oxford University Press.

Meakins, Felicity. 2014. Language contact varieties. In Harold Koch & Rachel Nordlinger (eds.), *The languages and linguistics of Australia. A comprehensive guide*, 365–416. Berlin: De Gruyter Mouton.

Meakins, Felicity. 2018. *Mixed languages*. In Mark Aronoff (ed.), *Oxford research encyclopedias: Literature*, 1–29. Oxford: Oxford University Press. https://doi.org/10.1093/acrefore/9780199384655.013.151

Meakins, Felicity & Carmel O'Shannessy. 2012. Typological constraints on verb integration in two Australian mixed languages. *Journal of Language Contact* 5(2). 216–246.

Meakins, Felicity and Jesse Stewart. In press. Mixed languages. To appear in: Salikoko Mufwene & A. M. Escobar (Eds.), *Cambridge handbook of language contact*. Cambridge: Cambridge University Press.

Mous, Maarten. 2003. *The making of a mixed language: The case of Ma'a/Mbugu*. Amsterdam: John Benjamins.

Muysken, Pieter. 2008. *Functional categories*. Cambridge: Cambridge University Press.

Myers-Scotton, Carol. 1998. A way to dusty death: The matrix language turnover hypothesis. In Leonore Grenoble & Lindsay Whaley (eds.), *Endangered languages: Language loss and community response*, 289–316. Cambridge: Cambridge University Press. doi:10.1017/CBO9781139166959.013

Myers-Scotton, Carol. 2002. *Contact linguistics, bilingual encounters and grammatical outcomes*. Oxford, UK: Oxford University Press.

O'Shannessy, Carmel. 2013. The role of multiple sources in the formation of an innovative auxiliary category in Light Warlpiri, a new Australian mixed language. *Language* 89(2). 328–353.

Pohl, Heinz-Dieter. 1995. Slowenisch-deutscher Sprachkontakt in Krain. Bemerkungen zur "Hubner Mischsprache", in Klaus Sornig et al. (eds.), *Festschrift für Norman Denison*, (Grazer Linguistische Monographien *10*), 315–322. Graz: Institut für Sprachwissenschaft. [new version: http://members.chello.at/heinz.pohl/Sprachkontakt_Zarz.pdf]

Rhodes, Richard A. 1977. French Cree – A case of borrowing. In *Actes du huitième congrès des Algonquinistes*, ed. William Cowan, 6–25. Ottawa: Carleton University. https://ojs.library.carleton.ca/index.php/ALGQP/article/view/696

Rhodes, Richard A. 2008. Ojibwe in the Cree of Métchif. In Karl Hele & Regna Darnell (eds.), *Papers of the Thirty-ninth Algonquian Conference*. 569–580 London, Ont.: University of Western Ontario. https://ojs.library.carleton.ca/index.php/ALGQP/article/view/1211

Sasse, Hans Jürgen. 1992. Theory of language death. In Mathias Brenzinger (ed.), *Language death: Factual and theoretical explorations with special references to East Africa*, 7–30. Berlin: Mouton de Gruyter.

Sekerina, Irina A. 1994. Copper Island (Mednyj) Aleut (CIA) A mixed language. *Languages of the World* 8. 14–31.

Thomason, Sarah G. 1996. Mednyj Aleut. In Sarah Grey Thomason (ed.), *Contact languages: a wider perspective*, 449–468. Amsterdam: John Benjamins.

Thomason, Sarah G. 2003. Social factors and linguistic processes in the emergence of stable mixed languages. In Yaron Matras & Peter Bakker (eds.), *The mixed language debate: Theoretical and empirical advances*, 21–39. Berlin: Mouton de Gruyter.

Thomason, Sarah Grey, and Terrence Kaufman. 1988. *Language contact, creolization, and genetic linguistics*. Berkeley: University of California Press.

Vakhtin, Nikolai. 1998. Copper Island Aleut; a case of language endangerment. In Leonore A. Grenoble and Lindsey J. Whaley (eds.), *Endangered languages: Language loss and community response*, 317–327. Cambridge: Cambridge University Press.

Van Gijn, Rik. 2009. The phonology of mixed languages. *Journal of Pidgin and Creole Languages* 24(1). 91–117.

Wakama, Carol Gloria. 1999. A mixed language in Okrika. Nigeria: University of Harcourt BA Thesis. http://www.rogerblench. nfo/Language/Niger-Congo/Ijoid/Kirike/Wakama%201999.pdf

Wilson, Aidan, Peter Hurst, and Gillian Wigglesworth. 2018. Code-switching or code-mixing? Tiwi children's use of language resources in a multilingual environment. In Gillian Wigglesworth, Jane Simpson & Jill Vaughan (eds.), *Language practices of Indigenous children and youth. The transition from home to school*, 119–145. (Palgrave Studies in Minority Languages and Communities). London: Palgrave.

Yarshater, Ehsan. 1977. The hybrid language of the Jewish communities of Persia. *Journal of the American Oriental Society* 97(1). 1–7.

Jesse Stewart and Felicity Meakins
Advances in mixed language phonology: An overview of three case studies

1 Introduction

Mixed languages have provided a fascinating platform for linguistic inquiry for the better part of four decades when initial works began to appear in the literature. From the 1990s to approximately the mid-2000s, interest in the mixed language debate peaked with a number of influential publications that aspired to make sense of this rare linguistic phenomenon. This research laid the foundation for numerous theoretical, empirical, and descriptive works that continue to refine what it means to be a "mixed language" and the importance of these languages in understanding language contact and language genesis. Nearly all studies involving inquiries into mixed languages centre on theoretical, empirical, or descriptive accounts of higher-level phenomena involving the mixing of lexicon, morphosyntax, semantics, in addition to socio-cultural phenomena that give rise to such extreme language mixing. However, beyond basic descriptions based primarily on impressionistic observations, one area of mixed language research that has been largely overlooked is that of phonology, and of greater theoretical interest, the phonetic repercussions of amalgamating two or more sound systems into a single language.

Mixed languages are unlike Creoles and other forms of language contact in that they are created for expressive purposes rather than out of communicative need. This is because the originators of mixed languages are already proficient bilinguals in the source languages. This fact raises a number of questions regarding how phonological material is arranged in the mixed language as the originators likely had some degree of proficiency in both source sound systems; unlike the originators of Creole languages who are often only proficient in one. This chapter provides a synopsis of the advances in mixed language phonology over the last decade based on three case studies involving Media Lengua, Gurindji Kriol, and Michif that have used empirical research involving acoustic measurements and psycholinguistic perception experiments.

Jesse Stewart, University of Saskatchewan, stewart.jesse@usask.ca
Felicity Meakins, The University of Queensland, f.meakins@uq.edu.au

https://doi.org/10.1515/9781501511257-003

1.1 Conflict sites

Investigating mixed language phonology, or the phonology of any contact language, begins with identifying *phonemic conflict sites* in the source languages' sound inventories. *Conflict sites* are areas of convergence in the grammars of two or more language varieties in contact where two or more forms compete to express a particular function. The identification of conflict sites is a useful diagnostic tool for determining the source grammar of code-switching vocabulary, lexical borrowings, structural gaps from incomplete or "unguided" L2 acquisition and areas of grammatical convergence (see e.g., Poplack 1993; Rosen 2007; Smith-Christmas et. al 2013). While conflict sites are commonly used to identify areas of convergence in the morphosyntax of contact grammars, phonemic conflict sites (i.e., areas of phonological convergence where two or more sounds compete for a position in the phoneme inventory of a language) provide the basis for identifying how a sound system in a contact grammar is formed. For example, if the ancestral language,[1] which makes up the bulk of a mixed language's phonology, contains phonemes /a, i, u/ and the introduced language contains phonemes /a, i, e, u, o/, /e/ and /o/ are considered phonemic conflict sites as speakers must decide what happens with these sounds (e.g., they could undergo assimilation to vowels of a similar quality or enter in the language as new phonemes). In fact, phonemic conflict sites make up the foundation of every comparative phonetic analysis in the mixed language literature to date, whether they are identified as such or not (see e.g., Rosen 2006, 2007; Jones, Meakins, and Buchan 2011; Buchan 2012; Jones, Meakins, and Mauwiyath 2012; Jones and Meakins 2013; Stewart 2014, 2015a, 2015b, 2018a, 2018b, 2020; Rosen, Stewart, and Sammons 2020; Stewart et. al 2018; Rosen et. al 2019; Stewart et. al. 2020). The following sections present phonological processes involved in "conventional" lexical borrowings (section 1.2), traditional descriptions and theoretical accounts of mixed language phonology (section 1.3), and empirical evidence of mixed language phonology using acoustic and perceptual data (section 1.4).

---

[1] The terms "ancestral" and "introduced" are used in a chronological sense with the former referring to the original homeland language (i.e., pre-contact), while the latter is the language introduced to this group, either through trade, colonization, or their own migration (i.e., post-contact).

1.2 "Conventional" contact language phonology

There is a large body of literature that describes what happens when two or more languages or dialects come into contact. As a group, contact languages typically exhibit similar types of changes; however, the degree of change can vary considerably. It has been shown that when contact takes place, extra-linguistic factors place one language variety in a more socially prestigious position over the other(s). In most cases the "introduced" language takes this position and has an unidirectional influence on the "ancestral" language (Fought 2010; Hickey 2010).

Cross-linguistically, linguistic elements show different degrees of susceptibility to transfer, for example nouns are borrowed more often than verbs and derivational morphology transfers more readily than inflectional morphology (Thomason 2010). However, one domain which is most often resistant to transfer is phonology. Under typical conditions, loanwords conform to the phonological constraints of the recipient language. This adaptation can affect a loanword at all levels of phonology (segmental, phonotactic, suprasegmental, morphophonological etc.) (Kang 2011). Because of their phonological assimilation, loanwords often become indistinguishable from the native lexicon (e.g., English speakers often pronounce 'karaoke' as [ˌkʰæɹiːˈoʊkʼɪ] and not as [karaoke̞] in Japanese, its language of origin) (Winford 2010). However, as the contact situation intensifies and learning becomes more "guided", phonological and phonetic features may also transfer from loanwords to the source language (e.g., Ossetic native vocabulary containing borrowed ejectives from neighbouring Caucasian languages) (Thomason 2010: 42). In very intense contact situations, sounds from the source language may even be borrowed into the recipient language's native vocabulary (Thomason 2010).

1.3 Traditional descriptions of mixed language phonology

Traditional phonological analyses and theoretical accounts of mixed languages claim that their phonological structure can be reasonably predicted based on how the language is arranged morphosyntactically. Such analyses essentially predict two possible outcomes where speakers of the mixed language either (1) adopt the phonology of the ancestral language or (2) preserve the phonologies of each source language (i.e., stratification). In the past, researchers have often tied the phonological outcome of mixed languages with their structural make up, which consist of three fundamental types (Bakker 2015; Meakins 2016; Meakins and Stewart accepted):
1) L(exical)-G(rammar) mixed languages
2) Converted languages
3) V(erb)-N(oun) mixed languages

In the first group, LG mixed languages, including Angloromani (see e.g., Hancock 1976, 1984; Matras, Gardner, Jones, and Schulmann 2007), Media Lengua (see e.g., Muysken 1981, 1997; Gómez-Rendón 2005) and Ma'á (see e.g., Mous 2003a, 2003b), phonology has been considered to be part of the grammatical system. This is based on the phonological regularization of lexical items from language A to that of the grammatical source language B (Bakker 2003). Therefore, the Spanish lexicon in Media Lengua would sound like that of Quichua (e.g., Media Lengua word of Spanish origin: *kiri-* [ˈkiri] 'want' vs. Spanish: *quere-* [keˈɾe] 'want'; Media Lengua word of Quichua origin (also borrowed in Spanish): *lluchu* [ʒuʧu] vs. Quichua: *lluchu* [ʒuʧu] vs. Spanish: *llucho* [ʎuʧo] 'naked'), and the Romani lexicon in Angloromani would sound like English.

The second group of mixed languages, known as converted languages, is categorised based on radical changes to its typology while maintaining its native vocabulary (Bakker 2003). Such typological changes are driven by the process of metatypy where the morphosyntax of language X in a bilingual speech community is restructured based on the morphosyntax of language Y (i.e., a type of extreme grammatical calquing) but the forms of the language essentially remain the same (Ross 2007). Little has been written about the phonological outcomes of these languages. However, for Modern Sri Lankan Portuguese (MSLP), Smith (1978) mentions that the vowel system is of Portuguese origin regarding number and place of articulation, yet the nasal contrast found in Portuguese had been eliminated in favour of the length contrast found in Tamil (e.g., /ẽ/ → /eː/).

The third group consists of V-N mixed languages such as Michif (see Bakker 1997), Mednyj Aleut (see Golovko 1990), and Gurindji Kriol (see Meakins 2011). Instead of showing a clear division between lexicon and grammar, these languages show splits between lexical and grammatical categories in the noun and verb systems. Unlike the phonological systems of the previous groups, both Michif and Mednyj Aleut are often analysed as having two "co-existing" phonologies. In the case of Michif, French phonology applies to French origin elements and Cree phonology applies to Cree origin elements (e.g., Michif of French origin: *li grañ* [ləgʁæ̃] vs. French: *le gran* [ləgʁæ̃] 'the big'; Michif of Cree origin: *shooshkwaaw* [ʃoːʃkwaːw] vs. Cree *sôskwâw* [soːskwaːw] 'it's slippery') (Rhodes 1986; Bakker 1997; Bakker and Papen 1997). Rosen (2007), however provided a synchronic description of the Michif phonological system suggesting that it was unnecessary to focus on the source languages to accurately describe its underlying structure. Regarding Mednyj Aleut, Russian borrowings maintain Russian phonology while the rest of the language maintains an Aleut phonological structure (Thomason 1997). Similarly, in Gurindji Kriol, words from Gurindji maintain a three-vowel contrast whereas words from Kriol (an English derived creole) maintain a five-vowel contrast (Jones, Meakins, and Mauwiyath 2012).

Van Gijn's (2009) analysis, based on descriptions of Media Lengua, Callahuaya, Mednyj Aleut, and Michif, concludes that the phonology of a mixed language can be predicted based on the unmixed phonological domains and where they appear on the prosodic hierarchy (see Nespor and Vogel 1986). Therefore, mixed languages with an agglutinating structure such as Media Lengua would conform to the phonology of the ancestral language, which provides the grammar, as the vast majority of words in the language contain elements from both languages (e.g., Spanish stems and Quichua suffixes). However, Michif, formed from a polysynthetic language (Plains Cree) and a fusional language (Métis French), contains a greater number of "unmixed" words because verb phrases (mainly of Plains Cree origin) remain separated from noun phrases (mainly of French origin). As such, van Gijn claims that French phonological rules can be applied to French origin noun phrases (NP) and Cree phonological rules can be applied to Cree origin verb phrases (VP).

Turning to the prosodic hierarchy, van Gijn explains that since Media Lengua and Michif contain elements from both source languages at higher prosodic levels (e.g., the intonational phrase and above) suprasegmental material should be identifiable from both languages. However, at the mid-levels of the prosodic hierarchy (e.g., the phonological phrase and prosodic word), he suggests that Media Lengua should conform to Quichua phonology since the language still shares elements at these levels. In contrast, Michif would still be considered "divided" (e.g., NPs and VPs are nearly always separate prosodic words). Finally at the lower levels (e.g., syllable and foot[2]), van Gijn suggests that both Media Lengua (also see Muysken 2013) and Michif should be stratified phonologically.

1.4 Empirical studies involving mixed language phonology

While van Gijn's (2009) analysis reflects various impressionistic aspects of the surface-level phonologies of mixed languages, it falls short at predicting the actual phonetic production and perceptual realities of these languages. From a phonetic stand point, mixed language phonology is a complex arrangement of the source language phonologies. Analyses of Media Lengua (Stewart 2014, 2015a,

---

[2] Van Gijn does not include the foot level in his analysis though Muysken (2013) does.

2015b, 2018b, 2019), Gurindji Kriol (Jones, Meakins and Mauwiyath 2011, 2012; Buchan 2012; Jones and Meakins 2013; Stewart et al. 2018, Stewart, Meakins, Algy, Ennever, and Joshua, 2020), and Michif (Rosen, 2006, 2007; Rosen et al., 2020; Rosen et al. 2019) suggest that there exists a propensity for phonological material to assimilate to the phonology of the ancestral language (e.g., Quichua for Media Lengua, Gurindji for Gurindji Kriol, and Cree for Michif). In other words, the language, which was acquired originally as an L2 (the introduced language) essentially conforms to the L1 phonological system of the ancestral language in much the same way a mid to late bilingual[3] might acquire the phonology of their L2.

At the same time, the introduced language appears to feed in phonological aspects that appear beneficial for maintaining contrasts. However, the arrangements of the source phonologies do not always conform to traditional notions of adaptive dispersion models which predict that when a new category is established, crowding of the phonetic space occurs causing dispersion in order to maintain contrasts (Liljencrants and Lindblom 1972; Lindblom 1986, 1990; Johnson 2000; Livijn 2000; Flege 2007). Instead we observe near-mergers, overlapping categories, categorical assimilation, categorical maintenance, and overshoot of target categories at the segmental level, in addition to prosodic assimilation, possible preservations of archaic patterns, and innovation at the suprasegmental level.

It should also be noted that the three mixed languages discussed below have some striking similarities across their phoneme inventories. In each case, the ancestral language (Quichua, Gurindji, & Cree) has a comparatively small vowel inventory and the stop series contains no voicing contrast (voiceless stops only). In contrast, the introduced languages (Spanish, Kriol, and French) have larger vowel inventories and voicing contrasts in their stop series. Given these similarities across each language and the number of studies conducted on vowels and stops in these mixed languages, we have the benefit of a number of cross-linguistic comparisons, which will be discussed in section 2. The following sections present case studies involving Media Lengua (section 2.1), Gurindji Kriol (section 2.2), and Michif (section 2.3).

---

[3] Guion (2003: 106) defines a mid bilingual as a person who acquires their L2 between the ages of 9–13 and a late bilingual after the age of 15.

2 Case studies

2.1 Media Lengua

Media Lengua (ISO 639-3: mue) is a LG mixed language with an extraordinary degree of relexification, surpassing 90% in the Imbabura dialect (see 1). The primary lexical basis for Media Lengua is Rural Andean Ecuadorian Spanish while the primary grammatical basis is Imbabura Quichua spoken in the southern region of Lago San Pablo. Media Lengua, like Quichua, is an agglutinating SOV language with highly regular morphology. In (1), the bolded elements in the IPA transcription are of Spanish origin while those in normal font are of Quichua origin. Translations in Rural Spanish and Quichua are provided for comparison.

(1) *Yoca esperashami breve volvimungui.*
 jo-ka **espera**-ʃa-mi **breβe** **bolβi**-mu-ngi
 1-TOP wait-FUT-VAL quickly return-TRANS-2
 'Yo te esperaré, vuelve breve.' (Rural Spanish)
 'Ñukaca shuyashami utiya tigramungui.' (Quichua)
 'I'll wait for you, come back quickly.'
 (Consultant #50)

2.1.1 Source language inventories

The Native Imbabura Quichua phoneme inventory is made up of 18 consonants (Table 1) and 3 vowels (Figure 1). Rural Andean Spanish spoken in Ecuador contains 19 consonants (Table 2) and 5 vowels (Figure 2). Comparing the phoneme inventories from both languages, 12 possible phonemic conflict sites can be identified; 5 from Quichua (/h, z, ʒ, ʃ, ɸ/) and 7 (/b, d, g, e, o, r, ʎ/) from Spanish. To date, all 7 conflict sites from Spanish have been analysed using quantitative methods.

2.1.1.1 Quichua
Imbabura Quichua differs from other Quechuan dialects in that it has collapsed a number of sounds into /ʒ/; most notably the lateral approximant /ʎ/, and the voicing of /ts/ in post-nasal positions (Cole 1982; Toapanta and Haboud 2012; Stewart 2019). Moreover, there is little evidence of an aspirated stop series in Imbabura Quichua and ejective stops and uvular stops are not

Table 1: Consonant inventory for Imbabura Quichua.

	Bilabial	Labiodental	Dental	Alveolar	Postalveolar	Retroflex	Palatal	Velar	Glottal
Plosive	p		t̪					k	
Nasal	m		n				ɲ		
Tap				ɾ					
Fricative		f		s	ʃʒ	ʐ		x	h
Affricate				tʃ					
Approximant							j		w
Lateral Approximant				l					

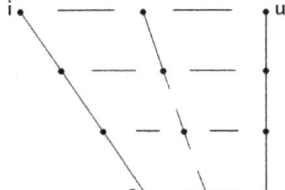

Figure 1: Vowel inventory for Imbabura Quichua.

Table 2: Consonant inventory for Rural Andean Spanish spoken in Ecuador.

	Bilabial	Dental	Alveolar	Postalveolar	Palatal	Velar
Plosive	p b	t̪ d̪				k g
Nasal	m	n			ɲ	
Trill			r			
Tap			ɾ			
Fricative	ɸ		s	ʃ*		x
Affricate				tʃ		
Approximant					j	w
Lateral Approximant			l		ʎ	

*non-native Spanish words.

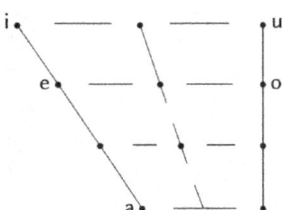

Figure 2: Vowel inventory for Rural Andean Spanish spoken in Ecuador.

found in Ecuadorian dialects of Quichua. Any sound that might resemble a trill [r/ʀ] in other dialects is pronounced as a voiced retroflex [ʐ] in Imbabura as well (e.g., *arrarray* 'it's so hot!').

The native vowel system of Imbabura Quichua consists of three corner vowels (/i, u, a/), which are sometimes described as /ɪ, ʊ, a/ (see e.g., Guion 2003). Unlike other Quechuan dialects, Ecuadorian Quichua does not contain the allophonic rule that lowers the high vowels to [e] and [o] when preceded by a uvular consonant (/q/) (e.g., Cuzco [kuzqo]) (Adelaar and Muysken 2004: 196).

2.1.1.2 Spanish

Spanish spoken throughout Ecuador varies greatly with a large number of regional dialects and sociolects spoken throughout the country. Those in the Andean region show some degree of convergence with Quichua while those on the coast (Equatorial dialects) reflect those of northern Peru and southern coastal Colombia (Boyd-Bowman 1953). For example, unlike other dialects of Spanish, speakers in Ecuador are able to identify differences between /t͡ʃ/ vs. /ʃ/ as the latter has entered the language through a number of Quichua borrowings (e.g., *shungo* 'heart', *shunsho* 'silly/fool', *mashi* 'friend'). Table 2 provides the phoneme inventory for Andean Spanish; other similarities with Quichua will be discussed in section 3.

The vowels in Andean Spanish are typically analysed as a five-vowel system consisting of three corner vowels in addition to a mid-vowel series. However, empirical evidence from Guion (2003) shows that late L2 bilinguals (L1 Quichua) often raise the mid vowel series or collapse it entirely with the high vowels suggesting that the system functions with three vowels.

2.1.2 Obstruents

The stop voicing phonemic conflict site in Media Lengua (/p-b/, /t-d/, /k-g/ from Spanish & /p/, /t/, /k/ from Quichua) provides an example of complete integration of an introduced sound contrast into the phonology of a mixed language where the ancestral language had no such contrast. In a study on stop production in Media Lengua involving 2456 elicited tokens produced by 19 speakers (12 women/7 men) recorded in their homes, Stewart (2018a) showed that Media Lengua speakers consistently produce voiced stops in Spanish origin words with long negative voice onset times (VOT) that reflect those of L1 speakers of Rural Spanish (1,060 tokens from 6 women/ 4 men) in all three places of articulation (Figure 3, left). The VOT of voiced stops of Spanish origin in Quichua (1564 tokens from 12 women/8 men) were shown to be significantly longer than those produced in Media Lengua or Rural Spanish and a substantial number of tokens also underwent weakening (/b/ → [β] 28%; /d/ → [ð] 4%; /g/ → [ɣ] 47%), which was not seen to such a degree in the Media Lengua (/b/ → [β] 4%; /d/ → [ð] 0.5%; /g/ → [ɣ] 4%), though partially in Rural Spanish group (/b/ → [β] 9%; /d/ → [ð] 4%; /g/ → [ɣ] 46%) (see Stewart, 2015b). For the voiceless series, Media Lengua speakers showed non-significant differences with Quichua speakers and Rural Spanish speakers in the production of short-lag (unaspirated) VOT, with the except of Rural Spanish [k], which only differed by 7 ms (Figure 3, bottom right).

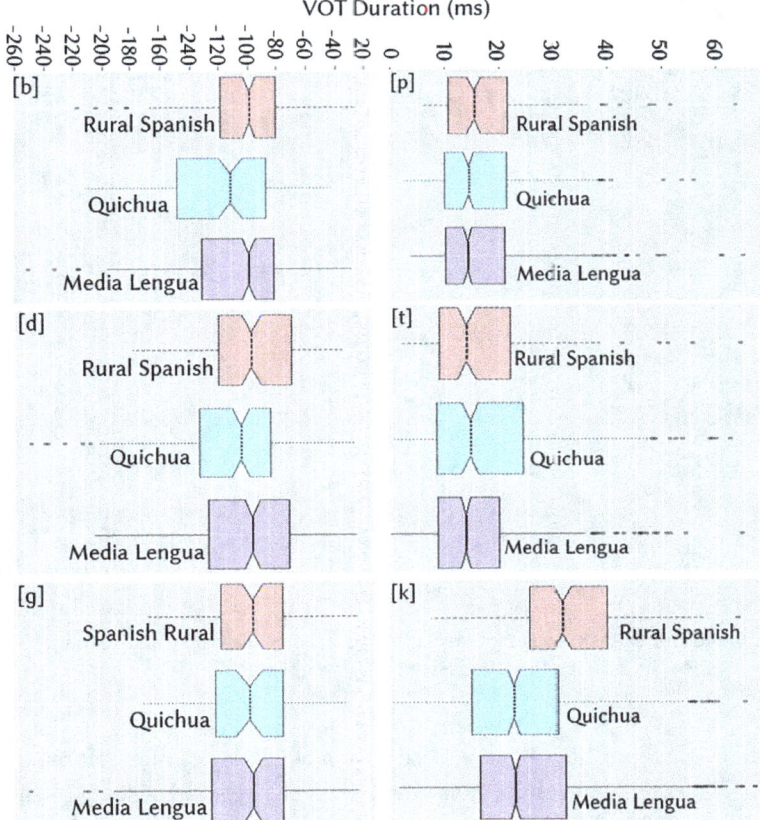

Figure 3: VOT comparisons for Media Lengua (solid, 9478C2) and Rural Spanish (dotted, FD8F86) voiced stops (left), and Media Lengua and Quichua (dotted, 5BCFF9) voiceless stops (right) based on Stewart (2018a).

To establish whether the production differences between voiced and voiceless stop play a functional role in the phonology as contrastive phonemes or whether Media Lengua speakers are simply assimilating Spanish-like voiced stops without considering categorical boundaries, Stewart (2015b) conducted a two alternative forced-choice (2AFC) identification task experiment with 10 participants. The experiment involved paired stimuli with gradually modified VOT durations of word-initial stops in minimal pairs across 10-step continua from a prototypical voiced stop to a prototypical voiceless stop (e.g., *peso-beso* 'weight-kiss', *tía-día* 'aunt-day'). Results from this experiment show that listeners identified significant differences in the voiced stops (Figure 4, step 1) from the voiceless stop

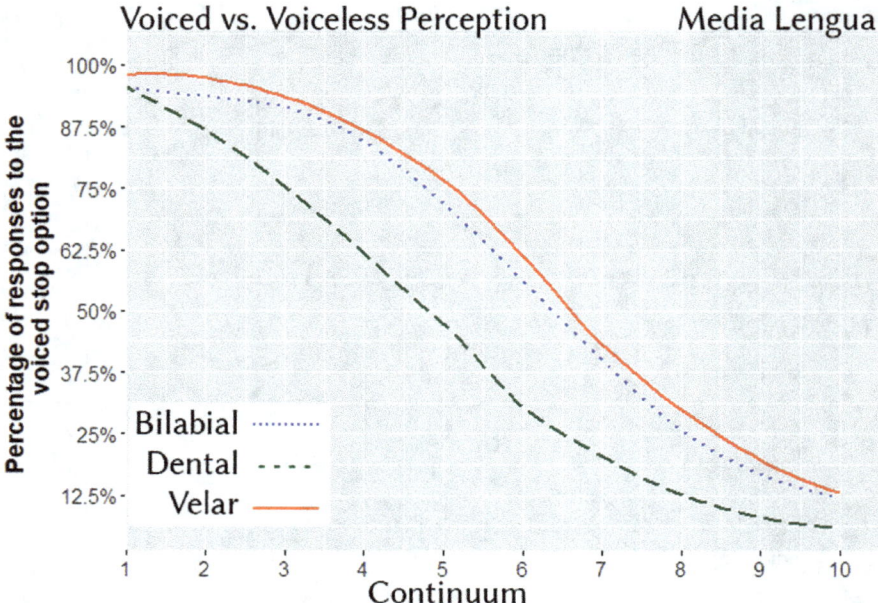

Figure 4: 2AFC identification task results for Media Lengua listeners averaged across the 10-step continua for each place of articulation based on Stewart (2015b).

(Figure 4, step 10) with a high degree of consistency across all three places of articulation.[4] The combined results from these studies suggest that Media Lengua speakers have fully adapted the stop voicing contrast both productively and perceptually from Spanish lexical borrowings.

2.1.3 Liquids

Another phonemic conflict site in Media Lengua involves the Spanish liquid consonants /r/ (trill) and /ʎ/ (palatal lateral approximant). In a phonetic analysis of this conflicting area of phonological convergence, Stewart (2019) shows

---

4 Notice that the categorical boundaries (the 50% point) for all three places of articulation in Figure 4 fall at -20 ms (+/− 2 ms). For the velars this appears at step 5 and for the dentals and bilabials at step 7. The visual difference in the figure is simply a graphing effect caused by superimposing all three places of articulation together, which reveals the different VOT range of the velars compared to the dentals and bilabials. This difference in range is caused by aerodynamic effects that make positive VOTs longer in more retracted places of articulation.

that /r/ and /ʎ/ have direct, one to one correspondences with native Quichua fricatives /ʐ/ and /ʒ/, respectively. As such, the Spanish origin sounds in Spanish origin words have been completely replaced by their Quichua fricative counterparts in Media Lengua. This wholesale assimilation was observed in all 19 of the Media Lengua-speaking participants with ratios of 104:1 [ʒ: ʎ] and 129:0 [ʐ: r].[5] An example of /r/ → /ʐ/ can be observed in Figure 5 with a standard trill on the left, identified by the closure and aperture phases which create regions of low and high energy across the wave form and spectrogram, respectively, throughout the segment, and the voiced fricative on the right, identified by the unimpeded frication throughout the segment (see Stewart 2019 for more details on the acoustic correlates of these segments).

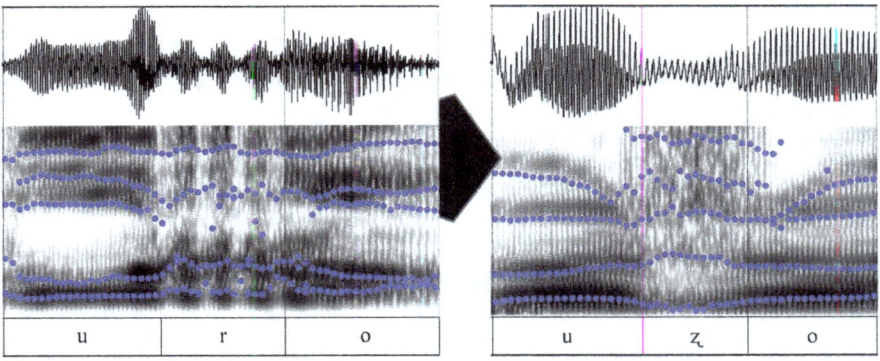

Figure 5: The standard Spanish trill produced in the word burro [ˈburo] 'donkey' (left) with 4 closure and 3 aperture phases vs. the standard Media Lengua retroflex fricative produced in the word burromi [buˈʐomi] 'donkey-val' (right).

An example of /ʎ/ → /ʒ/ is illustrated in Figure 6. In both images, the segment in question is flanked by approximants as the tongue is fronted from [o] towards the palate and postalveolar positions for the target segments before being once again retracted for the second [o]. One observable acoustic correlate that sets these sounds apart is the dispersion of the formant trajectories in the second half of the segment in Figure 6 (left), caused by lateral noise, whereas Figure 6 (right) has uninterrupted formant trajectories. Unlike the obstruent results, which showed a clear case of adoption by Media Lengua speakers, the Spanish origin liquids

---

[5] Data gathered in this section was collected from the same participants during the same field sessions described in 2.1.2.

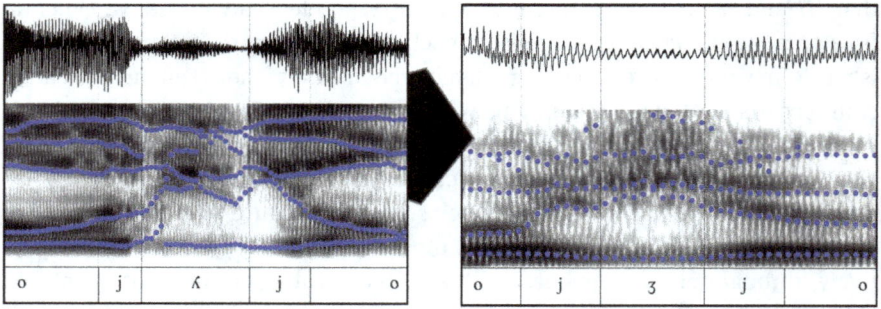

Figure 6: The Standard Spanish palatal lateral approximant produced in the word pollo [ˈpoʎo] 'chicken' vs. the standard Media Lengua postalveolar fricative produced in the word pollo [ˈpoʒo] 'chicken'.

provide a clear case of introduced phonemes undergoing assimilation to sounds in the ancestral language's phonology.

2.1.4 Vowels

The final phonemic conflict site discussed for Media Lengua, at the segmental level, involves its vowel system. In this case, Media Lengua speakers are confronted with two additional mid vowels (/e/ & /o/) entering the language through Spanish borrowings. For vowel production, Stewart (2014) describes a complex stratified system involving Media Lengua vowels based on their language of origin (Quichua & Spanish). This analysis involved F1 and F2 formant measurements from Quichua origin vowels (/i, u, a/) and Spanish origin vowels (/i, u, e, o, a/) from 2515 elicited tokens, recorded in the speakers' homes, from 10 speakers (6 women/ 4 men). Results showed that Quichua-source and Spanish-source high and low vowels of the same quality (/i, a, u/) co-exist as near-mergers (covert contrasts) in Media Lengua, which are only distinguishable from each other based on minute variances uncovered in the statistical analysis (see Figure 7). Yet, the Spanish-source vowels disperse away from the Quichua-source vowels is such a way that reflects the directions predicted by models of adaptive dispersion (see Liljencrants and Lindblom 1972; Lindblom 1986, 1990; Johnson 2000; Livijn 2000) (i.e., Spanish-source corner vowels are ever so slightly lower in F1 frequency for the high vowels /i/ and /u/, and ever so slightly higher in F1 frequency for the low vowel /a/).

For the Spanish-source mid-vowels (/e, o/) and Spanish-source (and by proxy Quichua-source) high vowels (/i, u/), Stewart (2014) revealed both systems

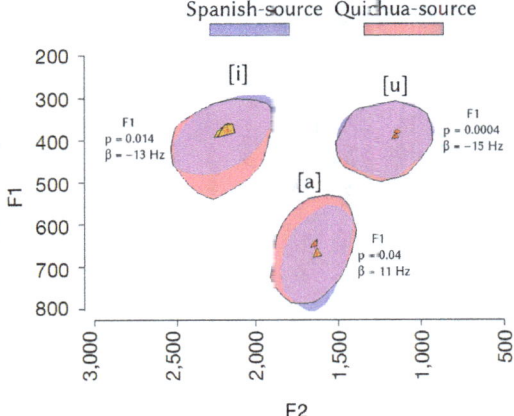

Figure 7: Fifty percent concentrations (large polygons) and averages (small centre polygons) of the overlapping Spanish-source (#9A9CFA) and Quichua-source (#FA9AAE) corner vowels in Media Lengua, based on Stewart (2014).

co-exist in Media Lengua with considerable overlap (see Figure 8). However, the differences in F1 frequency between the mid and high vowels were shown to be significant with an average distance of 41 Hz (0.36 Bark). This value falls just beyond the threshold of 0.3 Bark identified by Kewley (2001) for formant discrimination for formant values between 200 and 3000 Hz.

Based on this analysis, Stewart (2018b) asked whether Media Lengua listeners could aurally identify differences between mid- and high-vowels within these overlapping spaces. Similar to the experiment conducted by Stewart (2015b), a 2AFC identification task experiment was run with the same 10 participants but with the minimal pairs: *piso-peso* [ˈpi.so – ˈpe.so] 'floor-weight'; *pipa-pepa* [ˈpi.pa – ˈpe.pa] 'pipe-seed'; *lona-luna* [ˈlo.na – ˈlu.na] 'tarp-moon'; *poma-puma* [ˈpo.ma – ˈpu.ma] 'jug-puma'. Results from this experiment show that Media Lengua listeners identified significant differences between the mid vowels (Figure 9, step 1) and the high vowels (Figure 9, step 10) with a high degree of consistency across both the front and back series.[6]

---

[6] Notice that the categorical boundaries (the 50% point) for both vowels in Figure 9 have an F1 average between 469 Hz and 452 Hz; a difference of only 17 Hz. For the front vowels, this appears between steps 3 and 4, while for the back vowels this appears at step 5. The visual difference in the figure is simply a graphing effect caused by superimposing both front and back vowels together.

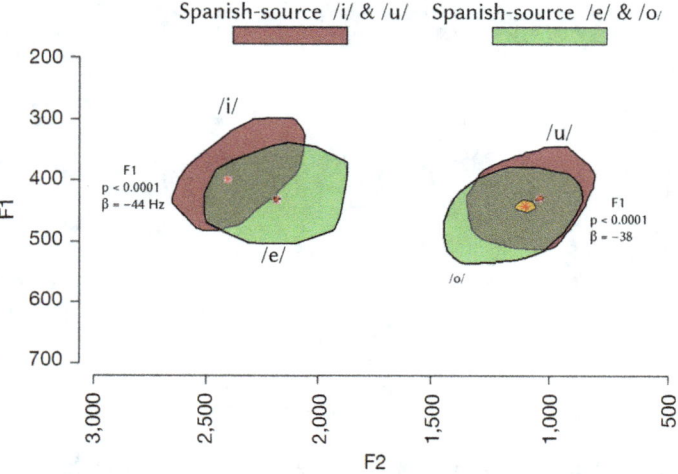

Figure 8: Fifty percent concentrations (large polygons) and averages (small centre polygons) of the overlapping Spanish-source high (#B97373) and Spanish-source mid (#79C87E) vowels in Media Lengua, based on Stewart (2014).

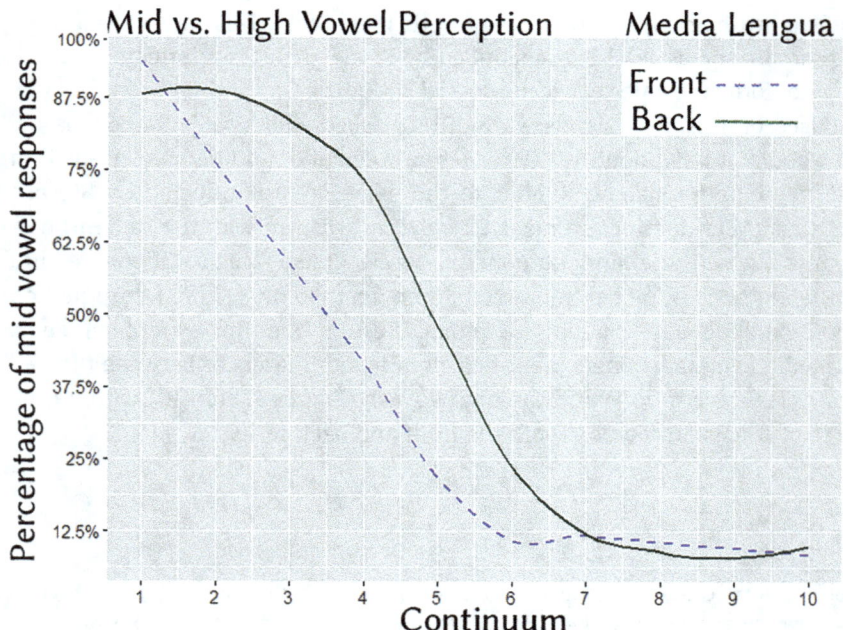

Figure 9: 2AFC identification task results for Media Lengua listeners averaged across the 10-step continua for the front (dashed) and back (solid) vowel series, based on Stewart (2018b).

Media Lengua, unlike Gurindji Kriol and Michif is often described as a mixed language with few stratified elements at the phonological level (Muysken 1997; Gómez-Rendón 2005; van Gijn 2009). However, the results from these studies call into question such analyses since Media Lengua appears to have adopted specific sounds (the voiced stop series described in 2.1.2), assimilated others (the liquids to fricatives described in 2.1.3), and operates two vowel systems with considerable overlap (described in 2.1.4). The next section (2.1.5) briefly describes intonation in Media Lengua.

2.1.5 Suprasegmentals

Regarding prosodic features in Media Lengua, Stewart (2015a) provides a description of intonation patterns based on fundamental frequency (f0) contours. This analysis suggests that the vast majority reflect intonation patterns in Quichua (see Cole 1982) and other Quechuan languages (see O'Rourke 2007) and those that did not were argued to either be innovations or archaic patterns not found in present day Quichua dialects geographically close to where Media Lengua is spoken. Additionally, no patterns were identified that reflected Spanish-like prosody, that were not already shared with Quichua.

2.2 Gurindji Kriol

Gurindji Kriol (ISO 639-3: gjr) is a V-N mixed language spoken in the Victoria River District of northern Australia. It emerged approximately 40 years ago through pervasive code-switching through intense contact between north Australian Kriol (an English-lexifier Creole, Roper Kriol is the classic variety) and Gurindji (a Pama–Nyungan language). Gurindji Kriol is currently spoken by Gurindji people in the communities of Daguragu and Kalkaringi, and by Bilinarra and Ngarinyman people in two communities north of Kalkaringi – Pigeon Hole and Yarralin. Unlike Media Lengua, Gurindji Kriol originates in both lexical and structural borrowings from both source languages with Gurindji providing the bulk of nominal phrase elements and Kriol providing the bulk of the verbal phrase elements. The lexicon of Gurindji Kriol is also quite mixed with an approximate 1:3 split between Kriol origin lexicon, Gurindji origin lexicon, and synonymous forms from both source languages. In (2), the bolded elements in the second line are of Kriol origin while those in normal font are of Gurindji origin. Translations in Kriol and Gurindji are provided for comparison.

(2) *Dat warlakungku bin baitim dat marluka futta.*
 dat waṟlaku-ŋgku **bin bait-im dat** maṟluka **fut**-ta
 the dog-ERG   PST bite-TR the old.man foot-LOC
 '*Dat dog bin baitim dat olman la fut.*' (Kriol)
 '*Warlaku-lu katurl payarni marluka jamana-la.*' (Gurindji)
 'The dog bit the old man on the foot.'

2.2.1 Source language inventories

The Gurindji phoneme inventory is made up of 17 consonants (Table 3) and 3 vowels with a marginal length distinction (Figure 1). Roper Kriol contains 29 consonants (Table 4) and 5 vowels with a length distinction (Figure 2). Comparing the phoneme inventories from both languages, 17 possible phonemic conflict sites can be identified; 1 from Gurindji (/c/) and 16 from Kriol (/b, t̪, ḍ, d, ɖ, g, f, s, ʃ, h, ʧ, ʤ, e, o, eː, oː/). To date, 10 of these conflict sites have been analysed using empirical methods (/b, d, g, f, s, e, o, eː, oː, ʤ/).

2.2.1.1 Gurindji
Gurindji, like many other Australian languages, is limited in its number of manner of articulation contrasts in its obstruent inventory. However, this is made up for with a high number of place of articulation contrasts (5 in Gurindji, but up to 6 or 7 in other Australian languages) (Fletcher and Butcher 2014).

The vowel system of Gurindji consists of three vowels with a marginal length contrast, which are described in Figure 10, as /ɪ, ʊ, ɐ/ (see Jones et al 2012: 309).

2.2.1.2 Kriol
Kriol shares a very similar inventory to that of Gurindji; however, some researchers suggest that the Roper dialect spoken in the community of Ngukurr contains a stop voicing contrast (Baker, Bundgaard-Nielsen, and Graetzer 2014) in addition to a fricative and an affricate series. Yet, varieties of Kriol with little contact with their lexifier languages have been shown to lack fricatives all together (Sandefur 1979, 1984, 1986; Sandefur and Harris 1986).

According to Jones, Meakins and Buchan (2011) the vowel inventory of Kriol spoken in Katherine contains five-vowels (see Figure 11). However, varieties with little contact with their lexifier languages have been shown to contain three vowels (Sandefur 1979).

Table 3: Consonant inventory for Gurindji based on (Meakins et. al 2013).

	Bilabial	Labiodental	Dental	Apico-Alveolar	Postalveolar	Retroflex	Pre-Palatal	Velar	Glottal
Plosive	p		t̪	t		ʈ	c	k	
Nasal	m		n̪	n		ɳ	ɲ	ŋ	
Trill				r					
Tap				ɾ					
Approximant						ɻ	j	w	
Lateral Approximant				l		ɭ	ʎ		

Table 4: Consonant inventory for Roper Kriol based on Baker, Bundgaard-Nielsen, and Graetzer (2014).

	Bilabial	Labiodental	Dental	Apico-Alveolar	Postalveolar	Retroflex	Pre-Palatal	Velar	Glottal
Plosive	p b		t̪ d̪	t d		ʈ ɖ		k g	
Nasal	m			n		ɳ	ɲ	ŋ	
Trill				r					
Tap				ɾ					
Fricative		f		s	ʃ				h
Affricate				tʃ dʒ					
Approximant						ɻ	j	w	
Lateral Approximant				l		ɭ	ʎ		

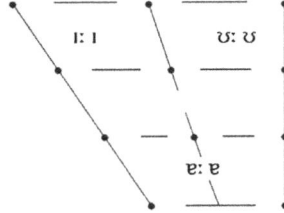

Figure 10: Vowel inventory for Gurindji (based on Jones, Meakins and Buchan 2011).

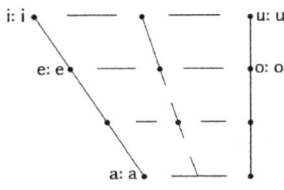

Figure 11: Vowel inventory for Kriol (based on Jones, Meakins and Buchan 2011).

2.2.2 Obstruents

Similar to Media Lengua, the stop voicing phonemic conflict site in Gurindji Kriol includes /p-b/, /t-d/, /k-g/ from Kriol, and /p/, /t/, /k/ from Gurindji. For Gurindji Kriol, English origin words in the Kriol lexicon are of greatest interest as English is originally responsible for bringing these contrasts into the language. Unlike Media Lengua, production of the voiced series of stops in Gurindji Kriol provides an example of mixed assimilation and integration, of an introduced sound contrast into the phonology of a mixed language, where the ancestral language had no such contrast (Jones and Meakins 2013). The production results of stops in word-initial position (Figure 12) from Jones and Meakins (2013), involving 330 tokens produced by 5 women, showed that speakers produce the bilabial series with short lag VOT no matter the language of origin. For the alveolar series, results show a high degree of variation in the VOT durations of Kriol origin /t/, ranging from long lag values (approx. 64 ms) to short lag values (approx. 0 ms). The VOT of both Kriol /d/ and Gurindji origin /t/ are produced with short lag values (approx. 21 ms & 18 ms respectively). The VOTs of the velar series show a gradient trend with Kriol origin /k/ being longer than Kriol origin /g/ and Gurindji origin /k/ being the shortest. However, averages of all three suggest they are all produced with relatively short lag values (max. approx. avg. 39 ms). Jones

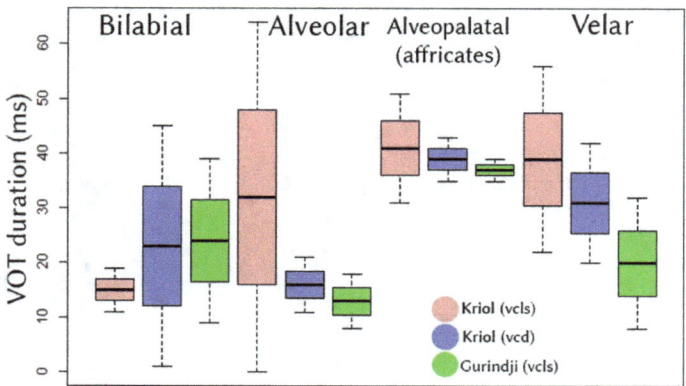

Figure 12: Word-initial VOT durations across place of articulation in Gurindji Kriol based on language of origin (EDA8A8 for voiceless stops of Kriol origin, 6478D1 for voiced stops of Kriol origin, and 66C24A for voiceless stops of Gurindji origin). This figure is roughly based on Figure 1 from Jones and Meakins (2013).

and Meakins (2013) also measured the VOT of affricates /tʃ/ and /dʒ/ in word-initial position. Their results show similar values no matter the language of origin (approx. avg. 39 ms +/– 2 ms).

Jones and Meakins (2013) also measured VOT durations from word-medial stops in addition to their closure durations. Their results (Figure 13A) for VOT show that Kriol origin /p/, with short lag VOT, differed significantly from both Kriol and Gurindji origin /b/ and /p/ with negative VOTs. However, little variation was revealed for the alveolar and velar series based on language of origin. For the affricates, VOT measurements from Kriol origin voiceless /tʃ/ were shown to be long lag, while Gurindji origin /tʃ/ were shown to be negative (Kriol origin voiced /dʒ/ was not analysed in their study).

Closure durations showed the same tendencies as the word-medial VOT durations (Figure 13B). Here, the bilabial closures for Kriol origin voiceless /p/ were significantly longer than those of Kriol origin /b/ and Gurindji origin /p/; the latter two being roughly similar in duration. Likewise, there was little variation between closure durations in both the alveolar and velar series based on language of origin. Reflecting the medial VOT durations once again, the closure durations for the affricates differed significantly with Kriol origin voiceless /tʃ/ being much longer than Gurindji origin /tʃ/.

Regarding perception of Gurindji Kriol stops by native speakers, Stewart et al. (2018) suggest a voicing contrast may currently be developing with increasing contact with mainstream English. Like the Media Lengua perception studies, a 2AFC identification task experiment was conducted. Fifty-nine participants took part

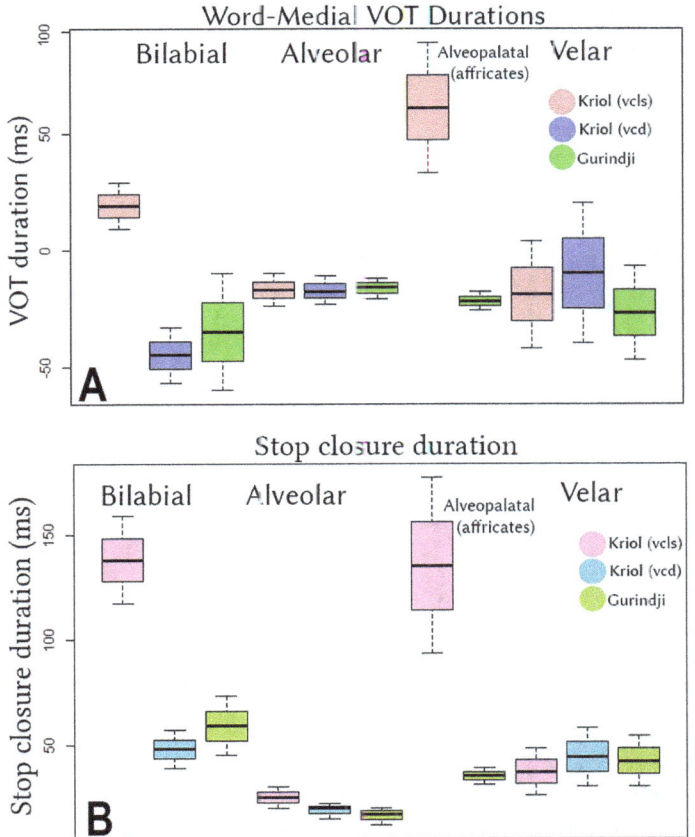

Figure 13: Image A illustrates word-medial VOT durations across place of articulation in Gurindji Kriol based on language of origin (EDA8A8 for voiceless stops of Kriol origin, 6478D1 for voiced stops of Kriol origin, and 66C24A for voiceless stops of Gurindji origin). This figure is roughly based on Figure 4 from Jones and Meakins (2013). Image B illustrates closure duration of word-medial stops across place of articulation in Gurindji Kriol based on language of origin (EDA8CE for voiceless stops of Kriol origin, 64B4D1 for voiced stops of Kriol origin, and A8C24A for voiceless stops of Gurindji origin). This figure is roughly based on Figure 5 from Jones and Meakins (2013).

in this study which used modified VOT values between prototypical voiced and voiceless stops ([p-b], [t-d], [k-g]) in word-initial position, across 7, 10-step continua. In-line with Jones and Meakins' (2013) observations for word-medial VOT and closure production, Stewart et al.'s (2018) perception results revealed that listeners are able to perceive consistent differences in voicing between bilabial stops ([p-b]), while results were more variable for the alveolar and velar

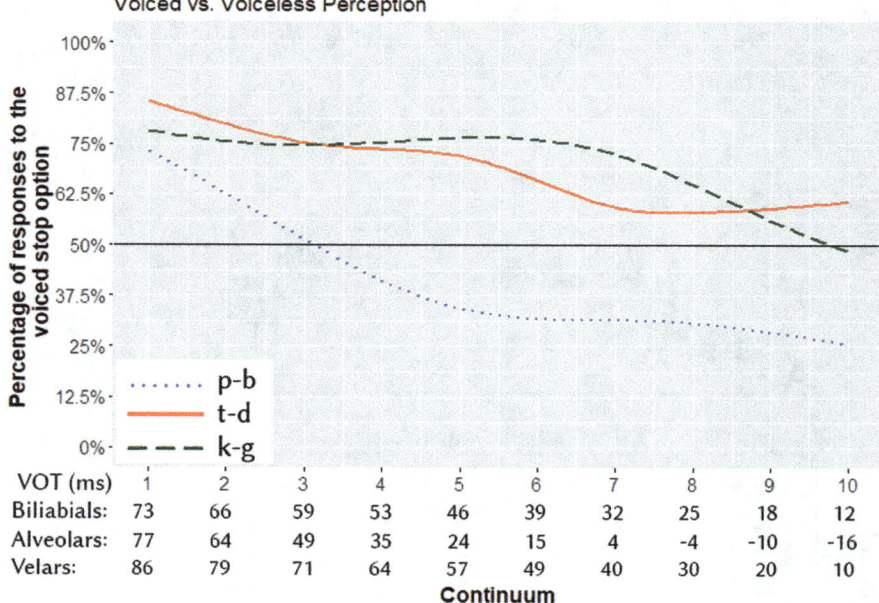

Figure 14: 2AFC identification task results for Gurindji Kriol listeners averaged across the 10-step continua for each place of articulation based on Stewart et al. (2018).

stimuli, ([t-d] & [k-g]), with only an estimated 39% of the participants able to identify consistent differences (see Figure 14).

A similar story can be told for fricatives /f/ and /s/ in Gurindji Kriol. Butcher (2006) shows the majority of Australian languages, including Gurindji, lack phonemic fricatives, however Sandefur (1979) shows the production of fricatives in Kriol is highly variable with their stop counterparts. Buchan (2012) specifically addresses the possibilities of production contrasts between voiceless fricatives and stops ([f-p] & [s-t]) with an analysis of maternal speech in Gurindji Kriol. While trends suggest variability across place/ manner of articulation, mother's speech of word-initial fricatives became more regularised, when communicating with older children. According to a perceptual study of this same conflict site by Stewart et al. (submitted), perception of [f-p] and [s-t] were also quite variable with just over half the participants showing a strong contrast between the pairs while the other half either had consistent responses to the fricative stimuli but random responses to the stops. Yet others only showed consistent responses to the fricatives. Kriol listeners showed similar results.

2.2.3 Vowels

According to Jones, Meakins and Buchan (2011) Gurindji Kriol has interacting source vowel systems consisting of /ɪ, ɐ, ʊ/ from Gurindji and /ɪ, e, æ, ɔ, ʊ, ɐ, iː, ɜː, oː, ʉː, ɐː/ from English, which have subsequently reduced to /ɪ, ɛ, ɐ, ɔ, ʊ/ in Kriol via the original pidgin language. With data from 894 spontaneous speech tokens taken from a single female speaker, Jones, Meakins and Buchan (2011) demonstrated there exists greater formant (both F1 & F2) overlap in the mainstream Australian English-source front vowels /æ/ and /e/ and back vowels /ʉː/ and /oː/ in Gurindji Kriol compared to their English cognates – a result which may suggest that Gurindji Kriol is expanding its vowel inventory from its original ancestral (Gurindji) inventory. However, Jones, Meakins and Buchan (2011) also show that the duration differences between the Gurindji Kriol lengthening contrasts (e.g., /ɪ/ and /iː/) are also reduced compared to those in Standard Australian English.

While van Gijn's analysis does not include Gurindji Kriol to support his theory of mixed language phonology, the language is categorised as a V-N mixed language like Michif. Therefore, there should be greater stratified elements at the phonological level. However, the results from these studies suggest that Gurindji Kriol has a mix of overlapping categories (e.g., emergent vowels currently operating with considerable overlap in the production domain, described in 2.2.3), assimilated categories (e.g., /t-d/ & /k-g/ in the perceptual domain, described in 2.2.2), and integrated categories (e.g., the /p-b/ contrast in the perceptual domain described in 2.2.2).

2.3 Michif

Michif (ISO 639-3: crg) is a V-N mixed language spoken sparsely throughout Manitoba, southern Saskatchewan and North Dakota (see Mazzoli 2019). It emerged in the early 19th century through intermarriages between First Nations women and French speaking fur traders. Unlike, Gurindji Kriol, the introduced language (French) is responsible for the bulk of nominal phrase elements, while the ancestral language (mainly Plains Cree) provides the bulk of the verb phrase, additionally, the origin of the majority of the lexicon coincides with the origin of the phrase. In (3), the bolded elements in the IPA transcription are of French origin while those in normal font are of Cree origin. A French translation is provided for comparison.

(3) *Gaa wiichihow mamaan avik loovraazh daan la mayzoon.*
 ga: wiːtʃihao **mamã: avek l-oːvraːʒ dã: la mezõ:**
 1.FUT help.3 mom with DET-work in DET.F house
 'J'aiderai à ma maman avec l'ouvrage/ménage dans la maison.' (French)
 'Nika wîcihâw nikâwiy ta kîsihtât wâskahikan atoskêwin.'[7] (Cree)
 'I'll help my mom with the housework.'
 (Gabriel Dumont Institute 2009)

2.3.1 Source language inventories

The Plains Cree phoneme inventory is made up of 10 consonants (Table 5) and 4 vowels with a length contrast in three positions (Figure 15). Canadian French contains 21 consonants (Table 6) and 17 vowels, with several nasal and length contrasts (Figure 16). Comparing the phoneme inventories from both languages, 41 possible phonemic conflict sites can be identified; 10 from Cree (short vowels: /i, u, a/, the long vowel: /eː/, glottals: /ʔ, h/, and alveolars: /t, n, s, ts/, which are realised as dentals in French) and 31 (/b, t̪, d̪, g, n̪, ɲ, ŋ, r, ʀ, f, v, s̪, z̪, ʃ, ʒ, ts̪, dz̪, ɥ, l̪, y, ẽ, ø, ɛː, ɛ, œ, œ̃, ã, ɑ, o, õ, ɔ, ə/) from French.

Table 5: Consonant inventory for Plains Cree based on Wolfart (1973).

	Bilabial	Dental	Alveolar	Postalveolar	Palatal	Velar	Glottal
Plosive	p		t			k	ʔ?
Nasal	m		n				
Fricative			s				h
Affricate			ts				
Approximant					j	w	

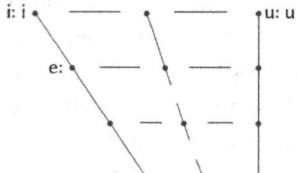

Figure 15: Vowel inventory for Plains Cree based on Wolfart (1973) and Muehlbauer (2012).

---

7 Translated by Randy Morin.

Table 6: Consonant inventory for Canadian French based on Walker (1984).

	Bilabial	Labiodental	Dental	Alveolar	Postalveolar	Palatal	Velar	Uvular
Plosive	p b		t̪ d̪				k g	
Nasal	m		n̪			ɲ	ŋ	
Trill				[r]				ʀ
Tap								
Fricative		f v	s̪ z̪		ʃ ʒ			
Affricate			t̪s̪ d̪z̪					
Approximant						j ɥ	w	
Lateral Approximant			l̪					

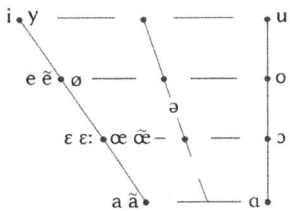

Figure 16: Vowel inventory for Canadian French based on Santerre (1974) and Walker (1984).

2.3.1.1 Plains Cree

Like most Algonquian languages, Plains Cree lacks phonemic voicing contrasts in the obstruent series. Plains Cree also differs from other varieties of Cree (e.g., Swampy, Moose, Northern, etc.) in that it lacks the rhotic /r/, and the postalveolar /ʃ/ and approximant /l/ (labial-dental [ð] in some varieties) are produced as /s/ and /j/, respectively. However, Plains Cree has a rich inventory of consonant clusters and diphthongs.

According to Wolfart (1973) and Muehlbauer (2012), the vowel inventory of Plains Cree contains three vowels with a lengthening contrast in every position with an additional long mid-front vowel (/eː/). The description of the back vowel varies among authors who describe it as high (/u/), mid-high (/o/), or lax (/ʊ/) (see Muehlbauer 2012 for a complete analysis).

2.3.1.2 Canadian French

French spoken throughout Canada varies greatly with a large number of regional dialects and sociolects. However, unlike Spanish spoken in Ecuador, there is little influence from First Nation languages on the French phonological system. Table 6 provides the phoneme inventory for Canadian French with a few prominent allophones which differ from European varieties.

Unlike the other languages described hereto, the vowel inventory of Canadian French is extensive and contains contrasts consisting of rounding, length, and nasalisation, which vary in their place of articulation. Figure 16 provides the vowel inventory for Canadian French.

2.3.2 Obstruents

Michif has a similar stop voicing phonemic conflict site to that of Media Lengua, with a voicing contrast from the introduced language (French /p-b/, /t-d/, /k-g/) and a single series of voiceless unaspirated stops from the ancestral language (Cree /p/, /t/, /k/). In a study on stop production in Michif, involving 446 tokens gathered from oral descriptions of the Pear Film (Chafe, 1980) from 10 speakers (5 women/5 men), Rosen et al. (2019) showed that, unlike Media Lengua, Michif speakers consistently produced short-lag unaspirated French-origin stops with VOTs in a similar range as Cree-origin unaspirated stops (Figure 17). The authors note that while some deviation appears (i.e., the median notches in Figure 17 do not line up perfectly), the actual median values of all three groups only differ by 18 ms; a VOT range that is normally considered to be non-contrastive for voiceless and voiced stops.

2.3.3 Vowels

The originators of Michif dealt with highly complex source vowel systems. While it is often not mentioned in the literature, numerous English lexical items also exist in Michif which could hypothetically bring the total number of vowels to 37, if speakers operationalised all three systems.[8] Even though this size of vowel inventory is not documented in the world's languages, many researchers claim that Michif's phonology is stratified (see e.g., Bakker and Papen 1997; and subsequent work based on this analysis). To test this claim, Rosen et al. (2020) investigated phonological stratification with an acoustic analysis of F1 and F2 formant frequencies and vowel duration. Their results, involving 2,678 tokens collected from the same data detailed in section 2.3.2, reveal that only two French vowels appear to

---

8 Including 12 Canadian English vowels.

Advances in mixed language phonology: An overview of three case studies — 85

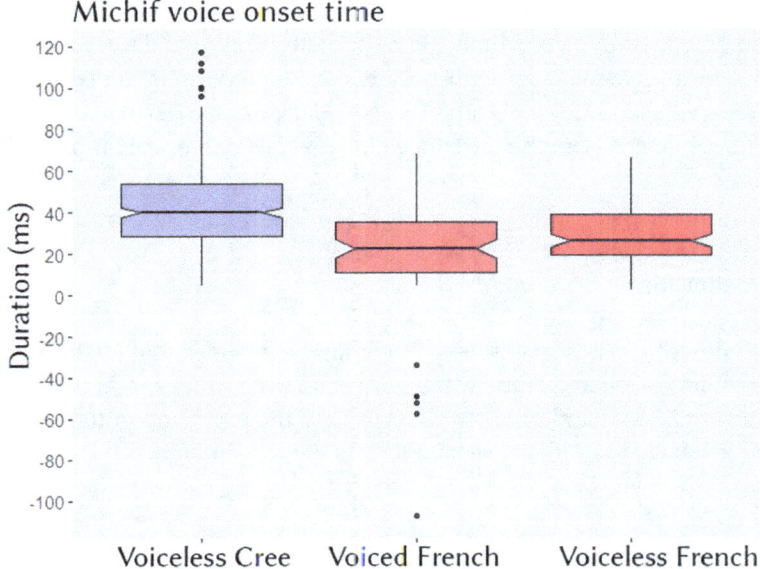

Figure 17: Michif VOT based on source language.

differ significantly from their Cree counterparts (/ɛ, ɔ/) while the rest undergo assimilation to the Cree system. This leaves Michif with 9 manageable vowels with acoustic spaces that differ significantly from other neighbouring vowels (see Figure 18).

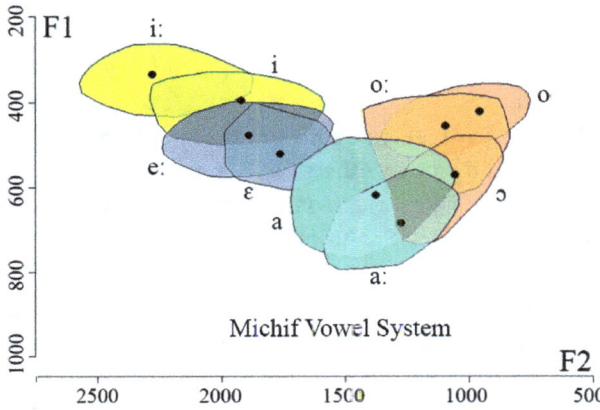

Figure 18: Michif vowel system based on Rosen et al. (2020).

Their results reveal once again that the ancestral language in a mixed language plays a primary role in providing phonetic material as Michif's vowel system largely reflects that of Cree, with only two mid-low vowels added from French. Moreover, results from this study reveal yet again that assimilation vs. integration of phonemes from the introduced language is not a straightforward process.

2.3.4 Suprasegmentals

Rosen (2006) describes stress patterns in Michif and concludes that Michif is a combination of both Cree and French stress systems. Her results suggest Michif stress assignment is very similar to that of Cree with the exception of the word level where the language is quality sensitive, as is the case in French.

3 Discussion

The results from the acoustic studies presented in this chapter suggest that stratification at both the segmental and suprasegmental level is more complicated than a simple clear-cut division between source languages. Many of the different phonological arrangements found throughout these acoustic analyses are non-conventional in the sense that in order to maintain clear perceptual differences between phonemes, categorical dispersion would be expected (e.g., /i/ and /e/ categories with clear vowel space separation or stop categories with VOT durations limited to a unique range with little overlap). On the other hand, if a given phonemic contrast is not important in a mixed language, assimilation would be expected. Instead, one finds overlapping categories and near-mergers (e.g., Media Lengua vowels), categories that are only perceptually contrastive in one position and not in others (e.g., Gurindji Kriol stop voicing contrasts), weaker degrees of categorical identification than would be expected for fully contrastive phonemes (e.g., Gurindji Kriol stop-fricative contrasts), and partially integrated systems (e.g., the Michif vowel system).

The combined results of these studies also suggest that when stratification is observed, it is most likely the result of various underlying acquisition, cognitive, and structural processes and not simply an awareness of source-language divisions (as appears to be the case with higher-level linguistic phenomena involving the mixing of lexicon, morphosyntax, semantics). Such processes could include, but may not be limited to, the age of acquisition of the introduced language during the creation of the mixed language, proficiency in or exposure to one, both, or none of the source languages, and extra-linguistic influences of the source languages (e.g., prestige), and the level of functional load required to maintain an optimum level of phonemic and prosodic contrasts in the mixed language. Because of these realities, the phonetic outcomes of mixed language sound inventories reflect the speech of mid- to late-bilinguals in that phonological conflict sites are either not fully acquired, assimilated, or acquired, but not to the same degree as would be expected by monolingual native speakers. This is apparent in how mixed languages overwhelmingly conform to the phonological system of the ancestral source language spoken before the introduced language was present.

The fact that some contrasts are adopted while others are not might also indicate that cognitive factors function to shape the phonological system of a mixed language; factors that could be beneficial for distributing functional load, levelling out phoneme frequency, and allowing for a greater number of contrasts leading to greater phonological optimization. However, the unpredictable outcome of a mixed language's phonological system should not come as a surprise since the phonological shells of entire linguistic systems and/or categories undergo transfer to a new system in a remarkably short period of time before becoming nativised.

Plans are in the works to test the functional load hypothesis with Media Lengua, which could be expanded to other mixed languages. Phonetic studies are also planned for Ma'a (Tanzania), work by Gonzales (see e.g., Gonzales 2017, 2018) is shedding light on the vowel system of Philippine Hybrid Hokkien (Philippines), Bundgaard-Nielsen and O'Shannessy are working on phonetic aspects of Light Warlpiri (Australia), and additional phonetic studies are planned for Gurindji Kriol. These studies will allow us to further test and refine our hypotheses.

Are the phonologies of mixed languages special? In short, not particularly. Impressionistically, mixed languages, Creole languages (especially when not in contact with their lexifiers), and borrowings found in virtually every language show a propensity to conform to the phonological make up of their ancestral source language(s) e.g., Media Lengua sounds like Quichua ([kiɾi-] *not* [keɾe-] for *quer-* 'want'), Michif sounds like Cree ([li fizi] *not* [le fyzi] for *les fusils* 'the rifles'), Haitian Creole reflects its substrate languages (namely Fon) in pronunciation ([ʃãm] *not* [ʃãbʀ] for *chambre* 'room'), and English borrowings in monolingual Spanish often conform to Spanish phonology ([fʷul] *not* [fʊɫ] *full* for 'full'). Moreover, like the acoustic analyses of mixed languages presented hereto, phonetic analyses of both Creoles and "conventional" borrowings show sounds do not confirm in a binary fashion (e.g., assimilation vs. integration). For example in Cavite Chabacano, a Spanish lexified Creole with a Tagalog substrate,

Lesho (2013) shows that mid vowels in unstressed positions are raised in Cavite Chabacano and overlap their Tagalog origin high vowel counterparts, yet mid and high vowel categories remain separate in stressed positions. While Quichua does not reflect Media Lengua exactly in its borrowing tendencies, regarding phonetic material and perception, overlapping mid- and high-vowels are still present. For Australian Kriol, listeners tested using the same stop-fricative identification task experiment as the Gurindji Kriol listeners, showed greater degrees of contrast but not to the same extent that would be expected if the contrast played an important role in the phonology of the language (Stewart et al. 2020). Additional examples abound in the literature which are too numerous to list here. Again, these realisations all point towards acquisition and cognitive processes that determine the arrangement of a phonological system in a contact language more than a simple awareness of divisions based on language of origin of a given lexical item or phrase.

Abbreviations

3	third person
DET	determiner
ERG	ergative
F	feminine
FUT	future
LOC	locative
PST	past
TOP	topic marker
TR	transitive
TRANS	translocative
VAL	validator marker

References

Adelaar, Willem & Pieter Muysken. 2004. *The languages of the Andes*. Cambridge UK: Cambridge University Press.

Baker, Brett, Rikke Bundgaard-Nielsen & Simone Graetzer. 2014. The obstruent inventory of Roper Kriol. *Australian Journal of Linguistics* 34(3). 307–344. http://dx.doi.org/10.1080/07268602.2014.898222.

Bakker, Peter. 1997. *A language of our own: The genesis of Michif, the mixed Cree-French language of the Canadian Métis*. New York: Oxford University Press.

Bakker, Peter. 2003. Mixed languages as autonomous systems. In Yaron Matras & Peter Bakker (eds.), *The mixed language debate: Theoretical and empirical advances*, 107–149. Berlin: Mouton de Gruyter.

Bakker, Peter. 2015. Typology of mixed languages. In Alexandra Y. Aikhenvald & R. M. W. Dixon (eds.), *The Cambridge handbook of linguistic typology*, 217–253. Cambridge: Cambridge University Press.

Bakker, Peter. & Robert Papen. 1997. Michif: A mixed language based on Cree and French. In Sarah G. Thomason (ed.), *Contact Languages: A Wider Perspective*, 295–363. Amsterdam: John Benjamins.

Boyd-Bowman, Peter. 1953. Sobre la pronunciación del español en el Ecuador. *Nueva Revista de Filología Hispánica* 7(1–2). 221–233.

Buchan, Heather. 2012. *Phonetic variation in Gurindji Kriol and Northern Australian English: A longitudinal study of fricatives in maternal speech.* University of Wollongong PhD Dissertation, Wollongong, New South Wales: Thesis Collection 1954–2016.

Butcher, Andy. 2006. Australian Aboriginal languages: Consonant-salient phonologies and the "place of articulation imperative." In Jonathan Harrington & Marija Tabain (eds.), *Speech production: Models, phonetic processes and techniques*, 187–210. New York: Psychology Press.

Chafe, Wallace. 1980. *The pear stories: Cognitive, cultural, and linguistic aspects of narrative production.* Norwood, New Jersey: Ablex Publishing Corporation.

Cole, Peter. 1982. *Imbabura Quichua.* Amsterdam: North-Holland Publishing Company.

Flege, James E. 2007. Language contact in bilingualism: phonetic system interactions. *Laboratory Phonology* 9, 353–380 Berlin: Mouton de Gruyter.

Fletcher, Janet & Andrew Butcher. 2014. Sound patterns in Australian English. In Harold Koch & Rachel Nordlinger (eds.), *The languages and linguistics of Australia: a comprehensive guide*, 91–138. Berlin: De Gruyter Mouton.

Fought, Carmen. 2010. Linguistic contact. In Raymond Hickey (ed.), *The handbook of language contact*, 229–319. West Sussex: Wiley-Blackwell.

Gabriel Dumont Institute. 2009. *Michif phrases.* Gabriel Dumont Institute. Retrieved December 12, 2010, from http://www.metismuseum.ca/michif_dictionary.php?ic=18.

Golovko, Eugeni. 1990. Aleut in contact: The CIA enigma. *Acta Linguistica Hafniensia* 22. 97–125.

Gómez-Rendón, Jorge. 2005. La Media Lengua de Imbabura. In Hella Olbertz & Pieter Muysken (eds.), *Encuentros y conflictos: Bilingüismo y contacto de lenguas en el mundo andino*, 39–58. Madrid: Iberoamericana.

Gonzales, Wilkinson Daniel. 2017. Language contact in the Philippines: The history and ecology from a Chinese Filipino perspective. *Language Ecology* 1(2). 185–212. https://doi.org/10.1075/le.1.2.04gon.

Gonzales, Wilkinson Daniel. 2018. *Philippine Hybrid Hokkien as a postcolonial mixed language: Evidence from nominal derivational affixation mixing.* Singapore: National University of Singapore MA Thesis.

Guion, Susan. 2003. The vowel systems of Quichua-Spanish bilinguals: Age of acquisition effects on the mutual influence of the first and second languages. *Phonetica* 60. 98–128.

Hancock, Ian. 1976. The pidginization of Angloromani. In George N. Cave (ed.), *New directions in creole studies*, 1–23. Georgetown: University of Guyana.

Hancock, Ian. 1984. Romani and Algoromani. In P. Trudgill (ed.), *Language in the British Isles*, 367–383. Cambridge: Cambridge University Press.

Hickey, Raymond. 2010. Language contact: Reconsideration and reassessment. In Raymond Hickey (ed.), *The handbook of language contact*, 1–29. West Sussex: Wiley-Blackwell.
Johnson, K. 2000. Adaptive dispersion in vowel perception. *Phonetica* 57. 181–188.
Jones, Caroline & Felicity Meakins. 2013. Variation in voice onset time in stops in Gurindji Kriol: Picture naming and conversational speech. *Australian Journal of Linguistics* 33. 196–220. https://doi.org/10.1080/07268602.2013.814525.
Jones, Caroline, Felicity Meakins & Heather Buchan. 2011. Comparing vowels in Gurindji Kriol and Katherine English: Citation speech data. *Australian Journal of Linguistics* 31. 305–326.
Jones, Caroline, Felicity Meakins & Shujau Mauwiyath. 2012. Learning vowel categories from maternal speech in Gurindji Kriol. *Language Learning* 64. 1052–1078. https://doi.org/10.1111/j.1467-9922.2012.00725.x.
Kang, Yoonjung. 2011. Loanword phonology. In Mark van Oostendorp, Colin Ewen, Elizabeth Hume & Keren Rice (eds.), *Companion to phonology*, 2258–2281. Berlin: Wiley-Blackwell.
Kewley-Port, Diane. 2001. Vowel formant discrimination II: Effects of stimulus uncertainty, consonantal context, and training. *Journal of the Acoustical Society of America* 85. 1726–1740.
Lesho, Marivic. 2013. *The sociophonetics and phonology of the Cavite Chabacano vowel system*. The University of Ohio PhD Dissertation, Colombus, Ohio: OhioLINK.
Liljencrants, Johan & Björn Lindblom. 1972. Numerical simulation of vowel quality systems: The role of perceptual contrast. *Language* 48. 839–862.
Lindblom, Björn. 1986. Phonetic universals in vowel systems. In John Ohala & Jen Jaeger (eds.), *Experimental phonology*, 13–44. Orlando, Florida: Academic Press.
Lindblom, Björn. 1990. Explaining phonetic variation: A sketch of the H&H theory. In W. Hardcastle & Alain Marchal (eds.), *Speech production and speech modeling*, 403–439. Dordrecht: Springer Science & Business Media.
Livijn, Peder. 2000. Acoustic distribution of vowels in differently sized inventories – hot spots or adaptive dispersion? *PERILUS* 23. 93–96
Matras, Yaron, Hazel Gardner, Charlotte Jones & Veronica Schulmann. 2007. Angloromani: A different kind of language? *Anthropological Linguistics* 49(2). 142–184.
Mazzoli, Maria. 2019. Michif loss and resistance in four Metis communities (Kahkiyaaw mashchineenaan, "All of us are disappearing as in a plague"). *Zeitschrift für Kanada-Studien* 69. 96–117.
Meakins, Felicity. 2011. *Case marking in contact: The development and function of case morphology in Gurindji Kriol*. Amsterdam: John Benjamins.
Meakins, Felicity. 2016. Mixed languages. In *Oxford research encyclopedia of linguistics*. Oxford: Oxford University Press.
Meakins, Felicity, Patrick McConvell, Erika Charola, Norm McNair & Lauren Campbell. 2013. *Gurindji to English dictionary*. Batchelor: Batchelor Press.
Meakins, Felicity & Jesse Stewart. Accepted. Mixed Languages. In Salikoko Mufwene & Ana María Escobar (eds.), *Cambridge handbook of language contact*. Cambridge: Cambridge University Press.
Mous, Maarten. 2003a. The linguistic properties of lexical manipulation and its relavance for Ma'á. In Yaron Matras & Peter Bakker (eds.), *The mixed language debate: Theoretical and empirical advances*, 209–236. Berlin: Mouton de Gruyter.
Mous, Maarten. 2003b. *The making of a mixed language: The case of Ma'a/Mbugu*. Amsterdam: John Benjamins.

Muehlbauer, Jeffrey. 2012. Vowel spaces in Plains Cree. *Journal of the International Phonetic Association* 42(1). 91–105.
Muysken, Pieter. 1981. Halfway between Quechua and Spanish: The case for relexification. In Arnold R. Highfield & Albert Valdman (eds.), *Historicity and variation in creole studies*, 52–69. Ann Arbor: Karoma Publishers
Muysken, Pieter. 1997. Media Lengua. In Sarah G. Thomason (ed.), *Contact languages: A wider Perspective*, 365–426. Amsterdam: John Benjamins.
Muysken, Pieter. 2013. Two linguistic systems in contact: Grammar, phonology, and lexicon. In Tej Bhatia & William Ritchie (eds.), *The handbook of bilingualism and multiculturalism*, 193–215 (2nd edn.). Malden, MA: Blackwell Publishing.
Nespor, Marina & Irene Vogel. 1986. *Prosodic phonology*. Dordrecht: Foris Publications.
O'Rourke, Erin. 2007. Intonation in Quechua: Questions and analysis. Paper presented at the International Congress of Phonetics Sciences' (ICPhS) Satellite Workshop on 'Intonational Phonology: Understudied or Fieldwork Languages', Universität des Saarlandes, Saarbrücken.
Poplack, Shana. 1993. Variation theory and language contact. In Dennis Preston (ed.), *American dialect research: An anthology celebrating the 100th anniversary of the American Dialect Society*, 251–263. Amsterdam: John Benjamins.
Rhodes, Richard. 1986. Métchif: A second look. In William Cowan (ed.), *Proceedings of the 16th Congress of Algonquianists*, 287–296. Ottawa: Carleton University.
Rosen, Nicole. 2006. Language contact and Michif stress assignment. *Sprachtypologie und Universalienforschung (STUF)* 59. 170–190.
Rosen, Nicole. 2007. *Domains in Michif phonology*. University of Toronto PhD Dissertation. Toronto, Ontario: TSpace.
Rosen, Nicole, Jesse Stewart, Michele Pesch-Johnson & Olivia Sammons. 2019. Michif VOT. Paper presented at the Proceedings of the 19th International Conference of Phonetic Sciences (ICPhS), Melbourne, Melbourne.
Rosen, Nicole, Jesse Stewart & Olivia Sammons. 2020. A comparative analysis of Michif, Métis French, and Cree vowel spaces. *Journal of the Acoustical Society of America*. https://coi.org/10.1121/10.0001009.
Ross, Malcolm. 2007. Calquing and metatypy. *Journal of Language Contact* 1(1). 116–143. https://doi.org/doi.org/10.1163/000000007792548341.
Sandefur, John R. 1979. An Australian Creole in Northern Territory: A description of Ngukurr-Bamyili dialects (Part 1). *Work Papers of SIL-AAB*. Darwin: SIL, Australian Aborigines Branch.
Sandefur, John R. 1984. *Papers on Kriol: The writing system and resource guide*. Darwin: SIL.
Sandefur, John R. 1986. *Kriol of North Australia: A language coming of age*. Darwin: SIL.
Sandefur, John R. & John Harris. 1986. Variation in Australian Kriol. In Joshua Fishman (ed.), *The Fergusonian impact*, 179–197. Berlin: Mouton de Gruyter.
Santerre, Laurent. 1974. Deux E et deux A phonologiques en français québécois: Etude phonologique, articulatoire et acoustique des oppositions de timbre et de durée. *Cahier de Linguistique* 4. 117–145.
Smith, Ian R. 1978. *Sri Lanka Creole Portuguese phonology*. Trivandrum: Kerala University Co-operative Stores Press Ltd.
Smith-Christmas, Cassie, Peredur Webb-Davies, M. Carmen Parafita-Couto & Gary Thoms. 2013. *How do Gaelic – English bilinguals deal with grammatical conflict? Evidence from mixed nominal constructions*. Report for Soillse. Sleat, Isle of Skye: Soillse.

Stewart, Jesse. 2014. A comparative analysis of Media Lengua and Quichua vowel production. *Phonetica* 71. 159–182. https://doi.org/10.1159/000369629.

Stewart, Jesse. 2015a. Intonation patterns in Pijal Media Lengua. *Journal of Language Contact* 8. 223–262.

Stewart, Jesse. 2015b. *Production and perception of stop consonants in Spanish, Quichua, and Media Lengua*. University of Manitoba PhD Dissertation, Winnipeg, Manitoba: DSpace:.

Stewart, Jesse. 2018a. Voice onset time production in Spanish, Quichua, and Media Lengua. *Journal of the International Phonetic Association* 48(2). 173–197. https://doi.org/doi.org/10.1017/S002510031700024X.

Stewart, Jesse. 2018b. Vowel perception by native Media Lengua, Quichua, and Spanish speakers. *Journal of Phonetics* 71. 177–193. https://doi.org/10.1016/j.wocn.2018.08.005.

Stewart, Jesse. 2020. A preliminary, descriptive survey of rhotic and approximant fricativization in Northern Ecuadorian Andean Spanish varieties, Quichua, and Media Lengua. In Rajiv Rao (ed.), *Spanish Phonetics and phonology in contact: Studies from Africa, the Americas, and Spain*. Amsterdam & Philadelphia: John Benjamins. https://doi.org/10.1075/ihll.28.05ste.

Stewart, Jesse, Felicity Meakins, Cassandra Algy, Thomas Ennever & Angelina Joshua. 2020. Fickle fricatives: Obstruent perception in Gurindji Kriol and Roper Kriol. *Journal of the Acoustical Society of America*. *147*(4). https://doi.org/10.1121/10.0000991.

Stewart, Jesse, Felicity Meakins, Cassandra Algy & Angelina Joshua. 2018. The development of phonological stratification: Evidence from stop voicing perception in Gurindji Kriol and Roper Kriol. *Journal of Language Contact* 11(1). 71–112.

Thomason, Sarah G. 1997. Mednyj Aleut. In Sarah G. Thomason (ed.), *Contact languages: A wider perspective*, 449–468. Amsterdam: John Benjamins Publishing Co.

Thomason, Sarah G. 2010. Contact explanations in linguistics. In Raymond Hickey (ed.), *The handbook of language contact*, 29–47. West Sussex: Wiley-Blackwell.

Toapanta, Jesus & Marleen Haboud. 2012. Quichua of Imbabura: A brief phonetic sketch of fricatives. *International Journal of Linguistics* 4(1). https://doi.org/10.5296/ijl.v4i2.1474.

van Gijn, Rik. 2009. The phonology of mixed languages. *Journal of Pidgin and Creole Languages* 24. 91–117. https://doi.org/10.1075/jpcl.24.1.04gij.

Walker, Douglas C. 1984. *The pronunciation of Canadian French*. Ottawa, Ontario: University of Ottawa Press.

Winford, Donald. 2010. Contact and borrowing. In Raymond Hickey (ed.), *The handbook of language contact*, 1–29. West Sussex: Wiley-Blackwell.

Wolfart, H. Christoph. 1973. *Plains Cree: A Grammatical Study*. Philadelphia: American Philosophical Society.

Evangelia Adamou
How sentence processing sheds light on mixed language creation

1 Introduction

Linguists are increasingly paying attention to the ways bilinguals may alternate between two languages in one situation and with a single interlocutor, and how, under some specific sociolinguistic circumstances, systematic code-switching may lead to the genesis of a novel, mixed language. Furthering the naturalistic evidence on mixed languages, I suggest that the study of sentence processing and of language switching costs can shed light on the creation of mixed languages. I illustrate this proposal through results from sentence processing of a so-called "fused lect" (Adamou 2010 following Auer 1999) or "unevenly mixed language" (Adamou and Granqvist 2015), comprising a majority of Romani linguistic material combined with the conventionalized use of Turkish elements, including verbs and verb morphology (Adamou and Shen 2019). Though in the study by Adamou and Shen (2019) the focus was on the importance of the Romani data for the discussion of language switching costs, in the present paper, I discuss these results with respect to the process of formation of mixed languages. In the remainder of this introduction, I present a brief overview of the literature on mixed languages (in 1.1.) and language switching costs (in 1.2.). In 1.3. I argue for the advantages of combining the two research paradigms with benefits for both fields: on the one hand, allowing to deepen our

---

Acknowledgements: I would first like to thank the participants in the experimental study as well as Sabiha Suleiman, president of the Women's Association 'Hope' in Greek Thrace, who made this research possible. I would also like to thank my co-author of the 2019 article, Rachel Shen, for the statistical analyses and discussion of the experimental design. The original research received support from the program Investments for the Future funded by the French National Research Agency (ANR-10-LABX-0083). A preliminary version of the present paper was presented at the conference "From language mixing to fused lects", organized by Peter Auer and Nikolay Hakimov at FRIAS, Freiburg University in 2017. I am grateful to the organizers for their invitation and to the participants of the conference for useful suggestions. Finally, I would like to thank the anonymous reviewers of this article for their insightful comments as well as the editors of the volume, Maria Mazzoli and Eeva Sippola, for inviting me to contribute on this topic and for their precious feedback during the reviewing process.

Evangelia Adamou, CNRS, evangelia.adamou@cnrs.fr

https://doi.org/10.1515/9781501511257-004

understanding of mixed languages, on the other hand, to understand more fully human cognition and the effects of cultural and linguistic variation.

1.1 Mixed languages

In past decades significant progress has been made in documenting "mixed languages" and understanding their formation (see among others Thomason and Kaufman 1988; Bakker and Mous 1994; Thomason 1995; Bakker 1997; Muysken 1997; Auer 1999; Myers-Scotton 1998, 2002; Matras 2000, 2003). Mixed languages can be broadly defined as "the result of the fusion of two identifiable source languages, normally in situations of community bilingualism" (Meakins 2013: 159).

At present, two well-established structural types of mixed languages have been identified (Meakins 2013):
a) G(rammar)–L(exicon) mixed languages, which draw the grammar from one language and the lexicon from another, for example, Ma'á, a Bantu language spoken in Tanzania with elements from Cushitic languages (Bakker and Mous 1994).
b) V(erb)–N(oun) mixed languages, which exhibit structural mixing, with nouns from one language and verbs from another. A good example of V-N mixed languages is Michif, a Cree-French mixed language spoken by the Métis (Bakker 1997). Michif combines the verb system from Cree and the noun system from French. Other well-known examples of V-N languages are the two Australian mixed languages, Gurindji Kriol (Meakins 2012) and Light Warlpiri (O'Shannessy 2013).

The process of mixed language genesis has been the locus of heated debate in the early studies. Some researchers considered mixed languages as the product of extraordinary mixing processes, for example, of language intertwining (Bakker and Mous 1994), or lexical re-orientation when the ancestral language anchors the predication (i.e., provides the inflection of the finite verbs) and selective replication when the socially dominant language anchors the predication (Matras 2000, 2003), eventually going through transitional stages in the anchoring of the predication as observed at the level of the discourse (Matras et al. 2007). Other researchers suggested instead that mixed languages emerge following the conventionalization of code-switching patterns (Auer 1999; Myers-Scotton 2002). According to Myers-Scotton, intrasentential code-switching, that is, code-switching at the level of the clause, comprises any number of words from the Matrix Language, the language that sets the grammatical frame, and at least one word from the Embedded Language, the language that mainly contributes content morphemes. Myers-Scotton (1998) proposed that mixed languages are created when there is a "Matrix Language Turnover" which is interrupted; this is dubbed "Arrested Matrix Language Turnover". Moreover, Myers-Scotton (2002: 105, 269) tentatively suggested that speakers may go through a stage of "composite code-switching" during which, within a single clause, they draw the Matrix Language from more than one source. Auer (1999), in turn, hypothesized that "code-switching", that is, the meaningful alternation between two languages that can index aspects of the situation or of the speaker, becomes "code-mixing"[1] when generalized in a bilingual community, and then eventually gives rise to a "fused lect" followed by an independent "mixed language". Auer's fused-lects are defined as follows: "the use of one 'language' or the other for certain constituents is obligatory in FLs [fused lects]; it is part of their grammar, and speakers have no choice" (Auer 1999: 321). Although Auer (1999) cites evidence from the Sinti dialect of Romani to illustrate fused lects, Adamou (2010) argued that Greek Thrace Romani data offer a more adequate example for this stage as the Turkish verbs are neither clearly borrowings nor code-switching insertions. The Romani-Turkish data have since been integrated in the discussion of fused lects, adding the possibility that in the process of language fusion, some elements may be obligatory, while others may still alternate (see Auer and Hakimov 2020). Finally, mixed languages differ from fused lects as they comprise innovative grammatical patterns, which did not exist in the source languages (for evidence of this last stage see Meakins 2013; O'Shannessy 2013).

Recently, the analysis of the language use of older and younger cohorts in the community provided decisive evidence in support of the view that mixed languages result from the intensification of general contact phenomena such as code-switching (McConvell and Meakins 2005; Meakins 2012; O'Shannessy 2012). More evidence in support of intermediate stages preceding the creation of independent mixed languages come from two distantly related Romani varieties spoken in Greece and in Finland. In these Romani varieties, morphologically intact verbs from the languages they are in contact with, Turkish and Finnish respectively, are inserted into a Romani-dominant speech by all proficient Romani speakers (Adamou 2010; Adamou and Granqvist 2015).

From a sociolinguist perspective, the creation of mixed languages is favored in highly bilingual communities, in particular, when there are conflicting processes of language shift and language maintenance (Thomason and Kaufman 1988; O'Shannessy 2012; Meakins 2013). McConvell and Meakins (2005) describe how Gurindji Kriol was formed under very specific sociopolitical changes

---

1 Note that a variety of definitions of code-mixing can be found in the literature.

that radically modified the community's language attitudes and the existing language mixing model. Bakker (1994: 24) noted that mixed languages can also be created in mixed households, as is the case of Michif.

Although some mixed languages arise from the conventionalization of code-switching, they exhibit characteristics that greatly differ from classic code-switching. This can be illustrated with an example from a V-N mixed language from Australia, Light Warlpiri. In Light Warlpiri most verbs come from English/Kriol, verb structure comes from both Warlpiri and English/Kriol, and nominal structure from Warlpiri (O'Shannessy 2013).[2] See example (1).

Light Warlpiri (Australia) < Warlpiri (in plain) and English/Kriol (in bold)
(1) *Junga mayi nyuntu* **yu-m** **go** *wati-kari-kirl mayi?*
 true Q 2SG 2SG.S-NFUT go man-other-COM Q
 'Is it true that you went with another man?' (O'Shannessy 2013: 330)

Insertions of verbs with verb morphology in a clause otherwise consisting of lexical and grammatical elements from the other language depart from classic forms of code-switching where isolated words are generally morphologically integrated (Poplack and Dion 2012). Specifically, the use of non-integrated verbs from a given language inserted in the speech of another language is cross-linguistically rare (Wohlgemuth 2009). Myers-Scotton and Jake (2014, 2017) suggest that bilinguals either prefer non-finite verbs from the Embedded Language or morphologically integrated Embedded Language-verbs with the inflection of the Matrix Language. The 4-M model,[3] in particular, predicts that agreement in code-switching will always come from the Matrix Language (Myers-Scotton 2002). According to Myers-Scotton and Jake (2017), the reason why Embedded

---

[2] In addition, Light Warlpiri exhibits a new auxiliary that draws on Warlpiri, English, and Kriol. Also Kriol verbs select ergative case marking from Warlpiri.
[3] The 4-M model distinguishes four types of morphemes: "content morphemes", "early system morphemes" (e.g., determiners, derivational prepositions, particles in phrasal verbs, derivational and plural markers in noun phrases, some tense and aspect markers in verbal clauses, subordinating and coordinating conjunctions), and two types of "late system morphemes": "bridges" (e.g., elements that join together two NPs and complementizers that join together two clauses) and "outsiders" (e.g., agreement morphemes and some case markers). In terms of the speech production model, there is a distinction between the "Mental Lexicon" (i.e., lemmas underlying morphemes), the "Lexical-Conceptual" level (i.e., where content morphemes and early system morphemes are elected), and the "Formulator" (i.e., the production mechanism that puts together the larger constituents that indicate the structure of the clause). While content morphemes and early system morphemes are salient in the Mental Lexicon, late system morphemes are not salient until the level of the Formulator.

Language-verbs do not keep Embedded Language-morphology in code-switching could be due to the fact that their production would be "more costly" as speakers would need to check agreement in addition to checking at the lexical-conceptual level. Although the authors do not make any predictions in terms of processing costs, this is an interesting hypothesis that can be discussed in the light of the results reported in the study by Adamou and Shen (2019). In the following section, I present an overview of previous studies on language switching costs.

1.2 Language switching costs

Among research questions that remain open is whether the simultaneous use of two languages is associated with cognitive costs. Using experimental methods, several studies indicate high costs, whether in production or in comprehension (see among others Soares and Grosjean 1984; Grainger and Beauvillain 1987; Meuter and Allport 1999; Thomas and Allport 2000; Jackson et al. 2001; Alvarez et al. 2003; Costa and Santesteban 2004; Proverbio et al. 2004). However, recent studies increasingly show that there are either low or no costs associated with "language" switching (see among others Moreno et al. 2002; Jackson et al. 2004; Ibáñez et al. 2010; Gullifer et al. 2013; Mosca and Clahsen 2016; Adamou and Shen 2019; Johns, Valdés Kroff, and Dussias 2019).

To understand the conflicting evidence, one needs to distinguish between simultaneous use of two languages when the speaker/comprehender is translating (Ibáñez et al. 2010) from simultaneous use when the speaker/comprehender is forced to switch between languages artificially, from simultaneous use when she is code-switching (Chan et al. 1983; Gullifer et al. 2013). For example, professional translators (who need to comprehend sentences in one language and produce them into another language) or frequent codeswitchers (who need to comprehend sentences in one or more languages and produce a response using sentences from that same pair of languages) will not exhibit the same costs as speakers who do not have the habit of translating or code-switching.

In addition, code-switching stimuli need to be as close as possible to the communication habits of the codeswitcher as otherwise unexpectedness effects may arise (Moreno et al. 2002). For example, it is important to use auditory stimuli when code-switching is generally performed in oral. Moreover, extensive research on code-switching has shown that bilinguals tend to conform to specific patterns of code-switching and that, despite variability, not all possible combinations of elements from two or more languages are attested among codeswitchers. It is therefore equally important that the experimental stimuli respect switch sites, length of switch, and constraints such as the use of verbal inflectional morphology from one language or another, etc. In the past, the stimuli used in many studies on sentence processing were artificial, for example, single switched words were inserted into longer sentences along with their native morphology, something that, as the previous section showed, is rather rare in classic code-switching that the participants of these studies are accustomed to (e.g., for nouns in Moreno et al. 2002; Proverbio et al. 2004; for nouns and verbs in Hatzidaki et al. 2011).

The importance of taking into consideration the communicational habits of the speakers/comprehenders in the study of the bilingual brain is expressed by Abutalebi and Green (2016). In Green and Abutalebi (2013) the authors elaborate the "adaptive control hypothesis" that assumes that the language control network is flexible enough to adapt to the needs of the interactional setting. Specifically, Green (1998, 2011) claims that bilinguals who codeswitch frequently in their everyday lives rely on the joint activation of the two languages, whereas bilinguals who do not frequently codeswitch rely on their language control network. More recently, Adamou and Shen (2019) and Johns, Valdés Kroff and Dussias (2019) showed that language switching costs align with the general code-switching habits of the members of a speech community as documented in corpus studies. Though speech communities are idealizations that serve as analytical tools, there is ample empirical evidence showing that children tend to acquire linguistic patterns similar to those that they were exposed to, and that adult speakers tend to converge with the productions of the individuals they interact with, whether in the long run or temporarily during an interaction.

1.3 Combining the two research paradigms (i.e., mixed languages and language switching costs)

At present, there is no research on processing among speakers of mixed languages. Indeed, research on mixed languages has primarily relied on the analysis of ecologically valid data that allow for the examination of the constraints and social significance of the mixed languages. In contrast, in experimental approaches to bilingual sentence processing researchers rely on controlled data produced in a laboratory environment with natural corpus data sometimes being used as basic frequency data.

This lack of processing studies among speakers of mixed languages is also due to the difficulties of conducting experimental research outside the laboratory as well as the need to adapt the research paradigms to groups who are not accustomed to this sort of task, and certainly not in a language that is not tied to formal education. Indeed, studies on the effects of literacy on oral language processing show consistent differences between literate and illiterate subjects (see Tarone and Bigelow 2005 for an overview), and yet research on bilinguals who are illiterate in both languages is virtually non-existent. An encouraging sign is that researchers are now starting to adapt successfully experimental and, in particular, psycholinguistic methods in the field (see O'Shannessy and Meakins 2012; Lipski 2016; Adamou and Shen 2019; Adamou 2021). However, I would like to stress here that these experimental studies were conducted following a first stage of extensive participant observation that allowed the researchers to discover the research questions that were relevant for the languages under study and not merely transpose research questions from well-studied languages.

I believe that taking into consideration lesser-documented forms of language mixing from a greater variety of groups can contribute to our understanding of bilingual processing at several levels. At a descriptive level, studying language processing among bilingual speakers of conventionalized code-switching and mixed languages will allow us to better understand how these contact varieties are processed. At a theoretical level, widening the typological database by considering rare forms of code-switching and language mixing may shed some light on the reasons why such language contact outcomes are cross-linguistically rare by disentangling the cognitive and the sociolinguistics factors. Moreover, for research on bilingual cognition to reflect cultural and linguistic diversity, it should move beyond the populations that are currently being studied extensively, the so-called "Western, educated, industrialized, rich, and democratic" populations or WEIRD (see Henrich, Heine, and Norenzayan 2010 for the use of this acronym to refer to the exceptional nature of such samples and call for more research in the field of human psychology among "non-WEIRD" populations).

To illustrate some of the contributions of this approach, I focus on the first experimental evidence that come from a typologically rare form of code-switching as spoken by Romani-Turkish simultaneous bilinguals residing in the Thrace region of Greece (Adamou and Shen 2019).

2 The Romani data in relation to the discussion on mixed language creation

2.1 Background on the mixed Romani-Turkish variety

Several corpus-based studies have shown that Muslim Roma from Greek Thrace are using Turkish verb morphology with Turkish verbs inserted into Romani dominant speech (Adamou 2015; Adamou and Granqvist 2015; Adamou 2016).

The resulting mixed variety is referred to by its speakers as *Xoraxane Romane* 'Turkish Romani' and no negative values are associated with it. Part of the Romani-Turkish recordings were quantitatively analyzed (Adamou and Granqvist 2015). The resulting corpus, of approximately 6,000 word tokens, comprises data from story-telling and interviews with the researcher as well as in-group conversations between 21 Roma speakers recorded in the community. The corpus was transcribed, aligned to the sound, annotated for sentences, words, morphemes, and parts of speech. Words and morphemes were tagged for language as a heuristic tool to discover the precise ways in which the two languages are combined while remaining agnostic about whether individuals processed them as alternations of two languages or as a single one, a question that was later tackled in Adamou and Shen (2019). More specifically, words and morphemes were tagged as "Romani" when the annotator could identify them as being of Indic origin or borrowed from past-contact languages. By contrast, words from the two current-contact languages that the speakers use in their everyday lives, were tagged as either "Turkish" or "Modern Greek". A fourth tag, "multiple", was applied to words for which more than one languages of origin were possible.

Analysis of this corpus reveals a numerically-dominant language, Romani, as speakers use on average roughly 15% Turkish words from all parts of speech with the exception of free pronouns. Adamou (2016) and Bullock et al. (2018) observe that the ratio of all tokens is a good proxy to determine the Matrix Language of the majority of sentences in a corpus. However, they also note that these ratios cannot predict the language that determines word order or the language of morphology. Indeed, in the Romani-Turkish corpus, though word order is consistently Romani, there is a split in morphology: while Turkish nouns inflect in Romani for case, number, and gender, like Romani nouns do, Turkish verbs systematically combine with the Turkish person, tense-aspect-modality morphology, and valency morphemes, as opposed to Romani verbs that combine with Romani verbal morphology (Adamou and Granqvist 2015). Adamou and Arvaniti (2014: 228) further note that speakers adopt mixed strategies of phonological adaptation for the Turkish lexical material when speaking in Romani-Turkish.[4] An example illustrating the use of Turkish verbs in Romani-Turkish is provided in (2).

---

[4] For example, Romani speakers use several Turkish vowels that are not part of Romani phonology (e.g., [y ɯ œ]), and yet they do not use Turkish /h/ in either Ottoman-period borrowings (e.g., *maala* 'neighborhood' from Turkish *mahal*), or in more recent borrowings, (e.g., *apo* 'pill' from Turkish *hap*). Also, they do not use vowel harmony when the nouns are integrated into Romani morphology; for Turkish clusters, including in the verbs, metathesis is frequent (e.g., Turkish *anlamayacak* 'he/she will not understand', becomes [alˈnamaˌdʒak]).

(2) Greek Thrace Romani: Turkish in bold

ep	*me*	*ka*	*dikh-av*	*kale*
always	1SG.NOM	will	look-1SG	them

me	**da**	**səndəm**		
1SG.NOM	FOC	tired.PRET.1SG		

me	**da**	*mang-av*	**dineneəm**	
1SG.NOM	FOC	want-1SG	rest.OPT.1SG	

'Am I **always** the one to look after them? I'm **tired** of it! Me **too**, I want to **rest**.' (Adamou and Shen 2019: 3)

Recall that according to the Matrix Language Frame model, the Matrix Language is the language that supplies the system morphemes, in particular the outsiders in the subsequent 4-M model, namely agreement verb morphology and some case morphemes as they establish the relationship between an argument and a verb. In example (2) one has to acknowledge the use of two Matrix Languages as there is agreement between the subject (Romani pronoun with Romani nominative case) and the finite verb 'tired' (in Turkish). In addition, there is agreement between the subject (Romani pronoun with Romani nominative case) and the Romani deontic finite verb 'want' (with present tense and indicative mood) as well as its complement clause verb, the Turkish finite verb 'rest' (with optative mood). In Romani-Turkish, the use of agreement verb morphology from two languages, Romani and Turkish, and case from only one of them, Romani, can be observed not only within a single clause, but overall throughout the spontaneous interactions. The opposite pattern, however, is not attested: for example, clauses comprising Turkish pronouns with Romani finite verbs are not encountered. This points to the existence of specific, conventionalized patterns in the way the two languages can be brought together in a clause or in the discourse.

The combination of Turkish verbs with Turkish verb morphology and Romani and Turkish nouns with Romani morphology is reminiscent of so-called V-N mixed languages where the verbs come from one language and the nouns from another. And yet, Adamou and Granqvist (2015) observe that the mixing process is not complete as only a small ratio of verbs come from Turkish (i.e., 12%), while the majority of verbs come from Romani and combine with Romani verb morphology. Although comparable frequency data are not available, full-fledged mixed languages such as Light Warlpiri and Gurindji Kriol are said to "derive their lexicon relatively evenly from their source languages" (O'Shannessy and Meakins 2012: 384). Adamou and Granqvist (2015) therefore suggest that the Romani data are representative of the early stages of mixed languages, as documented for the Australian languages (McConvell and Meakins 2005;

O'Shannessy 2012). Unlike what happened in the Australian languages, the mixing process has been interrupted in Romani.

Indeed, Myers-Scotton (2013) suggests the following scenario discussing the Romani-Turkish data from Adamou (2010): "That is, the explanation would be that Romani speakers were in the process of shifting to Turkish, but that this was a Matrix Language Turnover that was arrested. For socio-psychological reasons, the shift stopped." (Myers-Scotton 2013: 40). Adamou and Granqvist (2015) agree that an Arrested Matrix Language Turnover could account for the Romani-Turkish variety. They hypothesize that a shift to Turkish in the late 19th century may have been interrupted in the early 20th century when the Ottoman Empire collapsed. At that time, new borders modified the traditional mobility of Roma populations who were involved in trade throughout the Ottoman Empire. The area of Thrace eventually became part of the Greek State in the 1920s. This change gave rise to an entirely different sociopolitical setting where Turkish became the minority language and Greek the language of the State. A strong argument in favor of the formation of the Romani-Turkish variety in the early 20th century comes from the fact that similar patterns of Romani-Turkish mixing are documented in other contemporary Romani-speaking communities in the Balkans in which Turkish has no longer been spoken for the past hundred years. The fact that Turkish is still spoken nowadays in Greek Thrace is therefore not what gives rise to the Romani-Turkish variety that we observe, but merely allows the mixing to be further developed with new lexical additions and innovations.

More generally, similar mixing processes as the one documented in Greek Thrace can also be found in a number of Romani dialects in contact with a variety of languages. For example, Crimean Romani (Elšík and Matras 2006: 135) and several other Romani dialects spoken in the Balkans (Friedman 2013) use Turkish verbs similarly to Thrace Romani. Finnish Romani also draws verbs from Finnish together with Finnish morphology (Adamou and Granqvist 2015). North Russian Romani (Rusakov 2001), Soviet Romani, and Lithuanian Romani (Elšík and Matras 2006: 135) all draw verbs from Russian and use them together with Russian morphology. See an example from the written corpus of Soviet Romani, in (3), demonstrating that the process is highly conventionalized as it is also put into writing.

(3) Soviet Romani: Russian in bold
 Amə **organizuj-em** bar-ə sovetsk-a xulaib-əna
 we.NOM organise-PRS.1PL big-NOM.PL Soviet-NOM.PL enterprise-NOM.PL
 'We organize large Soviet enterprises.'
 (Nevo Drom, No. 1, 1931; excerpt from a million-word corpus of Soviet Romani texts from the 1920s-1930s; p.c. by Kirill Kozhanov)

The use of these rare mixing processes in a variety of Romani dialects that have no contact with one another suggests that sociolinguistic factors may be at play, shared by all the above-mentioned Romani communities. For example, these tightly knit, trade-related Romani communities exhibit extensive and intensive bilingualism, as opposed to other Romani rural communities with different communication habits (Adamou 2010).

We now turn to present a brief overview of the sociolinguistic context in the Romani community of Drosero in Greek Thrace and the rich linguistic repertoires that can be encountered (for a first account see Adamou 2010). Nowadays, the Romani community under study is settled at the outskirts of the town of Xanthi, in Drosero; see map in Figure 1. The community is large, with more than 7,000 members. Most Roma from Drosero have low socioeconomic status, with high rates of unemployment. People generally work in small trades or as seasonal workers while men are also working in ships.[5]

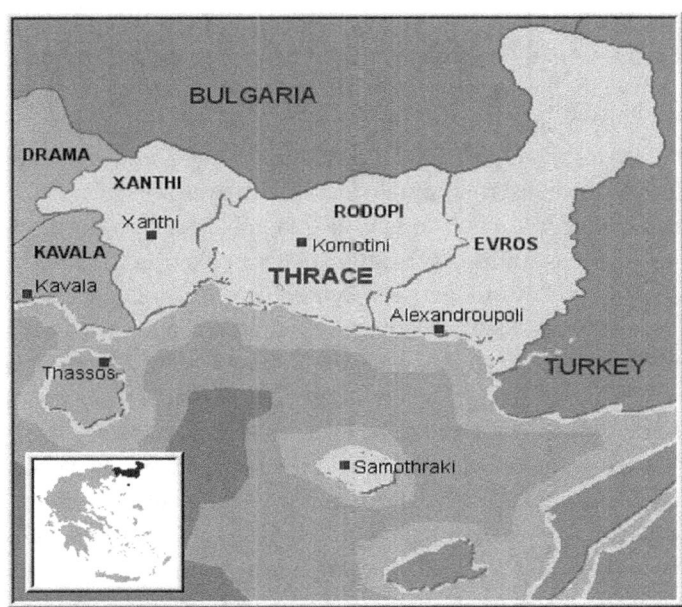

Figure 1: Map of Thrace, Greece. The study was conducted in the town of Xanthi.

---

5 See *Little Home* (https://vimeo.com/294901471), a short film resulting from participatory digital story-telling among Roma youth in Drosero who film and interview several members of the community about their profession. In a second short film, *Aver Than* 'Other Place' (https://vimeo.com/294780272), teenagers talk (in Xoraxane Romane) about how they view life in their

The mixed Romani-Turkish variety is the home language and the language of in-group communication. Most children receive input in this Romani-Turkish variety, in the (extended) family, in the community of Drosero as well as in other Muslim Romani communities in Greek Thrace, for example, in the Romani community settled in the outskirts of the town of Komotini as intermarriages and exchanges between members of these communities are frequent. Roma from Drosero also use Romani with other Romani-speaking communities in Greek Thrace (such as Christian Roma merchants, *Dasikane Roma*), and beyond (in other Greek cities or in the Balkans). The Romani variety they use in these interactions is not the Romani-Turkish variety, *Xoraxane Romane*, in that they are careful to avoid the Turkish lexicon, and in particular the Turkish verbs. Indeed, metalinguistic commentaries indicate that speakers of Romani-Turkish may be conscious of the Turkish/non-Turkish origin of the lexicon they use as they also speak Turkish. For example, Adamou and Arvaniti (2014: 226) note that their consultants recognized 'kavako 'tree' as a borrowing from Turkish and considered more appropriate for the recordings the use of the 'Romani' form ko'patʃi, even though they were not aware that the latter was of Romanian origin as Romanian is not currently spoken in the community.

In addition, most Roma children from Drosero also receive input by their families and community members in Turkish. Even though this Turkish variety has not been the object of extensive study, it can be tentatively described as a combination of the local Balkan Turkish variety, as traditionally spoken by other Muslim communities in Greek Thrace, and the varieties spoken in Turkey, as trade and visits to nearby Turkey are increasingly frequent. A distinction, however, needs to be made between Roma who have had simultaneous exposure to Turkish and Romani-Turkish (i.e., before the age of 3), those who had sequential exposure to Turkish (i.e., after the age of 3), and those who had early exposure to Turkish with little to no exposure to Romani-Turkish. Indeed, at present, a wave of shift to Turkish is ongoing in the community and is completed among several Romani families. To understand such a language shift from the traditional minority language, Romani(-Turkish), to another minority language, Turkish, and not the official language of the Greek State, Greek, one needs to keep in mind that Turkish has become in recent years an important language for the identity of Muslim Roma as it is strongly related to the Muslim religion. This is supported by the fact that Turkish is also recognized as the language of the Muslim Minority in

---

community. The production was possible with funding from the French National Research Agency (ANR) for the programme Empirical Foundations of Linguistics (ANR-10-LABX-0083), in collaboration with the Greek NGO Caravan Project and the local Romani NGO Hope.

Greek Thrace (since 1923 by the Lausanne Treaty) and as such is the main language of education in several minority schools in the area. Although there are no official statistics and the situation is constantly changing, extensive fieldwork allows me to conclude that most Roma from Drosero do not attend these minority schools. With the exception of the families who use Turkish in daily life, Turkish is generally used in the traditional market, the *bazaar*, interactions with the religious authorities, as well as with other Turkish-speaking members of the Muslim Minority (Turks and Pomaks, i.e., traditionally Slavic-speaking populations who are also shifting to Turkish; see Adamou 2010).

Last but not least, Roma children from Drosero receive input in Modern Greek, mainly from outsiders, for example, when they accompany their families to work or to the city, that is, in communicational settings outside of Drosero. Greek, which is the language of the Greek State, is also used in the administration, services outside of the community, and formal education. However, access to schooling is strongly affected by the broader social exclusion and discrimination that Romani communities are confronted to both at the local and at the national level, despite the efforts that are made at the level of the European Union. School attendance among Muslim Roma is low and as a result illiteracy is common among Roma over the age of 40. Though the situation is changing, the youth still frequently drop out before completing middle school.

After this introduction, we now turn to discuss the experimental evidence.

2.2 Experimental data on sentence processing of Romani-Turkish

In this section, I summarize the results regarding processing costs of mixed Romani-Turkish sentences comprising Turkish non-integrated verbs (Adamou and Shen 2019). The experimental Romani-Turkish data in Adamou and Shen (2019) have been analysed with respect to the literature on code-switching processing costs, but in this paper I will discuss them in the light of the literature on mixed languages.

Indeed, based on the review presented in the previous sections, one can hypothesize that mixed languages would be processed like unilingual speech, that is, speech with no switching. But how would intermediate stages such as fused lects be processed? Would they be processed similarly to unilingual speech, to code-switching, or differ from both? Figure 2 illustrates this question.

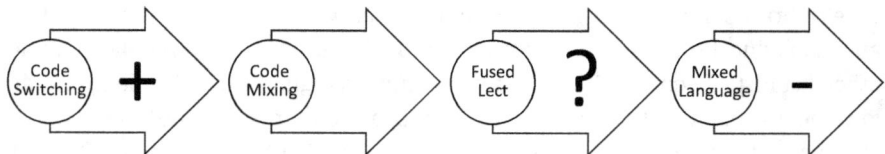

Figure 2: What processing costs for fused lects?

Two research questions have driven the study in Adamou and Shen (2019).

Research question 1: Do mixed Romani-Turkish sentences have higher processing costs than unilingual Turkish sentences? This question can be reformulated as follows: Is conventionalized language mixing (i.e., a fused lect) associated with high processing costs when compared to unilingual speech?

Predictions: In line with several studies on language switching costs, the mixed Romani-Turkish sentences should be associated with higher processing costs than unilingual speech. However, in line with the studies on code-switching that show no costs and knowing that Adamou and Granqvist (2015) consider Romani-Turkish mixing to be stabilized and predictable there should be no additional processing costs.

Research question 2: Are verbs from Turkish with Turkish morphology processed more slowly when they are in a unilingual Turkish sentence environment or in a mixed Romani-Turkish sentence environment? We can add: Are there any processing costs when this type of morphological non-adaptation is highly conventionalized in the community?

Predictions: Adamou and Shen (2019) predict higher costs in line with the studies that have shown language switching costs. Adamou and Granqvist (2015) hypothesize that the verbs from the contact language in Romani are systematic and therefore predictable. According to this analysis, Turkish verbs should be processed with low costs, similar to unilingual speech. Here, I would like to introduce another prediction based on Myers-Scotton and Jake (2014, 2017) who have argued that non-finite verbs are preferred in code-switching because they are associated with low costs in production, that is, they require checking at the lexical-conceptual level but not at the level of syntactic and argument structure. Based on this hypothesis, the prediction would be that the morphologically non-integrated verbs that occur in Romani will show high processing costs in production and possibly also in comprehension; it is only the latter that was tested in Adamou and Shen (2019).

To address these two research questions Adamou and Shen (2019) compared the reaction times (RTs), of the Roma participants on two tasks using auditory stimuli: a picture choice (Experiment 1) and a word recognition task in sentence context (Experiment 2). In behavioral studies, RTs correspond to the time participants take to respond to a stimulus. Slower RTs are interpreted as evidence of more difficulties in processing, that is, higher processing costs. In both experiments, participants were presented with four types of sentences: (a) conventionalized Romani-Turkish mixing involving Turkish verbs with Turkish morphology, (b) all Turkish sentences, (c) sentences with Romani-Turkish code-switching, that is, with morphologically non-integrated words in lengthy switches (Poplack and Dion 2012), and (d) sentences in Romani with Turkish borrowings, that is, morphologically integrated verbs (Poplack and Dion 2012). Version a offers mixed Romani-Turkish sentences as used in the language of the family and the community. Version b is in the language towards which the shift is currently taking place and that is acquired at home and in the community. Versions d and c are atypical in the community, but they are not ungrammatical since they occur in other Romani communities of the Balkans with which the speakers of Greek Thrace are in contact. Given that sentences of Versions a and b are the most natural in the community, Adamou and Shen (2019) expected that the reaction times would follow the order d > c > b ≥ a. See an example of each version in (4).

Romani in regular font; Turkish in bold; Greek underscored.
(4) 'The neighbours were having parties very often. They drank, ate (and danced) until late.'

Version a: Mixed Romani-Turkish (as spoken in the community)
a. e   **komʃ**-je   but   **seki** ker-en-as   <u>ylend-ja</u>
    DEF.PL   neighbour-PL   very   often   make-3PL-IMPF   party-PL
    itʃ-er-di-ler   xa-n-as   but   **getʃi**   sao   gie
    drink-AOR-PST-PL   eat-3PL-IMPF   very   late   every   day

Version b: all Turkish (in the local variety of Turkish)
b. **komşu-lar   ör   gün   eğlence   yap-ıyor-lar-dı**
    neighbour-PL   every   day   party   make-PROG-3PL-PST
    İç-er-di-ler   ye-r-di-ler   ör   gün   çok   geç   vakt   a kadar
    drink-AOR-PST-PL   eat-AOR-PST-3PL every   day   very   late time   until

Version c: Romani with Turkish code-switching (not attested in the community)
c. **komʃu**-lar   er   gyn   ker-en-as   <u>eglendʒe</u>
    neighbour-PL   every   day   make-3PL-IMPF   party
    onlar itʃ-er-di-ler   xa-n-as   kel-en-as   dʒi   but   **getʃi**
    3PL   drink-AOR-PST-PL   eat-3PL-IMPF   dance-3PL-IMPF   until   very   late

Version d: Romani with Turkish borrowings (not attested in the community)

d. e   **komʃ**-je   er   **gyn** ker-en-as   **eglendʒe**-a
    DEF.PL   neighbour-PL   every day   make-3PL-IMPF   party-PL
    itʃki-al-en-as   xa-n-as   kel-en-as   but   **getʃi**
    drink-LVM-3PL-IMPF   eat-3PL-IMPF   dance-3PL-IMPF very late

Sixteen sentences were used, each one constructed in four versions. A norming study for the four versions of the sentences was conducted among Romani speakers from the community. Results confirmed that Versions a and b are the most natural sentences whereas Versions c and d are the most unnatural.

In addition, the stimuli were constructed depending on the language preference of the verbs as observed in the spontaneous conversations. Five sentences included a Turkish verb that is more frequently used in Turkish than in Romani[6] within the community ("Turkish", i.e., 'to marry', 'to return', 'to read', 'to write', 'to think'), six sentences included a Turkish verb that is attested in the corpus once and for which the Romani variant is more frequently encountered ("Romani", i.e., 'to come', 'to go', 'to leave', 'to get', 'to do/fix', 'to put'), and five sentences included a Turkish verb that is used with equal frequency in both Turkish and in Romani ("variable", i.e., 'to wait', 'to work', 'to understand', 'to drink'). The motivation for controlling language preference comes from usage-based approaches. Indeed, according to a usage-based approach to language, utterances are composed of smaller units, whether these are words or constructions, which are stored in the speaker's mind. When the input aligns with a comprehender's expectations, there are no processing costs, but when it clashes with them, processing costs are entailed (Jaeger and Snider 2013; MacDonald 2013). Predictions were therefore as follows (for the Romani-Turkish version): the verbs preferably used in Turkish will be associated with short RTs (their use is expected and no processing costs will occur), the verbs preferably used in Romani will be associated with longer RTs (their use in Turkish is unexpected and processing costs will occur), and the verbs that are used in either Romani or Turkish will be associated

---

[6] Note that speakers of Romani-Turkish generally know the Romani verb as they are in contact with speakers from a variety of Romani dialects, including those that do not borrow extensively to Turkish. However, use of the Romani verb when speaking Romani-Turkish in cases where the Turkish verb is more frequent will be considered as a marked choice. This is particularly straightforward for verbs that have a meaning related to cultural-religious practices, as for example for the verb 'to marry', which they will use in Turkish as it is related to a Muslim religious ceremony, while also knowing the verb that other Christian Romani communities are using throughout Greece, which may in turn be a borrowing to Greek.

with long RTs (their use in Turkish is plausible but not necessarily expected and processing costs will occur).

2.2.1 Experiment 1

Experiment 1 is an online, bimodal picture-sentence matching task with auditory stimuli. It aimed at testing the reaction times of the Romani participants when listening to the various sentences presented above. Thirty seven trilingual Romani-Turkish-Greek speakers participated in the experiment. All were residents of the community of Drosero in Xanthi and had similar low socioeconomic status, and all but one had low education levels, with ages ranging from 13–51 [$M = 22.59$, $SD = 11.13$].

The experiment was conducted on a computer using Open Sesame (Mathôt, Schreij and Theeuwes 2012). Participants had to select the picture that appeared to be more closely related to the meaning of the audio stimuli by pressing a button on the computer.

For the analysis, linear mixed models (lmer) were constructed using the "lme4" package (Bates et al. 2015) in R (R Core Team 2013). The dependent variable was the RT, and the independent variables were "Language preference" of the verb and "Versions". The "Subjects", "Sentences" and "Duration" of audio files were coded as random factors (for more details on the statistical analyses see Adamou and Shen 2019).

Analysis of the results showed that the participants responded the fastest for the unilingual Turkish sentences (version b, see an example in 4b), followed by the Romani-Turkish mixed sentences (version a, see an example in 4a) and the codeswitches (version c, see an example in 4c). Although participants were free to press the button at any moment, RTs indicate that they did not press the button before listening to the Turkish verbs; it was therefore possible to also consider language preference of the verb in the analysis. When taking into consideration the RTs with respect to the language preference of the verbs in the naturalistic corpus, it appeared that the verbs that are more frequently used in Turkish when speaking Romani-Turkish were associated with the fastest responses, whether the sentence was in all-Turkish or in Romani-Turkish. When verbs are more frequently used in Romani but the stimuli included the verb in Turkish, the RTs were slower during processing of the mixed Romani-Turkish sentences than during the processing of the all-Turkish sentences. This indicates that the use of these verbs in Turkish when speaking Romani was unexpected. Finally, the slowest RTs were registered when the Turkish verbs in the stimuli correspond to verbs that are used both in Romani and in Turkish in spontaneous conversations. This indicates that variation in language choice is associated with higher processing costs in comprehension.

2.2.2 Experiment 2

This experiment was designed to determine whether the morphologically non-integrated Turkish verbs have higher processing costs when they occur in a Romani environment than in a unilingual Turkish environment. It was an online word monitoring task with auditory sentence stimuli where participants search for a pre-designated target word while listening to language input. This method allows us to investigate the nature, the position or the context in which the target word is found. Participants were instructed to press the button as soon as they would listen to a specific word (i.e., the target word), in the middle of a sentence. The target word was cut from the original recording and pasted into the instruction sentence. Participants would then listen to a lead-in sentence followed by the critical sentence that included the prime word, which was immediately followed by the target word; see Table 1. Adamou and Shen (2019) considered that if processing a finite verb in two different languages entails costs, then comprehenders would exhibit longer RTs. In contrast, there would be less or no costs when processing a finite verb in a single language. As can be

Table 1: Stimulus examples from Experiment 2 (Romani in regular font; Turkish in bold; Greek underscored).

Version	Auditory stimuli for the sentences: 'The neighbours were having parties very often. They drank and danced until late.'	Target word	Prime word
a. Mixed Romani-Turkish	E komʃje but **seki** kerenas ylendja. **Itʃerdiler** xanas but **getʃi** sao gie.	Xanas	**Itʃerdiler**
b. All Turkish (local variety)	**Komşular ör gün eğlence yapıyorlardı. İçerdiler yerdiler ör gün çok geç vakt a kadar.**	**Yerdiler**	**İçerdiler**
c. Romani with Turkish code-switching	Komʃular **er gyn** kerenas **eglendʒe**. **Onlar itʃerdiler** xanas kelenas dʒi but **getʃi**.	Xanas	**Itʃerdiler**
d. Romani with Turkish borrowings	E komʃje **er gyn** kerenas **eglendʒe**a. Itʃkialenas xanas kelenas but **getʃi**.	Xanas	Itʃkialenas

seen in Table 1, the prime word, a verb from Turkish with Turkish verb morphology, was practically the same in Versions a, b, and c, and differed slightly in Version d. In Versions a, c, d, the target word was the same (Romani verb with Romani verb morphology), but different in the unilingual-Turkish Version b (Turkish verb with Turkish verb morphology, similar to the prime word). A recorded follow-up comprehension question was played in Greek to make sure that the participants processed the sentences and were not merely focused on the search of the target word.

Forty nine trilingual Romani-Turkish-Greek speakers participated in this task. Ages range from 13–50 [M = 24.10, SD = 11.5].

The experiment was again conducted using Open Sesame and statistical analyses were conducted using linear mixed models (lmer) as in Experiment 1. Analysis of the results shows that the RTs in the Romani-Turkish mixed Version a (see example 4a) are significantly shorter than the RTs in the codeswitched Version c (see example 4c) and the RTs in the version with the borrowings (Version d, see example 4d). A similar result is found for the all-Turkish Version b (see example 4b). Crucially, there are no significant differences between the mixed Romani-Turkish Version a and the all-Turkish Version b. This indicates that when preceded by a Turkish verb with Turkish verb morphology the target words are similarly processed whether they are Romani verbs with Romani morphology or Turkish verbs with Turkish morphology. In addition, although the result did not reach statistical significance, participants responded the fastest in mixed Romani-Turkish sentences when the Turkish verb that was the prime word is frequently used in Turkish in natural conversations taking place in Romani. In contrast, when the Turkish verb that was used as a prime word is generally used in Romani in real life, the all-Turkish sentences were faster than the sentences in mixed Romani-Turkish.

2.3 Discussion

Adamou and Shen (2019) set out to answer two research questions, slightly reformulated in the current paper to encompass discussions on mixed language formation and fused lects. The first research question was whether there will be higher processing costs associated with mixed sentences as opposed to unilingual speech. In line with several studies on language switching costs, Adamou and Shen (2019) predicted that the mixed Romani-Turkish sentences should be associated with higher costs than unilingual speech; this is expressed as follows based on the four versions of the experiment: d (borrowing) > c (codeswitching) > a (mixed) > b (unilingual). Alternatively, in line with Adamou and

Granqvist (2015) who consider Romani-Turkish mixing to be stabilized, they predicted similar costs in the mixed sentences as in the unilingual speech; d (borrowing) > c (code-switching) > b (unilingual) ≥ a (mixed). In Experiment 1 the order of RTs was d > c > a > b, confirming studies that show processing costs in switching. However, when language preference of the verbs in the natural speech of the community is taken into consideration, it appears that for the verbs that were more frequently Turkish in the corpus, mixed Romani-Turkish was as fast as Turkish unilingual sentences, thus confirming the predictions based on Adamou and Granqvist (2015) for the order d > c > b ≥ a.

The second research question was whether there are costs when processing verb morphology in one language though the rest of the sentence, and neighboring verbs, are in a different language. Again, based on the corpus studies that show conventionalization of the use of Turkish verbs with Turkish verb morphology in a Romani sentence environment, Adamou and Shen (2019) predicted the order d > c > b ≥ a. We could add a second prediction inspired by Myers-Scotton and Jake (2014, 2017) that there should be extra costs when speakers need to check agreement in addition to checking at the lexical-conceptual level. Though Myers-Scotton and Jake (2014, 2017) do not make any predictions in terms of processing costs and though their hypothesis concerns production and not comprehension, it is possible nonetheless to formulate a prediction on this basis. In this case, morphologically non-integrated verbs in Romani should show high processing costs, i.e., d > c > a > b. Results of Experiment 2 confirm the first predicted order d > c > b ≥ a, in line with corpus studies showing that Turkish verbs with Turkish verb morphology are highly conventionalized (Adamou and Granqvist 2015).

Overall, the experimental findings from Romani-Turkish processing lend support to usage-based approaches according to which cognition is shaped by usage (see among others Tomasello 2003 for language acquisition; Construction Grammar in Goldberg 2006; Exemplar Grammar in Bybee 2010; Backus 2015 for code-switching). Comprehenders therefore anticipate code-switching based on prior experience (Jaeger and Snider 2013; MacDonald 2013).

Results in Adamou and Shen (2019) confirm that differences in processing boil down to differences in the frequency of use of specific lexical items in natural speech. Although results from Experiment 1 indicate that the comprehension of unilingual speech is less costly than the comprehension of speech involving language switching, a closer look reveals that the sentences that were constructed as closely as possible to attested real-life productions were processed faster when Romani-Turkish mixing occurred than when the sentences were in all-Turkish. This means that cognitive costs depend on the degree to which a switch is expected or unexpected based on previous short-term and long-term language experience. Unusual switches entail longer processing times, most likely due to surprise, and regular switches are processed similarly to sentence stimuli involving a single language. Results from Experiment 2 confirm this analysis as Turkish verbs with Turkish verb morphology are processed similarly whether in a Romani-Turkish mixed sentence or in an all-Turkish sentence. Adamou and Shen (2019) conclude that highly proficient, simultaneous bilinguals do not experience any difficulties in inhibiting one language in order to process a non-integrated word from the other language in a mixed sentence as long as the mixing conforms to established practices in the community.

Let us now turn to discuss these findings with respect to the mixed languages debate. First, I argue that the Romani-Turkish data support the approach according to which fused lects are situated somewhere in between code-switching (or language mixing) and independent mixed languages (Auer 1999; McConvell and Meakins 2005; O'Shannessy 2012). Indeed, the Romani-Turkish data confirm the existence of a continuum in the conventionalization of language mixing, in this case depending on the degree of conventionalization of specific Turkish verbs, and help refine the category of fused lects as a dynamic stage in the continuum. Specifically, Turkish verbs which are frequently used in Turkish when speaking Romani-Turkish are processed as fast in mixed Romani-Turkish sentences as in unilingual all-Turkish sentences. We could therefore say that when speakers expect some specific verbs to be in Turkish, such as 'to marry' or 'to think', based on frequencies in real-life exchanges, then they are processed as though there was no switch, as if the speakers were processing unilingual sentences. This does not mean that they do not know another equivalent, used more frequently among other Romani communities, only that the non-Turkish equivalent is less likely to be used among (Muslim) Roma from Drosero. In contrast, we note higher costs when participants still have the possibility to choose between a Turkish and a Romani verb, such as 'to work' or 'to wait'. This means that the use of those Turkish verbs that still have a Romani equivalent are optional, they are not highly conventionalized yet.

Second, the Romani-Turkish data show that speakers may process the grammatical information of the verbs stemming from two different languages without any additional costs as long as those verbs, together with their morphology, have become conventionalized in the community. The slow RTs for the sentences that were constructed in an unusual manner for the community, for example by using Romani morphology with Turkish verbs, shows that what is important is not so much whether comprehenders will process an integrated or a non-integrated verb but whether they have the habit of listening to integrated or non-integrated verbs. In the terms of usage-based approaches, in language processing it does not make sense to distinguish between grammatical and lexical meaning, as units appear to be stored in memory at various levels of complexity.

In summary, the results of the Romani-Turkish mixing point toward differences in processing depending on frequencies of the language chosen for specific lexical items as established in natural speech. Regarding the continuum, one can therefore reformulate and say that a fused lect is composed of elements that are both highly conventionalized by speakers of a given community and elements that are not yet conventionalized. Figure 3 illustrates this continuum and shows that fused lects are as predicted an intermediate form between code-switching (or non-conventionalized switches) and mixed languages (or highly conventionalized uses of elements from two sources).

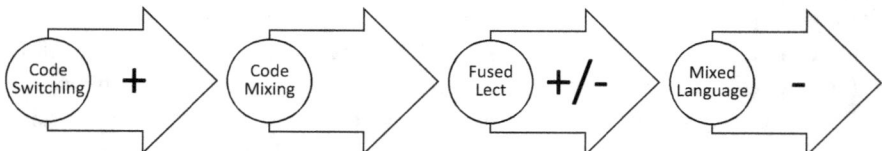

Figure 3: Processing costs for fused lects.

3 Conclusion

To conclude, in this chapter I have argued that the study of cognitive costs can shed light on the creation of mixed languages. The data come from a "fused lect" or an "unevenly mixed language" that is reminiscent of V-N mixed languages, but has not reached the stage of a mixed language as defined in the literature. Indeed, the mixing process has been interrupted, possibly following a change in the sociopolitical setting in the early 20th century. This offers a unique opportunity to observe a process of language mixing, viewed as a continuum, including a stage of compartmentalization in the domain of finite verb inflection that results from insertional code-switching (also see Auer and Hakimov 2020).

From a more theoretical perspective, I suggested that a fresh look at the mixed language data within usage-based approaches helps understand both the outcome and the process of mixed language creation. In terms of methodology, I hope that the present paper convincingly argued for the merits of the experimental method in the investigation of mixed languages. I consider that very exciting novel perspectives are open to the mixed language debate if we adapt the experimental methods of the research paradigm examining switching costs.

It still remains to be seen whether the specific hypothesis formulated in this paper, that mixed languages will have no processing costs, will be borne out by experimental evidence.

More generally, I suggest that in order to better understand the bilingual brain and cognition, we need to take into consideration lesser-documented ways of language mixing involving traditional bilingual communities that might have little exposure to prescriptive and standardized language contexts. The study of these populations raises several methodological hurdles as it may involve participants without any exposure to formal learning for either language, contrasting with most studies on language processing that involve languages with written traditions and exposure to formal teaching. The study conducted by Adamou and Shen (2019) shows that it is possible to overcome those obstacles by working in close collaboration with the communities, after long-term investigations of language practices in the community, and by adjusting our methods for the field.

Abbreviations

1	first person
2	second person
3	third person
AOR	aorist
COM	comitative
DEF	definite article
FOC	focus marker
Q	question marker
IMPF	imperfective
LVM	loan verb marker
NFUT	non-future
NOM	nominative
OPT	optative
PRS	present
PRET	preterit
PL	plural
PST	past
SG	singular

References

Abutalebi, Jubin & David W. Green. 2016. Neuroimaging of language control in bilinguals: neural adaptation and reserve. *Bilingualism: Language and Cognition* 19. 689–698.

Adamou, Evangelia. 2010. Bilingual Speech and Language Ecology in Greek Thrace: Romani and Pomak in contact with Turkish. *Language in Society* 39(2). 147–171.

Adamou, Evangelia. 2015. A corpus-driven analysis of Romani in contact with Turkish and Greek. In Eivind Torgersen, Stian Hårstad, Brit Mæhlum & Unn Røyneland (eds.), *Proceedings of the 7th International Conference on Language Variation in Europe (ICLaVE 7)*, 1–16. Amsterdam & Philadelphia: Benjamins.

Adamou, Evangelia. 2016. *A corpus-driven approach to language contact: Endangered languages in a comparative perspective*. Boston & Berlin: Mouton de Gruyter.

Adamou, Evangelia. 2021. *The adaptive bilingual mind: Insights from endangered languages*. Cambridge: Cambridge University Press.

Adamou, Evangelia & Amalia Arvaniti. 2014. Greek Thrace Xoraxane Romane (Illustrations of the IPA). *Journal of the International Phonetic Association* 44(2). 223–231.

Adamou, Evangelia & Kimmo Granqvist. 2015. Unevenly mixed Romani languages. *International Journal of Bilingualism* 19. 525–547.

Adamou, Evangelia & Xingjia Rachel Shen. 2019. There are no language switching costs when codeswitching is frequent. *International Journal of Bilingualism* 23. 53–70.

Alvarez, Ruben P., Philip J. Holcomb & Jonathan Grainger. 2003. Accessing word meaning in two languages: an event-related brain potential study of beginning bilinguals. *Brain and Language* 87(2). 290–304.

Auer, Peter. 1999. From Code-switching via Language Mixing to Fused Lects: Toward a dynamic typology of bilingual speech. *International Journal of Bilingualism* 3(4). 309–332.

Auer, Peter & Nikolay Hakimov. 2020. From language mixing to fused lects: The process and its outcomes. *International Journal of Bilingualism*. Online first: https://doi.org/10.1177/1367006920924943

Backus, Ad. 2015. A usage-based approach to codeswitching: The need for reconciling structure and function. In Gerald Stell and Kofi Yakpo (eds.), *Code-switching Between Structural and Sociolinguistic Perspectives*, 19–37. Berlin: Mouton de Gruyter.

Bakker, Peter. 1994. Michif, the Cree-French mixed language of the Métis buffalo hunters in Canada. In Peter Bakker and Maarten Mous (eds.), *Mixed languages: 15 case studies in language intertwining*, 13–33. Amsterdam: Institute for Functional Research into Language and Language Use.

Bakker, Peter. 1997. *A language of our own: The genesis of Michif, the mixed Cree-French language of the Canadian Métis*. New York: Oxford University Press.

Bakker, Peter & Maarten Mous. 1994. Introduction. In Peter Bakker & Maarten Mous (eds.), *Mixed languages: 15 case studies in language intertwining*, 1–11. Amsterdam: Institute for Functional Research into Language and Language Use.

Bates, Douglas, Martin Maechler, Ben Bolker & Steve Walker. 2015. Fitting Linear Mixed-Effects Models Using lme4. *Journal of Statistical Software* 67. 1–48.

Bybee, Joan. 2010. *Language, Usage and Cognition*. Cambridge: Cambridge University Press.

Bullock, Barbara, Gualberto Guzman, Jacqueline Serigos, Vivek Sharath & Almeida Jacqueline Toribio. 2018. Predicting the presence of a Matrix Language in code-switching. *Proceedings of the Third Workshop on Computational Approaches to Code-Switching*. 68–75.

Chan, Mun-Chee, Helen L. H. Chau & Rumjahn Hoosain. 1983. Input/output switch in bilingual code switching. *Journal of Psycholinguistic Research* 12. 407–416.

Costa, Albert & Mikel Santesteban. 2004. Lexical access in bilingual speech production: Evidence from language switching in highly proficient bilinguals and L2 learners. *Journal of Memory and Language* 50. 491–511.

Elšík, Victor & Yaron Matras. 2006. *Markedness and language change*. Berlin & New York: Mouton de Gruyter.

Friedman, Victor. 2013. Compartmentalized Grammar: The Variable (Non)-Integration of Turkish Verbal Conjugation in Romani Dialects. *Romani Studies* 23 (1).107–120.

Grainger, Jonathan & Cécile Beauvillain. 1987. Language blocking and lexical access in bilinguals. *Quarterly Journal of Experimental Psychology* A(39). 295–319.

Green, David W. 1998. Mental control of the bilingual lexico-semantic system. *Bilingualism: Language and Cognition* 1. 67–81.

Green, David W. 2011. Language control in different contexts: the behavioural ecology of bilingual speakers. *Frontiers in Psychology*. http://journal.frontiersin.org/article/10.3389/fpsyg.2011.00103/full (accessed 15 January 2019)

Green, David W. & Jubin Abutalebi. 2013. Language control in bilinguals: The adaptive control hypothesis. *Journal of Cognitive Psychology* 25. 515–530.

Goldberg, Adele E. 2006. *Constructions at work: The nature of generalization in language*. Oxford: Oxford University Press.

Gullifer, Jason W., Judith F. Kroll & Paola E. Dussias. 2013. When language switching has no apparent cost: Lexical access in sentence context. *Frontiers in Psychology* 4. 1–13.

Hatzidaki, Anna, Holly P. Branigan & Martin J. Pickering. 2011. Co-activation of syntax in bilingual language production. *Cognitive Psychology* 62. 123–150.

Henrich, Joseph, Steven J. Heine & Ara Norenzayan. 2010. Most people are not WEIRD. *Nature* 466. 29–29.

Ibáñez, Antonio, Pedro Macizo & Maria Teresa Bajo. 2010. Language access and language selection in professional translators. *Acta Psychologica* 135. 257–266.

Jackson, Georgina M., Rachel Swainson, Ross Cunnington & Stephen R. Jackson. 2001. ERP correlates of executive control during reported language switching. *Bilingualism: Language and Cognition* 4(2). 169–178.

Jackson, Georgina M., Rachel Swainson, Annie Mullin, Ross Cunnington & Stephen R. Jackson. 2004. ERP correlates of a receptive language-switching task. *The Quarterly Journal of Experimental Psychology* 57A(2). 223–240.

Jaeger, Florian & Neal Snider. 2013. Alignment as a consequence of expectation adaptation: Syntactic priming is affected by the prime's prediction error given both prior and recent experience. *Cognition* 127. 57–83.

Johns, Michael A., Jorge R. Valdés Kroff & Paola E. Dussias. 2019. Mixing things up: How blocking and mixing affect the processing of codemixed sentences. *International Journal of Bilingualism* 23. 584–611.

Lipski, John M. 2016. Palenquero and Spanish: A first psycholinguistic exploration. *Journal of Pidgin and Creole Languages* 31. 42–81.

MacDonald, Maryellen C. 2013. How language production shapes language form and comprehension. *Frontiers in Psychology*. http://dx.doi.org/10.3389/fpsyg.2013.00226 (accessed 15 January 2019).

Mathôt, Sebastiaan, Daniel Schreij & Jan Theeuwes. 2012. OpenSesame: An open-source, graphical experiment builder for the social sciences. *Behavior Research Methods* 44. 314–324.

Matras, Yaron. 2000. A functional-communicative approach. *Bilingualism: Language and Cognition* 3(2). 79–99.

Matras, Yaron. 2003. Mixed languages: Re-examining the structural prototype. In Yaron Matras and Peter Bakker (eds.), *The mixed language debate: Theoretical and empirical advances*, 151–76. Berlin: Mouton de Gruyter.

Matras, Yaron, Hazel Gardner, Charlotte Jones & Veronica Schulman. 2007. Angloromani: A different kind of language? *Anthropological Linguistics* 49(2). 142–184.

McConvell, Patrick & Felicity Meakins. 2005. Gurindji Kriol: A mixed language emerges from code-switching. *Australian Journal of Linguistics* 25(1). 9–30.

Meakins, Felicity. 2012. Which Mix? – Codeswitching or a mixed language? – Gurindji Kriol. *Journal of Pidgin and Creole Languages* 27(1). 105–140.

Meakins, Felicity. 2013. Mixed Languages. In Peter Bakker & Yaron Matras (eds.), *Contact languages: A comprehensive guide*, 159–228. Boston & Berlin: Mouton de Gruyter.

Meuter, Renata F. I. & Alan Allport. 1999. Bilingual language switching in naming: Asymmetrical costs of language selection. *Journal of Memory and Language* 40. 25–40.

Mosca, Michela & Harald Clahsen. 2016. Examining language switching in bilinguals: The role of preparation time. *Bilingualism: Language and Cognition* 19. 415–424.

Moreno, Eva M., Kara D. Federmeier & Marta Kutas. 2002. Switching languages, switching palabras (words): an electropysiological study of code switching. *Brain and Language* 80(2). 188–207.

Muysken, Peter. 1997. Media-Lengua. In Sarah G. Thomason (ed.), *Contact languages*, 365–426. Amsterdam: John Benjamins.

Myers-Scotton, Carol. 1998. A Way to Dusty Death: The Matrix Language Turnover hypothesis. In Lenore Grenoble & Lindsay J. Whaley (eds.), *Endangered languages: Language loss and community response*, 289–316. Cambridge: Cambridge University Press.

Myers-Scotton, Carol. 2002. *Contact linguistics, bilingual encounters and grammatical outcomes*. Oxford: Oxford University Press.

Myers-Scotton, Carol. 2013. Paying attention to morpheme types: making borrowability more precise. In Carole de Feral (ed.), *In and out of Africa languages in question*, 31–42. Louvain: Peeters.

Myers-Scotton, Carol & Janice L. Jake. 2014. Nonfinite verbs and negotiating bilingualism in codeswitching. Implications for a language production model. *Bilingualism: Language and cognition* 17(3). 511–525.

Myers-Scotton, Carol & Janice L. Jake. 2017. Revisiting the 4-M model: Codeswitching and morpheme election at the abstract level. *International Journal of Bilingualism* 21(3). 340–366.

O'Shannessy, Carmel. 2012. The role of codeswitched input to children in the origin of a new mixed language. *Linguistics* 50(2). 305–340.

O'Shannessy, Carmel. 2013. The role of multiple sources in the formation of an innovative auxiliary category in Light Warlpiri, a new Australian mixed language. *Language* 89(2). 328–353.

O'Shannessy, Carmel & Felicity Meakins. 2012. Comprehension of competing argument marking systems in two Australian mixed languages. *Bilingualism: Language and Cognition* 15. 378–396.

Poplack, Shana & Nathalie Dion. 2012. Myths and facts about loanword development. *Language Variation and Change* 24(3). 279–315.
Proverbio, Alice Mado, Giulianna Leoni & Alberto Zani. 2004. Language switching mechanisms in simultaneous interpreters: An ERP study. *Neuropsychologia* 42(12). 1636–1656.
R Core Team. 2013. R: A language and environment for statistical computing. R Foundation for Statistical Computing, Vienna, Austria. http://www.R-project.org/ (accessed 10 October 2013)
Rusakov, Alexander. 2001. The North Russian Romani dialect: interference and code switching, In Östen Dahl & Maria Koptjevskaja-Tamm (eds.), *Circum-Baltic languages*, 313–338. Amsterdam & Philadelphia: Benjamins.
Soares, Carlos & François Grosjean. 1984. Bilinguals in a monolingual and a bilingual speech mode: The effect on lexical access *Memory and Cognition* 12: 380–386.
Tarone, Elaine & Martha Bigelow. 2005. Impact of literacy on oral language processing. Implications for second language acquisition research. *Annual Review of Applied Linguistics* 25. 77–97.
Thomas, Michael S. C. & Alan Allport. 2000. Language switching costs in bilingual visual word recognition. *Journal of Memory and Language* 43. 44–66.
Thomason, Sarah G. 1995. Language mixture: ordinary processes, extraordinary results. In Carmen Silva-Corvalán (ed.), *Spanish in four continents: studies in language contact and bilingualism*, 15–33. Washington, DC: Georgetown University Press.
Thomason, Sarah G. & Terrence Kaufman. 1988. *Language contact, creolization, and genetic linguistics*. Berkeley: University of California Press.
Tomasello, Michael. 2003. *Constructing a language: A usage-based theory of language acquisition*. Cambridge, MA: Harvard University Press.
Wohlgemuth, Jan. 2009. *A typology of verbal borrowings*. Berlin & New York: Mouton de Gruyter.

Maria Mazzoli, Peter Bakker and Verna DeMontigny
Michif mixed verbs: Typologically unusual word-internal mixing

1 Introduction

The Michif language combines Plains Cree (autoglossonym *Nēhiyawēwin*) verbs and Metis French nouns. It also shows the influence of other languages, mainly Saulteaux and, more recently, English. Michif formed in the first decades of the 19th century in the area of the Red River basin (present-day Manitoba, Canada), along with the emergence of the Metis, a bicultural nation resulting from the encounter of French *voyageurs* and Indigenous women mainly of Ojibwe/Saulteaux descent (Bakker 1997). In all its varieties, Michif is severely endangered. In this paper, the term 'Michif' refers only to southern mixed Michif. Today, mixed Michif is spoken in traditional Metis communities in Manitoba, southern Saskatchewan, and North Dakota, by around 100–150 speakers between Canada and the USA (Mazzoli 2019).

In this paper, we illustrate the different Michif constructions that permit word-internal mixing in the verbal domain, and which morphological slots in the Michif verb template allow insertion of non-Algonquian material. We assess whether stem-internal mixing has added in any way to the non-lexical Michif verb morphology, and whether the stem-internal mixing attested in Michif differs in some way from similar phenomena in other mixed languages or comparable borrowing situations. The paper is structured as follows. In section 2, we provide a background of Michif as a mixed language. In section 3, we review the mixed stem types. In section 4, we discuss our data with respect to the Michif descriptive scholarship and the literature on mixed languages and language contact. The conclusions follow in section 5.

The data come from the Michif dictionary by Laverdure and Allard (1983) and, when the source is not specified, from Mazzoli's fieldwork corpus (collected in collaboration with Verna DeMontigny). The spelling conventions adopted here follow those used in Rosen and Souter (2009, 2015). All occurrences from Laverdure and

---

Acknowledgements: Maria Mazzoli conducted part of this research with the support of the University of Bremen and the European Union FP7 COFUND under grant agreement n° 600411. She thanks Nicole Rosen, Dale McCreery, Dennis Davey, David "Doc" Brian, Lawrie Barkwell, Harvey Pelletier, and Heather Souter. The authors also thank Marivic Lesho for proofreading the text, and the anonymous reviewers and Eeva Sippola for their helpful comments.

Maria Mazzoli, University of Groningen, m.mazzoli@rug.nl
Peter Bakker, Aarhus University, linpb@cc.au.dk
Verna DeMontigny, Michif Elder, kookume@msn.com

https://doi.org/10.1515/9781501511257-005

Allard (1983) are reported in their original form and reproduced in the new spelling. In the examples, Michif phrases/morphemes deriving from French are in italics, while Cree-derived phrases are in plain font. For the sake of readability, we will use the terms 'Cree' and 'French' to refer to Michif morphemes/words or phrases that are in fact derived from Plains Cree or derived from Metis French.

2 Background: Michif mixed structure

Michif resulted from the introduction of Metis French noun phrases into the structures of Plains Cree. Structurally, it is classified as a mixed Verb-Noun language (Bakker 2017; Meakins and Stewart to appear) that has a mixed lexicon and, arguably, also a mixed grammar. The great majority of its verbs are etymologically Cree, as well as the personal pronouns and the demonstratives. Virtually all Michif nouns, adjectives, and articles are etymologically French. Bakker (1997: 137–141) calculated that around 90% of the total number of nouns in Michif are of French origin, while the percentage of the Plans Cree verb roots ranges from 86% to 99%. Calculated using a (noun-dominated) 100-word Swadesh list, 52% of the entries have French roots and 29% are from Cree, while 19% of the entries have both Cree and French equivalents (Bakker 2019). However, in order to evaluate the mixed nature of Michif, it is crucial to assess also how mixed the *grammar* of Michif is. The three crucial questions to unpack and illustrate the mixed nature of Michif grammar are as follows:
1. Is the syntax of the noun phrase mixed?
2. Is the phonology of Michif mixed?
3. Is the morpho-syntax of the verb phrase mixed, or restructured with respect to Plains Cree due to contact with French?

Issue (1) has been addressed in the recent literature. Gillon and Rosen (2018) discuss it from a generative point of view and claim that Michif noun phrases have a mixed syntax, exhibiting mostly Algonquian-derived features and a few French-derived features (but cf. Thomason 2019). Sammons (2019) identifies Michif noun phrase structure as typologically unusual with respect to attested strategies of borrowing as well as to general systems of noun classification in the world's languages. Michif 'French sex-based' and 'Cree animacy-based' genders[1] are

---

[1] We use the term "sex-based" to indicate "feminine/masculine" as in French, and the term "animacy-based" to indicate "animate/inanimate" as in Cree. These labels are not to be interpreted as reflecting semantic distinctions.

surprisingly equivalent to their sources, with little simplification or development to arbitrary gender assignment. Even though the functional load of sex-based gender in Michif appears to be weakened (with respect to French and with respect to the load of the animacy-based classification), its productivity is confirmed by the existence of novel English forms with both genders (Sammons 2019: 231). Michif noun phrase syntax does not belong entirely either to French or to Cree but rather is mixed fairly evenly and shows an original and typologically rare set-up.

Issue (2) has received some attention in the recent literature as well. This work has brought a deeper understanding of the phonology of Michif, given the evident stratification of Michif lexicon. Papen (2017) recently reaffirmed the claim for a split phonology for Michif, while Prichard and Shwayder (2014) go against that claim. Concerning vowels, if Michif speakers operationalize two separate vowel systems at a time (Cree and French), this would bring the total number of vowels for Michif to 25. After examining the possible conflicting sites, however, Rosen, Stewart and Sammons (2020) identify only two French vowels that differ significantly from their Cree counterparts (/ɛ, ɔ/), while the rest are assimilated to the Cree system. According to this analysis, Michif's vowel system largely reflects that of Cree. However, their study does not include the nasal vowels.

The morpho-syntax of the Michif verb phrase (issue 3) is another relevant topic for a global assessment of the mixed grammar of Michif. The Michif verbal inflectional system is almost equivalent to that of Plains Cree, with very few modifications (Rhodes 1977; Bakker 1997: 261–263; Gillon and Rosen: 179–185). The general verb structure and derivational schemes are described by Mazzoli (2021), who illustrates a few restructuring processes with respect to Plains Cree. However, an account of mixed verb formations in Michif is currently missing in the literature, and the analysis provided in this paper sheds light on the constraints that originated mixed verbs. Cases of mixed Cree-French verb stems are relatively rare in Michif (Bakker 1997: 243–244; Antonov 2019). The paucity of French verbs in Michif has been attributed to the polysynthetic morphological type of the Michif verb, which is derived from Plains Cree (Bakker 1997: 246, 2006; Gillon and Rosen 2018: 15). "Polysynthesis" is a complex notion in typological linguistics (Fortescue, Mithun and Evans 2017). In the case of Michif, polysynthetic verb formation has to do with: (1) a high ratio of morphemes per word, (2) polypersonal agreement in the transitive verb, (3) a tendency to have non-root (bound) lexical affixes within the stem, (4) verb root serialization, (5) denominal formations, exclusively from French nouns (discussed in this paper in section 3.2), and (6) some forms of noun incorporation.

In Michif, as in Algonquian languages, there are four main verb stem classes based on the intersection of transitivity and animacy features. Each class requires different inflectional markers: inanimate intransitive (II), animate intransitive (AI), transitive inanimate (TI), and transitive animate (TA). To these, one can add semitransitive verb stems (Dryer 2007), which are semantically (ambiguously) transitive verbs that are morphologically intransitive but can take objects (abbreviated here as AI+O).

Mazzoli (accepted) provides a template in 12 slots for the Michif verb, which can be summarized as follows (cf. Goddard 1990; Wolfart 1996; Bakker 2006):

(1)   (prefixes) + (PREVERB) + [INITIAL+FINAL] + (DERIVATIVE) + [suffixes]
                               [STEM]

In this paper, our analysis of mixed verbs adopts the schema in 1, which distinguishes regarding role, position, and function between 'stem-internal finals' (in primary stems) and 'derivatives which modify stems' (in secondary stems). Morpho-phonologically, stem finals and derivatives behave differently: cases of hiatus are resolved differently within the stem (coalescence) and the stem's borders (epenthesis, vowel juxtaposition, cf. section 4.1). In 1, components that are necessary to form a grammatical verb form are in square brackets, while components that are optional are in parentheses. Underlined elements are slots that can be occupied by non-Algonquian (French and English) nominals. They are: the primary stem (before derivatives), the initial slot, and the preverb slot. In section 3, we provide a survey of mixed verbs in Michif.

3 French in the Michif verb

The Michif verb is essentially of Cree origin, but some French verbs are also attested. For instance, one finds French copular verbs (e.g. *sete* 'it was', *se* 'it is', *iyave* 'there was/were') and a few French stems. This section focuses on how French lexical material is inserted into a Cree verbal frame, resulting in mixed verbs which are inflected and derived like all the other Michif verbs of Cree origin.

The insertion of French material within Cree inflected verbs is generally one among several possibilities available to Michif speakers, as in:

(2)   *li   peer   ishiikat-ee-w   John pii Mari*
      DEF.M.S father.M.AN   bless.TA-DIR-IND.3>4   John and Mari
      'the priest blessed John and Mary (sprinkling holy water)'

(3) li   peer   biniaiktioon kii-miy-ee-w   John pii
    DEF.M.S father.M.AN blessing   PST-give.TA-DIR-IND.3>4 John and
    Mari miina
    Mari also
    'the priest gave a blessing to John and Mary (signing the cross with the hand)'

(4) li   peer   (li)   binii   kii-miy-ee-w
    DEF.M.S father.M.AN (the.M.S) blessing.M PST-give.TA-DIR-IND.3>4
    lii   zaañfaañ
    ART.PL children.AN
    'the priest gave a blessing to the children (signing the cross with the hand)'

(5) li   peer   li-binii-w   lii   zaañfaañ
    DEF.M.S father.M.AN NMLZ-bless-IND.3S ART.PL children.AN
    'the priest gives a blessing to the children (signing the cross with the hand)'

In (2), a Cree TA verb is used to denote the act of sprinkling holy water with an aspergillum; in (3), an analytic form made of the Cree TA verb for 'to give' and the French noun for 'blessing' is created; in (4), a similar analytical form is created using the Cree verb for 'to give' and the French nominalized infinitive *li binii* (lit. 'the to bless' < Fr. *bénir* 'bless'); and finally, in (5), a mixed verb is used, consisting of the infinitive French form of the verb 'bless' (*binii*) preceded by the singular masculine French article *li*. When mixed and non-mixed forms are available, speakers' familiarity with the competing forms varies greatly depending on their location and specific language use within their networks.

Example (4) *li binii* (lit. 'the to bless') and (6) *li brodii* (lit. 'the to embroider') 'the embroidery' illustrate a Michif-specific nominalization strategy that forms nouns out of French infinitive verbs (cf. section 3.1):

(6) nahayhtawwun li brodee chi-oushtawhk
    nayeehtaa-wan   li   brodii   chi-osht-aa-hk
    articulated-II.3S DEF.M.S embroidery.M CNJ-make-AI-INDEF.AC
    'embroidery is intricate' (lit. 'it is complicated to make embroidery')
    (Laverdure and Allard 1983: 147)

Mixed verbs with the insertion of non-Algonquian material have been created in most cases to fill lexical gaps with respect to introduced technologies, culture, and customs, as in (5), (6) and (7).

(7) bakwaat-ee-n (ee)-*li-surfii*-t *la* net *tultañ*
1.not.like-THE.TI-IND.1S (CNJ)-NMLZ-surf.AI-CNJ.3S DEF.F.S net.F always
'I don't like that s/he is browsing the net all the time' (< Eng. *surf* 'browse the internet')

All the mixed stems are intransitive (Antonov 2019). The large majority are animate intransitive (AI), and just two types among the mixed constructions discussed in this paper are intransitive inanimate (II) (viz. those with Cree final *-payi* and derivational suffix *-iw-an*). In all cases, the mixed stems conform to the inflectional and derivational paradigm common to the other Michif verbs (but cf. Bakker 1997: 243). The use of conjunct prefixes (8), personal pronominal prefixes (9), preverbs (10), derivational morphemes (11), obviation and possessed subject markers (12), person, number, possessed-subject, and animacy-based gender agreement (11), (12), (13) is regularly attested, and indicated in bold in the following examples:

(8) miyeuyiht-am *sooñ zhardaeñ* **ee-***zhalii*-ihkee-t
like.TI-THE.TI.3S 3POSS.M.S garden.M.INAN CNJ-nice-make.AI-CNJ.3S
's/he likes to make her/his garden nice' (< Fr. *joli* 'nice')

(9) **nd-***aschinii-***n** *avek mooñ mari*
1-argue.AI-IND.1S with 1POSS.M.S husband.M.AN
'I argue with my husband' (< Fr. *obstiner* 'to quarrel')

(10) **ati-***la-vyeey*-iwi-w
INCH-the.F-old.F-be.AI-IND.3S
'she is becoming an old woman' (< Fr. *la vieille* 'the old lady')
(Laverdure and Allard 1983: 176)

(11) bakwaat-ee-n *binii-***kaashoo-***chik li mooñd*
1.not.like-THE.TI-IND.1S bless.AI-MED.AI-CNJ.3PL DEF.S.M people.M
'I don't like that the people have been blessed' (< Fr. *bénir* 'to bless')

(12) pooree-iwuniyiw sa zhawmb
puurii-iw-an-**iyi**-w *sa zhaañb*
rotten-be.II-II-POSS.S-3S 3POSS.S.F leg.F.INAN
'gangrene set in her leg' (< Fr. *pourri* 'rotten')
(Laverdure and Allard 1983: 108)

(13) bakwaat-ee-n John pii Mari beegii-**chik**
1.not.like-THE.TI-IND.1S John and Mari stutter.AI-CNJ.3PL
'I don't like that John and Mary are stuttering' (< Fr. *bégayer* 'to stutter')

In general, either nouns or nominalised verbs are inserted into the Cree frame, but on a limited number of occasions, (etymologically) prepositional phrases are attested, introduced by the French article *li*. The French expression *en retard* 'delayed' (in bold in 14) is undoubtedly monomorphemic for Michif speakers.

(14) keemaekouhow ay-li **awn rtawr**-iwit awsha meena
kii-maakoh-oo-w   ee-*li-aañrtaar*-iwi-t
PST-press.TA-MID.RFLX.AI-IND.3S CNJ-NMLZ-in.late-be.AI-CNJ.3S
aasha   miina
already again
's/he was given a reprimand for being late again' (< Fr. *en retard* 'late')
(Laverdure and Allard 1983: 263)

There are four types of constructions that host French material:
a) French verbs nominalized in their infinitive form, and inflected as AI+O, e.g. *li-brodii*-w 's/he embroiders' (see section 3.1).
b) Denominal verb formation, where French nouns or nominalized adjectives are combined with the Cree derivatives, e.g. *la-maegr-iwi-w* 's/he is skinny' (see section 3.2).
c) French nominals or nominalized adjectives combined with Cree AI finals, e.g. *li-paapaa-i-payi-w* (see section 3.3).
d) French nominals in the preverbal slot (see section 3.4).

The great majority of the occurrences in our data pertain to either group (a) or (b) (section 3.1 and section 3.2). Occurrences of types (c) and (d) are less frequent.

3.1 The frame *li*-X-*ii*: French nominalized infinitives as AI+O Michif stems

French verbs are integrated in their infinitive forms as full Michif primary stems that can be further subjected to secondary derivation (cf. [11] and [18]–[21]). They are conjugated as animate intransitive verbs, irrespective of their original transitivity (15), (16), (17). The French stems invariably appear as infinitives, where the final long vowel -*ii* corresponds to the French infinitive marker -*er*, as noted by Bakker (1997: 242). In the examples in this section, we gloss the relics of the infinitive as 'INF'. In section 4.1, an alternative glossing will be proposed ('AI' animate intransitive). In addition, infinitive French forms are introduced by what is etymologically the masculine singular article *li-*, which marks nominalization and therefore is glossed as NMLZ. The nominalizer is occasionally dropped, e.g. in (17), (26).[2]

(15) bakwaat-ee-n ee-*li-brod-ii*-yaan
1.not.like-THE.TI-IND.1S CNJ-NMLZ-embroider-INF-CNJ.AI.1S
'I hate embroidering'
brodii AI< Fr. *broder* 'to embroider', ambitransitive

(16) kii-*li-sup-ii*-naan
2.PST-NMLZ-supper-INF-IND.AI.1.PL.INCL
'we (INCL) had supper'
supii AI < Fr. *souper* 'to eat supper', ambitransitive

(17) *sapraañ* kiihtwam chi-*arañzh-ii*-kaasho-t,
need.to again CNJ-arrange-INF-MED.AI-CNJ.3S
chi-*li-arañzh-ii*-yahk
CNJ-NMLZ-arrange-INF-CNJ.AI.1PL.INCL
'this has to be rearranged, we (INCL) have to rearrange it'
arañzhii AI+O < Fr. *arranger* 'to arrange', transitive

In (18–21), we observe an exception to the usual pattern, also identified in Antonov (2019: 33). The stem *dooñt-* 'to tame' (<Fr. *dompter*) is introduced by the nominalizer and ends in *-ii*, as in the other cases. However, the nominalized infinitive *li-dooñt-ii* is conjugated as a transitive animate verb in (18), and it takes direction marking (19), as well as passive (21) and medio-passive derivations (20). This is because the nominalized infinitive stem is further derived into a transitive verb through the derivational transitivizing suffix *-h*, which attaches regularly to animate intransitive stems in Cree and Michif (cf. Mazzoli 2021, here in section 4.4 and section 4.5).[3]

---

2 *Li* is not used in other contexts, especially before nominalized adjectives in denominal constructions, e.g. *la farin mweeñzii*-iwi-w (< Fr. *moisi*) 'the flour is moldy'; *li log purii*-iwi-w 'the log is rotten'; *tooñ kapoo purii*-iw-an 'your coat is rotten'.
3 A further example of a French infinitive conjugated as a TA is given in Antonov (2019: 33), taken from the GDI online Michif dictionary: *biniiwahwaaw* (original spelling: *biniiwahwow*), 'to bless someone', where the TA final *-ahw-* 'do by tool, external medium' is used. However, this seems to be an isolated occurrence.

(18) lidoonteehik tee zhvoo
 li-dooñt-ii-h-ik   tii   zhvoo
 NMLZ-tame-INF-TR-IMP.2S>3PL 2POSS.PL   horses
 'domesticate your horses'
 (Laverdure and Allard 1983: 78)

(19) *li-dooñt-ii*-h-ee-w   lii   zhvoo
 NMLZ-tame-INF-TR-DIR-IND.3>4 ART.PL horses
 's/he tames horses'

(20) *lii*   zhvoo   *li-dooñt-ii*-h-aa-w-ak
 ART.PL   horses NMLZ-tame-INF-TR-PASS.AI-IND.3-PL
 'the horses are tamed' (lit. 'they tame the horses')

(21) *li-dooñt-ii*-h-ikaasho-w   li   zhval
 NMLZ-tame-INF-TR-MED.AI-IND.3S DEF.M.S horse
 'the horse has been tamed'

Example (22) illustrates the use of the English verb stem *beeg* 'to beg', and highlights the emergence of a specific pattern:

(22) *sartaeñ* ga-waapam-aa-naan   (ee)ka chi-*li*-**beeg**-*ii*-t
 certain 1.FUT-see.TA-DIR-IND.1PL>3 NEG CNJ.FUT-NMLZ-beg-INF-CNJ.AI.3S
 pur larzhaañ
 for money
 'we (EXCL) will make sure that s/he will not beg for money'
 beeg-*ii* AI < beeg < Eng. *beg*, ambitransitive

The strategy for forming Michif AI stems from nominalized French infinitives becomes a frame to accommodate loan verbs from English. The abstract frame is given in (23), and below we give further examples with the English verbs *can, surf, collect* and *rob* (24)–(27) (the French frame is in italics, English loans in bold, and Cree in plain font).

(23) prefixes – *li* – **English verb** – *ii* – AI endings

(24) bakwawtaen shi-li can-iyawn daw li tawn payzawn
     bakwaat-ee-n   chi-*li*-**kan**-*ii*-yaan   daañ li
     1.not.like-THE.TI-IND.1S CNJ-NMLZ-can-INF-CNJ.AI.1S in   DEF.M.S
     taañ   *peezaañ*
     weather heavy
     'I don't like to can in humid weather'
     (Laverdure and Allard 1983: 137)
     kan-*ii* AI < kan < Eng. *can* 'preserve food', transitive

(25) *li*-**surf**-*ii*-w   *li*   *net*
     NMLZ-surf-INF-IND.AI.3S   DEF.M.S   net.M
     's/he is surfing the net'
     (Gillon and Rosen 2018: 129)
     surf-*ii* AI < surf < Eng. *surf*, ambitransitive

(26) saprawn chikalekteeyen wiya ouhchi
     sapraañ   chi-**kalekt**-*ii*-yen   wiiya   ohchi
     needed   CNJ-collect-INF-CNJ.AI.2S   him/her   from
     'you have to collect (wages) from her'
     (Laverdure and Allard 1983: 64)
     kalekt-*ii* AI < kalekt < Eng. *collect*, transitive

(27) noo keekishkayistam la bawnk aykee-li robeehk
     noo   kii-kishkeeyiht-am   la   baañk
     NEG PST-know.TI-THE.TI.3S   DEF.F.S   bank.F.INAN
     ee-kii-*li*-**rob**-*ii*-hk
     CNJ-PST-NMLZ-rob-INF-INDEF.AC.AI
     's/he was unaware of the robbery at the bank'
     (Laverdure and Allard 1983: 143, Papen 2005: 78)
     rob-*ii* AI < rob < Eng. *rob*, transitive

Examining the loan verbs from English, it is evident that the frame in (23) has grammaticalized as the pattern for verbal borrowing. In section 4.1, we discuss in more detail the role of *li*- and -*ii* in this emerging frame.

3.2 The bulk of Michif mixed verb stems: Denominal verb formation

Michif denominal verb constructions combine French nouns and the Cree derivatives *-iwi* 'to be', *-hkee* 'to make', and *-hkaashoo* 'to pretend'. Such constructions are sometimes analyzed in the literature as cases of (light verb) noun incorporation (Gerdts and Marlett 2008, Barrie and Mathieu 2016). We will discuss how Michif denominals relate to regular noun incorporation (henceforth NI), and to English-like denominal verb formation realized through conversion or category-changing derivatives (e.g. in English, *operation* > *operationalize*). Then, in section 4.1, we will discuss how Michif denominal verb formation fits into the general structure of the Michif verb that we presented in (1).

3.2.1 Mixed verbs with French nominals and Cree *-iwi* 'to be'

Animate intransitive forms with the Cree suffix *-iwi* 'be.AI' cover the copular meanings of attribution ('s/he is X-y'), ascription ('s/he is an X'), and identification ('s/he is X'). In Michif, *-iwi* combines with French (or English) noun phrases or nominalized adjectives only (29–32). Occurrences such as (28), with a Cree nominal, are almost unattested in Michif (cf. Laverdure and Allard 1983: 227, *koohkooshiwi-* 'be a pig', from Cree *kôhkôs*).

(28) mahîhkan-iwi-w
 wolf-be.AI-IND.3S
 's/he is a wolf'
 (Plains Cree, Wolfart 1996: 428)

(29) li pawpaw-iwiw pour see zawnfawn
 li-paapaa-iwi-w   pur sii   zaañfañ
 the.M.S-father-be.AI-IND.3S for 3POSS.PL children
 'he is the father of her children'
 (Laverdure and Allard 1983: 92)

(30) kaa-*li-beebii*-iwi-yaan
 CNJ-DEF.M.S-baby-be.AI-CNJ.1S
 'when I was a baby'

In denominal verb formation, the nouns appear with articles featuring sex-based gender (31–32) and the definite-indefinite distinction (33–34):

(31) no li kawnsayr-iwiw li toomer
 no li-*kaanseer*-iwi-w li *tumer*
 NEG the.M.S-cancer.M-be.AI-IND.3S the.M.S tumor.M.AN
 'the tumor is benign/not cancerous' (< Fr. *le cancer* 'the tumor')
 (Laverdure and Allard 1983: 40)

(32) la shayayr awn fayr ka-la rouy-iwiw
 la *shayeer aañ feer* ka-*la-ruy*-iwi-w
 the.F.S pail.F of iron FUT-the.F.S-rust.F-be.AI-IND.3S
 'the metal pail will rust' (< Fr. *la rouille* 'the rust')
 (Laverdure and Allard 1983: 278)

However, the use of a definite or an indefinite article and *aeñ ~ en* (masculine and feminine, respectively) is not indicative of a certain semantics, out of context. For instance, (33) and (34) are considered equivalent by DeMontigny, both meaning 'Lorna is an old lady'.

(33) Lorna *la-vyeey*-iwi-w
 Lorna the.F.S-old.F-be.AI-IND.3S
 (< Fr. *la vieille* 'the old woman')

(34) Lorna *en-vyeey*-iwi-w
 Lorna a.F.S-old.F-be.AI-IND.3S
 (< Fr. *une vieille* 'an old woman')

In addition, occurrences like (35) and (36) feature an indefinite concept but use *li-* to introduce the noun, so that the meaning of the determiner of the integrated noun phrase is weakened:

(35) noo gawmyeustaen ka-li besoon-oowiyawn
 no gaa-miyeuyiht-ee-n kaa-*li-besooñ*-iwi-yaan
 NEG 1.FUT-like.TI-THE.TI-IND.1S CNJ-the.M.S-twin-be.AI-CNJ.1S
 'I wouldn't like to be a twin' (< Acadian Fr. *le besson* 'the twin')
 (Laverdure and Allard 1983: 341)

(36) li bek seukree ayow [. . .] apray aykee-li meshawn-iwit
li   bek   seukree   ayaa-w   *apree*
DEF.M.S   beak.M   sugared   have.TA-3   after
ee-kii-*li-meshaañ*-iwi-t
CNJ-PST-the.M.S-mean.M-be.AI-CNJ.3S
'he has a sweet voice for his wife after being mean' (< Fr. adj. *méchant* 'mean')
(Laverdure and Allard 1983: 175)

3.2.2 Mixed verbs with French nominals and Cree *-iw-an* 'to be'

Inanimate intransitive forms with the II suffix *-iw-an* 'be.II-II.0' cover the copular meaning attributive ('it is X-y'), as in (37) and (38):

(37) la broo-iwun li laek
la-broo-iw-an   *li*   *laek*
the.F.S-froth.F-be.II-II.0 DEF.M.S   lake.M.INAN
'there is froth on the lake' (< Fr. ?)
(Laverdure and Allard 1983: 105)

(38) la brem-iwun
la-brem-iw-an
the.F.S-fog.F-be.II-II.0
'it is foggy' (< Fr. *la brume* 'the fog')
(Laverdure and Allard 1983: 99)

As in the case of *-iwi*, the article introducing the non-Algonquian material is always singular, and it agrees in sex-based gender with the noun it introduces.

3.2.3 Mixed verbs with French nominals and Cree *-(i)hkee* 'to make'

In Michif, the suffix *-(i)hkee~aa* meaning 'to make' combines with French nouns (39)–(40) or nominalized adjectives (41) to make AI stems:

(39) meena ka-li boudaen-ihkayw
miina ka-*li-budaeñ*-hkee-w
again FUT-the.M.S-sausage-make.AI-IND.3S
's/he'll sulk again' (< Fr. *le boudain* 'the blood sausage'; idiomatic expression)
(Laverdure and Allard 1983: 321)

(40) ga-*li-shmaeñ*-hkaa-n
1.FUT-the.M.S-road.M-make.AI-IND.1S
'I'll build a road'
(adapted from Rosen 2007: 205)

(41) miyeustum a lawntoor sa maizoon ay-li zhalee-ihkayt
miyeuht-am   *alaañtuur sa*   *meezooñ*
like.TI-THE.TI.3S around   3POSS.F.S house.F.INAN
ee-*li-zhalii*-hkee-t
CNJ-DEF.M.S-nice-make.AI-CNJ.3S
's/he likes to beautify her yard'
(Laverdure and Allard 1983: 38)

The introducing article agrees in sex-based gender with the noun, and an epenthetic -*i*- surfaces after consonant-final nouns like *bet* in (42):

(42) *la-bet*-ihkee-w
the.F.S-stupid-make.AI-IND.3S
'she is making silly things' (< Fr. *la bête* 'the silly, stupid woman')

The suffix -*(i)hkee* is not attested with Cree nouns (43):

(43) o-maskisin-ihkee-w   (< Plains Cree *maskisin* 'shoe')
3-shoe-make.AI-3S
'he/she makes shoes'

3.2.4 Mixed verbs with French nominals and Cree -*(i)hkaashoo* 'to pretend'

The Cree element -*(i)hkaashoo* means 'to pretend, to make oneself' and is common in Michif with Cree verb stems:

(44) paahpi-hkaashoo-w
    laugh-pretend.AI-IND.3S
    's/he pretends to laugh'

Most commonly, however, -(i)hkaashoo combines with French or English nominalized adjectives or nouns preceded by a definite article (45), and occasionally with French infinitives (46):

(45) *li-dzhaab*-ihkaashoo-w
    the.M.S-devil-pretend.AI-IND.3S
    's/he is acting like the/a devil' (< Fr. *le diable* 'the devil')

(46) *aschin-ii*-hkaashoo-w
    argue-INF-pretend.AI-IND.3S
    's/he is pretending to argue' (< Fr. *obstiner* 'to quarrel')

In the above examples of denominal formations, we have seen some French adjectives used in mixed verbs (35), (41)–(42). Adjectives are not incorporated in mixed constructions, but they are used in nominalized constructions in both genders (47)–(48). The French integrated into the Cree verb in Michif has the noun phrase as its base.

(47) gakway-la maegriwin
    gaakway-*la-maegr*-iwi-n
    1.try-the.F.S-slim-be.AI-IND.1S
    'I'm trying to slim down' (female subject)' (< Fr. *maigre* 'slim')
    (Laverdure and Allard 1983: 257)

(48) mitouni la prop-iwiw
    mitoni *la-prop*-iwi-w
    very DEF.F.S-proper-be.AI-IND.3S
    'she is very proper' (< Fr. *propre* 'clean')
    (Laverdure and Allard 1983: 243)

As far as gender is concerned, we have seen that nouns and nominalized adjectives agree in sex-based gender with their article. The article and the noun's masculine/feminine gender may also appear to agree with the subject's gender (47)–(48). However, when the subject is coded for non-natural sex-based gender, as in

(49), *la rosh* 'the stone', and (50), *ta shmiiz* 'your shirt', the agreement between the French article and the subject is blocked:

(49) *li-purii*-iwi-w   la   rosh
      the.M.S-rotten-be.AI-IND.3S   DEF.F.S   rock.F.AN
      'the rock is rotten'
      * *la-purii*-iwi-w *la rosh*

(50) *li-purii*-iw-an   ta   shmiiz
      the.M.S-rotten-be.II-II.0   2POSS.S.F   shirt.F.INAN
      'your shirt is rotten'
      * *la-purii*-iw-an *ta shmiiz*

3.2.5 Denominal verb formation and noun incorporation

We will now discuss how Michif formations with *-iwi*, *-hkee*, and *-hkaashoo* compare to denominal verbs with category-changing affixes and noun incorporation (NI). Denominal verb formation takes different shapes in the world's languages. In English (Clark and Clark 1979), there is a productive process of zero derivation that converts nouns into verbs, in a way that the meaning of the event is related to the noun in a variety of ways, and sometimes unpredictably. English, as well as other languages, also uses category-changing affixes like *de-*, *-ize*, *-ify*, and *-ate*. Speakers interpret affixes in denominal verbs in terms of semantic categories that permit redefinition of the internal semantics of the noun as a verb (Gottfurcht 2008). In Michif, denominal verbs appear in construction-specific environments, and they are never simple conversions. There are specific verbalizing morphemes that form a single word with the noun. The suffixed lexically intransitive verbs in the form of affixes are attached to nouns that are their predicative or direct arguments. A predictable meaning is associated with the construction in most cases.

     Denominal verb formation in Michif can also be compared to Noun Incorporation (NI). Mattissen (2017) and Jacques (2012: 1208) propose a strict definition of NI as the combination of a noun and a verb, on the condition that (1) the resulting construction constitutes a morphological and phonological word, which occurs in finite forms; (2) both the nominal and the verbal roots in question exist also as independent stems; and (3) the combination represents a productive pattern that is optional, with a non-idiomatic compositional meaning. However, incorporating languages show varying degrees of adherence to the definition (Fortescue, Mithun and Evans 2017). In the strict sense, NI does not occur in Michif, while it does occur in Plains Cree (Mellow 1990), albeit with limited productivity. In fact, in Michif, it is not possible to incorporate any French noun into a verbal Cree structure that includes an otherwise autonomous Cree verb stem. However, denominal verbs in many Algonquian languages have been treated as cases of NI (Mathieu 2013; Barrie and Mathieu 2016; Johns 2017 for Inuktikut), where the verbalizing suffixes function as light verbs that incorporate noun phrases. Although the Michif verbalizing suffixes in (29)–(50) do not occur as autonomous verb stems, the denominal constructions do meet the other requirements for NI. Michif denominal constructions constitute morphological words, since the noun is integrated within the Cree verb template. The combination is a productive pattern, as demonstrated by the use of French and English noun phrases, and its semantics is compositional (with the exception of a few idiomatic expressions, cf. [39]).

In summary, denominal verbs in Michif appear to share some features with NI, with the exception that Michif verbalizing suffixes are not independent verb stems. Verbalizing suffixes like *-iwi*, *-iw-an*, *-(i)hkee*, and *-(i)hkaashoo* function like light verbs that incorporate French noun phrases. Further research should explore the referentiality and (stranded) modifiability of the noun phrase in Michif denominal constructions, which are common attributes of incorporated nouns (Smit 2005).

3.3 French nominals combined with Cree finals

The Cree elements discussed in this section are identified as finals because they are found in Michif mainly in combination with Cree initials, differently from the denominal suffixes discussed in section 3.2.

3.3.1 French nominals with concrete finals of perception, AI (*-inaakoshi*) and II (*-inaakw-an*)

The morphemes *-inaakoshi* (animate) 'appears, looks like' and *-inaakw-an* (inanimate) 'appears, looks like' are intransitive finals of perception related to sight. They probably consist etymologically of a final related to vision and the eye, *-n-*, and a derivational morpheme of 'middle attributive predication', *-aakoshi* (AI) or *-aakw-an* (II). In Michif they combine with French elements:

(51) toolee-naakoshi-w
 awful-appear.AI-IND.3S
 's/he is/looks ugly' (< Fr. *tout laid*, lit. 'very ugly')

(52) *toolee*-naakw-an
awful-appear.II-II.0
'it is/looks ugly'

(53) *dilet*-inaakw-an
milk-appear.II-II.0
'it looks milky' (< Fr. *du lait* 'some milk')
(Laverdure and Allard 1983: 177)

These finals also commonly combine with Cree initials (e.g. *ishinaakoshiw* AI 's/he looks thus'; *shoohkinaakoshiw* AI 's/he looks strong'; *miyonaakwan* VII 'it is beautiful, it looks good', *teepinaakwan* VII 'it is still seen (in the distance)', 'it is still in sight').

3.3.2 French nominals combined with Cree concrete final -*payi* 'move.AI'

The morpheme -*payi* is a concrete final in Plains Cree and Michif that combines with a great variety of initials to form intransitive stems. As a stem-internal component, -*payi* has fuzzy semantics related to 'movement', 'change of state', and 'unexpected/sudden event' (54):

(54) *li   paeñ   ohpi-payi-w*
DEF.M.S   bread.M.AN   up-move.AI-IND.3S
'the bread leavens'

In Michif, unlike in Cree, -*payi* combines with a group of French nouns and nominalized adjectives introduced by *li*. There is an epenthetic vowel *i* between the consonant-final French material and the final -*payi*:

(55) li simawn ka-li jeur-ipayin
li   simaañ   ka-li-dzheur-i-payi-n
DEF.M.S   cement.M.INAN   FUT-the.M.S-hard-EPEN-move.II-II.0
'the concrete will harden'
(Laverdure and Allard 1983: 125)

(56) *li   zhardaeñ   ka-li-zhalii-payi-n*
DEF.M.S   garden.M.INAN   FUT-the.M.S-hard-move.II-II.0
'the garden will get nice'

(57) *liveer*-i-payi-n
winter-EPEN-move.II-II.0
'it will get winter'

(58) *mooñ   freer   kaa-li-paapaa*-i-payi-w
1POSS.M.S brother.M.AN CNJ-the.M.S-father-EPEN-move.AI-IND.3S
'my brother is going to be a dad'

In the Michif mixed constructions, the semantics of the final *-payi* are fully interpretable, and *-payi* functions as a kind of light verb, incorporating noun phrases (similarly to the ones in section 3.2).

3.3.3 French nominalized adjectives combined with Cree *-(i)shtikwaan-ee* 'head.AI'

The Michif element *-(i)shtikwaan-ee/aa* 'to have a head like' combines the Cree medial *-(i)shtikwaan* and the AI final *-ee/aa*. It is used in Michif in a limited number of occurrences where the stems are entirely from Cree (59)–(60):

(59) lee wawpishtikwawn
lii   waap-ishtikwaan
ART.PL light-head
'the blond people'
(Laverdure and Allard 1983: 45)

(60) machi-shtikwaan-ee-w
bad-head-AI-IND.3S
's/he is stubborn'

In a few occurrences, it combines with French elements:

(61) aen kanawr kaw-li vayr-ishtikwawnayt
aeñ   kanaar   kaa-li-veer-i-shtikwaan-ee-t
INDEF.M.S duck.M.AN CNJ-the.M.S-green-EPEN-head-AI-CNJ.3S
'a duck that has a green head, a mallard'
(Laverdure and Allard 1983: 170, Bakker 1997: 245)

Echoing the example in (61), DeMontigny proposed (62), commenting that this is a word she guesses "one could use", in confirmation of the productive nature of the word formation process:

(62) *ruzh*-i-shtikwaan-ee-w
red-EPEN-head-AI-IND.3S
's/he has a red head'

3.3.4 French nominals combined with the Cree abstract final *-ishi*

The morpheme *-ishi* is a Cree abstract final used to form AI verb stems. This final is widespread in Michif with Cree initials:

(63) noohtay mashkawishiw
noohtee-mashkaw-ishi-w
want-strong-be.AI-IND.3S
's/he wants to be strong'
(Laverdure and Allard 1983: 319, Bakker 1997: 240)

(64) gishkishin kaw-apisheeshishiyawn
gishk-ishi-n   kaa-apishiish-ishi-yaan
1.remember-AI-IND.1S CNJ-small-be.AI-CNJ.1S
'I remember my childhood' (litt. 'when I was little')
(Laverdure and Allard 1983: 61)

In Laverdure and Allard (1983), a few instances are attested of AI verbs composed by the stem *megr* and the AI final *-ishi*:

(65) maegrashin
megr-ishi-n
skinny-be.AI-IND.3S
's/he is skinny' (< Fr. *maigre* 'skinny')
Laverdure and Allard (1983: 23)

However, DeMontigny finds this final unacceptable with French nouns or nominalized adjectives. DeMontigny prefers *meg-iwi-w*, *li meg*, or *kaawaakatishi-w* to (65), and she considers (66)–(71) equally unacceptable:

(66) * *labet*-ishi-w
 (intended) 'she is stupid'

(67) * *liboss*-ishi-w
 (intended) 'he is bossy'

(68) * *libet*-ishi-w
 (intended) 'he is stupid'

(69) * *libet*-ishi-n
 (intended) 'I/you am/are stupid'

(70) * *lametres*-ishi-w
 (intended) 'she is a teacher'

(71) ?? *lipovr*-ishi-w
 (intended) 's/he is poor'

Therefore, in Michif, *-ishi* can be combined with Cree initials, but not with French noun phrases.

3.4 French used in the preverbal position

The adverbial specification of manner in *aeñ kwashooñ* 'a pig' or *kwashooñ* 'pig' is taken from the expression *kom aeñ kwashooñ* 'like a pig', shortened, and used in some Michif occurrences to modify a verb. These constructions are very rare. In (72), *kwashooñ* follows the personal pronoun prefixes for speech act participants in the independent order. It is also suffixed with *-i* either to avoid the consonant cluster or to form a preverb, as in the analysis by Mellow (1990), who referred to the equivalent Plains Cree structure as 'lexical noun incorporation':[4]

(72) ki-*kwashooñ*-i-miichisho-n
 2-pig-EPEN-eat.AI-IND.2S
 'you eat like a pig, greedily'

---

[4] *kohkoos-i-miitiso-w* (pig-i-eat.AI-IND.3S) 's/he eats like a pig' (Mellow 1990: 248).

In a similar fashion, *meelii-* (< Fr. *mêler* 'to mix') is used in (73) following the future marker *ka-*, and *ipee-* (< Fr. *épaix* 'thick') in (74):[5]

(73) ka-*meelii*-oshihtaa-n   li   morkii?
     FUT-mix-make.AI-IND.2S DEF.M.S plaster.M.INAN
     'will you mix the plaster?'
     (Laverdure and Allard 1983: 232)

(74) ipay-oushtaw la soup aen pchi braen
     ipee-oshihtaa   la   sup   aeñ   pchi   braeñ
     thick-make.IMP DEF.F.S soup.F.INAN INDEF.M.S little bit
     'thicken the soup a little'
     (Laverdure and Allard 1983: 331)

3.5 Summary

In Michif, a number of French nouns and nominalized adjectives and verbs are used in a Cree verbal frame. French infinitives are used as primary verb stems (section 3.1), and nominals can be derived into verbs through verbalizing suffixes that function like incorporating light verbs (section 3.2). On rarer occasions, French nominals are used as initials in combination with Cree finals (section 3.3) or as modifiers in a preverbal position (section 3.4) (cf. the general structure of the Michif verb presented in [1]).

4 Discussion

Michif allows several forms of word-internal mixing within the verb. We will now discuss the data presented in section 3 in the light of the descriptive literature on Michif and other Algonquian languages, and in relation to the literature on language contact.

---

[5] DeMontigny points out that this form is unknown to her. In her family, they would use *kishpakin*-a *la sup*.

4.1 Michif mixed verbs and their internal structure

4.1.1 Michif mixed forms and the general structure of the Michif verb

The French infinitive marker *-er* is the source of the long vowel *-ii* in occurrences like *li-binii* (DEF-bless, 'to bless') and *li-aranzhii* (DEF-arrange, 'to arrange'), which are AI+O verb stems in Michif (section 3.1). The stem is a nominalized infinitive, which is a Michif-specific strategy not possible in French. The analysis of English loans such as those in (24)–(27) raised the issue of the status of the long vowel *-ii* before the inflectional AI endings of the mixed verbs. Given that an exhaustive list of Plains Cree/Michif stem-internal finals is not currently available, it is unclear whether *-ii* is a productive Cree AI final.[6] Well-known Plains Cree abstract AI finals do include alternant *-ê/â* (e.g. *pîkishkw-ê-w*, *ni-pîkiskw-â-n*, 's/he speaks, I speak'), *-â* (e.g. *nip-â-w*, 's/he sleeps'), *-i* (e.g. *wâp-i-w*, 's/he has sight'), and *-ô* (e.g. *kit-ô-w*, 's/he calls'). Cowan (1990: 846) mentions an AI final in *-ii* for Plains Cree. The online Michif dictionary (Rosen 2019) lists fourteen AI verbs with stems ending in *-ii*, although it is not clear whether the final long vowel should be considered a category-defining final that assigns features of transitivity and animacy to the stems. Bloomfield (1984)'s Cree dictionary lists 87 verbs ending in *-îw*, all of them intransitive, and only eight of them animate. In Michif mixed stems, *-ii-* could be a non-Cree-derived final, born out of the reanalysis of the French infinitive *-er*, and functioning productively to form AI stems with non-Algonquian-derived elements, nominalized through the nominalizer *li-* (cf. also Gillon and Rosen 2018: 131–132).

French nominalized infinitives in these mixed formations are always transposed and inflected as animate intransitives (AI) in Michif. We confirmed this through eliciting conjunct inflected forms for each of the examples, which resulted in all the forms consistently inflected as AI. The reason why speakers interpret and inflect nominalized non-Algonquian infinitives as animate intransitive stems could be related to either:

1) The ease of interpreting the final long vowel of the French infinitives *-ii* into an AI final, due to its similarity to other Cree AI abstract finals consisting of vowels (i.e. Michif *-ee*, *-ee/aa*, *-aa*, *-oo*, *-i*).
2) The versatility of the AI verb inflection paradigm, given that in Cree and Michif a group of morphologically AI verbs can be syntactically transitive and take patients (Oxford 2017: 29).

---

[6] Jeffrey Muehlbauer made an excellent survey of them: https://www.academia.edu/304874/A_morpheme_index_of_Plains_Cree

3) The rich available paradigm for deriving transitives from intransitive stems (including the causative/valency increaser -*h* and other morphemes listed in Table 2 in Mazzoli 2021: 98–99; cf. also Bakker 2006).

In the case of the French denominal verb formation presented in section 3.2 (e.g., *li-paapaa-iwi-w*, [29]), the analysis of hiatus resolution between the French noun phrase and verbalizing suffixes like *-iwi* and *-iw-an* ('to be') indicate their relative positions with respect to the verb template in (1). In Michif and Cree (Wolfart 1996: 434), vowel hiatus is tolerated at the stem boundaries with the preverbs (to the left) and the derivatives (to the right). When the two components are internal to the stem, hiatus must be resolved through assimilation. This is consistent with other Algonquian languages, e.g. Oji-Cree (Slavin 2012: 242) and Ojibwe (Mathieu 2013). In the Michif examples in (75) and (76), the hiatus is not resolved, and we observe vowel juxtaposition between the vowel-final preverb *miyo-* and both the vowel-initial verb stems *ayaa-* 'to have' and *aapachi-* 'to use'. In both occurrences, *miyo-* 'good' is used as stem-external preverb that modifies primary verb stems:

(75) Bachees miyou-ayow
 Bachiis miyo-ay-aa-w
 Bachiis good-be-IND.3S
 'John is in good health'
 (Laverdure and Allard 1983: 354)

(76) miyou-awpachihikawshoow
 miyo-aapachih-ikaashoo-w
 good-use.TA-MED.AI-IND.3S
 'they take good advantage of him/her' (lit. 's/he is taken good advantage of')
 (Laverdure and Allard 1983: 18)

In (77) and (78), the hiatus is resolved through assimilation, and therefore the stem-internal initial *miyo-* assimilates with the finals *-ishi* and *-ee(yi)ht* to form the stems *miyoshi-* 'to be good' and *miyeuht-* 'to like':

(77) miyoshiw
 miyo-ishi-w
 good-be.AI-IND.3S
 's/he is good, s/he is nice'
 (Rosen 2019)

(78) Miyeustawkwun kakeeshoushihk
    miyo-ee(yi)ht-aakw-an   kaa-kiishoshi-hk
    good-do.by.think.TI-PRED.II-II.0 CNJ-be.warm.AI-INDEF.AC
    'It feels good to be warm'
    (Laverdure and Allard 1983: 19)

In denominal formations, if the combination between the French noun phrase and Cree verbalizing suffix resolves hiatus through assimilation, it indicates that the two components merge to form a new stem (i.e. they occupy the positions of initial and final). If French noun phrases and Cree verbalizing suffixes do not resolve the hiatus, then their boundary is not stem-internal.

The data on Michif denominal verbs show consistently that adjacent noun phrases and verbalizing suffixes tolerate hiatus and just show vowel juxtaposition (see [29]–[30], [36]–[37]). Therefore, the boundary in question patterns like a stem-external boundary rather than a stem-internal one: Michif denominal verbalizing suffixes, or light verbs, pattern like derivatives (and not finals) that apply to noun phrases used as primary stems.

In the cases described in section 3.3 of French nominals combining with Cree finals, the French material is used as an initial component in internally-mixed verbs. Nominals used in the preverbal position appear to be inserted into a stem-external position to the left of the stem.

In sum, only selected slots in the general Michif template allow for insertion of non-Algonquian material, and these are either (1) the primary stem, (2) the initial slot, or (3) the preverbal position.

4.1.2 French denominal verb formation: What noun phrase structure is incorporated?

The Michif mixed denominal constructions described in section 3.2 are special because the incorporated noun requires the presence of the article, which varies both in sex-based gender and definiteness:

(79) maachi-*li-vyeu*-iwi-w
    start-the.M.S-old.M.AN-be.AI-IND.3S
    'he is getting old'
    * *maachi-vyeu-iwi-w*

(80) ni-maachi-*la-vyeey*-iwi-n
 1-start-the.F.S-old.F.AN-be.AI-IND.1S
 'I am getting old' (female speaker)

(81) *en-vyeey*-hkaasho-w
 INDEF.F.S-old.F-pretend.AI-IND.3S
 '[somebody] is pretending to be an old lady'

The article *li* is used to nominalize and incorporate verbs or adjectives, sometimes in quite complex forms:

(82) la galet li vayr di gree-iwiw
 la   galet   li-veer-di-grii-iwi-w
 DEF.F.S bread.F.AN the.M.S-green-of-gray-be.AI-IND.3S
 'the bread is moldy'
 (Laverdure and Allard 1983: 181)

(83) la parsonn li pchee megr feb inawkoushiw
 la   parson   li-pchii-megr-feb-inaakoshi-w
 DEF.F.S person.F.AN the.M.S-little-skinny-weak-look.like.AI-IND.3S
 'the person looks puny'
 (Laverdure and Allard 1983: 245)

In other Algonquian languages, the noun phrases incorporated in similar formations require some structure. Mathieu (2013) argues that Ojibwe incorporated nominals are complex noun phrases that potentially include singular number marking, diminutive and pejorative morphology, and qualifying adjectives as well as possessives. In Michif, there are more restrictions on the specific nominal structure that can be incorporated into a verb. Definite articles do not denote definiteness of the incorporated noun phrase, as shown in (33)–(36). Animacy features of the noun may be retained, but there is no superficial agreement with any other elements of the noun phrase or the entire verb phrase. In fact, demonstratives are never incorporated into these denominal constructions in Michif (nor in Ojibwe, Mathieu 2013). Accordingly, (84b) and (85b) are ungrammatical:

(84) a. (ni-)*lur*-ihkaashoo-n
  (1-)bear.M.AN-pretend.AI-IND.1S
  'I am pretending to be a bear'

b. * *lur*-ana-ihkaashoo-n
bear.M.AN-that.AN-pretend.AI-IND.1S
(intended) 'I am pretending to be like that bear'

(85) a. ka-*la-meezooñ*-ihkee-w
FUT-the.F.S-house.F.INAN-make.AI-IND.3S
's/he is making a house'

b. * ka-anima-*la-meezooñ*-ihkee-w
FUT-that.INAN-the.F.S-house.F.INAN-make.AI-IND.3S
(intended) 's/he is making that house'

Possessives are not attested in our data in incorporated nominals, and numerals are not attested either.

Within the denominal mixed verbs, the plural article *lii* is unattested and ungrammatical, even with nouns that are otherwise attested and used almost exclusively in the plural:

(86) * *lii-bulet*-ihkee-w
ART.PL-meatball-make.AI-IND.3S
(intended) 's/he's making meatballs'
(Gillon and Rosen 2018: 134)

Apparently, Michif incorporated noun phrase structure is much less extensive than the structure incorporated in Ojibwe, since it does not include possessives and numerals (Mathieu 2013). Table 1 below sums up the noun phrase features incorporated in denominal constructions in Michif.

Table 1: Features of the incorporated noun phrase in Michif denominal constructions.

Feature	Attested	Specifics
articles	YES	mostly obligatory
definiteness (of the article)	YES	BUT it appears neutralized
gender (of the noun and the article)	YES	
animacy (of the noun)	N/A	
plurality	NO	ruled out as ungrammatical

Table 1 (continued)

Feature	Attested	Specifics
prepositions	NO	only forms like aañritaar, unanalysed by speakers and preceded by the nominalizer li-
demonstratives	NO	ruled out as ungrammatical
possessives	NO	not found in the data
numerals	NO	not found in the data

It is likely that denominals represented the first context for the formation of mixed French/Cree verb stems in Michif, and the great variety of these types of constructions demonstrates that denominal verb formation is a productive subset of the morphological Cree lexicon in Michif.

4.2 Typologically unusual patterns of borrowing and word-internal mixing in Michif

The presence of French elements in the Michif verb is marginal yet productively embedded in an Algonquian frame. The Cree polysynthetic verb frame is difficult to penetrate, probably due to the pivotal role of the stem-internal finals, which mark obligatory categorization with respect to transitivity and animacy, for all the stems to be inflected. Every non-Algonquian or mixed verb stem would have to receive this type of categorization to be able to be inflected. In what follows, we will compare the use of French nouns in Michif to phenomena of borrowing, code-switching, and other processes of word-internal mixing in other known mixed languages.

The patterns of use of French nominals in the Michif verb seem different from other known instances of borrowing, code-switching, or creole and mixed language formation. French nouns have been borrowed in Montagnais along with a variety of French determiners, like *la*, *les*, *l'* and even with *des* and *tes* as well as zero marking, although both the articles and the possessives were included as part of the phonologically integrated string of the borrowed French nouns in that language (Drapeau 1980). The same happened to some Michif nouns with the indefinite, definite, and plural determiners (e.g. *l/n/arzhañ* 'the money', *l/n/zotomobil* 'the car', and *l/nuuvraazh* 'the work'). However, Michif also has morphologically identifiable definite, indefinite, and plural determiners, and a set of possessives, which carry the overt marking of sex-based gender and number in the noun phrase. Moreover, in typical borrowing situations, loans are often assigned a default or a natural value of a nominal classificatory category (Kilarski 1997). For example, in Montagnais, in a more recent round of phonologically non-integrated borrowings by Montagnais-French bilinguals, the plural article *les* is used as a default to flag foreign borrowings, even when this would be incorrect in French (e.g. *les kafe* 'the coffee' Drapeau 1980). This is different from Michif, in which the sex-based gender of the French nouns in Michif is maintained productively and pretty much equivalent to its source, with only 14.4% of Michif gender values differing from their French equivalents (Sammons 2019: 232–234).

Michif differs from other known cases of intense borrowing from Romance languages, such as in Chamorro and Tetun Dili, which do not borrow gender from the European language. In general, it is uncommon for languages to borrow nouns with the markers of the original gender, and certainly not across the board as in Michif. The fact that Michif maintained the French gender system and that denominals are formed only on complex French noun phrases sets this language apart typologically from other contact languages (Good 2012, Corbett 1991).

Michif also shows peculiar behavior in denominal verb formation (section 3.2). The borrowing of nouns to form denominal verbs is known to be a common cross-linguistic process (Gardner-Chloros and Edwards 2007). Gerdts and Marlett (2008: 414) describe many languages from North America that employ denominal verb constructions as a productive source of borrowing, mentioning examples from Yaqui, Halkomelem, White Mountain Apache, Seri, and Nuuchahnulth. Valentine (2001: 419) notes productive denominal constructions from English bare nouns in Ojibwe with the light verbs *-ke* 'make' and *-i* 'have'. However, the majority of Ojibwe denominals are still formed from Algonquian nouns, while Michif forms denominal verbs only from French noun phrases. Also, borrowed nouns in denominal formations in Algonquian languages mostly feature the incorporation of bare roots (Gerdts and Marlett 2008: 415) and thus behave differently from Michif, in which the entire category of denominal verbs has been restructured and adapted to the incorporation of complex French noun phrases (Table 1 in section 4.1).

Moreover, Michif features a peculiar type of mixed verb combining French nominals and Cree finals. Due to their fuzzy semantics and uncertain productivity, Cree finals in Michif are not commonly used in mixed forms. However, the data illustrated in section 3.3 testify that some stem-internal Cree finals are attested in combination with French. That is the extent reached by word-internal patterns of mixing in Michif. Among the Algonquian languages, the only other known example is Mi'kmaq, which borrows verbs using the Algonquian final *-ewi-t* (Bakker and van der Voort 2017: 420).

The existence of constraints on borrowing in highly synthetic languages has been exaggerated in the literature (Bakker and van der Voort 2017). Our study adds to this by showing that borrowing is not blocked in polysynthetic languages. However, speakers do prefer borrowing nouns, while borrowing verbs into polysynthetic languages appears to be particularly uncommon. A cross-linguistically widespread strategy to inflect loan verbs is that of using an inflected verb of support (Matras 2007: 47; Wohlgemuth 2009; Haspelmath and Tadmor 2009, who survey borrowings in a sample of 41 languages, very few of which are polysynthetic). For example, in Montagnais, borrowed verbs are never integrated morphologically. The French verbs in Montagnais are uttered in their infinitive form and associated with the native forms of the verb *tuutam* 'to do' to help integrate the loan (Drapeau 1980, 1995). Michif adopted a different strategy, integrating the French nominalized infinitives into the Cree verbal structure. This triggered the reanalysis of the infinitives as bipartite stems with an originally created categorizing AI final *-ii* to accommodate English loans.

Theories of borrowing and language mixing have attributed the variability in the outcomes of language contact to the typological compatibility of the languages involved (Myers-Scotton 1993; Field 2002) and the existence of borrowing hierarchies, claiming, for instance, that nouns are the easiest to transfer, while inflectional morphology is the hardest (Muysken 2000). For word-internal mixing, the syntactic boundedness of the borrowed morpheme has proved to be a relevant factor, and Gardani (2008) observed that contextual inflection (agreement) is more difficult to borrow than inherent inflection (e.g. plural). Recent literature has singled out some cases of morphological inflectional borrowings among creole and mixed languages. For the mixed language Gurindij Kriol, Meakins (2011) provides evidence of the borrowing of contextual inflection, the most uncommon case of grammatical borrowing. Clements and Luís (2015) illustrate a case of exceptional morphological borrowing in Korlai Indo-Portuguese (a Portuguese-based creole language in contact with Marathi), which borrowed a Marathi non-finite verb form to create a new inflectional class, specifically for integrating loan verbs. The Korlai case is very similar to the Michif one, with the new AI final *-ii* having developed from the French infinitive marker *-er*. Michif patterns with cases of intense language contact and other known mixed languages, which further contribute to classifying Michif as a specific case of mixed language formation.

5 Conclusions

This paper adds a puzzle piece to the discussion of the mixed nature of Michif from the perspective of the morpho-syntax of the verb phrase, which is often considered to be entirely Cree-derived. Our analysis showed that the Cree verb structure persists when elements from non-Algonquian languages are integrated into Michif mixed verb formations. French influence on the Cree verb in Michif is mostly confined to lexical components within the verb, either as entire stems, as preverbs, and, in a few instances, as initials. However, at least two new functional morphemes appear to have emerged in Michif. The first is a new element -*ii*, which we argue to be an AI final, derived from the reanalysis of the French infinitive marker -*er*, and possibly influenced by Cree animate intransitive verbs ending in -*îw*. The second is the nominalizer *li-* that is prefixed to nominalized verbs or adjectives in noun phrases incorporated into a Cree verb frame.

Finally, we argued that Michif strategies of accommodating French nominals are typologically rare, also with respect to other contact languages, which places Michif among other cases of intense language contact and known mixed languages. In fact, unlike other Algonquian languages in contact with French, Michif adapted a variety of French nominalized verb stems to function as animate intransitive (AI) verbs. Also, while denominal verbs are commonly formed out of the bare roots of borrowed French nouns in many Algonquian languages, Michif replaced the entirety of denominal forms with new mixed constructions formed from complex French noun phrases and a set of Cree derivatives.

Abbreviations

0	inanimate subject
1	first person
2	second person
3	third person
4	third person obviative (fourth)
AC	actor
AI	animate intransitive
AN	animate
ART	article
CNJ	conjunct
DEF	definite
DIR	direct (TA)
EPEN	epenthetic vowel

EXCL	exclusive
F	feminine
FUT	future
II	inanimate intransitive
IMP	imperative
INAN	inanimate
INCH	inchoative
INCL	inclusive
IND	independent
INDEF	indefinite
INF	infinitive
M	masculine
MID.RFLX	middle-reflexive
MED	medio-passive
NEG	negative
NMLZ	nominalizer
O	object
PASS	passive
POSS	possessive
PL	plural
PRED	predicative attributive
PST	past
S	singular
SBJ	subjunctive
TA	transitive animate
THE	theme sign
TI	transitive inanimate
TR	transitive

References

Antonov, Anton. 2019. Loan verb integration in Michif. *Journal of Language Contact* 12(1). 27–51.

Bakker, Peter. 1997. *A language of our own: The genesis of Michif, the mixed Cree-French language of the Canadian Métis*. New York: Oxford University Press.

Bakker, Peter. 2006. Algonquian verb structure: Plains Cree. In Grazyna Rowicka & Eithne Carlin (eds.), *What's in a Verb?*, 3–27. Utrecht: LOT.

Bakker, Peter. 2017. Typology of mixed languages. In Alexandra Y. Aikhenvald & R. M. W. Dixon (eds.) *The Cambridge handbook of linguistic typology*, 217–253. Cambridge: Cambridge University Press.

Bakker, Peter. 2019. Review of Gillon, Carrie & Nicole Rosen, with Verna DeMontigny. 2018. Nominal contact in Michif. Oxford University Press. *International Journal of American Linguistics* 85(1). 163–165.

Bakker, Peter & Hein van der Voort. 2017. Polysynthesis and language contact. In Michael Fortescue, Marianne Mithun & Nicholas Evans (eds.), *The Oxford handbook of polysynthesis*, 408–427. Oxford: Oxford University Press.

Barrie, Michael & Eric Math eu. 2016. Noun incorporation and phrasal movement. *Natural Language and Linguistic Theory*, 34(1). 1–51.
Bloomfield, Leonard. 1984. *Cree-English lexicon. 2 Volumes*. New Haven: Human Relations Area Files.
Clark, Eve V. & H. H. Clark. 1979. When nouns surface as verbs. *Language* 55(4). 767–811.
Clements, Clancy J. & Ana R. Luís. 2015. Contact intensity and the borrowing of bound morphology in Korlai Indo-Portuguese. In Francesco Gardani, Peter Arkadiev & Nino Amiridze (eds.), *Borrowed Morphology*. 219–240. Amsterdam/Berlin: John Benjamins.
Corbett, Greville G. 1991. *Gender*. Cambridge: Cambridge University Press.
Cowan, William. 1990. Bloomfield, structuralism, and the Algonquian languages. In Hans-Josef Niederehe & E.F.K. Koerner (eds.), *History and historiography of linguistics: Proceedings of the fourth International conference on the history of the language sciences, Trier, 24–28 August 1987. Volume 2: 18th–20th Century*, [Studies in the History of the Language Sciences 51(2)]. 833–848. Amsterdam: John Benjamins.
Drapeau, Lynn. 1980. Les emprunts au français en montagnais. In *Inuktitut et langues Amerindiennes au Québec*. Special issue of *Cahiers de linguistique*, 10, 29–49. Quebec: Presses de l'Université du Québec.
Drapeau, Lynn. 1995. Codeswitching in caretaker speech and bilingual competence in a Native village of Northern Quebec. *International Journal of the Sociology of Language* 113. 157–164.
Dryer, Matthew. 2007. Clause types. In Timothy Shopen (ed.), *Language typology and syntactic description. Volume. I: Clause structure*, 224–275. Cambridge: Cambridge University Press.
Field, Fredric 2002. *Linguistic borrowing in bilingual contexts*. Amsterdam: John Benjamins.
Fortescue, Michael, Marianne Mithun & Nicholas Evans (eds.). 2017. *The Oxford handbook of polysynthesis*. Oxford: Oxford University Press.
Gardani, Francesco. 2008. *Borrowing of inflectional morphemes in language contact*. Frankfurt am Main: Peter Lang.
Gardner-Chloros, Penelope & Malcom Edwards. 2007. Compound verbs in codeswitching: Bilinguals making do? *International Journal of Bilingualism* 11. 73–91.
Gerdts, Donna & Stephen Marlett. 2008. Introduction: The form and function of denominal verb constructions. *International Journal of American Linguistics* 74. 489–510.
Gillon, Carrie & Nicole Rosen, with Verna DeMontigny. 2018. *Nominal contact in Michif*. Oxford: Oxford University Press.
Goddard, Ives. 1990. Primary and secondary stem derivation in Algonquian. *International Journal of American Linguistics* 56. 449–483.
Good, Jeff. 2012. Typologizing grammatical complexities: or Why creoles may be paradigmatically simple but syntagmatically average. *Journal of Pidgin and Creole Languages* 27(1). 1–47.
Gottfurcht, Carolyn A. 2008. Denominal verb formation in English. Evanston: Northwestern University dissertation.
Haspelmath, Martin & Uri Tadmor (eds.). 2009. *Loanwords in the world's languages: A comparative handbook*. Berlin: De Gruyter Mouton.
Jacques, Guillaume. 2012. From denominal derivation to incorporation. *Lingua* 122. 1207–1231.
Johns, Alana. 2017. Noun incorporation. In Martin Everaert & Henk C. van Riemsdijk (eds.), *The Wiley Blackwell Companion to Syntax*, 2nd ed. Hoboken, NJ: John Wiley and Sons, Inc.
Kilarski, Marcin. 1997. The case of the unmarked gender in loanwords. *Studia Anglica Posnaniensia*, 32. 89–99.

Laverdure, Patline & Ida Rose Allard. 1983. *The Michif dictionary*. John C. Crawford (ed.). Winnipeg: Pemmican Publications.
Mathieu, Eric. 2013. Denominal verbs in Ojibwe. *International Journal of American Linguistics* 79(1). 97–132.
Mattissen, Johanna. 2017. Sub-types of polysynthesis. In Nicholas Evans, Marianne Mithun & Michael Fortescue (eds.), *The Oxford handbook of polysynthesis*, 70–98. Oxford: Oxford University Press.
Matras, Yaron, 2007. The borrowability of structural categories. In Yaron Matras & Jeanette Sakel (eds.), *Grammatical borrowing in cross-linguistic perspective*, 31–73. Berlin: Mouton de Gruyter.
Mazzoli, Maria. 2019. Michif loss and resistance in four Metis communities (Kahkiyaaw mashchineenaan, "All of us are disappearing as in a plague"). *Zeitschrift für Kanada-Studien*, 69. 96–117.
Mazzoli, Maria. 2021. Secondary derivation in Michif: Beyond the traditional Algonquian template (presented with the glossed text of "La Sandrieuz" in Appendix). In Danae M. Perez & Eeva Sippola (eds.), *Postcolonial varieties in the Americas*, 83–182. Berlin: Mouton de Gruyter.
Meakins, Felicity 2011. Borrowing contextual inflection: Evidence from northern Australia. *Morphology* 21(1). 57–87.
Meakins, Felicity & Jesse Stewart. To appear. Mixed languages. In Salikoko Mufwene & Anna Maria Escobar (eds.), *Cambridge handbook of language contact*. Cambridge: Cambridge University Press.
Mellow, Dean. 1990. Asymmetries between compounding and noun incorporation in Plains Cree. In William Cowan (ed.), *Papers of Twenty-first Algonquian Conference*, 247–257. Ottawa: Carleton University.
Muysken, Pieter 2000. *Bilingual speech: A typology of code-mixing*. Cambridge: Cambridge University Press.
Myers-Scotton, Carol. 1993. *Duelling languages: Grammatical structure in codeswitching*. Oxford: Clarendon Press.
Oxford, Will. 2017. Algonquian grammar myths. *Toronto Working Papers in Linguistics* 39. 1–37.
Papen, Robert A. 2005. On developing a writing system for Michif. *Linguistica Atlantica* 26. 75–97.
Papen, Robert A. 2017. On confirming the split phonology hypothesis for Michif. Presented at the 49th Algonquian Conference, Université du Québec à Montréal.
Prichard, Hilary & Kobey Shwayder. 2014. Against a split phonology of Michif. *University of Pennsylvania working papers in linguistics* 20(1). 271–280.
Rhodes, Richard A. S. 1977. French Cree: A case of borrowing. In William Cowan (ed), *Actes du huitième congrès des algonquinistes*, 6–25. Ottawa: Carleton University.
Rosen, Nicole. 2007. Domains in Michif phonology. Toronto, ON: University of Toronto dissertation.
Rosen, Nicole & Heather Souter. 2009. *Piikishkweetak aañ Michif!* Winnipeg, Manitoba: Louis Riel Institute.
Rosen, Nicole & Heather Souter. 2015. *Piikishkweetak aa'n Michif!* [2nd ed.]. Winnipeg, Manitoba: Louis Riel Institute.
Rosen, Nicole. 2019. Michif Online Dictionary. http://michif.atlas-ling.ca/ (accessed 26 April 2020).

Rosen, Nicole, Jesse Stewart & Olivia Sammons. 2020. How 'mixed' is mixed language phonology? An acoustic analysis of the Michif vowel system. *Journal of the Acoustical Society of America* 147(4). 2989–2999.

Sammons, Olivia N. 2019. *Nominal classification in Michif*. Edmonton: University of Alberta dissertation.

Slavin, Tanya. 2012. The syntax and semantics of stem composition in Oji-Cree. Toronto: University of Toronto dissertation.

Smit, Niels. 2005. Noun incorporation in Functional Discourse Grammar. In Casper de Groot & Kees Hengeveld (eds.), *Morphosyntactic expression in Functional Grammar*, 87–134. Berlin: Mouton de Gruyter.

Thomason, Sarah Grey. 2019. Review of Gillon, Carrie & Nicole Rosen, with Verna DeMontigny. 2018. Nominal contact in Michif. Oxford University Press. *Language* 95. 806–811.

Valentine, Randolph. 2001. *Nishnaabemwin reference grammar*. Toronto: University of Toronto Press.

Wohlgemuth, Jan. 2009. *A typology of verbal borrowing*. Berlin: Mouton de Gruyter.

Wolfart, H. Christoph. 1996. Sketch of Cree, an Algonquian language. In Ives Goddard (ed.), *Handbook of North American Indians 17. Languages*, 390–439. Washington, DC: Smithsonian Institution.

Isabel Deibel
VO vs. OV: What conditions word order variation in Media Lengua?

1 Introduction

Every thought that a speaker wishes to communicate needs to be linguistically encoded in a specific linear order. While there are various possible orders of subject (S), verb (V) and object (O) in transitive declarative clauses, the majority of the world's languages follow two predominant word orders: (S)OV (565/1377, e.g. Quechua,[1] Basque, Japanese) and (S)VO (488/1377, e.g. English, Spanish), with some (189/1377, e.g. German, Dutch) allowing more than one predominant order (Comrie 1989; Dryer 2013; see also Goldin-Meadow et al. 2008; Langus and Nespor 2010; Schouwstra and de Swart 2014). If more than one order is possible in a language, variation in constituent order may be conditioned by pragmatic-stylistic factors (e.g. emphasis) or related to language contact.

This paper examines word order variation in Media Lengua, a mixed language spoken in Highland Ecuador. In the Imbabura province (Northern Ecuador), Media Lengua has been documented in three communities: Angla, Casco Valenzuela and Pijal. These three villages are close to San Pablo del Lago, lying within a radius of 5 mi/8 km. Many participants in the current data set as well as in data collected by other authors indicate that close family and commercial ties between these three communities may have led to the spread of Media Lengua from Pijal to Angla and Casco Valenzuela (Stewart 2011; Lipski 2016; Deibel 2019). In addition, previous research has noted that speakers in Pijal appear to have shifted more to Spanish (Gómez Rendón 2008b; Müller 2011; Lipski 2016).

---

[1] I will follow the convention employing the term Quechua to refer to the Quechua family, reserving Quichua (also, Kichwa) to denote the Ecuadorian dialect of Quechua.

Acknowledgements: This research was supported by a LeClaire (Lee) B. Watts Endowed Scholarship in Romance Languages, a Penn State Center for Global Studies Fellowship, and a Penn State *External Funding Incentive Award*. I am particularly grateful for the help of Gabriel Cachimuel, José María Casco and Antonio Maldonado during data collection, and I thank John M. Lipski and Rena Torres Cacoullos for their guidance and support with this project, and Jesse Stewart for providing helpful comments on an earlier version of this manuscript.

Isabel Deibel, The Pennsylvania State University, isabel.deibel@gmail.com

https://doi.org/10.1515/9781501511257-006

This configuration makes it possible to examine any community differences resulting from language shift in more detail. In other words, if degree of bilingualism is a significant predictor of linguistic performance, differences in speech patterns between the communities should reflect such differences in bilingualism.

Originally, Media Lengua was discovered in Central and Southern Ecuadorian regions (Cotopaxi, Cañar and Loja) in the late 1970s (Muysken 1981, 1997). However, it is doubtful whether these Media Lengua varieties are still spoken. Recent visits by multiple researchers to the field sites Muysken describes have been unsuccessful, and Muysken's documentation of the Cañar and Loja varieties is limited (Shappeck 2011; Stewart 2011; Lipski 2017). As concerns Media Lengua's formation, some authors have suggested that this hybrid language arose in the Cotopaxi province between 1920 and 1940 as a means of expressing an in-between identity as indigenous populations did not identify with either Quichua or Spanish culture (Muysken 1997: 374–376) and that, at least by the beginning of the 1960s (Gómez Rendón 2008b: 56), it may have been brought to Imbabura during railway construction work (Stewart 2015b). While its exact origins and formation remain controversial, there is a general consensus that it must have been formed quickly – that is, within a decade – and to some degree deliberately by bilinguals (Thomason 1995, 2003; Lipski 2016: 6).

From a structural perspective, Media Lengua is a quite unique phenomenon as its morphosyntax is essentially Quichua but over 90% of its lexical roots have been relexified from Spanish (Muysken 1981; Gómez Rendón 2008b). Consider (1–3), illustrating the replacement of Quichua lexical roots with Spanish ones and the retention of Quichua morphosyntax (bolded), as well as (4) for an example of connected speech. While some varieties of Quechua incorporate around 40% of Spanish borrowings (Bakker and Muysken 1994: 44), no documented varieties fall in between the most Hispanized Quechua and Media Lengua (Muysken 1997: 378). Thus, what is remarkable about Media Lengua is its extraordinarily large proportion of Spanish lexical roots and its systematicity. In contrast with Salcedo Media Lengua, the Media Lengua variety documented in the Cotopaxi region by Muysken (1981), Imbabura Media Lengua has been described as more morphosyntactically conservative (Gómez Rendón 2008b).

(1) Media Lengua: *Mujer-**ka*** *madera-**ta*** *casa-**man*** *lleva-**n***

(2) Quichua: *Warmi-**ka*** *kaspi-**ta*** *wasi-**man*** *apa-**n***
  woman-TOP wood-ACC house-to take-3SG

(3) Spanish: *La mujer lleva la madera a casa.*
'The woman is carrying the wood home.'

(4) *Ahipi mantequillata ponehun, emmm . . . un platopi ahi ponen. Ese salsata metehun hornoman. Sacan ya horneashkata. Ese moldeta sacahun, platopi ponehun, ya servingapa.*
'[She] is putting the butter there, ummm . . . [she] is greasing the plate there. [She] is putting that salsa into the oven. [She] is already taking the baked goods out [of the oven]. [She] is taking out the mold and is putting it on a plate in order to serve it.' (P5)

Importantly for the current study, this mixed language arose in an interesting linguistic environment where two languages with canonically opposite word order tendencies have been in contact since the early 16th century: Quichua, usually described as a head-final language with mainly (S)OV constituent order, and Spanish, prototypically regarded a head-initial language with mostly (S)VO word order. Possibly as a result of this prolonged contact, both Andean Spanish and Quechua allow some structural variation, including variation in linear order (Cole 1982; Haboud 1998; Camacho 1999; Escobar 2000, 2001, 2011; Sánchez 2003, 2010; Adelaar 2004; Muntendam 2008, 2009, 2013). Provided that Media Lengua conserves Quichua morphosyntax, it can be described as mainly (S)OV; however, in line with Quichua structural tendencies, this mixed language has been reported as displaying flexible word order as well (e.g. Muysken 1997; Adelaar 2004; Gómez Rendón 2008b; Stewart 2011, 2015a, 2015b). Example (5), taken from the current corpus, shows variation in word order in three consecutive sentences produced by the same speaker. (5a) and (5c) show OV word order; (5b) is an example of VO word order.

(5) (a) *camote-ta pela-hu-n*
sweet.potato-ACC peel-PROG-3SG
'[She] is peeling the sweet potato' (P4; 3:35).
(b) *aplasta-hu-n camote-ta*
squash-PROG-3SG sweet.potato-ACC
'[She] is squashing the sweet potato' (P4; 3:38).
(c) *camote-ta sazona-hu-n*
sweet.potato-ACC season-PROG-3SG
'[She] is seasoning the sweet potato' (P4; 3:46).

Thus, while variation in constituent order has been documented for all three languages involved in this contact situation, previous research has made no attempt to provide a detailed and systematic quantitative analysis of the conditioning factors of the two possible (OV/VO) word orders in Media Lengua. Rather, based on a comparatively small sample of 10 speakers from one community, previous research had discussed instances of "Spanish-like" VO word order in Imbabura Media Lengua as apparently contact-induced without providing descriptions of any conditioning factors nor exact distributions of patterns (Gómez Rendón 2008b: 77). This procedure is not sufficient to claim that contact-induced change has taken place (e.g. Poplack and Levey 2010) and does not consider any viable alternative explanations, such as pragmatic conditioning or other distributional factors. The current study sets out to define the variables conditioning VO and OV constructions by employing a quantitative approach: It will consider an array of cognitive factors that may influence the production of spoken speech with particular emphasis on their relation to word order. Since some of these factors have previously been linked to contact-induced change, the current paper will also examine whether the observed variation may indeed be linked to such effects of language contact, at least as concerns the factors coded for here. The factors selected for the current study target the nature of the object (the information status and animacy of the referent as they relate to topicality as well as the morphological markings surfacing on the object constituent), properties of the verb (the language of the verb root) and more general characteristics of the speech stream (clause type, presence of pauses and intervening material).

2 Cognitive parameters interacting with constituent order

2.1 Targeting the object: Topicality (information status and animacy of the referent)

Previous research has amply noted that "word order variation, both inter-linguistic and intra-linguistic, is not random, boundless, and unpredictable" (Downing 1995: 1), particularly when constituent order is regarded as a mechanism that signals the status and role of an object referent in discourse based on its degree of topicality (Givón 1983). Under this view, an object referent can be described as thematic or topical when it occurs repeatedly and is central to the discourse; since animate participants tend to be more persistent in discourse, they are also more topical (Payne 1990: 236; Arnold 2013). Thus, both referent persistence as well as referent animacy – two instantiations of topicality – play an important and interrelated role in word order variation.

In particular, reference is central to human language as speakers constantly refer to objects or people in the world around them (Kibrik 2011). As such, reference is an intrinsically discourse-centered phenomenon: Speakers may opt to refer to a particular referent – understood as "an image in a [speaker]'s mind" (Kibrik 2011: 5) – more than once and with different referential devices[2] (e.g pronouns referring to an anteceding proper noun), with distance or structural relationships between multiple mentions being flexible. Relevant for the current study is the notion that the accessibility of a referent, that is, the degree of activation of a particular referent in working memory, leads to particular referential choices, including different linear orders or assignment of subjects (Kibrik 2011: 53–55). Consider (5a) and (5b), again, where different linear orders are chosen with a repeated object, the sweet potato. Furthermore, referential choices have been shown to be modulated by addressee-design in that more or less explicit linguistic devices are used depending on how easily inferable a speaker judges an intended referent to be for the listener (Bell 1984; Arnold 2008). In terms of discourse position of new and persistent (i.e. previously mentioned) referents, it has been argued that new or unidentifiable referents will tend to occur later in the clause due to the processing difficulties they induce (MacDonald 2013; Rivas 2013; see also Du Bois 1987). These perspectives provide explanations for strategic noun phrase placement and need to be considered if word order variation is to be explained in detail.

Intrinsically linked to reference is animacy, a cognitive scale distinguishing humans, animals and inanimate objects, which is generally regarded as an important crosslinguistic factor in the conditioning of structural configurations (Yamamoto 1999). Yamamoto (1999: 22) provides a prototype categorization of animacy with human beings located at the center and animals and inanimate objects in more peripheral positions; other approaches to animacy consider similar hierarchical structures (Comrie 1989; Croft 2003). While factors such as definiteness or plurality have also been shown to interact with animacy (Hopper and Thompson 1980; Comrie 1989; Croft 2003), it is particularly relevant here to consider how object placement may vary depending on the animacy of a noun phrase.

---

[2] It is beyond the scope of this paper to discuss any differences in referential devices resulting from the pro-drop character of Quechua.

A myriad of studies has described that noun phrase placement (e.g. subject placement in intransitives) may be conditioned by animacy in that preverbally placed noun phrases tend to be human and post-verbally placed noun phrases tend to be non-human (e.g. Branigan, Pickering, and Tanaka 2008; Rivas 2013; Norcliffe et al. 2015). To be more precise, it appears to be the case that more accessible, frequent, animate or conceptually salient noun phrases tend to be mentioned earlier, which in some languages may involve selection for subjecthood (e.g. Gennari, Mirković, and MacDonald 2012; MacDonald 2013). From the perspective of language comprehension, sentence-initial animate noun phrases cue agent interpretations while inanimate noun phrases or animate noun phrases with patient-like features activate patient interpretations (Gennari, Mirković, and MacDonald 2012: 171). In SOV structures with two animate noun phrases, previous research has identified feature similarity between elements as the factor causing both production and comprehension difficulties and interference, as processing costs are increased when multiple noun phrases are available for selection in working memory (Gennari, Mirković, and MacDonald 2012; Kurumada and Jaeger 2015; Norcliffe et al. 2015). There are various structural strategies to alleviate this similarity-based interference:

1) One of the noun phrases may be omitted if a language's grammar permits this: Quechua grammar, for instance, licenses null-subjects as well as topic-familiar null-objects (Lefebvre and Muysken 1988; Sánchez 2010);
2) One of the noun phrases may be displaced so that noun phrases with matching features are separated by the verb or other constituents (Gennari, Mirković, and MacDonald 2012; Gibson et al. 2013);
3) Noun phrases may be function-marked with case markers (Gennari, Mirković, and MacDonald 2012; Gibson et al. 2013; Kurumada and Jaeger 2015).

These strategies become particularly important when events are reversible or the channel is noisy, and are in line with approaches highlighting the role of the speaker in striving to provide a robust linguistic signal that reliably conveys meaning to the listener (Gibson et al. 2013; Kurumada and Jaeger 2015; see also Hall, Mayberry, and Ferreira 2013). All these arguments reveal referent animacy as an important factor for word order variation.

Finally, for a description of Media Lengua, a mixed language containing Quichua grammar, it is relevant to consider the extent to which Quichua allows different linear orderings depending on topicality. While – to the best of my knowledge – no detailed functional analysis exists for Imbabura Quichua, Sánchez (2010) provides a minimalist description of word order variation in Southern

Quechua[3] tying different constituent orders to differences in information structure. Generally speaking, the canonical OV word order is employed when an utterance introduces new information; different word orders like VO involve the right periphery with some right-detached constituents showing specific phonological and prosodic properties while being morphologically unmarked for topic (and, sometimes, even case) (Sánchez 2010: 39–51, 90–94). In addition, the right periphery may be sensitive to salience in discourse and competing topics: Discourse-continuity licenses preverbal null arguments specified by right-detached material unmarked for topic; recovered topics, on the other hand, tend to surface with morphological topic markers in right-adjoined position (Sánchez 2010: 176–182). Sánchez (2010: 181, 229), thus, concludes that right detachment may result from disambiguating strategies.

The previous paragraphs already alluded to the relevance of morphological noun phrase markings in relation to referent persistence and animacy. For the current study, it is necessary to describe both functional morphological markers (here, the presence of the Quichua accusative marker -*ta*) and discursive morphological markers (the Quichua topicalizer -*ka*) in more detail.

2.2 Targeting the object: Quichua morphological noun phrase markings

The examples provided above show that both Imbabura Quichua and Media Lengua generally mark accusative case with the morpheme -*ta*; nominative case is morphologically unmarked (Cole 1982). In Spanish, both the accusative and the nominative case are morphologically unmarked, aside from differential object marking (e.g. Leonetti 2004; Iemmolo 2010). Colloquial Quichua has been described as allowing optional accusative case markers (King 2001), possibly due to language contact with Spanish (Gómez Rendón 2007, 2008a). Previous research on Pijal Media Lengua, however, has noted that it robustly marks direct objects with -*ta* (Stewart 2011: 49). From a crosslinguistic perspective, case marking is observably correlated with headedness and animacy (Gibson et al. 2013). In fact, OV languages are considerably more likely to distinguish case morphologically than VO languages (Dryer 2002). This is so because fixed word order in VO languages makes meaning recoverable, while OV languages

---

3 Imbabura Quichua is a dialect of Northern Quechua (together with other Ecuadorian dialects) while Southern Quichua includes dialects of Bolivia, Chile, Argentina, Cuzco and Southern Peru (Cole 1982).

need to rely on other mechanisms to ensure events are understood accurately. In order to recover event structures, case marking is, thus, clearly more useful on animate noun phrases than on inanimate noun phrases (Gibson et al. 2013; Kurumada and Jaeger 2015). Furthermore, previous research has shown that case marking eases comprehension and is particularly preferred when linear order fails to facilitate the interpretation of a sentence (Kurumada and Jaeger 2015). With flexible word order and no morphological markings, the listener is required to actively reconstruct grammatical relations in an utterance by drawing on semantics and real-world knowledge about the event (Bybee 2010: 208). However, if morphological markings are present, word order becomes available to encode discourse meaning rather than syntactic function (Frajzyngier and Shay 2016). Thus, examining whether case markings systematically co-occur with one or the other word order can speak to different grammatical functions of linear orders as well as reveal whether particular word order configurations may show traces of language contact.

As concerns information structure, Quichua uses morphological markers to signal topic (marked with *-ka*) and focus (marked with *-mi*). Cole (1982: 71) explains that, while topic marking with the morpheme *-ka* is not obligatory in Imbabura Quichua, it occurs frequently on post-verbal objects. Sánchez (2010: 71) specifies for Southern Quechua that direct objects tend to be marked with *-ka* when the subject of the clause was topicalized as well and that *-ka* occurs only on main clause constituents. This results from the fact that main clauses, contrary to subordinate clauses, are typically the locus where topic and focus may be encoded (see section 2.4). The only exception to this rule is that *-ka* in combination with the subordinators *-shpa* or *-jpi* indicates a conditional clause, with the marked constituent indicating old or background information (Cole 1982: 65). As mentioned above, the absence or presence of topic markers on right adjoined constituents may distinguish between (topic-unmarked) continuous topics and (topic-marked) recovered topics (Sánchez 2010: 176–182). Furthermore, prosodic differences may speak to the status of topics as well since topic-marked constituents appear to be part of the same intonational unit as the main clause while topic-unmarked constituents are prosodically separate (Sánchez 2010: 178–181, 225–228). Gómez Rendón (2007) describes any deletions of *-ka* in Imbabura Quichua as the result of contact-induced language change since Spanish does not morphologically mark topics; however, *-ka* has previously been observed in Quichua-dominant Spanish speech denoting similar functions as in Quichua, which calls into question whether its putative deletion in Quichua is indeed related to language contact or, rather, other factors (Lipski 2014). Tracing the presence or absence of *-ka* may, thus, help to distinguish between different kinds of topics as well as indicate potential effects of language contact.

2.3 Targeting the verb: Relexification

For a mixed language like Media Lengua, it is also relevant to consider whether the verb root itself is relexified from Spanish or maintains its Quichua phonological shape as this could possibly reveal a stratified lexicon.[4] Example (1) above displays the characteristic relexified verb root (*lleva-* < Sp. *llevar* 'to carry'); however, variation with Quichua roots (*apa-* 'to carry') can be observed in the present corpus as well – a phenomenon which remains to be studied in depth. According to Muysken's original description, Quichua lexical roots were systematically replaced by Spanish phonological shells, which "adopt[. . .] the meaning and use of the element in the receptor language for which [they are] substituted," during relexification (Muysken 1981: 55). It is possible that Spanish syntactic features were incorporated as well in this process of vocabulary substitution; in this case, the term *translexification* would be more appropriate (Muysken 1981: 61). Consequently, we may expect to observe a tendency for VO structures with Spanish-relexified verb roots and a tendency for OV with Quichua verb roots if word order is correlated with the etymological origin of the verb root.

The issue of whether Spanish-relexified lexical roots in Media Lengua could be distinguished from long-standing Spanish borrowings that already existed in Quichua at the time of Media Lengua's formation is complex. As mentioned briefly above, the number of Spanish borrowings in some varieties of Quechua reportedly reaches up to 40% – a number that appears to be much higher than the estimates for documented varieties of Ecuadorian Quichua (Lipski 2017). In fact, Lipski (2017: 235) informally estimates that the number of borrowings does not even reach the 5% mark for Imbabura Quichua, leading to a "quite pronounced" contrast between local Quichua and the high numbers of Spanish lexical items in Media Lengua. Since lexical roots in some cases maintain traces of intervocalic [z] (non-existent in present-day Spanish), this provides some evidence that Media Lengua is not created from scratch every time it is used (Lipski 2016). Due to the absence of research addressing this complexity from a psycholinguistic perspective, the current study makes no distinction

---

[4] The current study also inspected verb class and aspectual morphology as possible factors contributing to word order variation. Since no clear correlation between semantic verb class and word order could be identified, verb classes will not be further addressed here. Instead, each verb type (unique verb root) was considered for building the random effect structure in the logistic regression reported in section 4. In addition, due to the nature of the task, 85% (2331/2752) of all tokens in finite clauses were marked with an imperfective morpheme; the remaining 15% showed an inconclusive pattern. Future research should examine a different data set to isolate the contribution of these factors to word order variation.

between verb roots that may constitute long-standing borrowings in Quichua (e.g. Q. *trabahana* < Sp. *trabajar* 'to work' rather than Unified Quichua *llankana*) and relexified verb roots (ML. *trabahana*) as speakers may not be aware of the etymological source of these roots (see for a more detailed description of borrowings in Imbabura Quichua, Gómez Rendón 2008a; Gómez Rendón and Adelaar 2009).

2.4 Targeting the clause: Clause type, pauses and intervening material

In addition to the aforementioned properties of objects and verbs that can interact with constituent order, other characteristics of the speech stream such as clause type, presence of pauses or intervening material may also play a critical role in word order variation on the basis of their relationship to structural entrenchment. As concerns clause type, Bybee (2002) notes that subordinate clauses are less transitive than main clauses, contain background information unlikely to be topicalized and are overall more difficult to process, thus impeding linear permutations. Moreover, their ability to conserve structural idiosyncrasies, such as specific morphological properties, suggests that subordinate clauses are processed and stored as chunks despite the fact that they have certain properties in common with main clauses and may show the same word order (Givón 2001; Bybee 2002; Croft 2003). Main clauses, on the other hand, are pragmatically richer, less entrenched and hence less rigid in structure (Hopper and Thompson 1980; Bybee 2002; Croft 2003). Thus, examining whether word order variation occurs in main or subordinate clauses can inform whether pragmatic processes underlie this variation and how advanced potential typological changes may be in Media Lengua. In the latter case, subordinate clauses should show a significant tendency towards VO structures if changes are more advanced. As concerns Imbabura Quichua, previous research notes that word order in main clauses is relatively free while subordinate clauses appear to be more rigidly OV (Cole 1982).

While clause type relates to how structures are cognitively entrenched, pauses and intervening material have parallel effects on such entrenched structures: They both can be regarded as elements that may interrupt automated sequences because they increase the distance between two target items like a main verb and a subordinate verb inflected for mood or, as in the current data set, a verb and its direct object (Bybee 2002: 12). From this perspective, the presence of pauses can indicate that a particular structure is less cognitively entrenched as more highly automated constructions have often been shown to display effects of reduction

(Bybee 2010). Disfluencies occuring in non-canonical word order structures could then also indicate production difficulties (Arnold 2013). In addition, research on production patterns suggests that – independent of noun phrase complexity – disfluencies may facilitate the comprehension of new and unfamiliar referents as disfluencies are considerably more likely to appear with new referents than given referents, which have been primed at the conceptual, lexical and phonological level (Arnold 2008). In a similar vein, presence of additional linguistic material in a sentence has been found to have an effect on constituent placement (Rivas 2013). It may, thus, be likely that constituent placement differs if other linguistic material or disfluencies appear in the same utterance, particularly if they occur between verb and object.

3 The present Media Lengua corpus: Participants, data collection and procedure

Sixty-four participants (7 male) from three communities responded to a video description elicitation task in July 2016: Thirty-two were from Angla, 21 from Casco Valenzuela and 11 from Pijal. Sociolinguistic background information was only collected informally; however, most participants fall within an age range of approximately 25–55 years and use Quichua, Media Lengua and Spanish on a daily basis. As the data was collected within closely-knit rural communities, the current group of speakers should be fairly homogeneous in terms of socio-economic status. In other words, I assume that "linguistic patterns are community specific" (Torres Cacoullos and Travis 2018: 13) and that "an individual's personal ability is operative but is mediated by the norms of his speech community" (Poplack, Sankoff, and Miller 1988: 98). The data consist of approximately 15 minutes of recorded speech per participant. All participants were monetarily compensated for their time.

In order to elicit the present corpus, 22 short video clips were either extracted from the locally known movie *El pastorcito de Otavalo* 'The little shepherd from Otavalo' or from documentaries about the regions, showing locally known practices or traditions such as preparing a meal or dancing during the Festival of the Sun. All video clips were muted and cut so as to display a complete and coherent action. This form of data collection allows researchers to exert more control over the type of action, type of referent and ordering of events mentioned across participants than in free elicitation, leading to a more homogenous data set. Participants were instructed to describe what they were seeing in as much detail as possible using only Media Lengua. All responses were transcribed manually as individual transcription units provided that they were prosodically, semantically and/or syntactically coherent. This method is adapted from transcription methods targeting intonational units (e.g. Torres Cacoullos and Travis 2015) since in Quichua, the grammatical source language of Media Lengua, syntactic constructions can be considered to be dependent upon each other even when they do not belong to the same intonation contour (Sánchez 2010: 98).

A total of 3159 transcription units in the corpus contained object-verb complexes, that is, both an object and a verb were present in any given stretch of speech transcribed as a unit.[5] Governing verbs were defined as the closest verb that could govern the respective object semantically, even though these verb governors themselves might be non-finite and governed by a main-clause verb. The example in (6) illustrates this procedure (governor of the object 'popcorn' in bold):

(6) *Wawa-wa [[cangil-wa-ta **tosta-shpa**] dale-gpi] come-hu-n*
     Boy-DIM   popcorn-DIM-ACC toast-SUB   give-SWREF   eat-PROG-3SG
     'The little boy, having been given toasted popcorn, is eating' (P12).

The action of toasting is seen as the governor of 'popcorn' in (6) even though the entire syntagma is the embedded direct object governed by the giving action. The respective governor *tostashpa* was then coded as non-finite. Whenever reformulations led to the change of thematic role (such as direct object to adjunct or vice versa), the reformulation was considered as the intended form and coded as such.

All extracted tokens were coded for the factors described in section 2. Since most factors are binary (e.g. morphological markings are either present or absent), only the coding measures for information status and animacy of the referent and pause length merit a more detailed description. Table 1 presents all coding measures applied to the current corpus.

Information status of a referent, that is, whether it was mentioned repeatedly in discourse, was coded regardless of the previous syntactic position of a referent. To illustrate, if an object was introduced as the subject in a previous sentence, it was deemed persisting. Synonyms were included since they, just as pronouns, can refer to the same referent. It is important to note that this

---

[5] Exclusions: 237 units were uncategorizable due to unintelligible material or unclear syntactic relationships; 42 contained double constructions and target object or verb could not be clearly identified.

Table 1: Coding measures applied to the current corpus. Factor levels are indicated for each factor. Details justifying the inclusion of each variable can be found in the respective section.

Factors	n (levels)	Factor levels	See section
Word order	2	[OV; VO]	1
Community	3	[Angla; Pijal; Casco Valenzuela]	1
Referent information status	2	[New referent; persistent referent]	2.1
Animacy	2	[Animate; inanimate (including animals)]	2.1
Presence of case marker -*ta*	2	[Present; absent]	2.2
Presence of topic marker -*ka*	2	[Present; absent]	2.2
Verb Type	187	1 level for each unique verb root	2.3
Language of the verb root	2	[Spanish (relexified); Quichua (not relexified)]	2.3
Clause Type	2	[Main clause; subordinate clause]	2.4
Pauses (> 0.5 s)	2	[Present; absent]	2.4
Material intervening between verb and object	2	[Present; absent]	2.4

measurement does not take into account whether the participant may have seen a referent before but did not refer to it, leading to the activation of semantic networks and rendering referents inferable (see Myhill 2005: 474–476). In this, I follow Kibrik (2011: 376), who argues that from a linguistic perspective "attending to a referent is equivalent to mentioning it".

The current data set only contains a few examples of animals (all of them cows) as object referents. After initially treating them as a separate factor level, it was determined that their behavior with respect to the coding measures closely matched the behavior of inanimate objects. As a result, both levels, animals and inanimate objects, were collapsed for the current purposes.

Any pause longer than 0.5 s was measured and coded. This is in line with other corpus transcription methods indicating 0.5 s as a noticeable medium pause (Du Bois et al. 1993; Torres Cacoullos and Travis 2015). This measurement will be considered below as both a categorical variable (for crosstabulation purposes) and as a continuous variable (in order to determine any statistically significant length differences with respect to the two different word orders).

4 Results

The results indicate that VO word order occurred in 18% (577/3159) of all cases, in line with previous research (Muysken 1981, 1997; Gómez Rendon 2008b). Overall, the results suggest that Media Lengua's morphosyntactic frame remains largely intact: The majority of structures showed OV word order in main clauses, with accusative markers present in 98% of all cases (3088/3159).

A generalized linear mixed effects (logistic) regression was fit in R using the lme4-package with word order (VO/OV) as the dependent variable, referent information status, animacy, accusative case, intervening material, pause length and clause type as fixed effects and random intercepts by participant and verb type (Table 2) (Bates et al. 2015; R Core Team 2016). A likelihood comparison indicated that the inclusion of both random intercepts [AIC = 2528.1; Variance (Verb type) = 0.39; Variance (Participant) = 0.68] led to a significantly better fit of the model over the null model without the fixed effects [X^2 (6) = 230.54, p < .001] and over a model with only one random effect, respectively. Inclusion of the variables topic marker and language of the verb root did not contribute to a better fit of the model.

Table 2: Results of a generalized linear mixed effects (logistic) regression with word order (VO/OV) as response variable, referent information status, animacy, accusative case, clause type, intervening material and pauses as fixed effects and random intercepts by participant and verb type.

Fixed Effects	Estimate	Standard error	Z-value	p-value
Intercept (Ref:OV)	−2.89	0.33	−8.66	< .01
Persistent referents	1.06	0.12	8.98	< .01
Animate referents	0.94	0.18	5.27	< .01
Unmarked accusative case	0.74	0.32	2.33	< .02
Finite clauses	1.57	0.23	6.97	< .01
Intervening Material (absent)	0.63	0.64	3.55	< .01
Pauses (absent)	−1.56	1.56	−8.52	< .01

The results in Table 2 indicate that, with all predictors at their reference levels (new, inanimate referent, marked for accusative case, occurring in non-finite clauses, with intervening material and pauses present, the estimated odds of VO are smaller than the odds of OV [exp(−2.89) = 0.06]. Positive estimates of the coefficients indicate a higher likelihood of VO, that is, the odds of VO are significantly increased when referents are persistent and animate, unmarked for case, occur in a finite clause and when intervening material is absent.

Before examining the contribution of the linguistic factors, I will consider how word order usage varies across communities. A comparison of percentages of VO structures reveals that usage patterns in the different communities are relatively similar: Angla (18%, 307/1664), Casco Valenzuela (16%, 167/1031), Pijal (22%, 103/464). Figure 1 shows the distribution of VO uses by participant across all communities, that is, each participant's percentage of VO represents one data point.

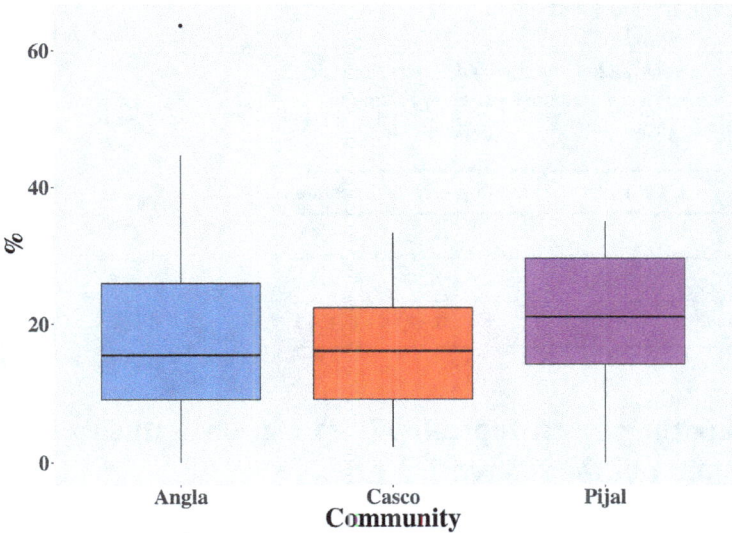

Figure 1: Percentage of participants' VO structures by community.

The large spread of values in the box-and-whisker plots indicates high participant variability across communities. Put differently, word order usage varies substantially among participants, regardless of community. The results of a t-test performed on the mean percentage of VO structures according to gender indicate no significant gender stratification of word order [t(11.78) = 1.29, p > .2; mean (VO, Females) = 18.77; mean (VO, Males) = 14.84]. Since participant groups across these 3 communities were not equally sized (Angla n = 32, Casco Valenzuela n = 21, Pijal n = 11) and only a few males could be interviewed at the time of data collection (Angla n = 2, Casco Valenzuela n = 3, Pijal n = 2), it may be possible that a clearer pattern may emerge with a larger participant sample, particularly from Pijal. Interestingly, the largest percentage of VO structures in Pijal used by one participant is 35% while some participants from Angla tend to use VO structures in more than 35% of all cases, as indicated by the longer whiskers and the outlier in the leftmost box in Figure 1. Since Pijal has been reported to have shifted more to Spanish, this is an unexpected result in light of the hypotheses put forth by other authors that VO structures in Media Lengua result from contact with Spanish (e.g. Gómez Rendón 2008b). For the current data set, a generalized linear mixed effect (logistic) regression predicting word order (VO/OV) by community with a random intercept by participant (Variance = 0.50) shows no significant difference between communities (Table 3). This model is not more accurate in predicting the data than a model with only participant as random intercept and no fixed effect.

Table 3: Results of a generalized linear mixed effects (logistic) regression with word order as response variable, community as fixed effect and a random intercept by participant.

Fixed Effects	Estimate	Standard error	z-value
Intercept (Ref: VO)	1.42	0.25	5.74
Angla	0.24	0.29	0.85
Casco Valenzuela	0.3	0.3	1.00

4.1 Targeting the object: Topicality (information status and animacy of the referent)

Cross tabulations of word order and information status of the object referent show that 55% (1741/3159) of all objects are mentioned for the first time in discourse and occur in OV structures (Table 4). Considering OV structures only, 67% co-occur with new referents (1741/2582) while only 33% co-occur with persistent referents (841/2582). As concerns VO structures, on the other hand, 56% (325/577) of them co-occur with a persistent referent while 44% (252/577) co-occur with new referents. Thus, objects that have been repeatedly mentioned in discourse show a significantly higher likelihood of occurring in VO structures [$X^2(1)$ = 113.26, p < .01, calculated with the values for referent status and word order in Table 4 without considering animacy distinctions].

As mentioned in section 2.1, it is relevant to consider the animacy of the referent with respect to the effect of information status revealed by the data. First, examining only the effect of animacy on word order structures in Table 4

Table 4: Distribution of referents across both word orders by referent information status and animacy.

Referent Status	Animacy	OV	VO	Total
New Referent	Inanimate	1612	206	1818
	Animate	129	46	175
Persistent Referent	Inanimate	706	237	943
	Animate	135	88	223
Total		2582	577	3159

shows that VO word order is significantly more likely if a referent is animate: Only 10% (264/2582) of all OV structures, compared to 23% (134/577) of all VO structures, occur with animate referents [$X^2(1)$ = 71.19, p < .01, calculated with the values for animacy and word order in Table 4 without considering referent status]. Figure 2, then, displays the relationship between referent status and animacy for VO structures. Animate objects are overall more likely to occur in VO structures than inanimate objects, regardless of their status in discourse [new animate objects: 26% (46/175); persistent animate objects: 39% (88/223)]. Repeated mention, however, significantly increases the proportions of either

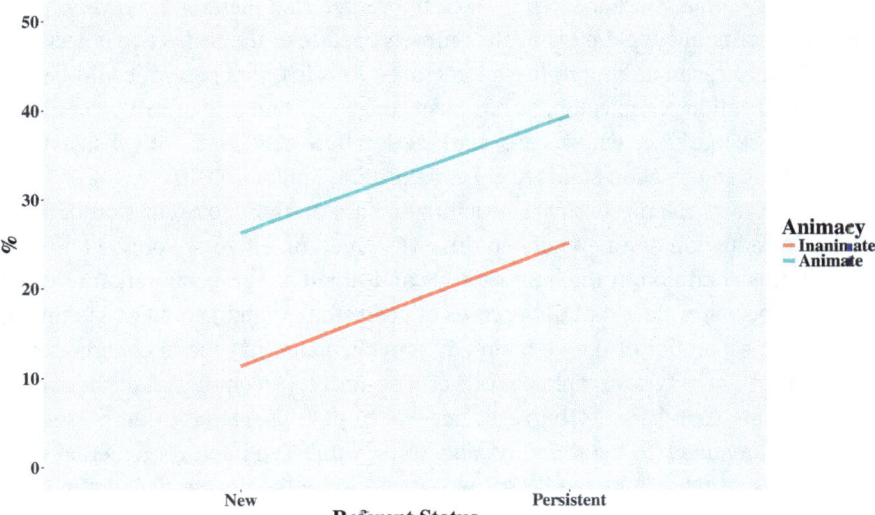

Figure 2: Percentage of VO structures by referent information status and animacy.

animacy category to occur in VO structures [$X^2(3)$ = 162.99, p < .01, with all values in Table 4].

Since animacy and information status are both related to topicality, the results presented here show a clear distribution of word order structures based on these pragmatic considerations.

4.2 Targeting the object: Quichua morphological noun phrase markings

With respect to the distribution of the accusative marker -*ta*, only 2% (71/3159) of all objects show no accusative case marking, see (7), (8) and (9) below. Yet, in order to be exhaustive, the distribution of the unmarked tokens will be examined in more detail as well. Table 5 displays a cross-tabulation of case-markers, object referent persistence and animacy. The distribution shows that unmarked animate referents are clearly dispreferred (4/3159). Instead, the majority of unmarked referents (42%, 30/71), are inanimate, newly mentioned and occur in the canonical OV structure. As explained above, inanimate objects are rarely selected as subjects of an utterance as their semantic features cue patient interpretations. Thus, case marking is expendable on inanimate objects, particularly when they occur in the spot that is usually occupied by objects (as they would in OV structures). As concerns persistent referents, case marking becomes redundant if – as in the majority of all cases – objects are marked as such upon their first mention. It is very likely that this redundancy, paired with the animacy feature of the respective object, led to the lack of case marking in these structures. As such, this pattern could be another ramification of topicality, as has been suggested similarly in works on differential object marking, where case marking is often correlated with dislocation, animacy and information status (e.g. Leonetti 2004; Iemmolo 2010).

In any case, the most crucial structure for case marking to occur would, thus, be the introduction of a new referent in a VO structure. There are only 9 observations in this condition in the entire corpus and, upon closer examination of these tokens, it becomes clear that in the cases of postverbal, unmarked, new, inanimate objects the semantics of the verb already provide a cue that the upcoming object would most likely be an inanimate object. The verb types employed in these constructions are *cosechana* 'to harvest', *ponena* 'to put', *quemana* 'to burn', *rallana* 'to grate', *prendena* 'to light' and *cogena* 'to pick up'. The hapax legomenon with the unmarked new, animate referent was found to be the phrase *they are burning the witch*, with previous discourse already making clear reference to a house that was being burned and in which a witch was located at the time of the fire.

Table 5: Distribution of case markers across both word orders by animacy and referent information status.

Accusative Case	Referent Status	Animacy	OV	VO	Total
Unmarked	New Referent	Inanimate	30	8	38
		Animate	0	1	1
	Persistent Referent	Inanimate	18	11	29
		Animate	2	1	3
Marked	New Referent	Inanimate	1582	198	1780
		Animate	129	45	174
	Persistent Referent	Inanimate	688	226	914
		Animate	133	87	220
Total			2582	577	3159

Common knowledge might also construe a witch involved in a burning action as a more likely object than subject.

Examples (7)–(9) present utterances containing VO and OV structures co-occurring with persistent object referents. Sentences (8) and (9) were produced by two different speakers but respond to the same video stimulus. Both participants had mentioned the gourd (marked overtly for accusative case) in previous utterances. It seems unlikely that the absence of the accusative marker in (9) is related to the occurrence of Sp. *ese* 'that' as there are many tokens of *ese* in the corpus together with case marked objects (see also Stewart 2013 for numerous examples).

(7) Persistent object referent (sweet potato) marked with accusative case in a VO structure:
mujer-ka   come-hu-n   camote-ta
woman-TOP   eat-PROG-3SG sweet.potato-ACC
'The woman is eating the sweet potato.' (P10)

(8) Persistent object referent (gourd) marked with accusative case in an OV structure:
sambo-ta   soga-wan   amarra-hu-n
gourd-ACC   rope-with   tie.up-PROG-3SG
'[He] is tying up the gourd with a rope.' (P55)

(9) Persistent object referent (gourd) unmarked for accusative case in a VO structure:

amarra-hu-n palo-pi ese sambo soga-wan
tie-PROG-3SG stick-on that sambo rope-with
'[He] is tying the gourd to the stick with a rope.' (P53)

I will now turn to examining the distribution of the Quichua topic marker *-ka*. Across the data set, the *-ka* was found to mark less than 2% of all objects as topics (61/3159), with 31% (19/61) of all occurrences in VO structures. Table 6 shows that 39% (18/46) of all persistent referents marked with *-ka* occur in VO structures. Recall that topic markings on persistent referents in VO structures in other Quichua varieties may distinguish between (topic-unmarked, prosodically separate) continuous topics and (topic-marked, prosodically linked) recovered topics. In the current data set, persistent referents in VO structures are marked with *-ka* in 6% of all cases (18/325), thus qualifying as recovered topics, while 94% (307/325) qualify as unmarked continuous topics. Future research is required to examine these structures from a detailed phonetic perspective.

Table 6: Distribution of referents across both word orders by referent status and topic marker.

Referent Status	Topic Marker	OV	VO	Total
New Referent	Unmarked	1727	251	1978
	Marked	14	1	15
Persistent Referent	Unmarked	813	307	1120
	Marked	28	18	46
Total		2582	577	3159

Figure 3 plots the percentage of VO structures according to the status of the referent and the presence of a topic marker. There is an overall increase in VO structures for both topic-marked and topic-unmarked objects as they persist in discourse, as described above in detail. Topic-marked objects, however, become more likely to occur in VO structures than unmarked objects if an object is persistent.

The distribution of topic markers across clause types (Table 7) shows that non-finite clauses are generally unmarked for topic, except for the 21% (13/61) of all topic markers that occur in non-finite conditional clauses with the subordinators *-shpa* and *-jpi*. These patterns are expected and align with the theoretical background presented in section 2.2.

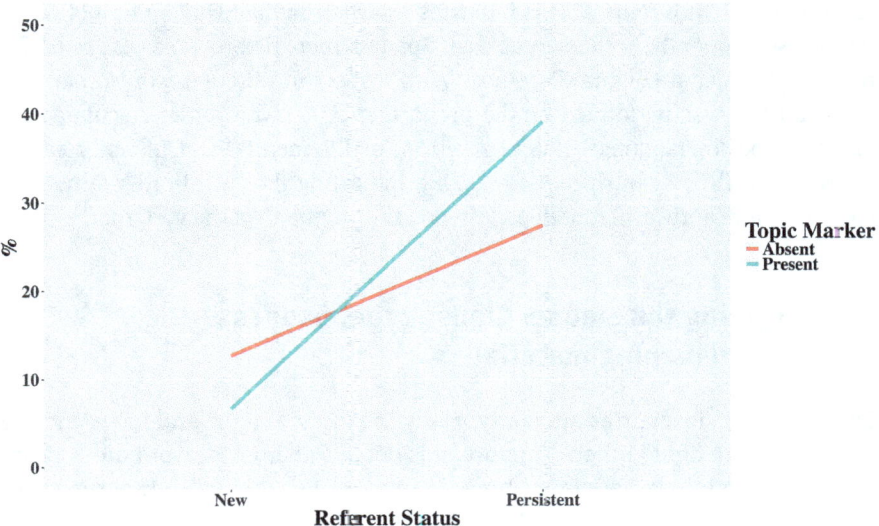

Figure 3: Percentage of VO structures by referent information status and topic marker.

Table 7: Distribution of topic markers by clause type.

	Clause Type	Finite	Non-finite	Total
Topic Marker				
Unmarked		2702	396	3098
Marked		48	13	61
Total		2750	409	3159

4.3 Targeting the verb: Relexification

In order to examine the distribution of particular word orders with Spanish relexified or patrimonial Quichua (non-relexified) verb roots, a total of 187 unique verb roots (i.e. verb types) were identified in the corpus. Of these verb types, 21% (39/187) were not relexified but maintained a Quichua root while 79% (148/187) occurred with a Spanish phonological shape. When all individual instances of each verb type are examined (that is, all tokens of all verb types), this amounts to 96% (3042/3159) of all verb tokens in the corpus employing a Spanish root. In other words, 21% of verb types (those with patrimonial Quichua roots) account for 4% of all verb tokens, while 79% (those with Spanish relexified roots) account for 96% of all verb tokens. This indicates that patrimonial Quichua roots occur much less frequently in the corpus than Spanish relexified roots, as expected for prototypical Media Lengua discourse. With respect to different word order patterns, a t-test was performed on the proportion of VO word order calculated for all verb types by language [t(56.42) = −0.54, p > .5; mean (VO, Quichua roots) = 20.99; mean (VO, Spanish roots) = 24.08], indicating that word order structures are not significantly different depending on the language of the verb root.

4.4 Targeting the clause: Clause type, pauses and intervening material

Since subordinate clauses are not typically the locus of topic and focus and are generally more rigid in their structure, it is not surprising that word order variation would mainly target main clauses. Only 4% (26/577) of all VO occurrences occur in non-finite clauses (Table 8); 21 of these 26 observations are either animate or persistent. As explained above, examining the distribution of pauses and intervening material between object and verb can reveal the degree of entrenchment of different word order patterns and the role lexical access difficulties may have played with respect to the use of different linear patterns.

Table 8: Distribution of word orders by clause type.

Clause Type	OV	VO	Total
Finite	2201	551	2752
Non-finite	381	26	407
Total	2582	577	3159

The results suggest that pauses and intervening material do not have a major impact on word order variation. Table 9 shows that only 6% (218/3159) of all utterances contain pauses larger than 0.5 s, the duration of a noticeable medium pause (Du Bois et al. 1993; Torres Cacoullos and Travis 2015), 90% (197/218) of which occur in finite clauses, as expected. There are significantly more pauses found in VO constructions [for all clauses: $X^2(1)$ = 81.46, p < .001; for finite clauses only: $X^2(1)$ = 78.86, p < .001]. However, the actual duration of pauses does not differ significantly by word order [t(213.78) = 0.6, p > .5; mean(OV) = 1.31 s; mean(VO) = 1.24 s] but on average tends to be shorter in VO structures. Moreover, the prediction that pauses tend to occur with new referents

Table 9: Distribution of word orders by presence of pauses.

Pauses (> 0.5 s)	Referent Status	OV	VO	Total
Pause	New Referent	95	56	151
	Persistent Referent	33	34	67
No pause	New Referent	1646	196	1842
	Persistent Referent	808	291	1099
Total		2582	577	3159

was borne out (Arnold 2008); pauses are also (nearly significantly) longer in constructions with new referents than with persistent referents [t(203.74) = 1.96, p < .06; mean(new) = 1.34 s; mean(persistent) = 1.13 s]. The 56 new referents that co-occurred with pauses in VO structures (adding up to less than 2% of the entire data set) could be interpreted as resulting from lexical access difficulties. In addition, the distribution of all detected pauses (n = 218) across word orders is not significantly different depending on referent status $[X^2(1) = 3.03, p > .08$; fisher's exact test: $p > .07]$.

Table 10 indicates that about 11% (359/3159) of all utterances contain intervening material between the object and the verb, 86% (308/359) of which occurred, again, in finite clauses. The distribution of intervening material across word orders is not statistically significant [for all clauses: $X^2(1) = 0.09, p > .7$; for finite clauses only: $X^2(1) = 0.03, p > .8$]. Intervening material in VO structures is mostly comprised of adverbs (n = 20), adpositional phrases (n = 22) or subjects (n = 9), and occurred in 71% (45/63) of all cases with a persistent object.

Table 10: Distribution of word orders by presence of intervening material.

Intervening Material	OV	VO	Total
Present	296	63	359
Absent	2286	514	2800
Total	2582	577	3159

5 Brief addendum: Could word order variation in Media Lengua be related to language contact?

While more research (including an analysis of Imbabura Quichua) is needed to determine the effects of language contact on structural variation in Media Lengua, the current data set allows us to tentatively re-examine several putative effects of language contact on word order variation and its correlation with other linguistic factors. Consider the following statements on the current contact setting, including Media Lengua:

- "Partiendo de que el orden típico del quichua es SOV, se asume que toda construcción del tipo SVO [en Imbabura Media Lengua] ha sido inducida por contacto con el castellano." [Given that SOV is the canonical Quichua word order, it is assumed that any SVO construction (in Media Lengua) is contact-induced]. (Gómez Rendón 2008b: 77, my translation)
- "In some cases [of relexification] the subcategorization features of the relexified (sic) item were adopted from [Spanish] as well, which led to word order changes in [Cotopaxi Media Lengua]." (Muysken 1981: 65)
- "In [Imbabura Quichua, . . .] there exists a clear tendency nowadays to Spanish-like SVO word order associated with the drop of topicalizer [-ka]." (Gómez Rendón 2007: 512)
- "Another [Imbabura Quichuan] structure influenced by Spanish is the marking of direct-object arguments [. . .] with *ta*. [. . .] [T]he accusative marker is systematically dropped on the direct objects, which contain either Spanish borrowings [. . .] or code switches [. . .]. Besides, the word order is SVO and *not* SOV as typical of [Imbabura Quichua]. There seems to be certain connection between dropped accusative markers, deviant word orders and heavy lexical borrowing. [However, . . .] SVO is subsidiary to SOV and the latter remains the most frequent word order, even in contact varieties. Notice that Spanish lexical material reinforces the tendency to drop the accusative marker in SVO constructions." (Gómez Rendón 2007: 487; emphasis in original)

Finally, with respect to Quechua-Spanish bilinguals from Peru, Sánchez (2003) states:

- "Functional interference [. . .] leads to changes in the syntactic and morphosyntactic representations of bilinguals such as SVO word order [and] dropping of the accusative marker -ta." (Sánchez 2003: 155)

To summarize, these claims state that VO word order is to be considered a contact-induced structure, which stands out due to its co-occurrence with dropped accusative and topic markers (a superficial structural similarity with Spanish) as well as with high numbers of Spanish lexical borrowings. Even some Peruvian Quechua-Spanish bilinguals may show these tendencies; other researchers, however, report that -*ta* is present in data collected in Ecuador and Bolivia while topic marking in these varieties is not obligatory (Cole 1982; Muntendam 2009).

The results presented in section 4 contrast with the statements linking VO word order to such effects of language contact: As was shown above, VO word order does not co-occur with a large number of dropped accusative case markers nor was there a statistically significant difference with respect to whether the verb was relexified or retained a Quichua root. In addition, since topic markers have been reported to be non-obligatory in Quichua, the lack of topic markers in the current Media Lengua corpus is not suspicious. Finally, even though one of the three communities examined here, Pijal, has reportedly shifted more to Spanish, no effect of this putative language shift on word order could be determined in the present data set. As a whole, the current data set does not provide sufficient evidence to confirm that VO word order in Media Lengua is the result of language contact nor of any online production errors (neither pause length nor distribution of intervening material was significantly different across the two linear orders). Rather, pragmatic effects can neatly account for these structures.

6 General discussion

The current study employed a functional approach to investigate the conditioning of word order variation in Media Lengua. A total of 18% (577/3159) of all structures showed VO word order, in line with previous research (Muysken 1997; Gómez Rendon 2008b). Even though one of the communities included in the data set, Pijal, has been reported to have shifted more to Spanish, the occurrence of VO structures across communities is not significantly different. Rather, when considering the structures used by each individual participant, it becomes apparent that certain participants tend to prefer OV structures, while others employ more VO structures.

As concerns the linguistic factors examined here, the results converge upon one general interpretation: Word order variation in this mixed language is significantly conditioned by pragmatic factors related to topicality. In particular, persistence and animacy of the object referent were shown to significantly increase the likelihood of VO structures in main clauses. This is in line with theoretical proposals arguing that animate entities are conceptually more accessible and are preferably placed in syntactically prominent positions – a strategy to ensure a robust linguistic signal in case the channel is noisy (e.g.

Branigan, Pickering, and Tanaka 2008; Gibson et al. 2013). In particular, the proposal that two animate noun phrases in SOV structures may result in similarity-based competition appears to be borne out by the data presented here, as animate object noun phrases qualify for post-verbal displacement (Gennari, Mirković, and MacDonald 2012; Norcliffe et al. 2015).[6] On the other hand, new inanimate referents tended to occur in the canonical object position, rather than later in the clause as suggested by other authors (e.g. MacDonald 2013), indicating that some languages may choose to mediate processing difficulties by placing newly introduced items in the respective most highly predictable syntactic position.

With respect to morphological noun phrase marking, the data revealed that VO word order does not co-occur with a large amount of dropped accusative case markers, providing evidence against an encoding of syntactic functions via word order choice and in favor of an encoding of discourse meaning. When case-marking is present, it serves to indicate the syntactic function of the marked noun phrase, which ensures that listeners construe events structures accurately. In fact, case marking was present nearly categorically across the entire data set with dropped markers co-occurring systematically with either persistent or inanimate referents. Case marking is redundant in such cases as referent function is predictable from context: There is a high chance that referents were marked as objects on their first mention and inanimate referents that occur in the canonical object position in OV structures do not cue agent interpretations. Thus, the few cases of dropped accusative markers observed in the current data set do not appear to be influenced by language contact with Spanish, which lacks such case markers. Given the minute distributional differences that were revealed for dropped accusative markers, it is not necessary to account for these instances as speech production errors but, rather, they may tentatively be interpreted as emerging topicality-based differential object marking (see also Leonetti 2004; Iemmolo 2010). This is an interesting finding as Quichua, contrary to Spanish, has generally not been described as a language that makes use of differential object marking (Bossong 2003; Sánchez 2012).

Topic markers, on the other hand, were absent in almost the entire data set but, when present, patterned together with pragmatic processes. Whether topic markers in the current data set are used strategically to mark different types of

---

[6] This conclusion needs to remain tentative as the distribution of (potentially pro-dropped) subjects in Media Lengua has not been studied.

topics, as suggested in Sánchez (2010), is a hypothesis that needs to be put to the test in subsequent phonetic analyses.

With respect to clause type, VO structures occurred mostly in main clauses, the locus where pragmatic meaning is generally encoded. The absence of a large amount of VO structures in subordinate clauses further suggests that no major typological changes have advanced to subordinate clauses. This is fully in line with previous literature discussing the conservative nature of subordinate clauses and their chunk-like processing (Bybee 2002). Since post-verbal objects in subordinate clauses, while infrequent, tended to be either animate or persistent referents, discourse related factors can once again account for the observed structural variation. In line with Bybee (2002), these subordinate clauses resemble main clause pragmatic patterns on a continuum between main and subordinate clauses. In addition, pauses and intervening linguistic material did not show a major effect on word order, suggesting that VO structures are not often the result of speech production errors or disrupted automated speech sequences.

Finally, the language of the verb root did not turn out to influence object placement: Contrary to proposals in previous literature, VO word order did not mainly occur with Spanish verb roots but word order structures were shown to not be significantly different depending on the language of the verb root. This suggests that Media Lengua's lexicon may not be stratified according to the etymological source of its lexical roots, at least as concerns syntactic representations (see also Deibel 2019 for a similar conclusion regarding adpositional phrases). Future research will be needed to disentangle variation targeting lexical roots in more detail. All in all, comparisons with local Quichua varieties may reveal a similar distribution and conditioning of word order (e.g. Muysken 1981, 1997; Sánchez 2010).

7 Conclusion

The results of the current study indicate that Media Lengua's morphosyntactic frame is overall intact, in line with previous descriptions of Imbabura Media Lengua as a more Quichua-conservative Media Lengua variety (Gómez Rendón 2008b; Deibel 2019). Discourse-related factors (topicality, in particular) were shown to govern various dimensions of word order variation, which highlights the importance of quantitative studies to reveal such variation. Overall, the results are in line with crosslinguistic word order tendencies and, possibly, with structural options present in local Quichua varieties. Furthermore, there was no evidence that VO word order in Media Lengua and its correlated factors were directly influenced by language contact with Spanish, at least as concerns the present data set. In conclusion, this underscores that mixed languages like Media Lengua may employ complex patterns of variation and that detailed functional analyses are required to reveal the conditioning factors behind such variation.

Abbreviations

ACC	accusative
DIM	diminutive
O	object
PROG	progressive
S	subject
SG	singular
SWREF	switch reference
TOP	topic
V	verb

References

Adelaar, Willem F. H. 2004. *The languages of the Andes*. Cambridge: Cambridge University Press. https://doi.org/10.1017/CBO9780511486852.

Arnold, Jennifer E. 2008. Reference production: Production-internal and addressee-oriented processes. *Language and Cognitive Processes* 23(4). 495–527. http://doi.org/10.1080/01690960801920099.

Arnold, Jennifer E. 2013. Information status relates to production, distribution, and comprehension. *Frontiers in Psychology* 4, 235, 1–3. http://doi.org/10.3389/fpsyg.2013.00235.

Bates, Douglas, Martin Mächler, Ben Bolker & Steve Walker. 2015. Fitting linear mixed-effects models using lme4. *Journal of Statistical Software* 67(1). 1–48. http://doi.org/10.18637/jss.v067.i01.

Bakker, Peter & Pieter Muysken. 1994. Mixed languages and language intertwining. In Jacques Arends, Pieter Muysken and Norval Smith (eds.), *Pidgins and Creoles: An Introduction*, 41–52. Amsterdam & Philadelphia: John Benjamins.

Bell, Allan. 1984. Language style as audience design. *Language in Society* 13(2). 145–204.

Bossong, Georg. 2003. Nominal and/or verbal marking of central actants. In Giuliana Fiorentino (ed.), *Romance objects: Transitivity in Romance languages*, 17–48. Berlin & New York: Mouton de Gruyter.

Branigan, Holly P., Martin J. Pickering & Mikihiro Tanaka. 2008. Contributions of animacy to grammatical function assignment and word order during production. *Lingua* 118. 172–189. http://doi.org/10.1016/j.lingua.2007.02.003.

Bybee, Joan. 2002. Main clauses are innovative, subordinate clauses are conservative: Consequences for the nature of constructions. In Joan Bybee & Michael Noonan (eds.), *Complex sentences in grammar and discourse: Essays in honor of Sandra A. Thompson*, 1–17. Amsterdam & Philadelphia: John Benjamins.

Bybee, Joan. 2010. *Language, usage and cognition*. Cambridge: Cambridge University Press.

Camacho, José. 1999. From SOV to SVO: The grammar of interlanguage word order. *Second Language Research* 15. 115–132.

Cole, Peter. 1982. *Imbabura Quechua*. Amsterdam: North-Holland Publishing.

Comrie, Bernard. 1989. *Language universals and linguistic typology: Syntax and morphology*. Chicago: University of Chicago Press.

Croft, William. 2003. *Typology and universals*. Cambridge: Cambridge University Press.

Deibel, Isabel. 2019. Adpositions in Media Lengua: Quichua or Spanish? – Evidence of a lexical-functional split. *Journal of Language Contact* 23. 404–439. https://doi.org/10.1163/19552629-01202006.

Downing, Pamela A. 1995. Word order in discourse: By way of introduction. In Pamela A. Downing & Michael Noonan (eds), *Word order in discourse*, 1–28. Amsterdam & Philadelphia: John Benjamins. https://doi.org/10.1075/tsl.30.02dow.

Dryer, Matthew S. 2002. Case distinctions, rich verb agreement, and word order type (comments on Hawkin's paper). *Theoretical Linguistics* 28. 151–157.

Dryer, Matthew S. 2013. Order of subject, object and verb. In Matthew S. Dryer & Martin Haspelmath (eds.), *The world atlas of language structures online*. Leipzig: Max Planck Institute for Evolutionary Anthropology. http://wals.info/chapter/81/ (accessed 27 November 2017).

Du Bois, John W. 1987. The discourse basis of ergativity. *Language* 63(4). 805–855.

Du Bois, John W., Stephan Schuetze-Coburn, Susanna Cumming & Danae Paolino. 1993. Outline of discourse transcription. In Jane A. Edwards & Martin D. Lampert (eds.), *Talking data: Transcription and coding in discourse*, 45–89. Hillsdale: Lawrence Erlbaum Associates.

Escobar, Anna M. 2000. *Contacto social y lingüístico: El español en contacto con el quechua en el Perú*. Lima: Pontificia Universidad Católica del Perú.

Escobar, Anna M. 2001. Contact features in Colonial Peruvian Spanish. *International Journal of the Sociology of Language* 149. 79–93. https://doi.org/10.1515/ijsl.2001.024.

Escobar, Anna M. 2011. Spanish in contact with Quechua. In Manuel Díaz-Campos (ed.), *The handbook of Hispanic sociolinguistics*, 323–352. Oxford & Malden: Wiley-Blackwell.

Frajzyngier, Zygmunt & Erin Shay. 2016. *The role of functions in syntax: A unified approach to language theory, description, and typology*. Amsterdam & Philadelphia: John Benjamins. http://doi.org/10.1075/tsl.111.

Gennari, Silvia P., Jelena Mirković & Maryellen C. MacDonald. 2012. Animacy and competition in relative clause production: A crosslinguistic investigation. *Cognitive Psychology* 65. 141–176. http://doi.org/10.1016/j.cogpsych.2012.03.002.

Gibson, Edward, Steven T. Piantadosi, Kimberly Brink, Leon Bergen, Eunice Lim & Rebecca Saxe. 2013. A noisy-channel account of crosslinguistic word-order variation. *Psychological Science* 24(7). 1079–1088. http://doi.org/10.1177/0956797612463705.

Givón, Talmy. 1983. Topic continuity in discourse: An introduction. In Talmy Givón (ed.), *Topic continuity in discourse: A quantitative cross-language study*, 1–41. Amsterdam & Philadelphia: John Benjamins.
Givón, Talmy. 2001. *Syntax: An introduction (1)*. Amsterdam & Philadelphia: John Benjamins.
Goldin-Meadow, Susan, Wing C. So, Asli Özyürek & Carolyn Mylander. 2008. The natural order of events: How speakers of different languages represent events nonverbally. *Proceedings of the National Academy of Sciences of the United States of America* 105(27). 9163–9168. http://doi.org/10.1073/pnas.0710060105.
Gómez Rendón, Jorge. 2007. Grammatical borrowing in Imbabura Quichua (Ecuador). In Yaron Matras & Jeanette Sakel (eds.), *Grammatical borrowing in crosslinguistic perspective*, 481–522. Berlin & New York: Mouton de Gruyter.
Gómez Rendón, Jorge. 2008a. Spanish lexical borrowing in Imbabura Quichua: In search of constraints on language contact. In Thomas Stolz, Dik Bakker & Rosa Salas Paloma (eds.), *Hispanisation: The impact of Spanish on the lexicon and grammar of the indigenous languages of Austronesia and the Americas*, 95–120. Berlin & New York: Mouton de Gruyter.
Gómez Rendón, Jorge. 2008b. *Mestizaje lingüístico en los Andes: Génesis y estructura de una lengua mixta*. Quito: Abya-Yala.
Gómez Rendón, Jorge & Willem F. H. Adelaar. 2009. Loanwords in Imbabura Quechua. In Martin Haspelmath & Uri Tadmor (eds.), *Loanwords in the world's languages: A comparative handbook*, 944–967. Berlin: Mouton de Gruyter.
Haboud, Marleen. 1998. *Quichua y castellano en los Andes ecuatorianos: Los efectos de un contacto prolongado*. Quito: Abya-Yala.
Hall, Matthew L., Rachel I. Mayberry & Victor S. Ferreira. 2013. Cognitive constraints on constituent order: Evidence from elicited pantomime. *Cognition* 129. 1–17. http://doi.org/10.1016/j.cognition.2013.05.004.
Hopper, Paul J. & Sandra A. Thompson. 1980. Transitivity in grammar and discourse. *Language* 56(2). 251–299.
Iemmolo, Giorgio. 2010. Topicality and differential object marking: Evidence from Romance and beyond. *Studies in Language* 34(2). 239–272. https://doi.org/10.1075/sl.34.2.01iem.
Kibrik, Andrej A. 2011. *Reference in discourse*. Oxford: Oxford University Press.
King, Kendall A. 2001. *Language revitalization processes and prospects: Quichua in the Ecuadorian Andes*. Clevedon: Multilingual Matters.
Kurumada, Chigusa & T. Florian Jaeger. 2015. Communicative efficiency in language production: Optional case-marking in Japanese. *Journal of Memory and Language* 83. 152–178. https://doi.org/10.1016/j.jml.2015.03.003.
Langus, Alan & Marina Nespor. 2010. Cognitive systems struggling for word order. *Cognitive Psychology* 60. 291–318. https://doi.org/10.1016/j.cogpsych.2010.01.004.
Lefebvre, Claire & Pieter Muysken. 1988. *Mixed categories: Nominalizations in Quechua*. Dordrecht: Kluwer Academic Publishers.
Leonetti, Manuel. 2004. Specificity and differential object marking in Spanish. *Catalan Journal of Linguistics* 3. 75–114. https://doi.org/10.5565/rev/catjl.106.
Lipski, John M. 2014. Syncretic discourse markers in Kichwa-influenced Spanish: Transfer vs. emergence. *Lingua* 151. 216–239. http://doi.org/10.1016/j.lingua.2014.07.002.
Lipski, John M. 2016. Language switching constraints: more than syntax? Data from Media Lengua. *Bilingualism: Language & Cognition*, 1–25. https://doi.org/10.1017/S1366728916000468.

Lipski, John M. 2017. Ecuadoran Media Lengua: More than a "half"-language? *International Journal of American Linguistics* 83. 233–262. https://doi.org/10.1086/689845.

MacDonald, Maryellen C. 2013. How language production shapes language form and comprehension. *Frontiers in Psychology* 4. 1–16. http://doi.org/10.3389/fpsyg.2013.00226.

Muntendam, Antje G. 2008. Crosslinguistic influence in Andean Spanish: Word order and focus. In Melissa Bowles, Rebecca Foote, Silvia Perpiñán & Rakesh Bhatt (eds.), *Selected proceedings of the 2007 second language research forum*, 44–57. Somerville, MA: Cascadilla Press.

Muntendam, Antje G. 2009. *Linguistic transfer in Andean Spanish: Syntax or pragmatics?* Urbana & Champaign: University of Illinois dissertation.

Muntendam, Antje G. 2013. On the nature of crosslinguistic transfer: A case study of Andean Spanish. *Bilingualism: Language and Cognition* 16(1). 111–131. http://doi.org/10.1017/S1366728912000247.

Muysken, Pieter. 1981. Halfway between Quechua and Spanish: The case for relexification. In Arnold Highfield & Albert Valdman (eds.), *Historicity and variation in creole studies*, 52–78. Ann Arbor: Karoma.

Muysken, Pieter. 1997. Media Lengua. In Sarah G. Thomason (ed.), *Contact languages: A wider perspective*, 365–426. Amsterdam & Philadelphia: John Benjamins.

Müller, Andrea H. 2011. *La media lengua en comunidades semi-rurales del Ecuador: Uso y significado social de una lengua mixta bilingüe*. Zürich: Universität Zürich Lizenziatsarbeit.

Myhill, John. 2005. Quantitative methods of discourse analysis. In Reinhard Köhler, Gabriel Altmann & Rajmund G. Piotrowski (eds.), *Quantitative linguistics: An international handbook*, 471–497. Berlin & New York: Walter de Gruyter.

Norcliffe, Elisabeth, Agnieszka E. Konopka, Penelope Brown & Stephen C. Levinson. 2015. Word order affects the time course of sentence formulation in Tzeltal. *Language, Cognition and Neuroscience* 30(9). 1187–1208. http://doi.org/10.1080/23273798.2015.1006238.

Payne, Doris L. 1990. *The pragmatics of word order: Typological dimensions of verb initial languages*. Berlin & New York: Mouton de Gruyter.

Poplack, Shana, David Sankoff & Christopher Miller. 1988. The social correlates and linguistic processes of lexical borrowing and assimilation. *Linguistics* 26(1). 47–104.

Poplack, Shana. & Stephen Levey. 2010. Contact-induced grammatical change: a cautionary tale. In Peter Auer & Jürgen E. Schmidt (eds.), *Language and space. An international handbook of linguistic variation. Volume 1: Theories and methods*, 391–419. Berlin: Mouton de Gruyter.

R Core Team. 2016. *R: A language and environment for statistical computing*. Vienna: R Foundation for Statistical Computing. http://www.R-project.org/ (accessed 8 January 2018).

Rivas, Javier. 2013. Variable subject position in main and subordinate clauses in Spanish: A usage-based approach. *Moenia* 19. 97–113.

Sánchez, Liliana. 2003. *Quechua-Spanish bilingualism: Interference and convergence in functional categories*. Amsterdam & Philadelphia: John Benjamins.

Sánchez, Liliana. 2010. *The morphology and syntax of topic and focus: Minimalist inquiries in the Quechua periphery*. Amsterdam & Philadelphia: John Benjamins. https://doi.org/10.1075/la.169.

Sánchez, Liliana. 2012. Convergence in syntax/morphology mapping strategies: Evidence from Quechua–Spanish code mixing. *Lingua* 122. 511–528. http://doi.org/10.1016/j.lingua.2011.10.004.

Schouwstra, Marieke & Henriëtte de Swart. 2014. The semantic origins of word order. *Cognition* 131. 431–436. http://doi.org/10.1016/j.cognition.2014.03.004.

Shappeck, Marco. 2011. *Quichua-Spanish language contact in Salcedo, Ecuador: Revisiting Media Lengua syncretic language practices.* Urbana & Champaign: University of Illinois dissertation.

Stewart, Jesse. 2011. *A brief descriptive grammar of Pijal Media Lengua and an acoustic vowel space analysis of Pijal Media Lengua and Imbabura Quichua.* Winnipeg: University of Manitoba MA thesis.

Stewart, Jesse. 2013. *Stories and traditions from Pijal: Told in Media Lengua.* North Charleston: CreateSpace.

Stewart, Jesse. 2015a. Intonation patterns in Pijal Media Lengua. *Journal of Language Contact* 8. 223–262. http://doi.org/10.1163/19552629-00802003.

Stewart, Jesse. 2015b. *Production and perception of stop consonants in Spanish, Quichua, and Media Lengua.* Winnipeg: University of Manitoba dissertation.

Thomason, Sarah G. 1995. Language mixture: Ordinary processes, extraordinary results. In Carmen Silva-Corvalán (ed.), *Spanish in four continents: Studies in language contact and bilingualism*, 15–33. Washington (D.C.): Georgetown University Press.

Thomason, Sarah G. 2003. Social factors and linguistic processes in the emergence of stable mixed languages. In Yaron Matras & Peter Bakker (eds.), *The mixed language debate: Theoretical and empirical advances*, 21–40. Berlin & New York: Mouton de Gruyter. https://doi.org/10.1515/9783110197242.2.

Torres Cacoullos, Rena & Catherine E. Travis. 2015. Gauging convergence on the ground: Code-switching in the community. *International Journal of Bilingualism.* 365–386. http://doi.org/10.1177/1367006913516046.

Torres Cacoullos, Rena & Catherine E. Travis. 2018. *Bilingualism in the community: Code-switching and grammars in contact.* Cambridge: Cambridge University Press.

Yamamoto, Mutsumi. 1999. *Animacy and reference: a cognitive approach to corpus linguistics.* Amsterdam & Philadelphia: John Benjamins.

Katja Hannß
Linguistic manipulations in Kallawaya

1 Introduction

In the paper, I will discuss linguistic manipulations of Kallawaya, a mixed and secret language of the Lake Titicaca region (Bolivia), spoken by male herbalists. I suggest that Kallawaya displays three types of linguistic manipulations: etymological manipulations, i.e. the borrowing of foreign lexical material; grammatical and phonological manipulations. Although the different types of Kallawaya linguistic manipulations appear to be unsystematic at first glance, I propose that they are actually not as irregular as it may seem. Instead, the linguistic manipulations in Kallawaya are applied according to the etymological origin of the lexical item being manipulated. This points to a high degree of linguistic awareness of the Kallawaya creators and speakers. Kallawaya resembles other secret languages with respect to both the types of linguistic manipulations attested in the language (e.g. phonological manipulation) as well as to the form linguistic manipulation takes (i.e. use of dummy suffixes and vowel substitution, for instance). Moreover, the linguistic manipulations found in Kallawaya are also comparable to deliberate changes made in non-secret languages. Thus, although Kallawaya is an illustrative example of linguistic creativity, it is by no means exceptional when it comes to deliberate changes made in order to keep the language unintelligible to outsiders.

The paper is organised as follows: in the remainder of this section, I will first introduce the Kallawaya and Pukina languages (sections 1.1 and 1.2), the latter being the alleged main lexifier of Kallawaya, before providing a brief

---

Acknowledgements: First and foremost, I would like to thank the editors as well as two anonymous reviewers for their inspiring comments and suggestions which helped to improve the paper. Also, I owe thanks to Eeva Sippola and Maria Mazzoli for inviting me to the Bremen Colloquium on Mixed Languages from which this volume developed. I am also very much indebted to the native speakers of Aymara and Quechua without whom I could never have checked the phonological manipulations. I would also like to thank my colleagues at the University of Cologne and elsewhere for their comments and critical remarks on previous versions of the manuscript. Special thanks go to Willem Adelaar, Simon van de Kerke and Arjan Mossel for their insightful comments on Quechua, Aymara and especially Pukina. I am also indebted to Else Gellinek for her careful reading of the manuscript. All remaining errors are mine. Research on Kallawaya was funded by the *Deutsche Forschungsgemeinschaft* (DFG; grant numbers HA 6340/2-1 and HA 6340/2-2).

Katja Hannß, Ludwig-Maximilians-Universität München, katja.hannss@lrz.uni-muenchen.de

https://doi.org/10.1515/9781501511257-007

introduction to the topic of linguistic manipulation (section 1.3). In section 2, I will discuss the linguistic manipulations of Kallawaya, starting with etymological manipulations in section 2.1, before turning to a description of grammatical manipulations in sections 2.2 to 2.2.2. A discussion of phonological manipulations is provided in section 2.3. Finally, in section 3, I will present a summarising discussion of my findings and my conclusions.

At this point, I would like to mention that there have been previous publications on the etymological composition and the formation of Kallawaya (see Hannß 2017, 2019). However, although parts of the following and especially those concerned with the etymology and the non-Quechua and non-Aymara grammatical markers of Kallawaya have been discussed before, a description of linguistic manipulations in Kallawaya would be incomplete without addressing etymological and grammatical manipulations. Therefore, I chose to include previously published findings on the etymology and the non-Quechua and non-Aymara grammar of Kallawaya here. In contrast to the previous publications, the focus of this paper lies on how the etymological composition and the non-Quechua and non-Aymara grammatical elements contribute to keeping Kallawaya secret – and thus it differs from the topics of the aforementioned publications.

1.1 The Kallawaya language

Kallawaya is a mixed and secret language spoken by traditional herbalists in the Bolivian highlands north-east of Lake Titicaca (Department of La Paz) (Muysken 2009: 147; see also Hannß 2019: 244). The herbalists' native language is Quechua, although they are usually described as bi- or even trilingual, having additional knowledge of Aymara and/or Spanish (Soria Lens 1951: 35; Oblitas Poblete 1968: 16; Muysken 1997: 428; Callahan 2011: 95). Use of Kallawaya is restricted to initiated men, while non-initiated men as well as women and children are not allowed to use the language. The Kallawaya language is used by the traditional herbalists during curing ceremonies and when they travel as itinerant healers (Muysken 2009: 148; Callahan 2011: 104; see also below). One of its main functions is thus to protect the herbalists' special knowledge about medicinal plants and herbs (Soria Lens 1951: 32; Saignes 1985: 200).

Despite a relative wealth of ethnographic and ethno-historical literature on the Kallawaya herbalists (see e.g. Bastien 1978; Oblitas Poblete 1978; Saignes 1985; Meyers 2002; among others), very little is known about how the Kallawaya language and culture came into being (Muysken 2009: 149). The name "Kallawaya" (or "Callahuaya" in its hispanicised form) is attested for pre-Spanish times, but its actual reference is quite uncertain. Saignes (1985: 190, referring to the *Relaciones Geográficas de Indias* [1573] 1965 and Garcilaso de la Vega *Historia General de Perú* [1617] 1944, 1960) and Meyers (2002: 47) relate the name to the province Carabaya or Calabaya, respectively, located north-east of Lake Titicaca.[1] Both authors (Saignes 1985: 188; Meyers 2002: 47) claim that the Kallawaya held a *señorío*; i.e. a territory there in pre-Inca times. The manuscript of Huarochirí (1598–1606; see Trimborn and Kelm 1967: 129), a colonial collection of Andean myths, as well as the chronicles by Guaman Poma de Ayala (1613, fol. 331 [333]; see Adorno 2004) and Santa Cruz Pachacuti (1613; cited in: Saignes 1985: 194; see also Saignes 1985: 194–195) mention a group called "Callahuaya" as carriers of the Inca's litter but they are not related to any herblore (Saignes 1985: 195). It remains unclear whether there is any historical relationship between the pre-colonial group(s) referred to as "Callahuaya" and the herbalists depicted in the 20th century sources.

The first mention of Kallawaya healers from Charazani, a centre of Kallawaya herbalism, only dates back to 1776 (Muysken 2009: 150), but it is unknown what language(s) they spoke.[2] As many references to the Kallawaya herbalists come from the 19th century, Muysken (2009: 150) estimates that the group of Kallawaya healers appeared only as recently as between 1750 and 1920. Note that this was a time when the use of Pukina was at least already declining (see section 1.2). Linguistic information on the Kallawaya language becomes available only from around 1950 onwards (see Table 1). These modern sources disagree on whether the Kallawaya language is used only in curing ceremonies or whether it can also be used in non-ritual, non-medicinal contexts. While Oblitas Poblete (1968: 13, 16) and Stark (1972: 199) claim that use of Kallawaya is restricted to rituals, Girault (1984: 24) states that Kallawaya is not limited to such contexts. A similar stance is taken by Callahan (2011: 104) who relates that "talking with their travel partners in the code enabled them [i.e. the Kallawaya herbalists; the author] to discuss suspicious people and situations, as well as escape plans in private". The overall design of the Kallawaya lexicon seems to support Girault's and Callahan's observations. With 2,289 lexical bases (see Table 2), the Kallawaya lexicon appears to be too comprehensive to represent a frozen language that is used only in formulaic and ritualised contexts. Moreover, Kallawaya makes productive use of compounding and reduplication, which suggests that the semantics of the lexical bases are accessible to the users of the language (see Hannß 2014: 176–177, 2019: 249). Both features are not typical for a frozen language. The present status of the

---

[1] In the text, Saignes (ibid.) gives 1944 as the year of the modern publication; in the references, however, he only provides the date of 1960. I list both publication dates here.
[2] Note that Girault (1984: 16) provides the date of 1766.

language, however, is uncertain: according to Muysken (2009: 147), it is debatable whether Kallawaya is still spoken today at all, while Anderson and Harrison (2007) provide the number of up to 200 remaining speakers. Similarly, Callahan (2011: 101) confirms ongoing use of Kallawaya. Despite this, the language is considered severely endangered (Adelaar 2007: 19). Little is known about how Kallawaya is transmitted. It is acquired only as a second language during the training to become a healer (Adelaar and Muysken 2004: 356), and Stark (1972: 199) claims that it "is passed on from father to eldest son" (but see Callahan 2011: 73, for a contrastive view). It is possible that each new generation of Kallawaya speakers slightly extended and/or modified the secret language that had been transmitted to them by their fathers, thereby creating a kind of "family tradition"; i.e. a particular way of using Kallawaya within one family of herbalists. These alleged modifications might be the addition of new words (borrowed and/or coined) and/or the making up of new linguistic manipulations. In this sense, speakers of Kallawaya would have also been creators at the same time. However, as linguistic documentation of Kallawaya spans only a little over 20 years (see Table 1); i.e. roughly one generation, this has to remain speculative. These "family traditions", however, would partly explain the relatively great variation attested within Kallawaya (Muysken 1997: 431–441, 2009: 150–151; Adelaar and Muysken 2004: 358; see also section 2.3) and especially within the lexicon. There is less variation when it comes to linguistic manipulations, which are – by and large – applied according to the etymological origin of an item (see section 3). If these etymological distinctions are still observed at least several decades (if not 100 or 200 years) after the language was first created, then this suggests a high degree of linguistic awareness not only on the side of the original creators of the secret language but also on the side of the speakers as portrayed in the linguistic sources on Kallawaya. Had the etymological distinctions become meaningless for the generations of Kallawaya speakers following the first creators one would expect a less clear picture of linguistic manipulations in Kallawaya. As it is, the linguistic manipulations are generally applied in accordance with the etymology of a lexical item. Note further that this ties in with the above-made suggestion that Kallawaya is not a frozen language (at least not at the time of documentation).

Although Kallawaya is a secret language, it is surprisingly well documented: between roughly the 1950s and the 1970s, approximately 17,190 word forms (including compounds, inflected and derived forms) and approximately 84 phrases were collected. However, we do not have texts in Kallawaya and thus almost the entire Kallawaya material is lexical (Muysken 2009: 152). There are no significant differences between the lexical and grammatical material within one source; however, between the sources, lexical as well as grammatical information may vary, in parts even considerably (see above). This may have to do with the above-mentioned family traditions, within which the Kallawaya language is presumably transmitted. Table 1 provides an overview of the sources on Kallawaya which, with the exception of Ponce Sanjinés (n.d) and Anderson and Harrison (2007), also provide the database for the investigation presented in the paper.

Table 1: Sources of Kallawaya (Muysken 2009: 151).

Author and date of publication	Year(s) of field work	Type of material
Ponce Sanjinés (n.d)	?	Unpublished field notes, approximately 50 words
Soria Lens (1951)	ca. 1950	Approximately 50 words
Oblitas Poblete (1968)	1950 and later	About 15 phrases, approximately 12,000 words, grammatical observations
Stark (1972)	ca. 1970	Approximately 130 words, grammatical analysis with one-word examples; no example phrases
Girault (1984)	1956–1965	Plant names and descriptions of their uses
Mondaca (1987)	? (late 1960s and/or 1970s?)	19 phrases, approximately 130 words, grammatical observations
Gifford and Lancaster (ca. 1988)	1982	General observations, 10 words
Girault (1989)	1956–1974	About 50 phrases, approximately 4,500 words, grammatical observations, some recordings
Torero (2002)	1966	Field notes
Anderson and Harrison (2007)	2007	Audio recordings
Total		**Approx. 84 phrases; approx. 17,190 word forms**

The parental languages of Kallawaya are Southern Quechua and allegedly Pukina. As is often the case with mixed languages, Quechua and Pukina are not genealogically related.[3] Some examples of Kallawaya follow (the grammatical material is

---

[3] Although the genetic classification of Pukina remains unclear, links to Arawakan languages have been suggested (Adelaar and van de Kerke 2009: 126).

from Quechua, the lexical material comes from Pukina, Aymara, Quechua-Aymara [see below], Uru-Chipaya or is etymologically opaque).

(1) soqerqoson p^hʔekamixeininta
    soqe-rqo-son p^hʔeka-mixe-i-ni-n-ta
    cure-PROMPT-1PL.INCL.FUT head-ache-NMLZ-EP-3SG.POS-DO
    'We are going to cure his/her headache.'
    (Mondaca 1987: n/p)

(2) k^hutunchiskuna   ʎaʎi uwaru sa^{w}juxpuni   achanko
    k^hutu-nchis-kuna   ʎaʎi uwaru sa^w-jux=puni acha-nko
    head.FIG-1PL.INCL-PL good fair   heart-POR=CONF be-3PL
    'Our authorities are of a very good heart.'
    (Oblitas Poblete 1968: 38)

Southern Quechua – classified as Quechua IIC (Adelaar and Muysken 2004: 184, 187) – provides the grammatical framework of Kallawaya (Stark 1972: 208; Adelaar and Muysken 2004: 357). Accordingly, the Kallawaya grammar is "almost identical to that of Cuzco Quechua" (Stark 1972: 208; see also Muysken 2009: 153, 157, 161, 162).[4] Only a few grammatical markers of Kallawaya are non-Quechua (and non-Aymara, non-Uru-Chipaya and non-Pukina, for that matter). I suggest that these are dummy suffixes and camouflaging markers (section 2.2). Also, the phonological system of Kallawaya resembles that of Quechua with the exception of the vowel system (Muysken 2009: 153). There, Kallawaya occasionally distinguishes vowel length, which is not phonemic in Southern Quechua (Adelaar and Muysken 2004: 195, 196). However, vowel length in Kallawaya is not systematic, as can be seen from the realisation of, for instance, 'man, male' as either *la:xa* or *laxa* (see also Hannß 2017: 223)

Extinct Pukina has been claimed to be the main lexifier of Kallawaya, contributing 70% to the Kallawaya lexicon (Stark 1972: 206). Stark's findings are based on the 200-word Swadesh list (Stark 1972: 206.). Unfortunately, the 200-word Swadesh list is not published along with Stark's article, so it remains somewhat uncertain how Stark reached the conclusion that 70% of Kallawaya are from Pukina. However, it seems likely that Stark attributed every lexical Kallawaya item that is not from Quechua, Aymara or Uru-Chipaya to Pukina

---

[4] A similar observation is made by Nelly Quispe, a Quechua native speaker, who also contributed to the questionnaire on phonological manipulations in Kallawaya (see Section 2.3). She notes that the Quechua as presented in the Kallawaya data is more reminiscent of Peruvian than of Bolivian Quechua (Nelly Quispe p.c.; November 2014).

(Hannß 2017: 236). The prominent role of Pukina in the investigation of Kallawaya probably goes back to the earliest available linguistic description of Kallawaya: Soria Lens (1951: 32, 35; see also Hannß 2017: 225) mentions that Kallawaya speakers refer to their secret language as "Pohena", which is, of course, highly reminiscent of the name Pukina (see also Muysken 2009: 147).[5] Accordingly, Soria Lens (1951: 35) provides a brief comparison of some Pukina and "Pohena"; i.e. Kallawaya terms some of which are clearly based on Pukina, such as Kallawaya *ikili* 'father' from Pukina *iki* 'father' (however, others are not, such as Kallawaya *tʃisma* 'five' and Pukina *takpa* 'five'). With this in mind, Stark's findings were readily accepted, although from a methodological point of view her approach is partly arguable. Accordingly, recent research (Hannß 2017) suggests (a) that the lexicon of Kallawaya is considerably more heterogeneous than assumed so far; and (b) that only about 5% of the Kallawaya lexicon can be clearly linked to Pukina, while the majority of all Kallawaya lexical bases remain etymologically opaque. As a consequence, Kallawaya does not have a clearly identifiable main lexifier language. Table 2 provides an overview of the etymological composition of the Kallawaya lexicon (see also Hannß 2017: 230).

Before detailing the Pukina language, I briefly introduce the other lexifier languages of Kallawaya. Aymara is the dominant language of highland Bolivia and the Kallawaya herbalists are surrounded by an Aymara-speaking population, which probably contributes to the relatively high degree of Aymara attested in the Kallawaya lexicon. The exact nature of the relationship between Aymara and Quechua has been a matter of ongoing debate (see Muysken 2012: 85). However, the two languages show some structural parallelisms and also share about 20% of their core vocabularies (Cerrón-Palomino 1994: 70, 147; Adelaar and Muysken 2004: 35). Uru and Chipaya belong to the isolated Uru-Chipaya language family and are (or were) spoken along the aquatic waterways of highland Bolivia (Wachtel 1986: 283). Uru (aka Uchumataqu) became extinct around 1950 (Hannß 2008). Chipaya is the only member of the language family that is still in use and it is spoken by approximately 1,000 people in the community of Santa Ana de Chipaya near Lake Coipasa in south-western Bolivia (Adelaar and Muysken 2004: 362–375, 622; Cerrón-Palomino 2006). Kunza (aka Atacameño) was spoken at the

---

5 Note that the Uru-Chipaya speakers also refer (or referred) to their language as "Pukina" (Lehmann 1929: n/p; Cerrón-Palomino 2006: 22). When the author of the paper conducted fieldwork in the community of Santa Ana de Chipaya in 2002, she was told that the Chipaya speakers (or at least some of them) call their own language "Pukina". This probably has to do with the fact that Pukina was a *lingua franca* of the southern Andes for a considerable span of time (see also Cerrón-Palomino 2006: 22). However, Uru-Chipaya is genealogically unrelated to Pukina (Cerrón-Palomino 2009: 32) (see also below).

Table 2: The etymological composition of the Kallawaya lexicon.[6]

Language	Lexical bases of Kallawaya (in numbers and %)	
Aymara	296	12.93%
Quechua	307	13.41%
Quechua-Aymara[7]	165	7.21%
Spanish	150	6.55%
Pukina	117	5.11%
Uru-Chipaya	26	1.14%
Kunza	7	0.31%
Ese Ejja (Takanan)	3	0.13%
Total known etymology	1,071	46.79%
Total unknown etymology	1,218	53.21%
Total	2,289	100%

northern Pacific coast of Chile and possibly in adjacent parts of Bolivia but is probably extinct now. It is considered an isolate (Adelaar and Muysken 2004: 375–385, 612). Lastly, the Ese Ejja language belongs to the Takanan language family, used in lowland Bolivia and neighbouring regions of Peru. According to Vuillermet (2012: 54, referring to Alexiades, Machuqui, and Monje 2009), there are more than 1,000 Ese Ejja speakers in Bolivia.

1.2 The Pukina language

In pre-colonial and early colonial times, the Pukina language, the alleged main lexifier of Kallawaya, was still widely used throughout the Andes (Adelaar and

---

6 For the etymological investigation of the Kallawaya lexicon which resulted in the numbers presented in Table 2, only lexical bases were considered but not compounded, derived or inflected forms, which are included in the number of 17,190 forms as given in Table 1 above (see also Hannß 2017). The Kallawaya lexicon is available online at: https://hdl.handle.net/11341/00-0000-0000-0000-1AD5-6 (Hannß 2015).
7 The label "Quechua-Aymara" refers to those lexical items that are identical in Quechua and Aymara, such as *wanaku* 'guanaco', for instance, and for which no unequivocal etymological origin can therefore be established.

van de Kerke 2009: 125). It was spoken in southern Peru, in large areas of Bolivia, and especially around Lake Titicaca, in the region where Kallawaya was to develop (Adelaar and Muysken 2004: 350; Adelaar and van de Kerke 2009: 125; see section 1.1). Pukina is closely associated with the Tiahuanaco Empire of Lake Titicaca, which flourished between 650 and 1050 A.D. (Adelaar and van de Kerke 2009: 126; Isbell 2012: 220). After the Tiahuanaco Empire had fallen, Aymara speakers reached Lake Titicaca and the neighbouring southern *Altiplano*, Bolivia's high plateau. It was only after Aymara had been implemented there that a Quechua-speaking population came to Lake Titicaca and the *Altiplano* (see Torero 2002: 387, 388; Sillar 2012: 310, 311, 313). The following spread of Quechua into until then Aymara-speaking areas was fuelled first by the Incas, establishing workers' colonies, and later by Spanish missionaries, who preached in Quechua (Albó 1995: 124; Cerrón-Palomino 2013: 327). These processes brought about the extinction of the Pukina language. The last mentions of Pukina speakers date back to the early 19th century (Adelaar and van de Kerke 2009: 125). It appears reasonable to assume that the Pukina language was in decline well before this date.

Pukina vanished with only scarce documentation. The only considerable Pukina material we are left with comprises 263 lexical bases, attested in a missionary document by Oré (1607; see also Grasserie 1894; Torero 1965, 2002; Adelaar and Muysken 2004; Adelaar and van de Kerke 2009). This document forms part of a collection of Christian texts that were translated into a number of indigenous languages, among them Pukina (Adelaar and van de Kerke 2009: 126). These data are of course somewhat problematic. First, the Pukina texts appear to be a mere (and in some cases less elaborate) translation of the Quechua equivalent (Adelaar and van de Kerke 2009: 127). Second, Christian texts introduced concepts like "sin", for instance, an adequate cultural and linguistic translation of which must frequently have failed. Accordingly, the resulting texts are often artificial to some degree. Finally, many Pukina terms from everyday life are unrecorded and hence unknown to us because of the religious nature of the Oré document. This makes an etymological classification of numerous Kallawaya words difficult, if not impossible. In the paper, Pukina items are first presented as written in the Oré manuscript (1607), followed by a modern transcription, based on Torero (2002).[8] Torero (2002: 416) transcribes doubtful cases ranging between /k/ and /q/ as <c> before /a, u/ and as <ck> before /e, i/. In such instances, I provide both transcription options: Pukina <guio> 'son, child', for instance,

---

8 I am indebted to Simon van de Kerke and Arjan Mossel for helping me to establish the correct orthographic representation by Oré.

is represented by Torero (2002: 449) as <ckiu>, while my transcription of this item is *kiu~qiu* (see Example 11a). Note that in the Oré manuscript /u/ is often represented as <v>, while /s/ may be rendered as <f> or <s> (see also Hannß accepted).

1.3 Linguistic manipulations

Within the study of mixed and secret languages, it is widely acknowledged that secret languages often display what has been called "manipulative constructions" (Matras 2000: 81), "manipulated speech" (Matras and Bakker 2003: 9) or "lexical manipulation" (Matras and Bakker 2003: 9; Mous 2003). Probably the most obvious and most widely attested linguistic manipulation is the insertion of lexical material from languages usually unknown within the respective dominant speech community (see Matras and Bakker 2003: 9), something which most (or possibly even all) secret languages rely on to some degree. However, descriptions of secret languages often also mention "camouflaging affixes and phoneme substitution" (Matras 2000: 81). This is found in Irish Shelta (Grant 1994), in the argot used by Egyptian entertainers (Nieuwkerk 1998) and in African secret languages (Storch 2011), for instance; it is also attested for Kallawaya. In the following, I refer to such disguise techniques as "linguistic manipulations" which describes the deliberate modification of a linguistic form; i.e. a lexical base, grammatical or phonological material which is somehow modified in order to make the resulting lexical, grammatical or phonological form unintelligible to outsiders.[9]

I suggest that Kallawaya shows three types of linguistic manipulations. Kallawaya has etymological manipulations where lexical material from several and partly unknown source languages is borrowed (see Table 2 and section 2.1). Furthermore, Kallawaya also makes use of dummy suffixes and camouflage markers. This is what I call grammatical manipulation (see section 2.2). Lastly, Kallawaya has phonological manipulation where phonological material gets substituted or deleted in order to make the phonological form of otherwise intelligible words unrecognisable (see section 2.3). It is the aim of the paper to provide an overview and a preliminary classification of the linguistic manipulations attested in Kallawaya.

---

9 The label "linguistic manipulation" is intended to capture the fact that manipulations are often not restricted to the lexicon but can occur in other parts of the language system as well (see Thomason 2007: 50; Section 3).

2 Linguistic manipulations in Kallawaya

In the following, I will describe the linguistic manipulations in Kallawaya In section 2.1, I will detail the etymological manipulations of Kallawaya, before turning to a description of grammatical manipulations throughout sections 2.2 to 2.2.2. Finally, phonological manipulations will be discussed in section 2.3.

2.1 Etymological manipulations

Etymological manipulation refers to the use of words in Kallawaya borrowed from languages unknown within the herbalists' dominant Quechua speech community (see Matras and Bakker 2003: 9; section 1.3). Quechua, Aymara and Spanish are spoken and understood widely throughout the Andean region and I therefore do not consider these languages to contribute to the secrecy of Kallawaya. Similar considerations apply to Uru-Chipaya terms in Kallawaya. The Uru-Chipaya languages are/were used in immediate neighbourhood to Pukina, Quechua, Aymara and Kallawaya (see section 1.1.). Most instances of Uru-Chipaya in the Kallawaya lexicon are therefore probably the result of regular language contact rather than of deliberate etymological manipulation. This leaves us with three types of lexical resources unknown in the herbalists' native Quechua speech community:
– Pukina items
– Etymologically opaque words
– Kunza and Ese Ejja words

The Pukina language was probably on its way to extinction when Kallawaya emerged (see sections 1.1 and 1.2). To the Kallawaya herbalists, the vanishing Pukina language must have appeared a most suitable source in order to create or otherwise embroider their secret code: as soon as Pukina was (almost) out of use, employing words from this language ensured a high degree of secrecy. However, as Pukina, Aymara and Quechua have been in contact with each other for several centuries, speakers have borrowed back and forth from these languages, resulting in a number of shared borrowings (Muysken 1997: 429, 430; Adelaar and Muysken 2004: 350, 352). Pukina items shared with Quechua and/or Aymara are disqualified as secret words as they are understood by speakers of Quechua and/ or Aymara (regardless of their ultimate origin). Therefore, only those Pukina words not shared by any other language but Kallawaya are considered an etymological manipulation. Of the 263 Pukina items known to us, 117 are attested in Kallawaya (Table 2 in section 1.1). Out of these, 43 items are shared only with

Kallawaya.[10] I propose that these 43 borrowings shared exclusively between Pukina and Kallawaya form the Pukina "lexical reservoir" (Matras 2000: 86) which Kallawaya speakers draw on to maintain secrecy (a list of these 43 Pukina-Kallawaya shared borrowings is provided in the Appendix). The Pukina words come from several semantic domains, such as agriculture, body parts, denominations of persons (such as 'friend', for instance), kinship terms, temporal relationships and numerals. The Pukina words are spread relatively evenly across these semantic domains, with one to four words per semantic domain. They can be the only lexical item in the Kallawaya lexicon to express a particular concept or they can exist alongside other terms that express the same concept (see Mous 2003: 214). Thus, for instance, the Pukina-based Kallawaya word *teka-~tʰeka-* is the only one to express the concept of 'to dream' (no. 35 in the Appendix), whereas Pukina-based *saʷ* 'heart, breast' (no. 30 in the Appendix) co-exists alongside the Aymara-based word *enke~enqe* 'heart, breast' and the Quechua-derived item *soko* 'heart, breast'. Among the 43 Pukina items shared only with Kallawaya, 17 Pukina words occur alongside other lexical items referring to the same concept (nos. 1–3, 5–7, 15, 19–20, 24, 28, 30, 36, 38–39, 42–43 in the Appendix), while 19 Pukina items are the only ones to express the concept in question (nos. 4, 9–10, 13–14, 16–18, 21, 23, 25–26, 31–35, 37, 41 in the Appendix). Seven cases cannot be clearly assigned to either group (nos. 8, 11–12, 22, 27, 29, 40 in the Appendix). This applies to, for instance, Kallawaya *okʔo~oko~oqo* 'moon, month' (from Pukina <vque> *uqe* 'moon'), where the notion of 'month' can additionally be expressed by the etymologically opaque word *kʰax* or by Aymara-based *pʰaxas*. The concept of 'moon', however, is uniquely expressed in the Kallawaya lexicon by Pukina-derived *okʔo~oko~oqo* (no. 22 in the Appendix).

This relatively small number of secret Pukina words in Kallawaya is significantly exceeded by the number of etymologically opaque items in the Kallawaya lexicon (see Table 2 in section 1.1). While it is quite likely that there are further unrecognised Pukina words among these etymologically opaque lexical items, linguistically speaking this is impossible to prove as these items could also originate in languages not yet considered in any etymological survey. Moreover, the etymologically opaque part of the Kallawaya lexicon could also include coined expressions and neologisms. An example for the latter is Kallawaya *pʔotoken*

---

10 In a previous publication (Hannß 2017: 235, 248–258), it was claimed that the number of borrowings shared exclusively between Pukina and Kallawaya amounts to 50. However, ongoing research on both Pukina and Kallawaya suggests that of the 50 Pukina-Kallawaya shared borrowings two are actually also shared with other languages, while for another five Kallawaya items the relation to Pukina is unclear. Thus, the number of 50 Pukina-Kallawaya shared borrowings was reduced to 43.

'horse', for which Quechua and Aymara either have a loan word, *caballo* 'horse' (from Spanish *caballo* 'horse') or use the general term for domesticated animals, *uywa*. Because of the severely restricted Pukina database, we cannot check the etymologically opaque Kallawaya items for further potential links to Pukina. However, what is important from the perspective of secrecy is that none of these etymologically opaque Kallawaya words shows any relationship to Quechua, Aymara, Uru-Chipaya or Spanish and, accordingly, cannot be understood by speakers of these languages. Thus, regardless of their actual etymological origin, the etymologically opaque items form the bulk of the secret lexicon of Kallawaya.

The class of Kunza and Ese Ejja words is the smallest of the three presented here (see Hannß 2017: 236–241). The condition upon which a Kunza or Ese Ejja term is considered secret is that it must not be a shared borrowing; i.e. it must not show any relation to either Quechua, Aymara, Pukina, Uru-Chipaya or Spanish lest the Kunza or Ese Ejja item in question traces back to one of the dominant (Andean) languages. Thus, only in those cases where a Kunza or Ese Ejja word in Kallawaya bears no phonological and semantic similarity to Quechua, Aymara, Pukina, Uru-Chipaya or Spanish, do I assume that it was Kunza or Ese Ejja that provided the term for Kallawaya. One such instance is Kallawaya su^wi 'arm, hand, finger', borrowed from Kunza *sui* 'hand, finger'. Kallawaya su^wi is not a loanword from Quechua, Aymara, Uru-Chipaya or Spanish; the Pukina word for 'hand' is <moha~muha> *muqa* and thus, too, is clearly different from Kallawaya. Another example is Kunza *lali* 'intestines, guts', which may have given rise to Kallawaya *lali* 'shortage' and *lali-ku-y* 'hunger', possibly by way of semantic extension, where the Kunza expression has been re-interpreted to refer to the sound and/or feeling of empty guts in Kallawaya. However, the Pukina lexical items for 'hunger' and 'intestines, guts' are unknown and the Kallawaya and Kunza expressions could thus also be shared borrowings, tracing back to Pukina.

With only three definite instances the number of Ese Ejja words in Kallawaya is low. The Ese Ejja items presented in the following have cognates in other Takanan languages. This strongly suggests that the items in question have their origins in the Takanan language family and were borrowed by Kallawaya. One example is Kallawaya *tʃʔaxu* 'bronchial tube, lung, trachea, windpipe', from Ese Ejja *e-ʃaho* 'lung'. The prefix *e-* of Ese Ejja *e-ʃaho* occurs frequently on body-part terms and is obligatory in the citation form, but otherwise is dropped in derivational processes, incorporation, juxtaposition and in possessive phrases (Vuillermet 2012: 299–300). This may account for its non-realisation in Kallawaya, as it is possible that Kallawaya speakers never came across the *e-*inflected form at all, because body parts are usually referred to within possessive phrases. Alternatively, Kallawaya speakers recognised the *e-*prefix as grammatical material and deleted it upon borrowing. The Ese Ejja phonemes [ʃ] and [h] have been adapted to Kallawaya phonology by way of [tʃ] and [x], respectively. Another borrowing in Kallawaya is Ese Ejja *ba* 'know', realised as *pʔa* 'believe' in Kallawaya. As Kallawaya does not have [b], the Ese Ejja sound becomes devoiced in Kallawaya. Finally, Kallawaya has *tʔipi* 'plate' from Ese Ejja *tepe~tipi* 'calabash', where 'calabash' probably refers to those fruits whose dried skin is used as a container, drinking vessel or, as is the case here, as a plate. The meaning of 'plate' in Kallawaya is thus a semantic re-interpretation of Ese Ejja 'calabash'. It is debatable whether Kallawaya *tʔipi* is an instance of etymological manipulation or rather reflects regular language contact in which the name of an object unknown in the receiving language gets borrowed.

Although there are only very few Kunza and Ese Ejja loans in Kallawaya, they include body-part terms. These are part of the core vocabulary of a language, which is usually more resistant to change than other and culturally more determined parts of the lexicon. If core vocabulary gets borrowed, this usually happens in situations of massive contact (Thomason 2001: 70). However, the low number of Kunza and Ese Ejja words in Kallawaya is not reminiscent of such a scenario. This strongly suggests that Kunza and Ese Ejja words were deliberately borrowed by Kallawaya speakers for reasons of secrecy.

2.2 Grammatical manipulations

Although the grammar of Kallawaya is almost identical to that of Southern Quechua (section 1.1), Kallawaya has a small number of grammatical markers that cannot be related to Quechua, Aymara, Spanish, Pukina or Uru-Chipaya (see Hannß 2019).[11] I suggest that these grammatical forms are dummy suffixes and camouflage markers, mainly or exclusively meant to disguise the phonological form and therefore the semantic content of the lexical bases they are attached to. These markers can be grouped into two classes:
1) Dummy suffixes without (barely) any grammatical function
2) Camouflage markers that may have a relatively clearly discernible grammatical function

---

11 Kallawaya also has two suffixes that are probably of Pukina origin but which are most likely frozen. One is the marker *-si*, a possible reflex of the Pukina ergative marker <-s> *-s* (Adelaar and Muysken 2004: 360), while the other one is the reflexive marker *-xa* (and its variant *-xi*). The form *-xa* is probably based on the Pukina reflexive marker <-sca> (for Pukina <sca->, see Adelaar and van de Kerke 2009: 135; for Kallawaya *-xa*, see Section 2.2.2). As reflexive *-xa* but especially *-si* differ from the other Kallawaya grammatical markers discussed here in that they are not dummy suffixes or camouflage markers, they will not be considered in the following.

Table 3 provides an overview of these dummy suffixes and camouflage markers.

Table 3: Dummy suffixes and camouflage markers of Kallawaya.

Class	Kallawaya marker	Function	Occurs preferably on words of . . . origin
Dummy suffixes	-tʃu~-tʃʔu	Dummy suffix on plant names	Spanish
	-xan~-kan~ -ken~-len	a) Dummy suffix b) Nominalizer	Aymara, Quechua
Camouflage markers	-ɲito	a) Agentivizer b) Adjectivizer	Pukina, opaque etymology
	u=~u:=	Negation	Pukina, opaque etymology
	-naxa	a) Some semantic relationship b) Abstract and generic nouns c) Nominalizer d) Resultative	Quechua-Aymara; Pukina; opaque etymology
	-sti	a) Adjectivizer b) (Near) synonyms	Pukina; opaque etymology

Before turning to an outline of these markers, I would like to explain briefly the terminological distinction I make between "dummy suffixes" and "camouflage markers" and the grounds on which this distinction rests. In my terminology used here, dummy suffixes add phonological material but no (or hardly any) grammatical meaning to the lexical base they attach to, whereas camouflage markers also add phonological material to the lexical base but additionally express some grammatical meaning (although this may be vague in cases).[12] It appears that in the literature both terms may be used to refer to the same type of manipulative device (see e.g. Matras 2000: 81; Mous 2003: 214). However, as Kallawaya has two classes of grammatical elements that clearly serve to disguise the form of the lexical base but which differ with respect to their grammatical impact, it appears useful to employ two different terms to describe these two different classes of grammatical markers in Kallawaya.

---

[12] This definition was partly inspired by Mous (2003: 214).

2.2.1 Dummy suffixes

The forms -tʃu~-tʃʔu and -xan~-kan~-ken~-len are dummy suffixes. The suffix -tʃu~-tʃʔu is found mainly on botanical denominations of Spanish origin (Examples 3a and b), and also, although less frequently, on zoological names (Example 4).[13] When -tʃu~-tʃʔu is attached, it replaces the last or the last two syllable(s) of the lexical base (see also section 2.3).

(3)   a. *manta-**tʃʔu*** 'mandarin' *mandarina* 'mandarin'   (Spanish)
      b. *kani-**tʃʔu*** 'cinnamon' *canela*   'cinnamon'   (Spanish)[14]

(4)   *xara-**tʃu*** 'small lizard' *xararanqʰu* 'small lizard'   (Aymara)

The etymological origin of -tʃu~-tʃʔu is unclear, although Quechua plant names also often end in -tʃu or -tʃuy (Willem Adelaar p.c.). It is possible that Kallawaya mirrors this pattern from the herbalists' native Quechua, but in contrast to Quechua, the Kallawaya suffix -tʃu~-tʃʔu clearly serves to disguise the otherwise widely intelligible Spanish plant names.

The form -xan and its variants -kan~-ken~-len are used mainly on words of Quechua or Aymara origin, although they can also occur on Spanish terms. Mostly, -xan~-kan~-ken~-len resembles -tʃu~-tʃʔu since its main function lies in disguising the Quechua, Aymara and Spanish words, without expressing any grammatical function (Examples 5a and b). The form -xan~-kan~-ken~-len either follows the base or it may supplant the last syllable of the base it is attached to (Examples 5a and b).

(5)   a. *miʎa-**xan*** 'ugly'   *miʎay* 'repulsive, disgusting'   (Quechua)
      b. *karte-**xan*** 'wallet' *cartera* 'wallet'   (Spanish)

However, in some cases it appears that -xan~-kan~-ken~-len has a nominalizing function, as demonstrated in Example (6).

(6)   *tʔeke-**len*** 'box' *tʔeqe-ɲa* 'to pack, to stuff'   (Aymara)[15]

---

[13] The language names in parentheses indicate the etymological origin of the lexical base in the right-hand column. The left-hand forms are always the Kallawaya terms.
[14] In Example (3a) the voiced bilabial stop [d] becomes devoiced in Kallawaya; in Example (3b), Spanish [e] undergoes vowel raising in Kallawaya.
[15] The form -ɲa is the Aymara infinitive marker.

2.2.2 Camouflage markers

Other grammatical markers of Kallawaya regularly have some grammatical function. This is the case with *-ɲito* which mostly expresses an agentivizing and, less frequently, an adjectivizing function. When attached to verbal bases, *-ɲito* marks an agentive, while the adjectival function is expressed when it follows a nominal base (Examples 7a and b). However, this is anything but a hard and fast rule and there are exceptions to this. Thus, when *-ɲito* follows *tʃusli* 'animal, (wild) beast, shy, livestock, cattle', for instance, it creates another agentive noun, *tʃusli-ɲito* 'cattle farmer', not an adjective. Note that the Pukina agentive marker is <eno> *-eno* (Adelaar and van de Kerke 2009: 136) and as such is formally unrelated to the Kallawaya agentivizer. An origin of Kallawaya *-ɲito* from Pukina <eno> *-eno* is therefore improbable.

(7) a. *isna-ɲito*   'traveller'
      <es~s>, *es-*   'go, travel'   (Pukina)
    b. *pixi-ɲito*   'oedematous'
      pixina~pʔixina~pʔixuna   'oedema, swelling, pustule'   (opaque)

In Kallawaya, negation is expressed by means of the marker $u=\sim u{:}=$. The short variant is the more common one, negating the semantic content of lexical bases as well as entire propositions (Examples 8a and b).

(8) a. *uʎaʎi*   b. *useqnitʃu soqʔeita*
      u=ʎaʎi   *u=seq(a)-ni=tʃu*   *soqʔe-i-ta*
      NEG=good   NEG=know-1SG=NEG   heal-NMLZ-DO
      'inept (lit.: 'not good')'   'I do not know healing.'
                                  (Mondaca 1987: n/p)[16]

The lengthened variant $u{:}=$ can be used as a lexical base itself, carrying discourse clitics and therein strongly resembling its Quechua counterpart *mana* 'no, not'. Compare Example (9a) from Kallawaya with (9b) from Quechua.

(9) a. *u:=puni*   b. *mana=puni*
      NEG=CONF   NEG=CONF
      'impossible'   'definitely not'
                   (Hoggarth 2004: 144)

---

[16] The negation marking enclitic =*tʃu* in (8b) comes from Quechua (Hoggarth 2004: 145).

In general, the morphosyntactic behaviour of Kallawaya *u=~u:=* is strongly reminiscent of the Quechua negation *mana* (Adelaar and Muysken 2004: 360) and it is quite likely that morphosyntactically Kallawaya *u=~u:=* was modelled after the Quechua negation.[17] In this context, it is remarkable that Kallawaya *u=~u:=* appears to be a bound proclitic element because such negation markers are unknown in the present-day Andean languages. However, although in most cases, negated forms are spelt as one word (see Examples 8a and b), suggesting that the researchers perceived elements like *uʎaʎi* 'inept' as a phonological unit, there are counter-examples in which negated elements are presented as orthographically separated from *u=~u:=*. Given the close structural resemblance between Quechua *mana* and Kallawaya *u=~u:=* it appears more plausible assuming that the latter is not a proclitic form, but rather an unbound negative particle, equalling Quechua *mana*. However, this has to remain uncertain as spelling in the sources is inconsistent and orthographic representation is not well suited for phonological statements.

The last two Kallawaya suffixes to be discussed are *-naxa* and *-sti*. Basically, the form *-naxa* has two functions: first, it expresses a somewhat vague semantic relationship between the lexical base and the form inflected with *-naxa*; second, it creates abstract and generic nouns. Examples (10a and b) are instances of the first function: while it is clear that there is some kind of semantic relationship between the lexical base and the *-naxa*-derived form, the exact nature of this relationship is hard to grasp.

(10) a. *sipi-**naxa**-ku-na* 'strangulate'
sipi- 'assassinate, kill, put out' (Quechua)
b. *sitʃi-**naxa**-na* 'to soak'
hitʃa-na 'to pour, spill (liquids or grains)' (Quechua?)

In this function *-naxa* may be related to Pukina for which at least once a verbal modifier <naha> *-naxa* is attested (Simon van de Kerke p.c.). However, as the precise meaning of the Pukina element remains unknown, likewise it will remain uncertain whether Kallawaya *-naxa* in its first function is in some way related to the Pukina marker.

---

17 There is no formal similarity between the Kallawaya negation marker *u=~u:=* and its functional equivalent in Pukina which is <apa~appa> or <ama>; the latter is used in prohibitives (Adelaar and van de Kerke 2009: 141). It is unlikely that the Kallawaya negation marker originates from Pukina.

In its second function, Kallawaya -*naxa* creates abstract and generic nouns. As such, one would expect -*naxa* to be restricted to verbal bases, but it also attaches to nouns, which then receive a more abstract or generic meaning (Examples 11a and b).

(11) a. *kea-**naxa*** 'offspring, seed'
 <guio>, *kiu~qiu* 'son, child'[13] (Pukina)
 b. *suĩ-**naxa*** 'machine, apparatus'
 suĩ 'hand, arm, finger' (Kunza)

Moreover, Kallawaya -*naxa* also has a nominalizing (Example 12a) and resultative-marking function (Example 12b), although both are less frequent.

(12) a. *xirkʔa-**naxa*** 'snag, nuisance'
 harkʔa- 'to obstruct, to block, to impede' (Quechua)
 b. *kʔumu-**naxa**-na* 'to hunch, develop a stoop'
 kʔumu-yku-y 'to tilt' (Quechua)

In its second function, Kallawaya -*naxa* may be a blend of the Quechua nominalizer -*na* (see Hoggarth 2004: 61–66) and the Kallawaya reflexive marker -*xa*. The latter is probably based on the Pukina reflexive marker <sca> (Adelaar and van de Kerke 2009: 135; see also section 2.2). Pukina has a tendency towards word-initial consonant clusters involving [s] which are regularly simplified in Kallawaya (Adelaar and van de Kerke 2009: 128). Thus, the Pukina form <sca> would be realised as *-*ka~-qa* in Kallawaya. As syllable-initial stops become fricatives in Bolivian Quechua (Bills, Vallejo, and Troike 1969: xviii; Willem Adelaar p.c.), *-*ka~-qa* is realised as -*xa* in Kallawaya. If Kallawaya -*naxa* indeed combines the Quechua nominalizer -*na* with the Pukina-based reflexive marker -*xa*, the semantic impact of the Quechua nominalizer -*na* is responsible for the nominalizing functions of Kallawaya -*naxa*, while the impact of -*xa* remains indefinable. It further suggests that Kallawaya has two homophonous forms of -*naxa*: one that might be based on the Pukina verbal modifier, expressing the unclear relationship between base and inflected form (see Examples 10a and b); and another one that has nominalizing functions (see Examples 11a to 12b). Lastly, it should be mentioned that -*naxa*, along with the agentivizer -*ɲito* and the negation marker *u=~u:=*, is one of the most productive suffixes in the Kallawaya database.

---

18 Arjan Mossel and Simon van de Kerke (p.c.) point out that in the respective context of the Oré manuscript this item should actually designate a female offspring.

The last suffix to be described, -*sti,* is also the one least clear. It occurs only seven times in the Kallawaya database and appears to express an adjectival meaning and creates (near) synonyms (Examples 13a and 13b). It is the latter function in which -*sti* resembles the above-mentioned markers -*tʃu~-tʃʔu* and -*xan~-kan~-ken~ -len.* However, in contrast to -*tʃu~-tʃʔu,* -*sti* does not have a preferred semantic domain. Moreover, it differs from -*tʃu~-tʃʔu* and -*xan~-kan~-ken~-len* as -*sti* occurs only on words of Pukina or opaque origin; i.e. on terms that are unintelligible anyway. Note, however, that -*sti* is not attested in the Pukina database.

(13) a. *nuki-**sti*** 'religious'
          nuki 'God, divine'   (opaque)
     b. *xitʃʔa-**sti*** 'shrewd, false, sham'
          xitʃʔa 'false, farce, informality, scheme'   (opaque)

With the exception of Kunza *suĩ-naxa* 'machine, apparatus' (Example 11b), no other Kunza or Ese Ejja items are inflected with any of the dummy suffixes or camouflage markers. This probably relates to a difference in quality between the Kunza and Ese Ejja words, on the one hand, and the Pukina and etymologically opaque items, on the other hand, as perceived by the herbalists (see also section 3). This once more suggests that the use of the dummy suffixes and camouflage markers as attested in Kallawaya points to a high degree of linguistic awareness on the side of the Kallawaya creators and speakers.

2.3 Phonological manipulations

Of the languages that contributed to the Kallawaya lexicon, only Quechua and Aymara show obvious phonological manipulations. Spanish, Ese Ejja and Kunza are not affected by phonological manipulations, while for Pukina and Uru-Chipaya this is unclear, though rather less likely (see also further below). Thus, the following presentation will be restricted to phonological manipulations of Quechua and Aymara lexical items in Kallawaya.

While it is possible to establish etymological and grammatical manipulations in Kallawaya when working with a written database, it is difficult or almost impossible to do the same for phonological manipulations. First, Kallawaya itself shows some variation when it comes to lexical bases and grammatical structures, which may have to do with the observation that the herbalists come from various communities within the Kallawaya region, not just from one village (Muysken 1997: 431–441, 2009: 150–151; Adelaar and Muysken 2004: 358; see section 1.1). Moreover, there is considerable orthographic variation across the sources. Thus, when relying on dictionaries and the Kallawaya written database alone, it is impossible to decide whether, for instance, Kallawaya *musk^{h}u-* 'plait' is a phonological manipulation of Quechua *misk^{h}u-* 'to twist wool or another element into a string' (which it is; see below), an orthographic misrepresentation or a local variation of Quechua *misk^{h}u-*.[19] Thus, in order to rule out – at least as far as possible – local variations and orthographic peculiarities as reasons for deviating Kallawaya words, I asked native speakers of Quechua and Aymara to judge the acceptability of potentially phonologically manipulated Kallawaya items. "Deviating" here means deviation from the lexical form as provided in the Quechua and Aymara dictionaries, especially Lira (1941), *Academia Mayor de la Lengua Quechua* (2005) and Lucca (1983). In a first step, I collected those Kallawaya words that phonologically and semantically resemble a Quechua or Aymara word but deviate from it in some phonological feature. In deciding what phonological features to look for in potentially manipulated Kallawaya items, I consulted the literature on other secret languages, such as Grant (1994), Nieuwkerk (1998), Mous (2003) and Storch (2011), in order to determine what kinds of linguistic manipulation are attested in other secret languages. I then checked the Kallawaya data to decide whether linguistic manipulations reported for other secret languages, such as vowel substitution, can be established for Kallawaya as well. The only possibly manipulated Kallawaya items chosen for the investigation were the ones that show regularly recurring patterns of deviations; i.e. single or rare cases of phonologically deviations were not considered. This resulted in the features of vowel and syllable substitution as well as syllable deletion being chosen for investigation. Another condition was that the Kallawaya words must show only one feature of phonological deviation; i.e. the Kallawaya items may differ in, for instance, a consonant from the allegedly underlying Quechua or Aymara form, but not in a consonant and a (deleted or substituted) syllable. If there is too much deviation, it becomes arguable whether the Kallawaya term in question is really based on the respective Quechua or Aymara word. In addition, the phonologically deviating Kallawaya terms must not show (considerable) semantic deviation from the presumable Quechua or Aymara source items. Thus, the above quoted example of Kallawaya *musk^{h}u-* 'plait' from Quechua *misk^{h}u-* 'to twist wool or another element into a string' is in accordance with these criteria as it differs only by one vowel from its Quechua base and the semantics of the two items are comparable. I am fully aware that this is a very cautious approach and the resulting database is rather small. It is quite possible that applying these narrow criteria excludes Kallawaya items that are

---

19 Example courtesy of Irma Alvarez Ccoscco.

actually instances of phonological manipulation from the database of phonologically manipulated Kallawaya terms. Thus, it is likely that the database of phonologically manipulated Kallawaya words is larger than the one I propose. However, these strict conditions are meant to increase the possibility that we are indeed dealing with the "same" word in Kallawaya and Quechua or Aymara and not with any chance similarity between a Kallawaya and a Quechua or Aymara item.

The Kallawaya terms thus identified were put into questionnaires, along with their presumable Quechua or Aymara bases and their Spanish translation.[20] In the questionnaires, I did not indicate whether a lexical item comes from Kallawaya or from Quechua or Aymara. These questionnaires were then presented to native speakers of Quechua and Aymara.[21] In the questionnaires as well as during the interviews, I asked the language consultants which of the two or three words appeared to be the correct one or whether both or all were correct; and whether some forms were used only by elderly people or only in particular regions. This way, it was possible to determine that some forms that look like phonological manipulation in Kallawaya are actually local variations. This is the case with, for instance, Aymara *kʔana* 'plait' and Kallawaya *kʔani* 'plait'. The Aymara dictionary of Lucca (1983: 878) only provides *kʔana* 'plait', but the Aymara language consultants agreed that both forms can be used. I interpreted only those Kallawaya words as phonological manipulations that the language consultants judged to be unacceptable as Quechua or Aymara words with respect to their phonological form and semantic content. Thus, for instance, Irma Alvarez

---

20 The questionnaire sent to Irma Alvarez Ccoscco in November 2013 did not yet contain the Spanish translation but only the Kallawaya and Quechua forms.

21 For Quechua, I owe thanks to Irma Alvarez Ccoscco and Nelly Quispe; for Aymara, I am indebted to Hortencia E. Condori Quispe, Dr. Teófilo Laime Ajacopa, Mag. Sc. Sotero Ajacopa Pairuani and Lic. Sorata Ajacopa. I contacted Irma Alvarez Ccoscco per email in November 2013 and sent her the questionnaire by email as well. I received the completed questionnaire from Irma Alvarez Ccoscco by email. All other language consultants were interviewed in person in November 2014 in La Paz, Viacha and Irohito (Department of La Paz, Bolivia). Note that in answer to the question for the consultants' native language(s), most consultants simply named "Quechua" or "Aymara" as their native language. Irma Alvarez Ccoscco further specified it by adding that she speaks Quechua Cuzco-Collao (i.e. Quechua IIC; Adelaar and Muysken 2004: 184) and Lic. Sorata Ajacopa also clarified that his native Aymara variety is central Aymara as spoken in La Paz. The term "Aymara central" is sometimes used in the literature to refer to the Aymara varieties spoken near Lima which are (almost) extinct (Adelaar and Muysken 2004: 170, footnote 4, 171; see also Cerrón-Palomino and Carvajal Carvajal 2009: 172). However, by stating that he refers to the Aymara variety as used in La Paz, Lic. Sorata Ajacopa makes it clear that he refers to the Bolivian Aymara variety and distinguishes his variety further from those spoken further north or south on the Bolivian high plateau.

Ccoscco judges the Kallawaya item *tʃʔuʎuku* 'cricket' to be unacceptable as a Quechua word with the meaning of 'cricket': in Quechua; it must be *tʃʔiʎiku* 'cricket' and *tʃʔuʎuku* with the meaning of 'cricket' is simply not acceptable.

In this way, I identified two basic types of phonological manipulations in Kallawaya: substitution and deletion of phonological elements. I will begin by outlining the substitution of vowels and syllables before turning to the deletion of syllables.

Substitution affects vowels and syllables. Although Quechua, too, shows vowel fluctuation between [i] and [a] (Adelaar and Muysken 2004: 198), the Kallawaya herbalists over-exploit this strategy from their native language in two ways. First, in Kallawaya not only [i] and [a] are affected by substitution but also other vowels that are not subject to vowel substitution in Quechua, such as [u] and [o] (Examples 14a and b; see also Kallawaya *tʃʔuʎuku* 'cricket' above). Second, words in Kallawaya are affected by vowel substitution that do not show vowel fluctuation in Quechua (Examples 15a and b).[22] Note that one or both stem vowels can show vowel substitution.

(14) a. *kʰumu-* 'chew, ruminate
       kʰamu- 'bite, chew'   (Quechua)
    b. *kʔoʎpo-* 'roll up'
       qʔaʎpa- 'roll up'   (Quechua)[23]

(15) a. *kusa-* 'amuse, play'
       kusi- 'have fun'   (Quechua)
    b. *pimpi* 'plain, pampas'
       pampa 'plain, pampas'   (Quechua)

Moreover, not only Quechua but also Aymara words are subject to vowel substitution although Aymara does not display vowel fluctuation.[24] The mechanisms

---

22 The upper examples come from Kallawaya, while the lower examples are from Quechua or Aymara. Elements affected by phonological manipulation are marked bold.
23 The difference between the velar stop in Kallawaya and the uvular stop in Quechua is not a phonological manipulation. Rather, the realisation of Quechua /q/ as /k/ in Kallawaya may reflect a certain variation in Bolivian Quechua itself (Bills, Vallejo, and Troike 1969: xvi) (see also Examples 18d and 19b).
24 Note, however, that the above cited instance of *kʔani* and *kʔana*, both meaning 'plait', suggests that Aymara may have vowel fluctuation after all, although possibly only where it has been in contact with Quechua (as is the case in the Titicaca area). However, this requires further investigation.

for vowel substitution in Aymara words are the same as for Quechua outlined above; i.e. not only [i] and [a] are affected but other vowels, too, and vowel substitution can occur in one or both stem vowels; the latter, however, is exceptional (Examples 16a and b).

(16)   a. *tʔiwi* 'sand'
        tʔiwu 'sand' (Aymara)
   b. *peke-* 'to sparkle, to glitter'
        paka- 'to sparkle, to glitter' (Aymara)

Not only vowels but syllables, too, display substitution. Most often the last or the last two syllables of a word are affected (see also Examples 3a to 4 in section 2.2.1). The tendency to modify base-final material may have to do with the overall suffixing structure of Kallawaya. Usually, the syllable(s) of the original Quechua or Aymara word are substituted by an equal number of camouflage syllables (Examples 17a and b) but occasionally the number of substituted syllables is higher or lower (Examples 17c and d).

(17)   a. *ajariri* 'mist'
        aqarapi 'dim snowfall' (Quechua)[25]
   b. *tʃoxna* 'wound, knock'
        tʃoxri 'wound, knock' (Aymara)
   c. *wislulu* 'oil'
        wiswi 'grease, oil, dirt' (Quechua)
   d. *kʔirki-* 'grind'
        kʔiririri- 'grind' (onomat.) (Quechua)

Kallawaya does not have a fixed set of camouflage syllables, unlike the fixed inventory of dummy suffixes and camouflage markers (see section 2.2) and any Quechua or Aymara syllable can be substituted by camouflage syllable(s) in Kallawaya.[26]

---

25 The realisation of the Quechua uvular stop [q] in Kallawaya as [x] results from the above-mentioned fricativization of syllable-initial stops in Bolivian Quechua (Bills, Vallejo, and Troike 1969: xviii; see Section 2.2.2).

26 This is also the reason why the dummy suffix *-tʃu~-tʃʔu* (Section 2.2.1) is not considered a phonological but a grammatical manipulation. Although the patterns of substitution are similar, the dummy suffix *-tʃu~-tʃʔu* has a largely invariant form and, moreover, attaches regularly only to botanical and zoological denominations. It differs therein from the kind of syllable substitution described above and is therefore classified as a grammatical manipulation.

As with the substitution of syllables, mainly base-final material gets deleted and deletion affects the last syllable of the Quechua or Aymara base. Consider Examples (18a to d).

(18) a. *waʎke* 'bag'
 *waʎke**pu*** 'pouch for carrying coca' (Aymara)
 b. *tʃʔiti*[27] 'sprinkle, splash'
 *tʃʔite**ka**-* 'sprinkle persons or objects with drops of liquid' (Aymara)
 c. *taka* 'post, stake'
 *taka**rpu*** 'post, stake' (Quechua)
 d. *kʔaūsi*
 'chew (a chewing gum)'
 *qʔaūsi**ʎu*** 'rubbery, elastic when chewing' (Quechua)

In Examples (19a and b) initial and internal material is deleted, although for Example (19a) it is arguable whether this presents an instance of deliberate phonological manipulation or rather results from contraction due to rapid speech.

(19) a. *tʃiriri* 'cicada'
 tʃiri tʃiri 'cicada' (Aymara)
 b. *xarankʰu* '(small) lizard'
 xararanqʰu 'lizard' (Aymara)

Lastly, I would like to point to some interesting cases where phonological manipulation results in Kallawaya items that are phonologically identical to Quechua or Aymara words but whose semantics differ. Thus, the form *wari*, meaning 'shout, scream, cry' in Kallawaya, probably from Aymara *warari* 'give cries of pain', means 'vicuña' in Aymara.[28] Equally, the form *kusa-*, in Kallawaya meaning 'amuse, play', derived from Quechua *kusi-* 'have fun' (see Example 15a), has the meaning of 'to roast' in Quechua.[29] Whether this is another intended effect of phonological manipulation or just a coincidental side-effect has to remain open.

Phonological manipulation in Kallawaya is unpredictable and it is so in at least two ways. First, it is unpredictable whether phonological manipulation will

---

[27] Vowel raising of Aymara [e] to Kallawaya [i] is not considered a phonological manipulation.
[28] I am indebted to Lic. Sorata Ajaccpa for pointing this out to me.
[29] I owe this observation to Irma Alvarez Ccoscco.

occur at all. Thus, Aymara p^hoka 'full, complete' becomes p^hoko 'full' in Kallawaya, but Aymara $pʔeke$ 'head' remains $pʔeke$ 'head' in Kallawaya, although the phonological structure of the two bases; i.e. p^hoka and $pʔeke$, is comparable. Whether phonological manipulation takes place or not is apparently independent of the phonological shape of the Quechua or Aymara lexical base. Second, it cannot be anticipated which form a phonological manipulation will take; i.e. whether a Quechua or Aymara lexical base will be affected by vowel substitution, syllable substitution or syllable deletion. Moreover, the form of the substituted vowel or syllable is equally unpredictable and there is no rule that would state that, for instance, Quechua [i] always becomes [a] in Kallawaya. Also, and as already mentioned above, there is no fixed set of camouflage syllables that are used in syllable substitution. Instead, the phonological form of the substituted syllable in Kallawaya appears to be randomly chosen. Thus, phonological manipulation in Kallawaya is the least systematic type of linguistic manipulation in Kallawaya.

It appears that Pukina words in Kallawaya are not affected by phonological manipulation. However, while in most cases, changes made to Pukina items in Kallawaya can be explained by the characteristics of (Bolivian) Quechua phonology, such as simplification of word-initial consonant clusters or fricativisation of syllable-initial stops (see section 2.2.2), in other cases the modifications are not so easily explicable.[30] Thus, it remains unclear why Pukina <scata> *skata~sqata* 'ten', for instance, becomes *xotʃa~xutʃa~k^hotʃa* 'ten' in Kallawaya and not just **kata*, **qata* or **xata*. As a tendency, monosyllabic Pukina bases become disyllabic in Kallawaya, maybe because many Quechua lexical bases are also disyllabic. Thus, for instance, the monosyllabic Pukina base <co> *qu* 'brother' is realised in Kallawaya as *sexo* 'friend, comrade, companion' (see no. 32 in the Appendix).[31] In adding seemingly random syllables, these Pukina words resemble the above presented Quechua and Aymara words where random syllables are substituted. However, other Pukina items do not show the same regularly observable phonological manipulations as discussed above for Quechua and Aymara. The picture is similar for Uru-Chipaya words in Kallawaya. In some cases, modifications of Uru-Chipaya items may be explained by adaptation to the phoneme inventory of Kallawaya which is similar to that of Southern Quechua (see section 1.1). Thus, Uru *tʃiɲ-* 'plait' is realised in Kallawaya as *tʃintʃi-* 'to plait' probably because Kallawaya does not allow for a palatal nasal to be in final position and usually requires a vowel in base-final position. However,

---

30 Adelaar and Muysken (2004: 357) point out that sound changes between Pukina and Kallawaya are not always regular.
31 The form <co> is based on Torero's transcription of Oré's Pukina form (Torero 2002: 453).

in other cases, modifications made to Uru-Chipaya words in Kallawaya appear to be unmotivated. This is the case for Uru *misi-* 'to hurt' (*mis-* 'to hurt' in Chipaya) and Kallawaya *mixi-* 'to hurt' (see Example 1). A phonological structure like *misi-* is acceptable in Kallawaya since it is also attested in Kallawaya *masi-* '(social) class', for instance. Therefore, the change from Uru-Chipaya *mis(i)-* 'to hurt' to Kallawaya *mixi-* 'to hurt' may be a phonological manipulation. However, the overall number of Uru-Chipaya words in Kallawaya which allow an interpretation as possibly phonologically manipulated items is rather small (there are only seven instances). Moreover, we also have to take into consideration that phonological deviances between Kallawaya and Uru-Chipaya may relate to an unrecorded Pukina item; i.e. phonologically deviating Kallawaya and Uru-Chipaya items may be actually shared borrowings, tracing back to Pukina, where the Pukina source item has just been realised differently in Kallawaya and Uru-Chipaya. Therefore, I suggest that most Uru-Chipaya items in Kallawaya are probably not subject to the same phonological manipulations as proposed for Quechua and Aymara words. As mentioned above, neither Spanish nor Kunza nor Ese Ejja items are affected by phonological manipulations and especially with respect to the latter two this give once more testimony to the linguistic awareness of the Kallawaya creators and speakers.

3 Summarising discussion and conclusion

In the preceding sections, I discussed etymological, grammatical and phonological manipulations of Kallawaya. Table 4 summarises the several types of linguistic manipulations and their etymological distribution in Kallawaya. Note, however, that this is a schematic and somewhat oversimplified representation of Kallawaya linguistic manipulations: in reality, the boundaries between the etymological origin of a lexical item and the linguistic manipulation by which it may be affected are not as clear-cut as presented in Table 4. The uncertain status of Uru-Chipaya with respect to phonological manipulations is indicated by a question mark (?).

Although this is a simplified representation, what transpires is that linguistic manipulations in Kallawaya are not as unsystematic as they may seem at first glance. Rather, it appears that the creators and speakers of Kallawaya show a high degree of linguistic awareness concerning the etymological origin of the lexical items of their secret language. That is, the Kallawaya creators and speakers must have recognised the different etymological origins of the lexical items that constitute the Kallawaya lexicon. They must have further understood that some words are foreign enough in themselves so as not to require any further disguise (Ese Ejja

Table 4: Schematic overview of linguistic manipulations in Kallawaya.

Linguistic manipulations	Etymological origin	Linguistic manipulations
dummy suffixes (grammatical manipulations)	Spanish	phonological manipulations
	Quechua	
	Aymara	
	Uru-Chipaya (?)	
lexical reservoir of secret words (etymological manipulations)	Pukina	camouflage markers (grammatical manipulations)
	etymologically opaque items	
	Kunza	
	Ese Ejja	

and Kunza words). And, lastly, they must have made up different rules according to which they manipulated the etymologically different lexical items (grammatical and/or phonological manipulations). Thus, it is ultimately the etymological origin of a lexical item that decides which type of linguistic manipulation is applied to the lexical item (or whether any further grammatical or phonological manipulation is applied at all; see the Kunza and Ese Ejja items). If the Kallawaya speakers as represented in the sources from approximately 1950 to around 1970 maintain the etymological distinctions made with respect to the linguistic manipulations, then this suggests that these speakers were still aware of the etymological origins of the lexical items of their secret language (see also section 1.1).

From a broader perspective, Kallawaya fits in nicely with other secret and non-secret languages that display deliberate changes (see Thomason 2007). Several secret and non-secret languages show deliberate changes for reasons of secrecy or to make a clear distinction to the speech of their neighbours' (Thomason 2007: 50, 51). These "[d]eliberate changes can be found in all grammatical subsystems, from the phonology to the morphology to the syntax and the lexicon, including lexical semantics as well as the forms of words" (Thomason 2007: 50), an observation that also applies to Kallawaya. Moreover, the types of deliberate changes found in other languages (secret or not) are at least partly attested for Kallawaya as well, such as the addition of affixes, sound changes, coinage of words, among others (see Thomason 2007: 50–53). Thus, within the admittedly small field of languages displaying deliberate changes, Kallawaya is not exceptional but rather a good example of linguistic creativity. The conscious use of deliberate linguistic manipulations gives testimony to how linguistic awareness and linguistic creativity of speakers can fashion a (secret) language.

Abbreviations

CONF	confirmative
DO	direct object
EP	epenthetic element
NEG	negation
NMLZ	nominalizer
PL	plural
POR	possessor
PROMPT	promptness
1SG	first person singular
1PL.INCL	first person plural inclusive
1PL.INCL.FUT	first person plural inclusive future
3SG.POS	third person singular possessive
3PL	third person plural
onomat.	onomatopoeic
~	variation

References

Academia Mayor de la Lengua Quechua. 2005. *Diccionario Quechua-Español-Quechua. Qheswa-Español-Qheswa. Simi Tcqe*. 2nd edn. Cusco, Peru: Gobierno Regional Cusco. http://www.illa-a.org/cd/diccionarios/DicAMLQuechua.pdf (accessed 13 September 2018).

Adelaar, Willem. 2007. Threatened languages in Hispanic South America. In Matthias Brenzinger (ed.), *Language diversity endangered*, 9–28. Berlin: Mouton de Gruyter.

Adelaar, Willem & Pieter Muysken. 2004. *The languages of the Andes*. Cambridge: Cambridge University Press.

Adelaar, Willem & Simon van de Kerke. 2009. Puquina. In Mily Crevels & Pieter Muysken (eds.), *Lenguas de Bolivia. Ámbito andino*, vol. 1, 125–146. La Paz, Bolivia: Embajada de Reino de los Países Bajos & MUSEF & Plural Editores.

Adorno, Rolena. 2004. *The Guaman Poma website. About the transcription and its critical apparatus*. http://www.kb.dk/permalink/2006/poma/info/en/foreword.htm and http://www.kb.dk/permalink/2006/poma/333/en/text/?open=idm46287306171424&imagesize=XL (accessed 17 April 2019).

Albó, Xavier. 1995. *Bolivia plurilingüe. Guia para planificadores y educadores*. Vol. 1 and 2. La Paz, Bolivia: Centro de Investigación y Promoción del Campesinado (CIPCA) & UNICEF.

Alexiades, Miguel N., A. Machuqui, & J. Monje (eds.). 2009. *Proceso de reivindicación territorial del pueblo Ese Ejja en el Bajo Heath boliviano. Bases para su sustentación, diagnóstico situacional y memoria actualizada (2006–208)* [sic!]. Riberalta, Bolivia: CIPEA (Capitanía Indígena del Pueblo Ese Ejja de la Amazonía), Portachuelo, Bolivia & CIRABO (Central Indígena de la Región Amazónica Boliviana).

Anderson, Gregory & David Harrison. 2007. *The Kallawaya language project*. https://livingtongues.org/kallawaya/ (accessed 13 September 2018).

Bastien, Joseph W. 1978. *Mountain of the condor. Metaphor and ritual in an Andean ayllu*. Long Grove, Illinois: West Publishing Company.
Bills, Garland D., Bernardo Vallejo C. & Rudolph C. Troike. 1969. *An introduction to spoken Bolivian Quechua*. Austin & London: The University of Texas Press.
Callahan, Mollie. 2011. *Signs of the time: Kallawaya medical expertise and social reproduction in 21st century Bolivia*. University of Michigan dissertation. https://deepblue.lib.umjch. edu/bitstream/handle/2027.42/84575/molliec_1.pdf (accessed 13 September 2018).
Cerrón-Palomino, Rodolfo. 1994. *Quechumara. Estructuras paralelas de las lenguas quechua y aimara*. La Paz, Bolivia: Centro de Investigación y Promoción del Campesinado (CIPCA).
Cerrón-Palomino, Rodolfo. 2006. *El chipaya o la lengua de los hombres del agua*. Lima: Fondo Editorial de la Pontificia Universidad Católica del Perú.
Cerrón-Palomino, Rodolfo. 2009. Chipaya. In Mily Crevels & Pieter Muysken (eds.), *Lenguas de Bolivia. Ámbito andino*, vol. 1, 29–77. La Paz, Bolivia: Embajada de Reino de los Países Bajos & MUSEF & Plural Editores.
Cerrón-Palomino, Rodolfo. 2013. *Las lenguas de los Incas: el puquina, el aimara y el quechua*. Frankfurt am Main: Peter Lang.
Cerrón-Palomino, Rodolfo & Juan Carvajal Carvajal. 2009. Aimara. In Mily Crevels & Pieter Muysken (eds.), *Lenguas de Bolivia. Ámbito andino*, vol. 1, 169–213. La Paz, Bolivia: Embajada de Reino de los Países Bajos & MUSEF & Plural Editores.
Garcilaso de la Vega, Inca. 1960 [1944] [1617]. *Comentarios reales de los Incas*, vol. 2. Madrid: BAE LXXIII.
Gifford, Douglas J. & Elizabeth Lancaster. ca. 1988. *Tradition and change among the grassroots of Callawaya indigenous medicine*. University of St. Andrews, Scotland: Centre for Latin American Linguistic Studies.
Girault, Louis. 1984. *Kallawaya, guérisseurs itinérants des Andes*. Paris: Éditions de l'ORSTOM.
Girault, Louis. 1989. *Kallawaya: el idioma secreto de los Incas: diccionario*. La Paz, Bolivia: UNICEF & Panamerican Health Organisation (OPS) & World Health Organisation (OMS).
Grant, Anthony. 1994. Shelta: the secret language of Irish Travellers viewed as a mixed language. In Peter Bakker & Maarten Mous (eds.), *Mixed languages: 15 case studies in language intertwining*, 123–150. Amsterdam: Institute for Functional Research into Language and Language Use.
Grasserie, Raoul de la. 1894. *Langue Puquina: textes Puquina. Contenus dans le Rituale seu Manuale Peruanum de Geronimo de Ore* [sic!], *publié à Naples en 1607*. Leipzig: Köhler.
Hannß, Katja. 2008. *Uchumataqu. The lost language of the Urus of Bolivia. A grammatical description of the language as documented between 1894 and 1952*. Nijmegen, the Netherlands: Radboud University PhD dissertation.
Hannß, Katja. 2014. Reduplication strategies in Kallawaya. In Swintha Danielsen, Katja Hannß & Fernando Zúñiga (eds.), *Word formation in South American languages*, 163–180. Amsterdam & Philadelphia: Benjamins.
Hannß, Katja (comp.). 2015. *An etymological dictionary of Kallawaya*. Language Archive Cologne. https://hdl.handle.net/11341/00-0000-0000-0000-1AD5-6 (accessed 31 January 2020).
Hannß, Katja. 2017. The etymology of Kallawaya. *Journal of Language Contact* 10(2). 219–263.
Hannß, Katja. 2019. Formation of the Kallawaya language. *Journal of Pidgin and Creole Languages* 34(2). 243–286.
Hoggarth, Leslie. 2004. *Contributions to Cuzco Quechua grammar*. Aachen: Shaker Verlag.

Isbell, William H. 2012. Middle Horizon imperialism and the prehistoric dispersal of Andean languages. In Paul Heggarty & David Beresford-Jones (eds.), *Archaeology and language in the Andes. A cross-disciplinary exploration of prehistory*, 219–245. Oxford: Oxford University Press.
Jiménez de la Espada, Marcos (ed.). 1965 [1573]. *Relaciones Geográficas de Indias – Perú*. Madrid: BAE CLXXXIII – CLXXXV.
Lehmann, Walter. 1929. *Vocabularion de la lengua Uro sacado por Dr. W. Lehmann, en el pueblocito de Hãnko Hãkē o sea Ũru ērũĩtũ* ("estancia de Ũros" el día 12 de octubre 1929. [sic!]. Ms. Berlin: Ibero-Amerikanisches Institut.
Lira, Jorge A. 1941. *Diccionario kkechuwa-español*. Tucumán: Universidad Nacional de Tucumán.
Lucca, Manuel de. 1983. *Diccionario aymara-castellano. Castellano-aymara*. La Paz, Bolivia: Comisión de Alfabetización y Literatura en Aymara.
Matras, Yaron. 2000. Mixed languages: a functional-communicative approach. *Bilingualism: Language and Cognition* 3(2). 79–99.
Matras, Yaron & Peter Bakker. 2003. The study of mixed languages. In Yaron Matras & Peter Bakker (eds.), *The mixed language debate: Theoretical and empirical advances*, 1–20. Berlin & New York: Mouton de Gruyter.
Meyers, Rodica. 2002. *Cuando el sol caminaba por la tierra. Orígenes de la intermediación kallawaya*. La Paz, Bolivia: Plural Editores.
Mondaca, Jaime. 1987. *La lengua callawaya. Apuntes de un cuaderno de campo*. University of St. Andrews, Scotland: Centre for Latin American Linguistic Studies.
Mous, Maarten. 2003. The linguistic properties of lexical manipulation and its relevance for Ma'á. In Yaron Matras & Peter Bakker (eds.), *The mixed language debate: Theoretical and empirical advances*, 209–235. Berlin & New York: Mouton De Gruyter.
Muysken, Pieter. 1997. Callahuaya. In Sarah G. Thomason (ed.), *Contact languages. A wider perspective*, 427–448. Amsterdam: John Benjamins.
Muysken, Pieter. 2009. Kallawaya. In Mily Crevels & Pieter Muysken (eds.), *Lenguas de Bolivia. Ámbito andino*, vol. 1, 147–167. La Paz, Bolivia: Embajada de Reino de los Países Bajos & MUSEF & Plural Editores.
Muysken, Pieter. 2012. Modelling the Quechua-Aymara relationships: structural features, sociolinguistic scenarios and possible archaeological evidence. In Paul Heggarty & David Beresford-Jones (eds.), *Archaeology and language in the Andes. A cross-disciplinary exploration of prehistory*, 85–109. Oxford: Oxford University Press.
Nieuwkerk, Karin van. 1998. Secret communication and marginality. The case of Egyptian entertainers. *Sharqiyyât* 10. 27–40.
Oblitas Poblete, Enrique. 1968. *El idioma secreto de los Incas (Vocabulario castellano-callahuaya)*. La Paz, Bolivia: Editorial 'Los Amigos del Libro'.
Oblitas Poblete, Enrique. 1978. *Cultura callawaya*, 2nd edn. La Paz, Bolivia: Ediciones Populares Camarlinghi.
Oré, Luis Jerónimo de. 1607. *Rituale seu Manuale Peruanum*. Naples: n/p.
Ponce Sanjinés, Carlos. n.d. unpublished field notes. n/p.
Relaciones Geográficas de Indias, see Jiménez de la Espada.
Saignes, Thierry. 1985. *Los Andes orientales: Historia de un olvido*. Cochabamba, Bolivia: Centro de Estudios de la Realidad Económica y Social.
Santa Cruz Pachacuti, Juan de. 1613. *Relación de las antigüedades de este Reyno del Pirú*. Madrid: BAE XXIX.

Sillar, Bill. 2012. Accounting for the spread of Quechua and Aymara between Cuzco and Lake Titicaca. In Paul Heggarty & David Beresford-Jones (eds.), *Archaeology and language in the Andes. A cross-disciplinary exploration of prehistory*, 295–319. Oxford: Oxford University Press.

Soria Lens, Luis. 1951. Pequeño vocabulario callawaya. *Boletín de la Sociedad Geográfica de La Paz* 71–72. 32–35.

Stark, Louisa R. 1972. Machaj-Juyay: Secret language of the Callahuayas. *Papers in Andean Linguistics* 1. 199–218.

Storch, Anne. 2011. *Secret manipulations: language and context in Africa*. Oxford Scholarship Online. DOI: 10.1093/acprof:oso/9780199768974.001.0001 (accessed 10 September 2018).

Thomason, Sarah G. 2001. *Language contact*. Edinburgh: Edinburgh University Press.

Thomason, Sarah G. 2007. Language contact and deliberate change. *Journal of Language Contact* 1. 41–62.

Torero, Alfredo. 1965. *Le Puquina, la troisème langue générale du Pérou*. Paris: Université de la Sorbonne dissertation.

Torero, Alfredo. 2002. *Idiomas de los Andes. Lingüística e historia*. Lima: IFEA & Editorial Horizonte.

Trimborn, Hermann & Antje Kelm (eds.). 1967. *Francisco de Avila*. Berlin: Gebr. Mann Verlag. http://publications.iai.spk-berlin.de/servlets/MCRFileNodeServlet/Document_derivate_00000250/Quellenwerke_VIII_Teil_01.pdf (accessed 17 April 2019).

Vuillermet, Marine. 2012. *A grammar of Ese Ejja, a Takanan language of the Bolivian Amazon*. Lyon: Université Lumière Lyon 2 dissertation. http://www.marinevuillermet.com/these/complete-thesis/ (accessed 13 September 2018).

Wachtel, Nathan. 1986. Men of the water: the Uru problem (sixteenth and seventeenth centuries). In John V. Murra (ed.), *Anthropological history of Andean polities*, 283–310. Cambridge: Cambridge University Press.

Appendix. Pukina-Kallaway shared borrowings

	Kallawaya lexical item	Meaning	Pukina lexical item
1.	atʃa-~atʃe-~xatʃa-	be, evidence, exist, to function, have, make, evidence, exist, be in the habit of doing s.th., succeed, live	<ascha> aʃa-: be, exist, be of use
2.	axna-~axne-~axni-	abandon, to pass, leave, distribute, forget, loose	<acro> akru-~aqru-: leave, abandon
3.	etka~etqa	brave, wild, vigorous, fury, bravery, hostile, inclement, anger, bad, set against, perverse, rage, ill feeling, strictness, serious, severe	<ento> ento: bad
4.	ikili~ikile	father, friend (fig.), brother, papa	<yqui, iqui, qui> iki: father, mister
5.	isna-	go, travel	<es-, s-> es-: go
6.	iti:-~itʰi-~xiti-	take, seize, hold up, possess, take root, take effect, to touch	<yti> iti: receive, take possession
7.	kaman~qaman	day, time	<camen, gamen> kamen: day
8.	katu	interior, deep	<catto, katto> kattu: interior
9.	kea~qea	baby, rearing, female, son, infant, offspring	<guio> kiu~qiu: son
10.	komsi~qomsi	dog, bitch	<conʃe> qunsi: dog
11.	komu~kumu ~kuni itʰi	all, total	<coma> kuma: all
12.	kʰi:~ki:	now, today, recent(ly)	<ca, kaa> ka:: now
13.	la:xa~laxa	man, male	<raago, rahago> ra:ko: male
14.	lili ko:n	testicle(s)	<con> qun: penis
15.	mata-~matʃi-	to clean	<mata, mati> mata-~mati-: to clean, clean, tidy
16.	me:~mi:~mil	people, individual, person, courtier	<maña, meñ, miñ, mñ> meɲ: man, people, indigenous

(continued)

	Kallawaya lexical item	Meaning	Pukina lexical item
17.	mili~mi:li	mother, mum	‹ymi, mi› imi~umi: mother, madam
18.	mini~mini:	name, to name	‹mana, men› men: name
19.	moxsa	meeting, gathering of people	‹mocsca, moxca› muqqa-: assemble, gather
20.	nisi~nitʃi	I, me	‹ni› ni: I
21.	okʰa-~uka-	buy, sell, to transfer, bankruptcy, realise, realisation, pay ransom for, to deal	‹vhcga, vqu› uka-: buy
22.	okʔo~oko~oqo	moon, month	‹vque› uqe: moon
23.	oxa-	eat, food, nourish, feed	‹occa, ohcga, oxa, vca, vxa› uqqa-: eat
24.	pakas	field, small farm, estate, region, land	‹ pacas, huacas, pacaʃʃo› pakas: land, world
25.	pil~pili~piʎi	four	‹sper› sper: four
26.	pipi	meat, flesh, muscle	‹pip, pipe› pip: meat, flesh, body
27.	raka-~raxka-~taxra-	to work, work, labour, to practice	‹tacsca› taqqa-: to work
28.	rex~rej	field, small farm, land	‹re, ree› re: field, small farm, land
29.	ruʎin	a person that becomes a relative and settles oneself in that place (i.e. in the house)	‹rullin› ruʎin: a certain relative
30.	saʷ	heart, breast	‹ʃee, ʃe e, ʃe he, fehe, ʃe› seʔe: heart
31.	saxa-~saqa-	fence in, close, lock in, wall up	‹ʃaga› saka-: to hide
32.	sexo	friend, sharecropper, comrade, caste, colleague, compatriot, companion	‹co› qu: brother
33.	soke~sokei ~soqʔe	cure, drug, medicine, remedy	‹focnu› soqnu: potion, brew

(continued)

	Kallawaya lexical item	Meaning	Pukina lexical item
34.	so:~so~su~su:~suju~sujo	two	\<so\> so: two
35.	teka-~tʰeka-	to dream	\<taha\> taxa-: to dream
36.	tutin	seven	\<stu\> stu: seven
37.	tʃʔa-	ado, fuss, shout, lament	\<cha\> tʃa-: cry out, demand
38.	uʎi-	to find, come across	\<vlli\> uʎi-: to reach, catch up with, achieve
39.	utan	field, small farm, land	\<vta\> uta: field, small farm, land
40.	xata-~xatʔa-	caress, desire, to like, enjoy, aspire to, want	\<hata\> xata-: desire, want
41.	xe:~xeito~xuitu~xi~xiʔi~kʰe:	llama	\<he\> xe: llama
42.	xotʃa~xutʃa~kʰotʃa	ten	\<scata\> skata~sqata: ten
43.	xuja-	chat, verse, say, speak, speech, language, modulate, narrate, word, tell, to report, report	\<holla\> xuʎa-: speak, say

J. Clancy Clements, Patrícia Amaral and Jordan Garrett
Social identity and the formation and development of Barranquenho

1 Introduction

The border region between Portugal and Spain, locally known as *A Raia* or *La Raya* 'the border, boundary', has been an area of several Portuguese-Spanish contact situations, in some cases, for centuries. In his fieldwork along the border, Clements (2009) reports that Portuguese-Spanish bilingualism is fairly common. Barranquenho – a hybrid variety spoken in Barrancos, Portugal for at least 150 years – emerged from the contact between speakers of Portuguese and Spanish and has received some attention from scholars dating back to the renowned philologist Leite de Vasconcelos's monograph published in 1955. Although this and more recent work by Navas Sánchez-Élez (1992, 1994, 1996, 1997, 2001) are mostly seminal in nature, this contact situation is only now becoming known to the wider audience in contact linguistics in more recent research.

In addition to several of the multiple settings in which contact varieties arise, the Barrancos situation is interesting because over the centuries the area has been claimed by both Portugal and Spain, many times, back and forth, leading to a prolonged language contact situation. There is evidence suggesting that as early as the 16th century there was Portuguese-Spanish contact in Barrancos. We review this evidence and then discuss various features that define Barranquenho, drawing on studies by Leite de Vasconcelos (1955), as well as those by Clements (2009), Clements, Amaral, and Luís (2008), Taylor (2014), Garrett (in press), all of which are based largely on a corpus of transcribed speech of 20 Barranquenho speakers. We then attempt to respond to the question about whether the details of the history of Barrancos help us define, or not, what type of contact variety Barranquenho is.[1]

---

[1] When using the terms *Portuguese* and *Spanish* here, we are referring exclusively to European Portuguese and Andalusian Spanish. However, with regard to clitic form and placement in Spanish, our generalizations apply to Spanish in general.

J. Clancy Clements, Indiana University Bloomington, clements@indiana.edu
Patrícia Amaral, Indiana University Bloomington, pamara@indiana.edu
Jordan Garrett, Indiana University Bloomington, garretjm@indiana.edu

2 Historical background of the Barrancos area

The history of Barrancos and the nearby Noudar castle goes back to the Middle Ages. For centuries the area was under the rule of the Moors who had conquered the Iberian Peninsula in the beginning of the 8th century. As the Christians began to organize themselves across the northern part of the peninsula, there were battles against the Moors but also battles among the different emerging political entities among the Christians. The players that concern us here are Portugal, Galicia, and Castile-Leon. From the 9th to the 12th century, the borders between what would become the three kingdoms just mentioned were fluid (Serrão and Marques 1990: 59–60). Portugal defined itself first as a county in 1094 and later as a kingdom in 1179 (Serrão and Marques 1990: 263; Marques 1998: 35–37). Over the ensuing 800+ years, the area encompassing Barrancos and the nearby Noudar was bounced between the kingdoms of Portugal and Castile several times (Coelho 1999). Beginning as early as the 13th century, Portugal and Castile signed two important border-related agreements or treaties: that of Badajoz and that of Alcañices. In the Badajoz agreement, the two political entities reached a decision to use the Guadiana River as the border between the kingdoms. As is apparent from Map 1

Map 1: The area of *A Raia* on the southern Portugal-Spain border relevant for our study.

above, this puts Barrancos and the nearby town of Moura in Castile. Maia (2001: 3) states that borders, especially in the Middle Ages, are best understood as *zonas-frontera* or 'border zones' rather than border lines, and that these zones were defined by a long string of castles from north to south. The castle closest to Barrancos is the Noudar castle, approximately eight kilometers away, and Noudar Castle and the Barrancos area have historically been considered as part of the same area.

Leite de Vasconcelos (1955: 6–7) notes that in a 1527 text Barrancos was said to have 73 inhabitants, the majority of whom were Castilians. Thus, we can assume that there was a strong Spanish-language presence there, at least from that point. From 1715 onward, the Noudar castle-Barrancos area has been part of Portugal, albeit not without complications of status. Throughout the 19th century, Portugal and Spain continued to struggle over their respective claims on the territory. The matter languished until 1886, when Portugal and Spain named delegations to negotiate the issue of possession. The diplomatic effort culminated in 1894 with the ratification of a Convention whereby Barrancos and Noudar castle became a definitive part of Portugal and in 1910 the castle was christened a national monument, ending once and for all the 800-year old territorial dispute.

Regarding the sociolinguistic relation between Portuguese, Castilian/Spanish, and the other dialects of the area (Galician, Asturian, Leonese), as Castile expanded its size and influence in the Iberian Peninsula, Castilian became the lingua franca of the reconquest effort and was generally considered a language of prestige as far back as the 12th century (cf. Lapesa 1981: 172–173, 189–192, 245–247). During his reign as king of Castile (1252–1284), Alfonso el Sabio 'the Wise' was a patron of the arts and of learning, responsible for a number of important publications, including translations of scholarly works. While many of the works Alfonso sponsored were in Galician/Portuguese, Castilian's status was further established as the more prestigious variety since the majority of scholarly production in Alfonso el Sabio's court was translated from or written in Castilian. Finally, Castilian was the first Romance language to have a grammar – Nebrija's (1492) *Gramática de la lengua castellana*.

With regard to the Barrancos area, its inhabitants have traveled regularly to Spain in the last century, for many reasons, chiefly to purchase consumer goods and seek better health care, apart from visiting friends and relatives (Navas Sánchez-Élez 1992, 1994, 1996, 1997, 2001). Even during the Spanish dictatorship (1939–1975), there remained a steady stream of contraband trade across the border, mostly from Spain to Portugal, which is true of the entire border. Since the Barranquenho women carried out most of the cross-border commerce, they maintained their variety of Spanish. And even after the Spanish dictatorship fell and the dictatorship in Portugal dissolved in 1974 through a peaceful revolution,

Barranquenho women still sought goods and services routinely on the Spanish side of the border.[2]

Today the situation is largely the same in a number of ways, given the geographic isolation of Barrancos. For example, Barrancos inhabitants reported in 2003 that there is a greater diversity of merchandise at less expensive prices in Spain than in Portugal. Thus, Barranquenho women still shop on a regular basis in Spain. Moreover, Barrancos has no hospital, thus its inhabitants go to Spain for emergency medical treatment and a Spanish doctor travels to Barrancos once a week to attend to the sick. Leite de Vasconcelos (1955: 7–8) reports that when he visited Barrancos in 1938, almost all the families claimed to be of Spanish heritage and that all inhabitants, whether literate or illiterate, spoke Portuguese and Spanish equally well. He also mentions cases of children who spoke Spanish to their mothers and Portuguese to their fathers, although he also notes that Portuguese was favored among the younger generation because of the influence of the schools.

The general pattern of this very brief overview is that, from very early on, Spanish has generally been more prestigious than Portuguese on the Iberian Peninsula. Leite de Vasconcelos (1955: 29–30) states that there was a document dated 1245 from which one can infer that in Noudar castle both Portuguese and Castilian were in use at that time. He also reminds us that in 1527 the majority of the Barrancos population was Castilian and it was only after the passage of much time and through political influence at the local level that more linguistic prestige was transferred to Portuguese in the sense that it became the language used in government, schools, and the church. This supports the view that, although Barranquenhos were more closely aligned with Portugal in more recent history, they maintain deep ties with Spain and Spanish. Of course, as the nation states became better defined in the 19th century, Portuguese became the language of instruction and of the church in Barrancos. And as more people attended school, they learned Portuguese.

From this unique sociohistorical and linguistic situation, in addition to the Portuguese and Spanish national cultures Barranquenhos have also created a separate, unique identity. Consequently, they maintain, as Leite de Vasconcelos (1955: 30) notes, three linguistic varieties: Barranquenho, their local variety, Spanish, the variety that historically they have ties with, and Portuguese, the

---

[2] It must also be mentioned that until the border became easier to cross, there was a substantial market in contraband goods, which the men typically carried out.

language of the nation in which they live. In another place in the same monograph (1955: 10), Leite de Vasconcelos comments:

> From Barrancos' geographical situation, the mixing of the village's inhabitants and the language they speak, they have acquired a certain character of traditional moral independence. When a villager from another [Portuguese] town such as Moura, Beja, etc. arrives [in Barrancos], the Barranquenhos say: "He's Portuguese, there comes a Portuguese," as if they were not Portuguese! But they also say about someone coming from Spain, "there comes a Spaniard!"' [our translation]

This independent character among the Barranquenhos is also reflected in certain defining aspects of their village culture. One of these involves bull fighting. In Barrancos' annual village festival, there are a number of bull fights and in these the bulls are still killed, as is the custom in Spain, although in Portugal the killing of bulls in bull fights is strictly prohibited. Being part of Portugal, this law also applied to Barrancos. However, the resistance to the law in Barrancos was intense. Several of the town's key citizens even traveled to Lisbon, presented their case before the national parliament for keeping their bullfighting tradition in Barrancos, and ultimately were successful in protecting a tradition that is deeply Spanish but no longer Portuguese in character.

3 Barranquenho as a hybrid variety

3.1 Barranquenho and hybridization

The literature on *mixed languages* is discussed in a number of publications (see Meakins 2013 for an overview of cases). From the evolutionary, population-genetic perspective, Croft (2000: 209–221) discusses mixed languages as cases of hybridization, of which he distinguishes three types. The first type is instantiated by code-switching and code-mixing (hybrid utterances). The second type is illustrated by varieties that form in language contact situations in which the languages are closely related (for example, the community of Uruguayans near/on the Uruguay-Brazil border who speak a Portuguese-Spanish mixed variety, see Waltermire 2006). In such cases, it is often difficult to tease apart which features come from one or the other language in contact, and sometimes it is impossible to do so. The third type is labeled by Croft 'mixed languages', for which he offers a brief discussion while also noting that the social and linguistic facts in such contact situations are complex (2000: 214). Based on the social situations resulting in mixed languages, Croft distinguishes three types: *mixed-marriage languages*, languages resulting from *death by borrowing*, and languages resulting from *semi-shift*. Mixed-marriage languages have emerged in communities where there are mixed marriages in which spouses speak genetically unrelated languages. As examples, Croft cites Mednyj Aleut (Russian finite VP morpho-syntax, 90% Aleut lexicon) and Michif (Cree verbs and VP morphology, French nouns and NP morphology) (See also Meakins 2013: 163). Croft does not provide examples of cases in which actual language death by borrowing has taken place, but cites cases in which extensive borrowing has occurred, such as in Asia Minor Greek (citing Thomason and Kaufman 1988: 215–222). Following Matras (2000), Croft adopts the term "functional turnover", whereby "the basic vocabulary and sometimes some grammatical affixes of the original are restricted to a secret or in-group register of the now-acquired language of the external group" (Croft 2000: 217). Other examples mentioned by Croft are Polish Romani and Spanish Romani, spoken by Roma who migrated to Poland and the Iberian Peninsula, respectively.[3]

The third situation in which a mixed language forms is, following Croft, semi-shift.

> In semi-shift, the speakers in a society appear to shift only part way to the external society's language. The semi-shift may be due to lack of full access to the external society's language, or may be a marker of a distinct social identity. The linguistic result of semi-shift is the minor image of functional turnover: the vocabulary is that of the external society's language, while many grammatical inflections . . . and most grammatical constructions . . . are at least in part those of the native-language society. (Croft 2000: 219)

In this contribution, we acknowledge that the complexities of contact situations that yield mixed languages are not easily pigeon-holed into a rigid classification. At the same time we also acknowledge that, to a certain degree, there have been and and still exist mixed marriages in Barrancos and that over the centuries there has been a shift from Spanish, which seems to have been the

---

3 As an example, Spanish Romani maintains Spanish grammar, with Romani vocabulary and certain grammatical features. The Spanish Romani example in (i) (adapted from González Caballero 1998:13–14) illustrates this: the function words *y* 'and', *su* 'his/her/their', the verbal suffix *-aba*, and the nominal pluralization marker *-s* (including the Spanish plural allomorphs *-s* and *-es*) are Spanish, and the underlined lexical items are Romani.

(i) | *Y* | <u>*na*</u> | <u>*teler*</u>-***aba***-*n* | <u>*chaboró*</u>, | *presas* | Isabel | <u>*sin*</u>-***aba*** | <u>*nanguí*</u>,
| | and | NEG | have-PST-3PL | child | because | Isabel | be-PST | barren
| | *y* | *o-s* | <u>*dui*</u> | <u>*chalado*</u>-*s* | *dur* | *andré* | ***su***-*s* | <u>*chibés*</u>-*es*
| | and | the-PL | two | advanced-PL | far | in | their-PL | day-PL

'And they had no child because Isabel was barren and both were very advanced in age.'

dominant language in the 16th century, to Portuguese, whereby a hybrid variety emerged.[4] In the next subsection, we present how Barranquenho is likely to have formed, and in section 4, we discuss some of the key traits of Barranquenho.

3.2 The formation of Barranquenho

Speakers of Barranquenho consider the variety they speak to be its own language. Assuming this to be true, the question arises about how Barranquenho has become its own linguistic variety. We know that in 1527 Barrancos arguably had a majority of Castilian speakers and a minority of Portuguese speakers. Some time between 1527 and the beginning of the 20th century Barranquenho developed, assuming as we do that when Leite de Vasconcelos visited the village in 1938 the variety was fully formed and could be identified as a distinct variety by its speakers. Yet, given the history of Barrancos, a reasonable assumption is that Barranquenhos have been bilingual in Portuguese and Spanish at least since the beginning of the 17th century, and possibly earlier. Based on what we will discuss in the next section, we suggest that Barranquenho is the result of Spanish-language traits being introduced into the Portuguese spoken by the Barranquenhos and that over time these traits came to form part of an emerging linguistic variety that conventionalized as Barranquenho. A major factor in the formation of this variety, we argue, is the rise of consciousness among the speakers of the village that they are unique. That is, they came to see themselves as distinct from the Portuguese and Spanish, as evidenced by the aforementioned quote provided by Leite de Vasconcelos. And although their identity as being culturally and linguistically unique has definitely been in place since the beginning of the 20th century, Barranquenhos still preferred Spanish to Portuguese and Barranquenho until recently. An 11-year-old informant reported in 2003 that, "the most aged people in Barrancos, the oldest, they almost all speak Spanish, they don't speak Barranquenho. It's now that

---

4 Rather than a new appraisal of Barranquenho as a mixed language, we consider the present contribution as an extension of our position in Clements et al (2008). We still acknowledge that Barranquenho is a native language of a unique community of speakers, having emerged in a situation of bilingualism and not used to bridge a communication gap, that it has split (though related) ancestry (Portuguese-Spanish), and that its lexicon is Portuguese to a great extent with key morphosyntactic structures from Spanish. In this contribution, we frame the discussion within Croft's framework, viewing Barranquenho as a result of semi-shift, and mixed marriages, to a certain extent.

they are beginning to speak Barranquenho".⁵ We assume that this was the case for practical reasons, as well as for reasons involving the prestige of Spanish.

At present Barranquenho is a cultural "badge" of the Barranquenhos. They maintain it because it marks them as culturally unique. It also serves to maintain and even promote their community cohesion. That Barranquenhos are aware of this is suggested by the following quote, taken from the same 11-year-old informant. Responding to the question about whom he speaks Barranquenho with and where, he says:

> Com uz amigu, na ehcola nãu, com uz amigu, com otra pesóa asim máih belha àh bêzi. ... Com a minha família fálu barranquênhu i com u mez amiguh, içu tudu. So na ehcola é que nãu fálu barranquênhu, fálu à bêzih.
>
> [I speak Barranquenho] with friends, in school no, with friends, with older people sometimes. ... With my family I speak Barranquenho and with my friends, and all. It's only in school that I don't speak Barrenquenho, I speak it at times.

In the next section, discuss some of the key features that define Barrenquenho as a contact variety.

4 Some defining features of Barranquenho

As noted, we argue that Barranquenho does possess traits that allow it to be classified, at least in part, both as a hybridized variety similar to Portuñol spoken in northern Uruguay (due to typological and genetic proximity of Spanish and Portuguese), and as a case of semi-shift whereby we find that Barranquenho survives and thrives aided in great measure by the degree to which it is maintained due to cultural and linguistic identity of its speakers. In addition, it contains grammatical constructions, as well as grammatical inflections, of Spanish origin, and an overwhelming part of the vocabulary from Portuguese. Specifically, Barranquenho exhibits the following features:
– Morphosyntax: the determiner and pronominal systems are a mixture of Portuguese and Spanish; clitic placement is Spanish that cannot be accounted for by appealing to variation found in the Ibero-Romance dialect continuum;⁶

---

5 The original reads: "I ah pesóah mái idoza de Barrancu, a mái belha falom quazi todah a ehpanhola, nãu falom barranquenhu. Agora é que já bãu falandu barranquenhu".
6 Meakins (2013: 160) attributes clitic placement in Barranquenho to variation in the dialect continuum, stating that, "it is not clear how the restructuring found in this variety would differ

- Lexicon: Portuguese with some use of Spanish pragmatically (e.g., Spanish *bueno* 'good' used as a discourse marker in Barranquenho); there are also Spanish verbal constructions in Barranquenho, such as *gustar* 'like' with dative experiencer vs. *gustar de* with nominative experiencer in Portuguese (*me gusta la música* vs. *gosto da música* 'I like music') (see Taylor 2014);
- Phonology: Barranquenho has seven vowel phonemes (a larger vowel system than Spanish, i.e. closer to Portuguese), but possesses phenomena, notably /s/ aspiration and/or deletion in coda position, that is part and parcel of Extremeño Spanish.

On the basis of these facts, with a focus on Barranquenho object clitics, Garrett (in press) argues that while Barranquenho may not be as clear-cut a mixed language as, say, the Spanish-Quichua mixed language spoken in Ecuador (Muysken 1997), it has properties that allow it to be classified, in Croft's terms, as a semi-shift mixed language. He also argues that it may be useful to consider the notion of a mixed language as a continuum rather than discrete: ". . . Such a conceptualization of mixed languages as continua as opposed to discrete categories should better represent the reality of mixed varieties and, as this study shows, when two typologically similar languages are in contact for an extended period of time, the resulting contact variety may show some but not all of these properties of prototypical categories" (in press: 27).

Some of the features of Barranquenho discussed in this section are found in the Portuguese dialect of the area, called Português Alentejano. Others, by contrast, are clear cases of influence from Spanish, but not within the context of a dialect continuum (see footnote 1 above). We discuss phonological, as well as morphological, morphosyntactic and lexical features, comparing them, where relevant, to the features of regional Portuguese and Spanish.

Whereas the Spanish vowel system consists of only the five oral phonemes /i, e, a, o, u/, no nasal phonemes, and all five vowels can appear in pretonic, tonic, and posttonic positions, in Portuguese there are nine oral phonemes /i, e, ɛ, ə, ɐ, a, ɔ, o, u/, of which [i, ə, ɐ, u] are found in pretonic and posttonic

---

from that found along a dialect chain". Due to the particular historical developments of the Iberian Peninsula from 711 to 1492, the dialect chain, or continuum, while robustly represented across the north of the peninsula, is not found in the southern half of the peninsula. In the 600+ year long reconquest, the kingdoms of Portugal, Castile-Leon, Navarre, Aragon, and Catalonia expanded southward and Castile increasingly took over territory from other kingdoms and became Spain. The disputes in and around Barrancos (in the southern half of the Iberian Peninsula) took place at a time when dialectal variation in Portugal and Spain was happening separately, divorced from any continuum.

non-final position and [ɐ, ə, u] in posttonic final position. In addition, Portuguese also has the five nasal phonemes /ĩ, ẽ, ɐ̃, õ, ũ/ (Mateus et al. 1989). Thus, the Portuguese vowel system has not only four more oral vowel phonemes than Spanish but also a series of nasal phonemes for which Spanish has no nasal counterparts. And given the different distribution of Portuguese vowels in stressed and unstressed positions, it is apparent that in unstressed position there is reduction and/or raising whereas in Spanish this is not the case.

Given these considerable differences in the vowel inventories between the two languages, and the sensitivity to stressed and unstressed position in Portuguese, a reasonable expectation would be that if there originally were predominately Castilian speakers in Barrancos, some Spanish traits would be introduced into the emerging variety that would later become Barranquenho. That is, we might expect to find a reduced vowel inventory in Barranquenho relative to Portuguese and/or a lack of vowel reduction and/or raising in unstressed position, or a possible lack of nasal vowels. However, neither Leite de Vasconcelos (see 1955: 19) nor we found such features in Barranquenho. That is, the speakers of Barranquenho whose speech we have studied have no apparent lack of reduction or lack of nasal vowels, nor is their oral vowel inventory reduced in any transparent way. What we do find, however, is vowel raising to [i] of /e/ in posttonic final position, as in the sentence in (1), where the standard Portuguese version is given under the sentence in Barranquenho.

(1) *Alguma   bezi   tibi   ẽỹ   São Marcu   da   Ataboêra.*
    Algumas vezes   estive em   São Marcos da   Ataboêra.
    Some   times   I was   in   Saint Mark of   Ataboêra.
    'Sometimes I was in Saint Mark of Ataboêra.' (F86:4)

Note that the posttonic final vowel in *bezi* [bé-zi] and *tibi* [tí-bi] have been raised to [i]. This phenomenon is a regional one, also found in the Portuguese dialect of the area.[7]

With regard to the consonants, Barrancos possesses various traits that are clearly not Portuguese but found in the varieties of Iberian Spanish, as well as more generally. Before discussing these, we compare the consonant inventories of Portuguese and Spanish, given in (2) and (3) respectively.

---

[7] To obtain an idea of the linguistic traits in the Alentejano speech, samples taken from Serpa were consulted, a town approximately 60 kms. south west of Barrancos. The sound files are made available by the Instituto Camões and are available at their website (http://www.instituto-camoes.pt/cvc/hlp/geografia/mapa06.html). Thanks to Ana Luís for the information on the audio files of the different Portuguese dialects.

(2) / p, b, t, d, k, g, w /
/ f, (v), s, z, ʃ, ʒ /
/ l, ɾ, r, λ, (ʀ) /
/ m, n, ñ /

(3) / p, b, t, d, k, g, w /
/ f, s, y, (λ) x /[8]
/ ʧ /
/ l, ɾ, r /
/ m, n, ñ /

Comparing the two consonant inventories, we see that Spanish has a reduced set of fricatives in that it lacks /v/, /z/, /ʒ/, and /ʃ/. Although Portuguese has three types of rhotics /ɾ, r, ʀ/, /ʀ/ is found in urban speech and, as we shall see, in the speech of the younger speakers, whereas /r/ is found in rural areas, which includes the region where Barrancos is located (cf. Cunha and Cintra 1984: 32). And although the Portuguese norm distinguishes between /b/ and /v/, this distinction is not found in several areas,[9] among which the Barrancos area is one. Thus, the fact that many Barranquenho speakers have /r/ instead of / ʀ / and do not distinguish /b/ and /v/ (e.g. *votar* [bo-tár]) is attributable to Alentejano, the variety of Portuguese spoken in the Barrancos area.

In Barranquenho, we find three phonology-related phenomena that are clearly due to contact with Extremeño Spanish. In Extremeño Spanish, as in Andalusian Spanish, the aspiration or deletion of [s] in coda position, and the deletion of word-final [ɾ] and [l] are commonplace (Hualde, Olarrea, and Escobar 2001: 337).[10] Similarly, we find that this phenomenon is also widespread in Barranquenho (see also Leite de Vasconcelos 1955: 43–44). Some illustrative examples are given in (4). For Barranquenho, the aspiration and deletion of [s] in coda position has attracted most attention, as is evident from the studies by Navas Sánchez-Élez (1992, 1994, 1996, 1997, 2001), while the deletion of word-final [ɾ] and [l]

---

8 Azevedo (1992: 332) lists the deaffrication of [ʧ] to [ʃ] (e.g., ['o-ʧo] vs. ['o-ʃo] for *ocho* 'eight'). as a characteristic trait of Andalusian Spanish. We note, however, that Hualde et al (2010: 402–403) does not list it among its traits. We assume that the deaffrication present is Andalusia is an independent development from the same phenomenon in Portuguese.
9 According to Cunha and Cintra (1984: 13), the borderline between /v/=/b/ and /v/≠/b/ goes from a region slightly to the south of Coimbra up to the region of Bragança and along the entire border starting from the south of Bragança. To the north of that line as well as to the east (hence including the border region) we find /v/≠/b/.
10 It is noteworthy that texts such as Lapesa (1981) and Penny (1991) do not mention the deletion of word-final liquids, but only refer to their neutralization.

have not been studied in detail. We found abundant examples of word-final [r] deletion, but no examples of [l] deletion in the same position. In Barranquenho, /s/ is maintained, as [z], across word boundaries where the syllable-final /s/ is resyllabified. An illustrative example of this common phenomenon in Barranquenho is given in (5). Leite de Vasconcelos (1955: 13–14) also mentions this as a trait of Barranquenho.[11]

(4) a. *Purque antiØ . . . nóØ não tinhamuØ   possi para*
  porque antes ..   nós não tínhamos   posses para
  pagáØ esa coiza i aquela mulhéØ com   qualquéØ
  pagar essa coisa e aquela mulher com qualquer
  coizinha que a genti le daba ela ficaba contenti
  coisinha que a gente lhe daba ela ficava contente.
  'Because before we didn't have the means to pay for that type of thing and that woman, she was content with whatever the people gave her.' (F86:10–11)
 b. *Eu trabalhu na ehcola, trabalhu com u primêru*
  Eu trabalho na escola, trabalho com o primeiro
  ciclu, sô auxiliáØ.
  ciclo, sou auxiliar.
  'I work in the school, I work with the first cycle (primary school), I'm an assistant.' (F33:9)
 c. *No, uh da nosa sala queremuØ fazéØ isu.*
  Nós, os da nossa sala queremos fazer isso.
  'We, the ones from our grade, we want to do that.' (M11:191)

(5) *A já **doj** zanuh*
  Há já dois anos
  'two years ago' (F19:96)

As mentioned above, Barranquenho speakers generally display no distinction between /b/ and /v/ and have /r/ instead of /ʀ/. However, some younger speakers, an 11-year-old boy and a 19-year-old girl, both have /ʀ/, but both a 14-year-old boy and a 24-year-old young man exhibit /r/. Thus, the possibility exists that the choice between /r/ and /ʀ/ is sensitive to sociolinguistic considerations and would need to be studied.

---

[11] Leite de Vasconcelos (1955: 48) notes that there is retention of –r when it appears intervocalically across word boundaries, as in *senhórAntónio* [se-ñó-ran-tó-njo] (< *senhor António).*

Finally, we saw above that Portuguese distinguishes between /s/ and /z/, whereas Spanish only possesses /s/. In Barranquenho, the speakers whose speech we examined maintained the distinction between /s/ and /z/ consistently.[12]

With regard to morphology, one might expect Barranquenho speakers' speech to contain irregular Spanish verb forms with frequently used verbs. That is, if Barranquenho speakers favored Spanish and were dominant in it until recently, we would expect to find forms such as Spanish *estuve* 'I was' instead of Portuguese *estive*. However, we seldom find this. In the speech of a 63-year-old speaker who regularly uses Spanish in his daily life, we find evidence of irregular Spanish verbs in his Barranquenho (e.g. *i ehtube trêzanu lá* [Portuguese: *e estive treze anos lá*] 'and I was thirteen years there'). Other than this and the aforementioned aspiration or deletion of the –s, (both /s/ and the plural morpheme {s}), our data do not reveal any other phenomena. For his part, Leite de Vasconcelos (1955) does not comment on any morphological phenomena other than Spanish forms of the same verb (*(s)tobe* from *estuvo* 's/he was' and the use of the diminuitive *–ito*, not found in speech samples that make up our corpus.

It is the morphosyntactic phenomena found in Barranquenho that reveal the strongest influence from Spanish. Between Portuguese and Spanish there is a clear contrast regarding how the progressive aspect is expressed. While Portuguese employs the construction *estar a* + verb-INF, as in *nós estamos a fazer o trabalho* 'we are doing the work', Spanish uses the construction *estar* + verb-GER, as in *nosotros estamos haciendo el trabajo* 'we are doing the work'. In Barranquenho, the more commonly used construction to express the progressive aspect is clearly the Spanish construction. Illustrative examples are given in (6).

(6) a. *Me casei tarde, **ehtaba já trabalhando**.*
'I married late, I was already working.' (F52:133–34)
b. *Nu se si sabi, ondi **ehtãu fazendu** u cini teatru.*
'I don't know whether you know, [the place] where they're making the theater.' (M11:126)
c. *. . . i minha irmã **ehtaba bailandu**.*
'. . .and my sister was dancing.' (F31:124)

Object clitic placement is another phenomenon where Barranquenho exhibits significant differences with Portuguese, but a commonality with Spanish. To be able to understand the significance of clitic placement in Barranquenho, it will

---

[12] Only one speaker, who had a Spanish-speaking boyfriend, occasionally devoiced /z/, as in [ká-sɐ] 'house' instead of [ká-zɐ].

help to explain briefly here how the phenomenon works in both Portuguese and Spanish.[13] In Portuguese, in main clauses proclisis is found after certain operators, such as negation markers (7) quantifiers (8), indefinite pronouns such as 'someone' (9), as well as certain adverbs (10).

(7) O João **não a** viu no cinema ontem.
 the João NEG her saw in-the movie theater yesterday
 'João didn't see her at the movie theater yesterday.'

(8) **Tudo a** chateia.
 all her bothers
 'Everything bothers her.'

(9) **Alguém me** telefonou ontem.
 someone me telephoned yesterday
 'Someone called me up yesterday.'

(10) **Apenas/Até** o João **te** reconheceu na televisão.
 only/even the João you.OBJ recognized in-the television
 'Only/Even João recognized you on TV.'

Proclisis in Portuguese is also obligatory if there is a non-canonical topicalized element in sentence-initial position, such as an object or an adjunct. An example is shown in (11).

(11) **Dele se** sabe pouca coisa.
 of-him PASS knows little thing
 'Of him little is known.'

In addition, proclisis is required in subordinate clauses, illustrated by the example in (12).

(12) Disseram-me **que** o João **a** viu no cinema ontem.
 told-3PL-me that the João her saw in-the movie theater yesterday
 'They told me that João saw her at the movie theater yesterday.'

---

13 Unless otherwise indicated, the information regarding clitic placement in Portuguese, Barranquenho, and Spanish is taken from Mateus et al. (1989) and Clements and Lorenzino (2006).

Thus, in Portuguese certain operators and certain pragmatically-driven word orders call for proclisis. This also holds for compound verbs (i.e. aux + verb) and modal constructions. Finally, proclisis is required in subordinate clauses, which is true of simple as well as compound tenses.

In contrast to the environments in which proclisis is the norm, enclisis is required in Portuguese finite matrix clauses in which there is no pragmatically-driven non-canonical word order and no presence of the aforementioned operators. Examples are given in (13–15).

(13) O João viu-*a* no cinema ontem.
 the João saw-her in-the movie theater yesterday
 'João saw her at the movie theater yesterday.'

(14) O João tem-*a* visto últimamente.
 the João has-her seen lately
 'João has seen her lately.'

(15) O João deve-*te* reconhecer. /deve reconhecer-*te*.
 the João should-you.OBJ recognize /should recognize-you.OBJ
 'João should recognize you.'

According to Luís (2004) and Washington (2015), enclisis in Portuguese appears to be expanding its domains, independently of age group, socio-economic class, or education level. Enclisis is becoming the default order in Portuguese, independently of what type of clause it appears in and what type of auxiliary verb or adverbial it appears with.

In Spanish, clitic placement obeys a different set of rules than those found in Portuguese. Proclisis is obligatory with finite indicative verb forms, with or without an auxiliary (cf. [16]) and negative imperative verb forms (cf. [17]).

(16) a. *Juanita* **lo** *compró*.
 Juanita it bought
 'Juanita bought it.'
 b. *Juanita* **lo** *ha comprado*.
 Juanita it has bought
 'Juanita has bought it.'

(17) *¡No **lo** hagas!*
    NEG it do-IMP-2SG
    'Don't do it!'

Enclisis in Spanish is obligatory in finite imperative verb forms (cf. [18]), and all non-finite forms (cf. [19]).

(18) *¡Haz**lo**!*
    do-IMP-it
    'Do it!'

(19) a. *Después de hacer**lo**...*
        after of do-INF-it
        'After doing it...'
    b. *Después de haber**lo** hecho...*
        after of have-INF-it done
        'After having done it...'
    c. *Buscándo**lo** por toda la casa...*
        looking.for-it through all the house
        'Looking for it throughout the house...'
    d. *Habiéndo**lo** buscado por toda la casa...*
        having-it looked.for through all the house
        'Having looked for it throughout the house...'

With many modals, proclisis or enclisis is found, as illustrated by the examples in (20).

(20) a. *Juan **te** debe ayudar.*
        Juan you.OBJ should help-INF
        'Juan should help you.'
    b. *Juan debe ayudar**te**.*
        Juan should help-INF you.OBJ
        'Juan should help you.'

The one environment in which Portuguese and Spanish object pronoun clitic placement does not coincide is in finite matrix clauses with no pragmatically-driven non-canonical word order and no presence of a proclisis-triggering element in Portuguese. In these cases, Portuguese exhibits enclisis and Spanish proclisis. The focus is on these particular environments in Barranquenho.

Garrett (in press) carried out a quantitative analysis of various morphosyntactic phenomena en Barranquenho that also included clitic placement. In the

Barranquenho corpus consisting of data from 20 speakers, he coded 895 object clitics and excluded reflexive and passive/impersonal *se* clitics. Table 1 shows the distribution of tokens, coded for order (proclitic or enclitic), Case (accusative or dative), number (sg. or pl.):

Table 1: Tokens extracted.

	Enclisis	Proclisis	Accusative	Dative	Singular	Plural
N	109[14]	786	280	615	856	39
%	12.18	87.82	32.29	68.72	95.64	4.36

Table 2 compares clitic placement in Barranquenho to Portuguese.

Table 2: Clitic placement in finite clauses that are enclitic in EP.

	Total	Proclisis	Enclisis
N	277	261	16
%	100	94.22	5.78

Based on our data, Barranquenho is seen to have a system in which clitic placement is overwhelming proclitic, regardless of the factors coded (case, number, and animacy), even though EP has been gravitating toward enclisis for well over a century (Luís 2004; Galves and Sousa 2005). The counts in Table 2 show this starkly: Barranquenho speakers produce proclitic orders 94% of the time (261/277) in contexts in which EP would display enclisis with finite verbs. When considering age and sex (see Table 3), the distribution is not statistically significant (χ^2 (df = 1, n = 16) = 0.87, p = .65). That is, the preference for proclisis in Barranquenho is not affected by the age or the gender of the speaker in our data sample.[15]

---

[14] Of the 109 tokens of enclitic orders, 93 appeared with an infinitival form that would condition enclisis in the same way in both Spanish and Portuguese. Thus, they were excluded from other counts.

[15] Garrett (in press) discusses other factors that affect proclisis vs. enclisis in Barranquenho, but we give here the main findings.

Table 3: Clitic systems by age and sex.

Age group	Speakers with only #Cl-V (% of gender)		Speakers with both #Cl-V; Cl-V (% gender)		Number of tokens with V-Cl (%)	
	M	F	M	F	M	F
< 29	1 (9.09)	3 (33.33)	2 (18.18)	1 (11.11)	3 (18.75)	1 (6.25)
30–54	1 (9.09)	1 (11.11)	3 (27.27)	2 (22.22)	6 (37.50)	2 (12.50)
55 +	3 (27.27)	1 (11.11)	1 (9.09)	1 (11.11)	2 (12.50)	2 (12.50)
Total per gender	*5 (45.45)*	*5 (55.55)*	*6 (54.55)*	*4 (44.44)*	*11 (68.75)*	*5 (31.25)*
Total (% of total)	*10 (50.00)*		*10 (50.00)*		*16 (100.00)*	

Regarding how Barranquenho came to have such a strong preference for proclisis, Garrett (in press) notes that it could be the result of incomplete second language acquisition, whereby Spanish speakers naturalistically learning Portuguese imposed Spanish clitic placement patterns onto the Portuguese variety they were targeting. Given that the village also has has a long history of being relatively isolated, the population shifting from Spanish to Portuguese would have been able maintained a naturalistically acquired variety of Portuguese without outside influences till the second half of the 20th century when education and infrastructure diminished the barriers of isolation. Independently of whether this or another hypothesis turns out to best account for Barranquenho clitic placement, the fact remains that today Barrancos currently has a multilingual population that maintains Barranquenho for social purposes such as identity or social cohesion (Clements 2009; Clements, Amaral and Luís 2011).

Garrett (in press) also discussed quantitatively the phenomenon of indirect object doubling, absent in Portuguese, present in Spanish, and frequently found in the Barranquenho data. Illustrative examples from Barranquenho speakers are shown in (21).

(21) a. i   eu   lhe   disse   à   rapariga
     and I   IO.3SG   said-1SG   to.the   girl
     'and I said to the girl . . .' (M64:64)
   b. i   lhe   pedi   a   uma   colega   minha.
     and   IO.3SG   requested-1SG   to   a   colleague   mine
     'and I asked a colleague of mine . . .' (F26:176)

Garrett extracted 70 cases of indirect doubling. The results are given in Table 4, where the doubling is listed according to clitic.

Table 4: Indirect object doubling.

	Total	lhe	le	me	te	nos	a
#Tokens	70	23	21	20	4	1	1
% of doubling	100.00	32.86	30.00	28.57	5.71	1.43	1.43

The results are interesting in at least one way. We know that in Barranquenho the indirect object clitic is realized as *le* /le/ (as in Spanish), as well as *lhe* /ʎe/ (as in Portuguese). Given that the construction is a Spanish one and not found in Portuguese, we might expect that when speakers produce the construction the Spanish clitic *le* would be used more often than the Portuguese clitic *lhe*. This turns out not to be the case. Rather, both distributions (21/70 for *le* and 23/70 for *lhe*) are significant, but the latter more so than the former.[16] That is, chi-square tests show that doubling with *le* is highly significant (χ^2 (df = 1, n= 895) =7.50; p = .005), but less so than doubling with *lhe* (χ^2 (df = 1, n= 895) =11.53; p = .001).

Recall that in Croft (2000: 220) a mixed language like Barranquenho may represent a semi-shift dynamic in which the majority of the lexicon is Portuguese while several structural properties are uniquely from the Spanish sub-/adstrate. This is in line with linguistic tendencies proposed for mixed languages but it may not be always the case. For instance, function words are often resistant to replacement. With such high degrees of correspondence between Spanish and Portuguese, and the high level of trilingualism among the speakers, they may not distinguish in Barranquenho between marking an indirect object with *le* or *lhe*. That is, *lhe* may have a perceptible phonetic distinction compared to the Spanish *le* but some speakers do not seem to make the distinction in the sense that their speech displays variable *lhe/le* variable use. This is shown in Table 5. Only one speaker exclusively doubles with *lhe*, while four use *le* exclusively and one produced no clitics. The remaining 14 speakers produced both clitics. Chi-square tests show that there were no significant differences between age group (χ^2 (df = 2, n= 895) = .70; p = .71) and gender (χ^2 (df = 2, n = 895) = 4.11; p = .13).

---

[16] The distinction between tokens of *le* and *lhe* was made by native Barranquenho speakers who transcribed the corpus. An acoustic analysis was not conducted.

Table 5: Individuals' indirect object doubling preferences.

Age group	Speakers that exclusively use le*	Speakers that exclusively use lhe**	Mixed speakers (use both)
< 29	2 (10.00)	0 (0.00)	4 (20.00)
30–54	2 (10.00)	1 (5.00)	5 (25.00)
55 +	0 (0.00)	0 (0.00)	5 (25.00)
Total (%)	*4 (20.00)*	*1 (5.00)*	*14 (70.00)*

*One participant didn't produce any cases of doubling (M:27)
**One participant produced *lhe* exclusively (F:35)

Several other morphosyntactic phenomena were attested in the data, but not frequently enough to examine them quantitatively. *Leísmo*, that is, the use of an indirect object clitic where a direct object clitic is called for, is found. There are nine tokens of an indirect object clitics used to refer to masculine animate direct object referent. Of the nine, five appeared with the verb *ajudar* 'help'. In Spanish, *ayudar* with *le* is exceedingly common, indeed the norm, but it is not attested (or at least not reported) in EP.[17] Leísmo is also found with other verbs in Barranquenho, as well. Garrett cites the example in (22) as a case in point.

(22) . . .que Deu **le** perdoi.
 . . .that God CL forgive.SUBJ.3SG
 '. . .that God may forgive him.' (M:83:44)

As for which clitic, *le* or *lhe*, was found in cases of *leísmo*, we find *le* six times and *lhe* three times. We consider the presence of *leísmo* in Barranquenho to be another example of the Portuguese lexical items in a Spanish-origin construction, which we take as further support that Barranquenho is a type of mixed variety.

Double pronominalization is another phenomenon involving clitics where Portuguese and Spanish differ. In Portuguese, double pronominalization involves a coalescence of the indirect object pronoun *lhe* and the direct object pronoun (*o, a, os, as*) to the monosyllabic clitic clusters *lho, lhos, lha,* and *lhas*. An illustrative example is shown in (23), from Barranquenho.

---

[17] So-called *lheísmo* or *leísmo brasileiro* is attested in Brazilian varieties but not in EP (Nascentes 1960; Schwenter 2014). However, in EP the dative pronoun is common with the verb *perdoar*, as in (22).

(23) eu **lh-o**   agradeço   eçe   dia quandu...
     I   CL-CL   thank-1SG that day when. . .
     'I thank him for it that day when. . .' (M:64:708)

In Spanish, the indirect object pronoun in double pronominalization has evolved from *le* via *že* [ʒe] to *se* and the direct object pronouns are *lo, los, la, las*. Thus, the corresponding combinations are *se lo, se los, se la, se las*. These combinations do not undergo any type of coalescence and thus are relatively more transparent than their Portuguese counterparts. While we find examples of both the Portuguese and Spanish models in the Barranquenho corpus, the more frequently occurring construction is the Spanish one. Illustrative Barranquenho examples are given in (24).

(24) a. *Eu achu   que **se lu** tenhu   que dizé...*
        I   think-1SG that CL CL   have-1SG that say-INF
        'I think that I have to say it to him. . .' (Id. F:28:443)
     b. *Arranjou   um   acordiom que **se   lhu   benderom.***
        arranged.3SG an   accordion that IO.3SG IO.DO.3SG-it sold-3PL
        'He arranged an accordion that they sold to him.' (F86:196–97)

Yet another Spanish trait found in Barranquenho is the non-anaphoric use of *se* in an impersonal or passive construction or as an aspectual marker, whereby *se* appears in preverbal position. This commonly found construction in Barranquenho is illustrated in (25–26). In the corresponding Portuguese construction, *se* would follow the verb.[18]

(25) **Se comia**   ali, **se tocaba**   zambomba.
     SE eat-IMPER there SE play-IMPER drum
     'They ate there, and they played drums.' (F86:196)

(26) *I   **se lhe**   daba   uma gorjeta para eli.*
     and SE IO.3SG give-IMPER a   tip   for   him
     'And he was given a tip.' (F57:142–143)

Leite de Vasconcelos (1955:39) mentions that this trait also appears in the Barranquenho texts available to him.

---

18 Regarding the different functions of non-anaphoric *se* in Spanish, see Clements (2006).

Argument structure is also an area in which Portuguese and Spanish differ, and thus where we can see the mixing of Portuguese lexicon with Spanish morphosyntax. In Spanish, the experiencer verb *gustar* 'like' codes the stimulus as subject and the experiencer as the indirect object, as shown in the example in (27).

(27) **Le**   gustan   la-s   manzana-s.
IO.3SG like-3PL the-PL apple-PL
'S/He like apples.'

By contrast, in Portuguese *gostar* 'like' the experiencer is coded as the subject of the sentence and the experiencer in a prepositional *de* 'of' phrase, as in (28).

(28) Gosta   d-a-s   maçã-s.
like-3SG of-the-PL apple-PL
'S/He likes apples.'

In (29), examples from Barranquenho are given, all coming from the same speaker.

(29) a. **eu gostaria**   também **de**   **falá**   um bocadinho milhó.
I would. like also COMP speak-INF a little better
'I would also like to speak a little bit better.' (F52:291)
b. *para eu fazé   uma coisa que a mim tanto*   **me gohtaba**...
for I do-INF a thing COMP to me so.much me like-IMPER
'for me to do a thing that I like so much . . .' (F52:76–68)
c. *A   primera beh   nãu* **le**   **guhtó** *muitu.*
the first time NEG IO.3SG liked much
'The first time, he didn't like it much.' (F19:113)

We find both argument structures in Barranquenho, often produced by one and the same speaker, such as in the examples in (29a, b). In fact, in her quantitative analysis of the use of *gustar/gostar* in Barranquenho with subject v. indirect object (IO) experiencer, Taylor (2014) also documented considerable inter-speaker variation in the use of the two constructions. She also found that, counter to expectations, the youngest group (11–18 years old) of the 20 speakers (from 11 to 83 years old) displayed a statistically significant preference for IO experiencer coding. That is, these Barranquenho speakers had incorporated the IO experiencer model into their variety more often. In addition, Taylor found that priming and the presence of an animate stimulus were statistically significant predictors of which argument structure was selected. That is, when the interviewer used *gostar/gustar* with a subject experiencer or with an IO experiencer, the interviewee followed suit.

As alluded to above, the presence of animate stimuli also favored the use of a subject experiencer. This could be accounted for by assuming that Barranquenho speakers may be sensitive to the link between animacy and conmesurate higher degree of potential agency. This would, of course, need to be further investigated before something more definitive could be said.

One last phenomenon deserves mention as a distinctive trait of Barranquenho. The word *bueno* 'good' ([bueno] or [buenu] in Barranquenho) is a discourse marker, much like *well* is used in English. In (30), we give a set of examples, taken from speakers of different sexes and ages. In Portuguese, the counterpart *bom* is not used as a discourse marker in the same way. This is one of the only single Spanish words found in Barranquenho. That is, there is little borrowing of lexical items from Spanish into Barranquenho.

(30) a. *I   depoih disi,   **buenu** ehta mulhé i   salta   ela asim.*
       and then   said-1SG good   this woman and jumps she like.this
       'And then I said, well, this woman here, and then she jumps like this.'
       (M24:442)

   b. *Quandu eu ehtaba na   França dizia: mete-te*
       when   I was   in-the France say-IMPER put-yourself
       *na   ehcola, **buenu** que   não aprendeu*
       in-the school good   COMP   NEG learned-3SG
       nem   o   nomi.
       not.even the name
       'When I was in France, she said "get in school!" Well, she didn't even learn the name [of the school].' (M64:101–02)

   c. *Um assuntu meu da   minha bida, não?*
       a matter my of-the my   life, NEG
       ***Buenu** poi eu anti   moraba   nu   campu, purque me*
       well   then I before live-IMPER   in-the country because my
       pai   morabom   nu   campu e   fui   criada
       parents live-IMPER-PL   in-the country and was-1SG raised-PPART
       nu   campu.
       in-the country
       'An episode of mine from my life, right? Well then, before I used to live in the country because my parents lived in the country and I was raised in the country.' (F33:71–72)

d. *Já   não me lembru   comu é esa cantiga,*
   anymore NEG REFL remember how is that song
   tã bunita   que é. **Buenu** *ali   tocabom*
   so beautiful COMP is good there play-IMPER-PL
   a   zambomba se bailaba.
   the drum   SE dance-IMPER-SG
   'I don't remember anymore how that song goes, as beautiful as it is. Well, they played the drum there and there was dance.' (F86:205–06)

In this section, we have reviewed some key features that make the variety spoken in the border town of Barrancos distinctive, traits attributable to the presence of Spanish, which historically has been and currently is spoken in the area. The traits we have described and illustrated are: the aspiration or deletion of syllable-final –s, deletion of word-final –r, the '*estar* verb + -ndu' construction for the progressive instead of '*estar a* + verb-INF', indirect object doubling, as in *le conté a meu pai* [lit. IO.1SG told-1SG to my father] 'I told my father', strong preference of proclisis of object clitics in main clauses, double pronominalization following the Spanish model, preplacement of non-anaphoric *se* clitic, the existence of the indirect object experiencer construction *gustar le a uno* [lit. like-INF IO.3SG to one] (along with the presence of the Portuguese subject experiencer construction *gostar de* [lit. like-INF of]), and the existence of *bueno* 'good' as a discourse marker. All these traits are traceable to Spanish. To conclude the paper, we take up the question about whether the presence of such traits allows Barranquenho to be classified as a mixed language.

5 Concluding remarks

From the historical overview, it is clear that Portuguese and Spanish in the Barrancos area have been in contact for centuries. This means that there has been a strong presence of stable bilingualism in Barrancos for at least 150 years if not more, before Barrancos definitively and undisputedly became part of Portugal at the beginning of the 20th century, and possibly before it was first made part of Portugal at the beginning of the 19th century.

The traits that define Barranquenho are notably the Spanish traits discussed in section 3.3. The aspiration or deletion of syllable-final –s and deletion of word-final –r are clear indications that Extremeño Spanish has had a major influence on Barranquenho. How would such traits make their way into this variety? It seems likely that such traits were carried into Portuguese by a population that was predominantly Spanish-speaking that applied the same rules to Portuguese coda consonants –*s* and –*r* that apply in Extremeño Spanish, as long as they were understood. We submit that reducing the Portuguese vowel system from nine to five or doing away with Portuguese nasal phonemes would have impeded intelligibility and thus the Spanish speakers avoided reducing the Portuguese vowel system or denasalizing vowels.

All other Barranquenho traits discussed in the previous section are those that do not undermine intelligibility: the '*estar* verb + *-ndu*' construction for the progressive, indirect object doubling, proclisis of indirect object clitics and non-anaphoric *se* in main clauses, double pronominalization, the use of *gustar le a uno* are arguably traits that are close enough to their Portuguese counterpart construction not to cause any problems. In the case of a clear adoption of a Spanish function word, the indirect object pronouns *le* and *les* are sufficiently close to their Portuguese counterparts and thus, we argue, would not create problems for comprehension. Thus, not only do Barranquenho speakers maintain the Spanish position of the indirect object pronouns but they also maintain the Spanish form *le* and *les*. With regard to Spanish lexical items found in Barranquenho, we note that with the exception of *buenu*, Spanish-language vocabulary is rarely used in Barranquenho and the occasions where Spanish is used are instances of code-switching. The items we did find were discourse connectors. For example, there's one example of Spanish *pueš* (< *pues*) 'well, then', but in the vast majority of cases, Portuguese derived *poi* (< *pois*) was used.

The creation of Barranquenho was in our view driven initially by predominantly Spanish-speaking people learning Portuguese because of socio-political circumstances. The maintenance and cultivation of Barranquenho is, we argue, a case of the development of a cultural identity sparked by the just-mentioned political circumstance. The Barranquenhos found that their cultural identity was neither entirely Spanish nor entirely Portuguese but a hybrid of the two cultures. As consciousness of this fact began to grow, a linguistic identity began to take form. What we have today in Barrancos, we suggest, is a linguistic variety that solidified out of a cultural identity that was shaped by local and socio-political developments.

This type of language mixture we submit, is a case of semi-shift. Recall that Croft (2000: 219) defines semi-shift as a situation in which

> the speakers in a society appear to shift only part way to the external society's language. The semi-shift may be due to lack of full access to the external society's language, or may be a marker of a distinct social identity . . . [T]he vocabulary is that of the external society's language, while many grammatical inflections . . . and most grammatical constructions . . . are at least in part those of the native-language society.

In our view, this characterization defines Barranquenho accurately.

Abbreviations

CL	clitic
COMP	complementizer
DO	direct object
IMP	imperative
IMPER	imperfect
INF	infinitive
IO	indirect object
NEG	negation
OBJ	object
PASSIVE	passive
PL	plural
PPART	past participle
PST	past
REFL	reflexive
SG	singular
SUBJ	subjunctive

References

Azevedo, Milton M. 1992. *Introducción a la lingüística española*. Englewood Cliffs, NJ: Prentice Hall.

Clements, J. Clancy. 2006. Transitivity and Spanish non-anaphoric *se*. In J. Clancy Clements & Jiyoung Yoon (ed.), *Functional Approaches to Spanish Syntax*, 236–264. London: Palgrave Macmillan.

Clements, J. Clancy. 2009. *The Linguistic legacy of Spanish and Portuguese*. Cambridge: Cambridge University Press.

Clements, J. Clancy, Patrícia Amaral & Ana Luís. 2008. Cultural identity and the structure of a mixed language. In *Proceedings of the 34th Annual Meeting of the Berkeley Linguistics Society* (special session on pidgins, creoles, and mixed languages), 1–10. Berkeley: University of California.

Clements, J. Clancy, Patrícia Amaral & Ana Luís. 2011. Spanish in contact with Portuguese: the case of Barranquenho. In Manuel Díaz-Campos (ed.), *The Handbook of Hispanic Sociolinguistics*, 395–417. Oxford: Blackwell.

Clements, J. Clancy, & Gerardo Lorenzino. 2006. The Contact Situation in Barrancos, Portugal. Paper presented at the *Annual Meeting of the Society for Pidgin and Creole Languages*, Albuquerque, NM, January 2006.

Croft, William. 2000. *Explaining language change. An evolutionary approach*. London: Longman.

Cunha, Celso & Luís F. Lindley Cintra. 1984. *Nova grammática do Português contemporâneo*. Lisbon: João Sá da Costa.

Coelho, Adelino de Matos. 1999. *O castelo de Noudar. Fortaleza medieval*. Águeda: Câmara Municipal de Barrancos.

Galves, Charlotte & Maria Clara Paixão de Sousa. 2005. Clitic placement and the position of subjects in the history of European Portuguese. *Amsterdam studies in the theory and history of linguistic science series* 4. 129–150.

Garrett, Jordan. in press. *Me gohtaba ehta linguaji barranquenha*: Variable object clitics in Barrancos, Portugal. In Timothy Guzton & Elizabeth Gielau (eds.), *East and West of the Pentacrest: Linguistic Studies in Honor of Paula Kempchinsky*. New York: John Benjamins.

González Caballero, Alberto. 1998. *El evangelio de San Lucas en Caló*. Annotated edition. Cordoba: Ediciones El Almendro de Cordoba, S. L.

Hualde, José Ignacio, Antxon Olarrea & Anna María Escobar. 2001. *Introducción a la lingüística hispánica*. Cambridge: Cambridge University Press.

Hualde, José Ignacio, Antxon Olarrea, Anna María Escobar & Catherine E. Travis. 2010. *Introducción a la lingüística hispánica*, 2nd edition. Cambridge: Cambridge University Press.

Lapesa, Rafael. 1981. *Historia de la lengua española*. Madrid: Gredos.

Leite de Vasconcelos, José. 1955. *Filologia barranquenha. Apontamentos para o seu estudo*. Águeda: Grafinal.

Luís, Ana. 2004. *Clitics as morphology*. University of Essex Ph.D. dissertation.

Maia, Clarinda de Azevedo. 2001. Fronteras del español: aspectos históricos y sociolingüísticos del contacto con el portugués en la frontera territorial. Paper presented at the *II Congreso Internacional de la Lengua Española: El español en la Sociedad de Información*, organized by La Real Academia Española and Instituto Cervantes, Valladolid, 16–19.

Marques, António Henrique de Oliveira. 1998. *Breve história de Portugal*, 3rd edn. Lisbon: Editorial Presença.

Mateus, Maria Helena Mira, Ana Maria Brito, Inês Duarte, and Isabel Hub Faria. 1989. *Gramática da Língua Portuguesa*. Lisbon: Caminho.

Matras, Yaron. 2000. Mixed languages: a functional-communicative approach. *Bilingualism: Language, and Cognition* 3(2). 79–99.

Meakins, Felicity. 2013. Mixed languages. In Peter Bakker & Yaron Matras (eds.), *Contact languages: A comprehensive guide*, 159–228. Berlin, Germany: De Gruyter Mouton.

Muysken, Peter. 1997. Media Lengua. In Sarah Thompson (ed.), *Contact languages: a wider perspective*, 365–426. Amsterdam and Philadelphia: John Benjamins.

Nascentes, Antenor. 1960. Lheísmo no português do Brasil. *Revista Letras*, 11. 108–113.

Navas Sánchez-Élez, María Victoria. 1992. El barranqueño: un modelo de lenguas en contacto. *Revista de Filología Románica* 9. 225–246.

Navas Sánchez-Élez, María Victoria. 1994. Canciones cantadas por los quintos de Barrancos. Un caso de contacto de lenguas. In Sílvio de Almeida Toledo Neto (ed.), *Variação linguística no espaço, no tempo e na sociedade: Proceedings of the Asociação Portuguesa de Linguística*, 147–182. APL/Edições Colibri.

Navas Sánchez-Élez, María Victoria. 1996. Importancia de los asentamientos humanos en la configuración de un área geográfica: El caso de la margen izquierda del Guadiana. In Juan M. Carrasco González & Antonioi Viudas Camarasa (eds.), *Proceedings of the Congreso Internacional Luso-Español de Lengua y Cultura de la Frontera, Cáceres*, 411–430. Cáceres: Universidad de Extremadura.

Navas Sánchez-Élez, María Victoria. 1997. Factores lingüísticos y extralingüísticos que determinan la alternancia de variantes de -/s/ en un dialecto luso-español, el barranqueño. *Revista de Filología Románica* 14. 391–410.

Navas Sánchez-Élez, María Victoria. 2001. Relaciones entre las hablas andaluzas y portuguesas meridionales próximas. *Revista de Filología Románica* 18. 171–185.
Nebrija, Antonio de. [1492] 1980. *Gramática de la lengua castellana*, edited by Antonio Quilis. Madrid: Editora Nacional.
Penny, Ralph. 1991. *History of the Spanish language*. Cambridge: Cambridge University Press.
Schwenter, Scott. A. 2014. Two kinds of differential object marking in Portuguese and Spanish. In Patrícia Amaral, & Ana Luís (eds.), *Portuguese-Spanish Interfaces: Diachrony, synchrony, and contact*, 237–260. Amsterdam: John Benjamins.
Serrão, Joel & A.H. de Oliveira Marques. 1990. *Nova história de Portugal. Portugal: Das invasões germânicas à "Reconquista"*, vol. 2. Lisbon: Editorial Presença.
Taylor, Jenna L. 2014. *Casting variability of a mixed language: Realizations of the verb* gustar *in Barranquenho*. Unpublished manuscript, Indiana University-Bloomington.
Thomason, Sarah G. & Terrance Kaufman. 1988. *Language contact, creolization, and genetic linguistics*. Berkeley: University of California Press.
Waltermire, Mark. 2006. *Social and linguistic correlates of Spanish-Portuguese bilingualism on the Uruguayan-Brazilian border*. University of New Mexico Ph.D. dissertation.
Washington, Hannah B. 2015. *Variable Object Clitic Placement: Evidence from European and Brazilian Portuguese*. The Ohio State University Ph.D. Dissertation.

Eeva Sippola
Ilokano-Spanish: Borrowing, code-switching or a mixed language?

1 Introduction

There are several well-known outcomes of language contact in the Philippines, including heavy lexical borrowing from Spanish into Philippine languages, the formation of the Chabacano creoles, and the widespread use of Taglish, a Tagalog-English code-switching variety. Based on a text sample taken from a letter in Schuchardt (1884), it has been suggested that a mixed language variety, Ilokano-Spanish, also existed in the Philippines; it would have been spoken by mestizos in the town of Vigan in the province of Ilocos Sur but died out by the end of the 19th century (Steinkrüger 2008: 226). This claim is echoed by Bakker (2017: 221) who calls it a Philippine Mestizo language (Ilokano-Spanish) in his structural classification of mixed languages. Ilokano (also known as Iloko, ilok1237, Northern-Luzon, Austronesian) is one of the largest languages of the Philippines by the number of speakers, spoken on the Northern parts of Luzon, while Spanish was the colonial language in the Philippines for over 300 years.

In this paper, I examine the Ilokano-Spanish text sample in order to assess the claim that it is an example of a mixed language. As very limited information on the author and the context of the letter is available, we only know that it was written in the late-19th century in the Philippines, the focus will be on a structural analysis of the text in question and a general overview of the sociohistorical context. The results of the structural analysis are compared to other documented Spanish contact varieties in the Philippines of that period, such as the creoles and pidgins (Lipski 2010; Fernández and Sippola 2017), code-switching practices in contemporary varieties such as Taglish (Bautista 2004), and other known mixed language systems (Meakins 2013; Bakker 2017).

Although the literature and data on mixed languages has increased over the past decades, and more of them have been identified (Meakins 2013: 159), their relatively low number is still an issue when it comes to making comprehensive statements about the existence and nature of this group as a class of languages. More information on the grammatical nature of these varieties and how they emerge in different types of social settings is therefore needed to address the central questions in the study of language contact and mixed varieties. Similarly,

---

Eeva Sippola, University of Helsinki, eeva.sippola@helsinki.fi

https://doi.org/10.1515/9781501511257-009

detailed studies on the history of different language contact situations in the Philippines can shed light on how the processes and outcomes involved might differ from more commonly studied contexts, such as those in the Atlantic and the Americas. So far, in many historical and linguistic works, there seems to be confusion about the characteristics of the Philippine contact varieties and the differences between them. Lipski (2010) explains the confusion to be due to the gradual processes of formation of the Philippine creole varieties, the high number of shared features among them, and that the similar borrowing processes have taken place in other Philippine languages. Also, for ideological reasons, contact languages are not seen as independent varieties. In addition, as shown more generally in historical sociolinguistics and contact linguistics (e.g. Arends 2017; van Rossem 2017; Ayres-Bennett 2018), a careful examination and critique of sources is crucial when trying to answer questions about the origins of contact varieties, such as the one under scrutiny.

2 Classifications of linguistic mixing

As a background for the study and for the purposes of classifying the text sample, I will offer a selection of definitions about borrowing, code-switching,[1] and mixed languages and what differentiates them. The differences between these processes generally depend on the perspective taken toward the language system and its stability. Mixed languages are stable codes, while code-switching is often understood as a situational practice. Borrowing is an outcome of language contact at the level of the language system. Code-switching can be seen on a diachronic continuum with respect to borrowing. Loans into one language often start off as synchronic codeswitches that gradually, through diachronic change, become established as part of the system. A borrowing is usually integrated into the recipient language's system, extending the vocabulary with new items, while code-switching usually takes the form of overt, unintegrated elements from different language varieties.

The first defining feature to distinguish between these classifications is thus that of the stability of a variety (Bakker 2017: 227). Code-switching patterns are common in multilingual settings, but they are generally not understood as stable practices or varieties. Mixed languages, on the other hand, are stable

---

[1] Code-switching is here understood as a practice, while the term code-mixing is reserved for the structural mixing in any variety or practice, from mixed languages to codeswitching practices. The terms are not used in opposition here but offer different vantage points to the mixing phenomena.

varieties that result from the fusion of two or more identifiable languages and present a split in the sources of their morphemes, which remains visible in their synchronic make-up. Varieties with heavy borrowing are often stable as well, in that despite the borrowing, no general shift or birth of a new language has occurred. In the case of Tagalog, for example, despite heavy borrowing, the grammatical structure has not been significantly affected.

The second area of definitions has to do with the social and historical factors, such as the level and nature of bilingualism. Bi- or multilingualism is common to all the processes, but there are again differences as to how these are understood. For code-switching to happen, the speaker needs to be bilingual, and the switching is often understood as happening at an *individual* level. Mixed languages on the other hand, are often identified as a phenomenon at the *community* level (Meakins 2013: 156). They emerge in situations of community bilingualism, and can sometimes lead to situations where the two languages participating in their formation are no longer present. Bilingualism is also needed for borrowing to happen, but borrowings can spread from bilingual individuals to the community level and then be taken on by monolingual speakers as well. Furthermore, severe social upheaval is often understood as an important factor in the formation of mixed languages (Meakins 2013: 186), whereas this factor has not been identified in communities where code-switching is common.

The third area has to do with identity functions. Mixed languages often develop in relation to the expression of identity, reflecting either a new social category or an ancestral group membership, often as a conscious linguistic operation led by a group of speakers (Meakins 2013: 181). Code-switching or borrowing can also have identity functions, where switches or borrowings index social affiliations (e.g. Auer 2005). Consequently, although identity is central to understanding the formation of a variety or a practice, this factor can be relevant to either stable varieties or more situational or stylistic codes, so it alone cannot be used to distinguish between them.

The sociolinguistic situations where certain structural mixing patterns are found can also be used to classify mixing types (see Table 1). For example, insertional code-mixing often happens in situations with asymmetric power relations, typically in postcolonial settings. Here the L1, the original language of the community, especially from a historical perspective, functions as the base language, and speakers often have limited proficiency in the L2, which is the new, introduced language (Muysken 2013a: 720).[2] In insertional code-mixing,

---

[2] It should be noted that communities do not always reflect the L1/L2 divide at the individual level. In situations of widespread bilingualism, the assignation of these labels can be challenging

Table 1: Sociolinguistic factors and strategies in code-mixing (adapted from Muysken 2013a: 720).

Code-mixing pattern	Sociolinguistic factors	Proficiency	Strategies
Insertion	Asymmetric power relations, postcolonial settings	Low proficiency in L2	L1 as the base language
Alternation	Political competition	High bilingual proficiency	Universal principles for combinations
Back-flagging	Language shift in second or third generation	High proficiency in L2	L2 as the base language

one language determines the overall structure into which constituents from another language are inserted. The process is constrained by categorical or semantic congruence, or equivalence between the inserted element and the properties of the slot into which it is inserted (Muysken 2000: 95, 230). Borrowing, code-switching, and mixed languages all show insertional patterns of mixing. Alternational mixing patterns are typical for communities with high levels of bilingual proficiency, where the languages in question are often in political competition. Code-switching typically shows alternational patterns; for example, Taglish alternational code-switching conforms to this situation to some degree (see 3.2). Here languages occur alternately, with the switch point being located at a major syntactic boundary, constrained by both grammatical and interactional factors (Muysken 2000: 96–97). Another relevant type identified in Muysken's (2000, 2013a) classification is back-flagging.[3] Back-flagging happens in situations of language shift in the second or third generation. The community's historical L1 is used to highlight aspects of ethnic or linguistic identities, although the speakers are generally more proficient in the L2 of the community. The structural types and the sociolinguistic processes connected to them make clear that with shift in time, the labels L1 and L2 can change for individuals and also communities, leading to situations where the assignment of these labels is challenging. Beyond the

---

and should be done taking several factors into account according to the research question and the point in time when the assignment is being made.

3 In addition, Muysken (2000) has congruent lexicalization as part of his typology. It is characteristic of communities with relaxed language norms and closely-knit networks, where the languages in question have a long history of contact. Speakers have high levels of bilingual proficiency, and the languages in contact share typological and/or lexical properties; this type is common for code-mixing between related languages and for dialect contact.

structural patterns of mixing, we can identify another extralinguistic feature for classification: power relations between the languages that affect the selection of the prestige language in the community.

An additional structural factor that is often used to argue for the differences between the types is the degree of mixing. Bakker (2017: 220) points out that there is no consensus about what degree of mixing is needed for a variety to be called a mixed language, although the degree of borrowing in heavy borrowing languages is nevertheless significantly lower than in documented mixed languages. In addition, borrowing does not generally affect words of the basic lexicon to the same degree as in mixed languages.

From the above it becomes clear that many extralinguistic and structural features and processes are shared between borrowing, code-switching, and mixed languages. The differences focus mostly on the perspective we take on a contact phenomenon, structural tendencies, and power relations in the communities where language contact takes place. A careful contextualization of the object in its social history is therefore needed when we want to classify a text sample.

3 Contact varieties in Philippine (post)colonial history

Over 150 languages are spoken in the Philippines. The great majority of these are local Philippine languages, but varieties of Chinese, Malay, and European colonial languages have also historically been spoken there. The centuries-long contacts between local and other languages have resulted in different contact outcomes. Although there has been lexical and grammatical influence from Malay and Chinese varieties, the attention here is given to contact situations starting in the colonial era, with special focus on Spanish and English – the languages that are relevant for the cases of mixing that are discussed in this chapter.

These examples (see Table 2 for an overview) show that Spanish and English have both similarities and differences with regard to contact outcomes. From these examples it is clear that trilingual mixing is common in the Philippines. It may well be that other mixing practices also existed during the Spanish colonial period, but the only samples available are very limited and often confusing (see, e.g., Lipski 2001, 2010).

Table 2: Examples of inter-ethnic contact varieties in Philippine history.

Variety	Mix	Type	Speakers	Time Period
Chinese Spanish Pidgin	Spanish, Hokkien,[4] Tagalog	Pidgin	Chinese merchants, no native speakers	Until early 20th century
Chabacano	Spanish, Tagalog, Cebuano, Hiligaynon	Creole	Native speakers from diverse social classes	18th century onwards
Taglish	Tagalog, English	Code-switching variety	Upper class, emerging native speakers?	1960s onwards
Hokaglish	Hokkien, Tagalog, English	Mixed variety	Filipino-Chinese community, no native speakers	From the American period?

3.1 Spanish contact varieties

The Spanish colonial period in the Philippines lasted for over three centuries, from the early 16th century to the end of the 19th century, but Spanish was never widely adopted as a colonial language by the majority of the native population. The reason has to do with the low numbers of Spanish-speaking migrants, which meant that there was no significant Spanish mestizo group or any possibility for demographic shifts among the general native population to take place (Lipski, Mühlhäusler, and Duthin 1996).

The socioethnic composition of the Philippines during the Spanish colonial period included different groups divided and administered according to their ethnic background and their relation to the Spanish (García de los Arcos 1999: 57): *españoles* 'Spanish' included those born in Europe or in the colonies, *indios* referred to the indigenous population of the Philippines, and *mestizos* could refer to either *mestizos de sangley* or *mestizos de español*. The former were descendants of the local indigenous population and the Chinese, while the latter were born out of unions of Spanish with other groups. These groups were also the basis for taxation, and to some degree, it was possible to change affiliation to a group by marrying into a different group or by other means (Wickberg 1964: 65–66). By the mid-19th century, the influence and size of the Chinese mestizo class had grown significantly: it was the largest non-indigenous group of the islands,

---

[4] I.e. Min Nan.

which led to the term *mestizo* coming to mean primarily Chinese mestizo (Wickberg 1964: 67, 80).

Spanish was the prestige language in the Philippines during the Spanish colonial era. It was spoken by the colonial administrators, the military and clergy, and the local indigenous and mestizo groups that occupied the highest positions in the colonial hierarchy. For most of the Spanish period, Spanish education was limited to a small elite, that of *españoles* and selected members of the *mestizo* and *indio* groups. The local population naturally spoke Spanish to differing degrees due to the continuing presence of the colonial language throughout the islands and the prestige attached to it, but the historical representations of these have clear traits of learner varieties (Lipski 2001: 133).

During the Spanish era, a number of contact varieties arose in different parts of the Philippines. The most well-known are Chinese Spanish Pidgin and the Philippine Spanish Creole varieties, collectively known as Chabacano. Chinese Spanish Pidgin served specific social functions in trade between different ethnic groups. The Chinese had an important economic position in the colonial Philippines. Their monopoly over food provision, retail trading, and artisanal works made them a crucial part of the everyday functions of the colony. In addition, they traded between coastal China and Manila as well as distributed the imports from Manila to other parts of Luzon (Wickberg 1964: 67). The Chinese Spanish Pidgin was a rather stable code, with some defining features such as unmarked verbs, the personal pronouns *mia* '1SG' and *suya* '2SG', the substitution of /r/ for [l], and clitics without referents in verbs (Reinecke 1937: 823; Lipski 2010: 9). It was used by Chinese merchants in commerce with the local population, or between these groups and the Spanish. It was not a native language nor was it used as a lingua franca between local population groups who shared a common native language (Lipski 2001: 132).[5]

The Chabacano varieties are today spoken in Zamboanga, Cavite City, and the town of Ternate, but similar varieties elsewhere in the archipelago have also historically been documented, although not in Vigan (Fernández 2011; Fernández and Sippola 2017: 305–307). Other names, such as *español de cocina* 'kitchen Spanish', *español de tienda* 'shop Spanish', and *lengua de Parian* 'language of the Parian'[6] were used to refer to Chabacano. This denomination sometimes also included other types of contact varieties to different degrees, which were often poorly described by Spanish narrators (Fernández 2011: 200).

---

5 Lipski (2001, 2010) calls the Chinese Spanish Pidgin "Kitchen Spanish", a denomination generally used for Chabacano.
6 *Parian* refers to the Chinese district in Manila or other towns, which were also centers for commercial activity.

Of interest here is to state that all the Chabacano varieties show clear creole traits in that their lexicon is for the most part of Spanish origin while the structure differs from it: the TAM system consists of preverbal aspectual particles and an invariant stem, gender is generally not marked in adjectives or nouns, the plural is marked with the Philippine plural particle *mga*, etc.

Although there is no agreement as to the exact origin and development of the creole varieties, we know that Chabacano was used by different socioeconomic groups in the time period that interests us, the 19th century, at least in Manila and Cavite. It was used in interactions between the Spanish and the local population as well as serving as an in-group language, such as in the restricted enclave of Ternate (Schuchardt 1884; Fernández 2011). Chabacano samples showing its variety of uses can be found in 19th century sources (Schuchardt 1884; Fernández and Sippola 2017). According to Fernández (2011, 2012), the crystallization of Chabacano was linked to the emergence of a new socioeconomic class, that of the Chinese mestizos. This socioeconomic group's position was a favorable one in that they paid less taxes than the Chinese, were more hispanized than the indigenous population, and overlapped with the leading indigenous class in the colonial hierarchy. The mestizos used local varieties of Spanish that at a point in time would have led to the consolidation of Chabacano as an in-group language for some and as a code of social promotion for others.

3.2 English contact varieties

After the Spanish period, when the United States took control of the Philippines, English quickly took over as the prestige language, and today it is used widely in the government, education, business, the media, and especially in urban areas of the Philippines (Thompson 2003: ch. 2). Today it is the official language of the Philippines, alongside the Tagalog-based Filipino. English has penetrated the personal and private lives of Filipinos, and some even learn it as a first language. Proficiency in English is often connected to socioeconomic status as those more proficient in the language tend to be in a higher socioeconomic situation (Borlongan and Hyuk Lim 2013).

The English contact has given rise to varying degrees of bilingualism and mixed codes. A lectal division of Philippine Englishes (Llamzon 1997) can be made with regard to their proximity or distance to Standard American English, but this is also influenced by social and cultural factors. As put by Gonzales (2017: 88): "The English used by a Filipina *tindera* or stall vendor would most likely be different from the English spoken by a middle-class

Filipina businesswoman. At the same time, the Philippine English spoken by Filipino-Chinese could be distinct from the English spoken by Filipino-Koreans or 'pure' Filipinos".

The most well-studied code-switching variety is Taglish, involving Tagalog and English (Bautista 1980).[7] It was first attested in the late 1960s as a creation of educated Filipinos and spread from the classroom to the general population via mass media, especially radio and TV (Thompson 2003: 41). Two types of Taglish code-switching are identified by Bautista (2004): the most common type is used by speakers with high levels of competence in both Tagalog and English, but deficiency-driven switching also exists. In general, Taglish is the code for informal communication, while the languages are kept apart in formal situations (Thompson 2003: 41).

Taglish is often characterized as an alternational type of code-switching, but when the base language is Tagalog, insertional mixing predominates. Here, English insertions into the Tagalog base tend to be limited to noun and noun phrase insertion, rejoinders, tags, and conjunctions (Bautista 1980; Thompson 2003: 153). When Tagalog insertions occur in the English frame, they tend to be limited to discourse items such as conjunctions, enclitics, linkers, the plural marker *mga*, the affirmative marker *oo*, and formulaic expressions (Bautista 1986). The latter type is occasionally called Engalog or Coño English. This variety tends to be used by a small group of elite English speakers who use Tagalog insertions as a way of indexing, or back-flagging, their Filipino identity (Smedley 2006: 40).

In addition, a mixed variety called Hokaglish or Salamstam-oe 'mixed language' has been documented (Zulueta 2007; Gonzales 2016, 2018). It is the use of Philippine Hokkien, Tagalog, and English in conversation where Philippine Hokkien dominates. Gonzales (2016: 112) proposes that the Filipino-Chinese communities would have been using this mixed variety for a long time, excluding the contemporary immigration from China. The variety is used for marking insider group identity among young Chinese-Filipinos and to signal a good socioeconomic position (Zulueta 2007).

4 A letter in Ilokano-Spanish

The text sample is a letter sent to the Spanish-language newspaper *La Oceanía Española* in 1884 and quoted in Schuchardt (1884: 125–126). We do not have

---

[7] Other mixed varieties involving English and other Philippine languages also exist, but since Taglish is the most well studied one, it will be the example studied here.

much information about it beyond what is explained by Schuchardt (1884). Schuchardt collected most of his material from correspondence with people located in creole-speaking areas, often colonial administrators or clergymen making use of diverse sources, including newspapers. *La Oceanía Española* was one of the channels Schuchardt used to collect material from the Philippines. The newspaper was one of the main publications in Manila at the time, with a daily edition between 1877 and 1899. In response to Schuchardt's inquiries, people from different parts of the Philippines wrote to the newspaper with opinions and samples of contact varieties of Spanish. One of the letters included the Ilokano-Spanish text, and Schuchardt (1884: 125, footnote 1) used it to show that "in certain places, the Malayization of Spanish words has no limits" when discussing the nature of the structural blending in the Spanish-Tagalog contact.

The text is a letter to a friend, and in it, two main topics of information are given: the author of the letter has been appointed chief of the *barrio* 'neighborhood', and the recipient's *comadre* 'godmother' or 'close friend' is pregnant and has also had an accident. Schuchardt (1884: 125, footnote 1) considers it a sample of the language used among the Mestizos in Vigan. The example lines are ordered as follows: first, the original text in Schuchardt (1884: 125–126) where the Tagalog lexical items are indicated with underlining; second, the same line in with Ilokano words in modern Ilokano orthography and morpheme division (when applicable); third, the gloss in English; fourth, the English translation; and fifth, the original Spanish translation from Schuchardt (1884).

(1) *Mi   estimado amigo*:
    Mi   estimado amigo:
    my   dear   friend
    'My dear friend:
    Mi estimado amigo:

(2) *iparticiparco   qca   á   nanombraranac   á*
    i-participar-ko kenka   a   na-nombrar-an-ak a
    TH-inform-1SG   2SG.OBL LK   PFV-nominate-V-1SG LK
    I inform you that I was appointed
    te participo que me han nombreado

(3) cabo del barrio   qt   sentirec   unay ti   caasanmo⁸
    kabo del barrio   ket   sintir-e-k   unay ti   ka-asan-mo
    chief of the barrio and feel-V-1SG   very the   NOM-absence-2SG
    chief of the barrio and I regret much your absence
    cabo del barrio y siento mucho tu ausencia

(4) ditoy porque   convidarenca   met   comá á
    ditoy porque   kumbida(r)-en-ka   met   komá a
    here   because   invite-V-2SG   also OPT   LK
    here because I would invite you also to
    aquí porque te convidaría también para

(5) maquipagdespachar   itoy bassit á   napreparar   ditoy balay.
    makipag-despatsar   itoy bassit a   na-preparar   ditoy balay
    JNT-serve   this little LK   PFV-prepare   here   house
    the little party here at home.
    despachar la preparación que tengo en casa.

(6) Unica á   noticia á   maiproporcionarca   qca:
    unica a   noticia a   mai-proporcionar-ka   kenka
    only   LK   news   LK   POT-deliver-2SG   2SG.OBL
    The only news I am able to deliver to you
    Unica noticia que te puedo proporcionar

(7) ni   comadrem   buntis   manen   qt   idi
    ni   komadre-m   buntis   manen   ket   idi
    ART   godmother-2SG   pregnant   again   and   before
    your close friend is pregnant again and when
    tu comadre está otra vez en cinta y un dia, cuando

(8) inda   cobraren   ti   buisna,   timmacbu   qt
    in-da   cobrar-en   ti   buis-na   timmacbu   ket
    go-3PL   charge-V   ART   tax-3SG   ran   and
    they went to collect the tax of hers, she ran and
    fueron á cobrarla el tributo, echó á correr y

---

8 Probably *caawanmo* (Steinkrüger 2008: 225, footnote 5).

(9) *natnag idiay* <u>batalan</u> *qt* <u>nabiac</u> *diay quiliquilina.*
natnag idiay batalan ket na-biac diay quiliquili-na
fell over.there porch and PFV-break that armpit-3SG
fell on the proch/roof and broke that armpit of hers.
se cayó en la azotea: consecuencia de este accidente fué la hendidura de su sobaco.

(10) *Na castigar ngarud, pues* <u>naarimuhanan</u> *la unay.*
na castigar ngarud pues naarimuhanan la(eng) unay
PFV punish then so thrifty only very
Then punished for being so stingy.
digno castigo de su avaricia.

(11) *Toy amigo qt servidormo Z*
toy amigo ket servidor-mo Z
this friend and servant-2SG NAME
This friend and servant of yours Z.'
Tu amigo y servidor Z.

5 Mixing practices

5.1 Structures and types of mixing

The letter contains 65 words of Spanish, Ilokano, and Tagalog origin. The Spanish component includes verbs in infinitive form, nouns, conjunctions, and a possessive pronoun. The Spanish nouns *amigo* 'friend', *cabo del barrio* 'chief of the barrio', *comadre* 'godmother', and *servidor* 'servant' are related to social roles. Some of these, such as *comadre* and *amigo* have also been borrowed to Philippine languages. The Spanish verbs do not pertain to basic lexical verbs, but also indicate a variety of social meanings and many of them have been borrowed to modern Ilokano, sometimes with semantic changes (*sintir* 'to resent', *kumbida(r)* 'invitation', *agkumbida* 'to invite', *despatsar* 'to sell, to dismiss, to dispatch', *agkobra* 'to collect a payment', *kastigar* 'to punish', cf. Rubino 2000).

The grammatical affixes and clitics are from Ilokano and indicate thematic roles, person, verbalizers,[9] and TAM meanings. The word order of the main

---

9 The common suffixes that are here glossed as verbalizers are used, among other things, to transitivize nouns in Ilokano.

Table 3: Mixed verbs in the Ilokano-Spanish letter.

Verb	Spanish root	Ilokano affix
iparticiparco	participar 'share'	i- 'TH', -co '1SG'
nanombraranac	nombrar 'name'	na- 'PFV', -an- 'V', -ac '1SG'
sentirec	sentir 'feel'	-ec '1SG'
convidarenca	convidar 'invite'	-en 'V', -ca '2SG'
maquipagdespachar	despachar 'take care of'	maquipag- 'JNT'
napreparar	preparar 'prepare'	na- 'PFV'
maiproporcionarca	proporcionar 'provide'	mai-'POT' -ca '2SG'
cobraren	cobrar 'charge'	-en 'V'
na castigar	castigar 'punish'	na(-) 'PFV'

clauses is verb-initial, as in the Philippine languages in general and Ilokano in particular (Rubino 2005: 331). Ilokano and Spanish do not differ in typological terms as to how subjects are marked: in both languages subjects are (generally) marked as suffixes (Dryer 2011) However, there are no full noun or independent pronominal subjects in the text that would be expressed. In Ilokano, clauses with predicative adjectives do not have a copula and show a predicate-initial pattern (Rubino 2008: 519). Similarly, there is no copula in (7) *ni comadre-m buntis manen* [ART-friend-2SG pregnant again] 'your friend is pregnant again', but the sentence is not predicate-initial. In (10), *naarimuhanan la unay* [thrifty only very] 'being very stingy', the subject is not expressed.

The greeting formula in line (1) is in Spanish, while the closing (11) shows a mixed structure. In the closing, only the nouns are in Spanish, while the demonstrative pronoun *toy* 'this', the conjunction *qt* [ket] 'and', and the possessive suffix *-mo* are expressed with Ilokano items.

The Tagalog elements mentioned in Schuchardt (1884: 125–126) are five in number and are mostly lexical elements (*buntis* 'pregnant', *buis(na)* '(her) tax' < Tag. *buwis* 'tax', *timmacbu* 'ran' < Tag. *tumakbo*, *batalan* 'porch', *nabiac* 'broke' < Tag. *nabiyak*, and *naarimuhanan* 'thrifty'). A note accompanying the text mentions that these words are from Tagalog, and according to some Ilokanos, only used in Vigan (Schuchardt 1884: 126 footnote).

The types of mixing patterns observed are generally insertional, with Spanish lexical items inserted into an Ilokano frame. An alternational pattern is found in the opening paragraph in Spanish, which alternates with the mixed code with an Ilokano frame in the main body of the letter. No creole or pidgin traits are attested, beyond general borrowing patterns that can also be found in these types of languages.

5.2 Sociohistorical characteristics

Sociohistorical context might give us some clues as to the nature of the text and its author. The level and nature of bilingualism and access to Spanish in the community where the letter was written is central. No information on the author of the letter is available, but it was probably sent from Vigan, a city in Ilocos Sur, in the northern part of the island of Luzon. Vigan is known for its Spanish heritage as well as for the fact that it was an important trading center between northern Luzon and Chinese traders from the Fujian province in China. The city had an important Chinese mestizo population and a *pariancillo* 'Chinese district' (Doeppers 1972). As the frame of the letter is for the most part in Ilokano, it is probable that the author was a fluent speaker of that language. We also know that the person who sent the letter to the newspaper, and probably held a close relationship with the author and/or recipient of the letter, if not actually one of them, was a reader of a Spanish-language newspaper, and thus fluent in this language, and belonged to a class that participated in the cultural activities of colonial society. There are no cues as to the ethnicity of the author in the letter itself, but due to his participation in Spanish-speaking cultural activities and his knowledge of Ilokano, he might have belonged to the Chinese or Spanish mestizo groups, or been an upper class *indio*. These groups had access to education in Spanish, and members of these groups would have occupied minor administrative positions such as *cabo del barrio*.

Did the mixed variety have identity functions? The mixed code was used in a letter of personal intimacy, which gives us some clues based on the use of other contact varieties of the time. Several examples from the Filipino elites of that time, both from mestizo and *indio* groups, and elsewhere show that the creole varieties were used in personal communication as an in-group language. These members of the elite had (full) access to Spanish as well, which they used in educational and official institutions (Fernández 2013). However, another correspondent to *La Oceanía Española* wrote in Chabacano that the letter sent from Ilocos is merely the language used by the people in the food stalls and selling vegetables,[10] not the elevated, beautiful kitchen Spanish, i.e. the

---

10 *el lengua del mangá saluyot, propio de carindería, donde ta ende el mangá gulay* in the original.

creole Chabacano, that Schuchardt was looking for (Schuchardt 1884: 123). This note tells us more about the creole variety than the Ilokano-Spanish text, showing that it was already consolidated and associated positively with a certain identity. Yet, it is unlikely that a market seller of the lower social classes, with more limited access to Spanish, would have corresponded with a friend by writing letters. Due to the text type, a personal letter, it is thus probable that both the writer and the recipient had access to Spanish. Also, using a mixed code could have served identity functions, as in the creole varieties.

The power relations affecting the selection of the prestige language are well documented from the colonial period in question. It is clear that Spanish had the highest level of prestige. Although the Philippine independence movement had already started to develop, the Filipino revolutionaries used Spanish as their home language and in cultural and social life (Fernández 2013: 371).

5.3 Degrees of mixing

As to the degree of mixing found in the text, a simple calculation of the written words separated by a space shows the following patterns: the majority of the words (37) are from Ilokano, and we can attest a lower number of Spanish (12) and Tagalog (6) words, while there are in total nine mixed words with a Spanish root/stem and Ilokano affixes.[11] The total number of words is too low to give any valid calculations about the degree of mixing, but the Spanish component occupies less than 30%, even if the mixed words with Ilokano affixes are included.

A look into the degrees and types of borrowings in other Philippine languages gives us some context. Spanish has had extensive lexical influence on Tagalog and other Philippine languages, and Bowen (1971: 948) connects the degree of borrowing with the amount and type of contact between Spanish and the Philippine languages. The more extensive the contact, the more the cultural penetration of Spanish can be observed. The most studied language with a borrowed component is Tagalog, which has been estimated to have borrowed between 10 and 30 percent of its lexicon from Spanish (Bowen 1971; Wolff 2001). No studies of Spanish or English borrowings in Ilokano are available, but Panganiban (1961: iii) estimates that the Tagalog case is similar to other major languages of the Philippines, including Ilokano. A look into Ilokano dictionary (Rubino 2000) reveals that many of the Spanish lexical items in the sample letter have actually been incorporated into modern Ilokano (see 5.1). This means

---

11 The letter Z symbolizing the author of the letter is left out of this calculation.

that the degree of mixing of elements from different languages in the analyzed text is quite similar to general observations on the extent of borrowing into Philippine languages. It should be kept in mind, however, that the realization of these percentages in individual texts might naturally be very different.

As to the types, the Spanish borrowings in Tagalog are most visible in nouns, the counting system, the calendar, the expression of time, and greetings. Even for some core semantics that are seen as the least borrowable in language contact, Tagalog has borrowings that have fully or partly replaced the original forms, e.g. *braso* 'arm' and *kantá* 'song' from Sp. *brazo* and *cantar* 'to sing' (Baklanova 2017). The lexical borrowings also include function words, such as the modal verb *puwede* 'can, be able to' (< Sp. *puede* 'can-3SG.PRS'), other modal particles, such as *siguro* 'probably' and *sigurado* 'certain' (< Sp. *seguro* 'certain' and *asegurado* 'guaranteed'), and elements in comparative constructions, where the Spanish-origin comparative *más* 'more' is used. It is difficult to estimate the penetration of the Spanish words into the basic lexicon of the mixed code in the letter but looking at the semantics of the Spanish items present, they are rather far removed from the items generally included in basic word listings. In addition, it is probable that a local fully immersed in the Ilokano-speaking surroundings of Vigan would have known the Ilokano words that the Spanish words in the text replaced. The Spanish items are greeting and farewell formulas, occasional nouns or noun phrases (*cabo del barrio*, *única á noticia*, and *comadre*), two conjunctions, and – differently from Tagalog – verbs that function as the stem for Ilokano affixes. To explain the selection of these specific Spanish words, we have to look elsewhere. For the Spanish borrowings in Tagalog, Stolz (1996) and Wolff (2001) have suggested that the use of the colonial language was a means of acquiring power in colonial Philippine society. Social lexical items in the Ilokano-Spanish text, such as the opening formula and verbs with social meanings, as well as elements of discourse organization (e.g., conjunctions), would therefore be easily borrowed.

Similar examples of codes with heavy borrowing are, for example, the hyperformal English of Indian officers in colonial India (Babu English, Kachru 2006: 266–267) and the formal register of Tetum in East Timor (Williams-van Klinken 2002), with an exceptionally high number of items of the colonial languages.[12] The mixing in these codes appear to be especially associated with formal, written, and administrative language and not with domains more prevalent in informal daily communication, due to the fact that they were acquired to the communicative repertoires of language users who acquired and used the

---

[12] I thank the anonymous reviewer for pointing out these similarities.

colonial language formally for official administrative tasks. Similarly, in other Philippine contact varieties, the degree and type of mixedness has been said to correlate with the social position of the speaker and the domain of use (see section 3).

5.4 From borrowing to code-switching

Some of the mixing patterns observed in the text show similar patterns to recent borrowings from English into Tagalog or Filipino. They are abundant in everyday speech and connected to the code-switching practices of urban bilinguals (Baklanova 2017: 40). Baklanova explains that the code-switching variety, Taglish, functions as a model for borrowings into the speech of monolinguals. The most frequent intrasentential switches in Taglish are also borrowed by Tagalog/Filipino monolinguals and incorporated into the Tagalog vocabulary used in a variety of contexts, from everyday speech to more specific domains.

The degree of the integration of a borrowing into Tagalog can be assessed by different means. For example, in written text, Tagalog speakers often handle nonce borrowings as foreign words with italics or by putting a hyphen between the Tagalog prefix and the English root, as in (12a, b). In the Ilokano-Spanish text, the Spanish items are fully integrated in the writing, except for the marker *na* in (10), which is written separately before *castigar* 'punish', although all other verbs present affixation.

(12) Tagalog with English borrowings (Baklanova 2017: 40)
 a. *Nagtungo sila sa Iloilo City at doon sila na-stranded*
  headed 3PL to NAME and there 3PL V-stranded
  'They headed to Iloilo City and there they got stranded.'
 b. *kina-shock ko talaga*
  CAUS.PFV-shock 1SG really
  'I was really shocked.'

Assimilated borrowings are integrated either phonetically, morphologically, or semantically (Baklanova 2017: 42). Based on a written text, not much can be said about phonetic assimilation in the Ilokano-Spanish code, nor are there clear examples of semantic assimilation. Morphologically assimilated words are simplified into indivisible root words and used for further derivation, as in Tagalog *istambáyan* 'a place where idlers gather' and *istambayán* 'to loiter'. The Ilokano items in the mixed text do not show derivational modifications to Spanish borrowings, as the base is always a Spanish verb, and thus the affixes do not serve derivational functions such as changing word class (see Table 3). Verbal affixation similar to the Ilokano-Spanish text is found in (12a, b) with *na-stranded* 'got stranded' and *kina-shock* 'was shocked'. The latter example is from a famous Philippine media figure and is also found quoted as *kina-shocked* in other news sources,[13] showing that the borrowing of the English verb has not yet been fully integrated into Tagalog.

In the code-switching variety Taglish, beyond noun insertion, switches happen at equivalence points (Bautista 1980: 200). These equivalence points are, e.g., the English prepositional phrase and the Tagalog *ng*-genitive phrase or the *sa*-oblique phrase and prepositional phrases in general. Bautista (1980: 178) used word order and major vs. minor constituents to establish the base language for the switch to happen. In the Ilokano-Spanish text, the types of mixing that are found include noun and conjunction insertion, verb stem insertion (Table 3), and alternational switches pertaining to the greeting and closing formulas (1)–(2), (10)–(11). The main difference is that Taglish is generally described as alternational switching, while it is clear that the Ilokano-Spanish text mostly favors insertional patterns within clauses and phrases.

5.5 A mixed language?

Was the Ilokano-Spanish text a sample of a mixed language spoken by the mestizos of Vigan? In the previous pages, we have explored the sociohistorical conditions typical of that time and of other contact varieties in the Philippines, as well as the sample's structural characteristics. In order to assess the nature of the Ilokano-Spanish letter, its sociohistorical framing can be discussed in the light of a general overview of the structural types of mixed languages and typical sociolinguistic factors is presented in Table 4 (based on Muysken 2000, 2013a) as well as mixing patterns (see Table 1).

When a lexifier language has a very limited presence in the community, it is often the L1 that takes the role of the base language. This kind of situation is typical of Media Lengua in the Quechua-speaking communities, for example, where Spanish has only a limited presence. In the case of Spanish in the Philippines, the lexifier language had a relatively limited presence in the everyday life of the masses, although Spanish was used by colonial elites of different ethnic backgrounds. It is also true that the Ilokano-Spanish situation reflects bilingual settings

---

[13] E.g. https://news.abs-cbn.com/entertainment/04/19/14/when-did-bistek-kris-start-dating (accessed 11 November 2019).

Table 4: Sociolinguistic factors and strategies in mixed languages (adapted from Muysken 2013a: 720).

Type of mixed language	Sociolinguistic factors	Strategies
L1-oriented mixed languages, e.g. Media Lengua	Lexifier language with a very limited presence in the community	L1 base language
Compromise mixed languages, e.g. Michif	Bilingual settings with a clear division between the two languages	L1/L2 base language
L2-oriented mixed languages, e.g. Gurindji Kriol	'New' language provides essential components through language shift	L2 base language

with a clear division between the two languages: Ilokano for the everyday domains of native Filipinos and Spanish for the colonial administration, which was made up of both colonial mestizo/indio elites and native Spanish speakers. Muysken (2013a: 720) sees these bilingual situations as typical of compromise mixed languages, such as Michif, where the base language can either be the L1 or the L2 of the community. The third type in Muysken's (2013a) typology requires a situation of community language shift. We know that the general native population in Luzon never shifted to Spanish, so this would only be possible had the mestizo group shifted to Spanish and then resorted to Ilokano elements for identity purposes, which does not seem probable based on the mixing patterns of the text and the Ilokano frame.

The structures of mixing in the sample resemble lexical borrowing in modern Tagalog, and to some extent the insertional types of mixing found in the code-switching varieties of Taglish and Hockaglish. However, no clear alternational patterns more typical of contemporary code-switching are found in the text. In the letter, the pattern of mixing is clearly Spanish and Tagalog lexical insertions into an Ilokano base. The insertional pattern is also typical of certain mixed languages, such as Media Lengua, as pointed out by Steinkrüger (2008: 227). Media Lengua (which has Quechua grammar and Spanish lexicon) is one of the mixed languages that display primarily lexical mixing, together with Ma'á/Mbugu (Bantu grammar and Cushitic lexicon) and Angloromani (English grammar and English and Romani lexicon), although in it, Romani lexicon is rather sporadic and always optional (Matras 2010). For all these cases, the creation of a separate identity after language shift is crucial. In the Ma'á/Mbugu case, the expression of a non-Bantu identity led to the creation of the mixed language (Mous 2013), while Angloromani is used to express group cohesion and solidarity (Matras et al. 2007: 173, 177). In the case of Media Lengua, young migrant workers' contact with Hispanic urban society set them apart from the peasant community in the areas where Media Lengua is spoken, and it is now an intragroup language not understood by outsiders (Muysken 2013b).

Like the speakers of Media Lengua, the writer of the letter, likely a mestizo from Vigan, was not necessarily that different from other Filipinos, but identification with the colonial Spanish and hispanized elites could have been an incentive to set them apart. There are other parallels as well. As in the Tagalog case, many dialects of Quechua contain Spanish words due to the centuries of contact. In the case of Media Lengua, however, it is relatively easy to set the mixed language apart from these dialects due to the degree of mixing. In Media Lengua, 90% of Quechua roots, including basic vocabulary, have been replaced by Spanish roots (Muysken 2013b). As we saw in 5.3, the degree of mixing cannot be reliably estimated based on mere 65 words of the Ilokano-Spanish letter, although the borrowings and the pattern of incorporation into Ilokano point towards heavy borrowing. In addition, for a variety to be categorized as a mixed language, it should be seen as a stable code. Both code-switching varieties and borrowing permit more fluctuation. However, the issue of stability is impossible to answer based on a single letter and without more contextual information than what is available. Although there are some overlaps between the functions, strategies, and patterns of mixing in the text and the known mixed languages, the overall balance does not permit us to rule out a one-off performative function of the text or its use as a stylistic resource in the written communication.

6 Conclusions

This paper offers detailed information about an Ilokano-Spanish text previously claimed to be an example of a mixed language, showing that it presents mixing that is characteristic of Ilokano with heavy borrowing from Spanish. Motivation for this type of mixing could have included social positioning within the colonial hierarchy and participation in Spanish cultural life, as well as possibly serving identity functions for a mestizo group. Comparison to other mixed codes from the Philippines, including both creoles and code-switching varieties, shows that based on this isolated sample, it is difficult to state conclusively if we are dealing with a case of a mixed language, code-switching, or borrowing. All of these varieties can be used to express identity, but the lack of information about the author and other domains of use for this code allows room for little more than speculation. Despite the challenges presented by this limited sample, however, detailed case studies such as the one presented here can contribute to the debate on processes of language mixing and the boundaries between different language types where grammatical analysis of the mixing practices is complemented with social factors.

Abbreviations

ART	article
JNT	joint action
L1	first language
L2	second language
LK	linker
NOM	nominalizer
OBL	oblique
OPT	optative
PFV	perfective
POT	potentive
SG	singular
TH	theme
V	verbalizer

References

Arends, Jacques. 2017. *Language and slavery. A social and linguistic history of the Suriname creoles*. Amsterdam: John Benjamins.
Ayres-Bennett, Wendy. 2018. Historical sociolinguistics and tracking language change. In Wendy Ayres-Bennett & Janice Carruthers (eds.), *Manual of Romance sociolinguistics*, 253–279. Berlin: De Gruyter.
Auer, Peter. 2005. A postscript: code-switching and social identity. *Journal of Pragmatics* 37. 403–410.
Bakker, Peter. 2017. Typology of mixed languages. In Alexandra Y. Aikhenvald & R.M.W. Dixon (eds.), *The Cambridge handbook of Linguistic Typology*, 217–253. Cambridge: Cambridge University Press.
Baklanova, Ekaterina. 2017. Types of borrowings in Tagalog/Filipino. *Kritika Kultura* 28. 35–54.
Bautista, Maria Lourdes S. 1980. *The Filipino bilingual's linguistic competence: A model based on an analysis of Tagalog-English codeswitching*. Canberra: Australian National University.
Bautista, Maria Lourdes S. 1986. English-Pilipino contact: A case study of reciprocal borrowing. In Wolf-Dietrich Bald & Wolfgang Viereck (eds.), *English in contact with other languages: Studies in honour of Broder Carstensen on the occasion of his 60th birthday*, 491–510. Budapest: Akadémiai Kiadó.
Bautista, Maria Lourdes S. 2004. Tagalog-English codeswitching as a mode of discourse. *Asia Pacific Education Review* 5(2). 226–233. https://doi.org/10.1007/BF03024960.

Kachru, Braj B. 2006. English in South Asia. In Kinglsey Bolton & Braj B. Kachru (eds.), *World Englishes: Critical concepts in linguistics*, vol. 2, 255–310. London & New York: Taylor & Francis.

Borlongan, Ariane Macalinga & Joo Hyuk Lim. 2013. Philippine English. In Bernd Kortmann & Kerstin Lunkenheimer (eds.), *The electronic world atlas of varieties of English*. Leipzig: Max Planck Institute for Evolutionary Anthropology. http://ewave-atlas.org/languages/75 (accessed 31 July 2019).

Bowen, Donald. 1971. Hispanic languages and influences in Oceania. In Thomas Sebeok (ed.), *Current trends in linguistics 8: Linguistics in Oceania*, 938–953. The Hague: Mouton.

Doeppers, Daniel. 1972. The development of Philippine cities before 1900. *The Journal of Asian Studies* 31(4). 769–792. doi:10.2307/2052101.

Dryer, Matthew S. 2011. Expression of Pronominal Subjects. In Matthew S. Dryer & Martin Haspelmath (eds.), *The world atlas of language structures online*, Chapter 101. Munich: Max Planck Digital Library. http://wals.info/chapter/101 (accessed 22 July 2019).

Fernández, Mauro. 2011. Chabacano en Tayabas. Implicaciones para la historia de los criollos hispano-filipinos. *Revista Internacional de Lingüística Iberoamericana* 9,1(17). 189–218.

Fernández, Mauro. 2012. Leyenda e historia del Chabacano de Ermita. *UniverSOS: Revista de Lenguas Indígenas y Universos Culturales* 9. 9–46 & 65–70. http://www.uv.es/~calvo/amerindias/numeros/n9.pdf (accessed 23 July 2019).

Fernández, Mauro. 2013. The representation of Spanish in the Philippine Islands. In José Del Valle (ed.), *A political history of Spanish: The making of a language*, 364–379. Cambridge: Cambridge University Press.

Fernández, Mauro & Eeva Sippola. 2017. A new window into the history of Chabacano. Two unknown mid-19th century texts. *Journal of Pidgin and Creole Languages* 32(2). 304–338.

García de los Arcos, María Fernanda. 1999. Grupos éthnicos y clases sociales en las Filipinas de finales del siglo XVIII. *Archipel* 57. 55–71.

Gonzales, Wilkinson Daniel Wong. 2016. Trilingual Code-switching Using Quantitative Lenses: An Exploratory Study on Hokaglish. *Philippine Journal of Linguistics* 47. 106–128.

Gonzales, Wilkinson Daniel Wong. 2017. Philippine Englishes. *Asian Englishes* 19(1). 79–95.

Gonzales, Wilkinson Daniel Wong. 2018. *Philippine Hybrid Hokkien as a postcolonial mixed language: Evidence from nominal derivational affixation mixing*. National University of Singapore MA thesis. http://scholarbank.nus.edu.sg/handle/10635/151219 (accessed 1 August 2019).

Lipski, John. 2001. The place of Chabacano in the Philippine linguistic profile. *Estudios de Sociolingüística / Sociolinguistic Studies* 2(2). 119–163.

Lipski, John. 2010. Chabacano y español: resolviendo las ambigüedades. *Lengua y Migración* 2(1). 5–41.

Lipski, John, Peter Mühlhäusler & F. Duthin. 1996. Spanish in the Pacific. In Stephen Wurm, Peter Mühlhäusler & Darrel Tryon (eds.), *Atlas of languages of intercultural communication in the Pacific, Asia and the Americas*, II.1., 271–298. Berlin and New York: Mouton de Gruyter.

Llamzon, Teodoro. 1997. The phonology of Philippine English. In Maria Lourdes S. Bautista (ed.), *English is an Asian language: The Philippine context, Proceedings of the conference held in Manila on August 2–3, 1996*, 41–48. Australia: Macquarie Library.

Matras, Yaron. 2010. *Romani in Britain: The Afterlife of a Language*. Edinburgh: Edinburgh University Press.

Matras, Yaron, Hazel Gardner, Charlotte Jones & Veronica Schulman. 2007. Angloromani: A Different Kind of Language? *Anthropological Linguistics* 49(2). 142–184.

Meakins, Felicity. 2013. Mixed Languages. In Yaron Matras & Peter Bakker (eds.), *Contact languages: A comprehensive guide*, 159–228. Berlin: Mouton de Gruyter.

Mous, Maarten. 2013. Mixed Ma'a/Mbugu. In Susanne Maria Michaelis, Philippe Maurer, Martin Haspelmath & Magnus Huber (eds.), *The survey of pidgin and creole languages. Volume 3: Contact languages based on languages from Africa, Asia, Australia, and the Americas*. Oxford: Oxford University Press.

Muysken, Pieter. 2000. *Bilingual Speech. A typology of code-mixing*. Cambridge: Cambridge University Press.

Muysken, Pieter. 2013a. Language contact outcomes as the result of bilingual optimization strategies. *Bilingualism: Language and Cognition* 16(4). 709–730.

Muysken, Pieter. 2013b. Media Lengua. In Susanne Maria Michaelis, Philippe Maurer, Martin Haspelmath & Magnus Huber (eds.), *The survey of pidgin and creole languages. Volume 3: Contact languages based on languages from Africa, Asia, Australia, and the Americas*, 143–148. Oxford: Oxford University Press.

Panganiban, José Villa. 1961. *Spanish loan-words in the Tagalog language*. Manila: Bureau of Printing.

Reinecke, John E. 1937. *Marginal Languages. A sociological survey of the creole languages and trade jargons*. New Haven: Yale University dissertation.

Rubino, Carl R. Galvez. 2000. *Ilocano dictionary and grammar. Ilocano-English, English-Ilocano*. Honolulu: University of Hawai'i Press.

Rubino, Carl. 2005. Iloko. In Alexander Adelaar & Nikolaus P. Himmelmann (eds.), *The Austronesian languages of Asia and Madagascar*, 326–349. London; New York: Routledge.

Rubino, Carl. 2008. Ilocano. In Keith Brown & Sarah Ogilvie (eds.), *Concise encyclopedia of languages of the world*, 518–521. New York: Elsevier.

Schuchardt, Hugo. 1884. Kreolische Studien IV. Ueber das Malaiospanische der Philippinen. In *Sitzungsberichte der philosophisch-historischen Classe der Kaiserlichen Akademie der Wissenschaften, Wien 105*, 111–150.

Smedley, Frank. 2006. *Code-switching and identity on the Blogs: An analysis of Taglish in computer mediated communication*. Auckland: Auckland University of Technology MA thesis.

Steinkrüger, Patrick O. 2008. Hispanization processes in the Philippines. In Thomas Stolz, Dik Bakker & Rosa Salas-Palomino (eds.), *Hispanisation: The impact of Spanish on the lexicon and grammar of the indigenous languages of Austronesia and the Americas*, 203–236. Berlin: De Gruyter Mouton.

Stolz, Thomas 1996. Grammatical hispanisms in Amerindian and Austronesian languages. *Amerindia* 21. 137–160.

Thompson, Roger M. 2003. *Filipino English and Taglish: Language switching from multiple perspectives*. Amsterdam: John Benjamins.

van Rossem, Cefas. 2017. *The Virgin Islands Dutch Creole textual heritage: Philological perspectives on authenticity and audience design*. Utrecht: LOT.

Wickberg, Edgar. 1964. The Chinese mestizo in Philippine history. *The Journal of Southeast Asian History* 5(1). 62–100.

Williams-van Klinken, Catharina. 2002. High registers of Tetun Dili: Portuguese press and purist priests. In Cynthia Allen (ed.), *Proceedings of the 2001 conference of the Australian Linguistic Society*. http://www.als.asn.au (accessed 3 January 2020).

Wolff, John. 2001. The influence of Spanish on Tagalog. In Klaus Zimmermann & Thomas Stolz (eds.), *Lo propio y lo ajeno en las lenguas austronésicas y amerindias: procesos interculturales en el contacto de lenguas indígenas con el español en el Pacífico e Hispanoamérica*, 233–253. Madrid: Iberoamericana.

Zulueta, Johanna. 2007. "I speak Chinese but . . ." Codeswitching and identity construction among Chinese-Filipino youth. *Caligrama (São Paulo. Online)* 3(2). http://www.revistas.usp.br/caligrama/article/view/65395/68006 (accessed 16 July 2019).

Elizabeth Herring Dudek and J. Clancy Clements
Jopara as a case of a variable mixed language

1 Introduction

Among the Spanish-speaking countries in South America, Paraguay is unique in that since the beginning of the colonization period both the Indigenous language of the area, Guarani, and the colonial language, Spanish, have maintained official status. There are several reasons for this. During the 16th century, when the area was being settled by Castilians, virtually no European women accompanied the Spanish-speaking conquistadors and settlers (Potthast 2015). Later on, mostly during the 17th century, the area developed into the main center of Jesuit missionary work (Caraman 1976). Jesuit priests educated the Guarani people, introducing them to Christianity, European culture, and, of course, the Spanish language. By the time the Jesuits were expelled in 1767, Paraguay had an educated Indigenous population but few settlers and urban centers because the territory was poor in mineral wealth. Paraguay became an increasingly minor colony, remaining that way until Spanish colonial rule was overthrown in 1811 and José Gaspar Rodríguez de Francia became the first leader of the country in 1813. Rodríguez de Francia was an isolationist and sought to eliminate racial difference by issuing a decree in 1814 that no European man could marry a European woman. Rather, marriages had to be mixed, which was a continuation of a practice already prevalent in Paraguay. As we argue, the practices of isolationism and miscegenation had an impact on the maintenance of Guarani and Spanish in significant ways, which have given way to the variably conventionalized mixture of the two languages, today called Jopara.

By considering the social history of the area and the morphosyntax of Jopara, we hope to provide a clearer image of the impact of historical factors on the present-day reality of Jopara. Understanding where and how Jopara emerged can help us gain a better understanding of its role today as the default variety used by the Paraguayan public. Whereas previous work has largely discussed Jopara as a code-switching register (Estigarribia 2015) or a register of either Paraguayan Spanish or Guarani, relegated to specific informal contexts only, we argue here that there is solid evidence in favor of classifying it as a mixed language in itself.

Elizabeth Herring Dudek, D'Youville College, dudeke@dyc.edu
J. Clancy Clements, Indiana University Bloomington, clements@indiana.edu

https://doi.org/10.1515/9781501511257-010

In the next section, we present some historical context on the emergence of Jopara. We then discuss where Jopara fits into current classifications of mixed languages found in the literature followed by a presentation and discussion of morphosyntactic characteristics of Jopara, and argue for Jopara as a mixed-marriage mixed language using data from various sources. We use the corpus used in Herring (2015), which is a compilation of over 50 hours of spontaneous conversational speech and story telling collected in 2010 and 2011, as well as over 8,000 tweets collected from Twitter in July 2014. The data in the corpus reveals just how variable and mixed Paraguayan language use is, such that at times it is impossible to determine whether the speaker is using Spanish or Guarani. For this reason, we argue that Jopara is its own variety, and that the corpus represents Jopara language use. As the reader will see, although there is considerable variability in the Jopara corpus, most examples containing a predicate (verb plus arguments) are expressed entirely in Guarani or in a Spanish-based lexicon with Guarani morphology.

2 Guarani and the historical background of Paraguay

2.1 The roles of women and the status of Guarani culture and language in the history of Paraguay

Since Paraguay's founding, the practices of isolationism and miscegenation have been the norm. Although in the history of colonial and post-colonial Paraguay women have played a crucial role in the creation and maintenance of bilingualism, their role can be traced further back to pre-colonial Guarani culture, at which time the society was polygamous (Potthast 2015). Given that the area was not rich in precious metals, Spaniards who settled in the area during the colonial period arrived poor and remained so, and thus could not afford the cost of bringing European wives (Klee and Lynch 2009).

For their part, it was a common practice of the Indigenous population in Paraguay to gift Guarani women to the Spaniards as a demonstration of good will and in order to form alliances. Women in Guarani culture were, among many other things, the main agricultural laborers. Thus, the Spanish soldiers not only received *piezas* "pieces, items" – the term they used to refer to women given as gifts – but also a large portion of the work force (Ganson 1990). This subjugation of Paraguayan women and the resultant formation of new family units were often referred to as harems, due to the unequal proportion of men to women living in individual homes. Additionally, unmarried couples living under one roof were common and widely accepted (Potthast-Jutkeit 1991).

After Paraguay's independence, Rodríguez de Francia followed an isolationist policy. He closed the border to all traffic in and out of Paraguay, with rare exceptions for purposes of trade. As a result of this isolationist stance and the policy requiring marriage to be between white European men and Indigenous women, a large portion of the population became mestizo[1] very quickly. A side effect of Rodríguez de Francia's isolationist practice was that access to new ideas and education opportunities was cut off during his time in power (1813–1840). The ruling Paraguayan elite were, thus, members of the mestizo population who worked their way up to elite status, rather than Europeans. Given the mestizo heritage of the elite, Paraguayans lived in a two-language contact situation and Guarani enjoyed equal status with Spanish (Ganson 1990; Potthast-Jutkeit 1991; Nickson 2009).

Since the practice of co-habitating in familial units without marriage was commonplace in Guarani culture, many couples chose not to marry in order to avoid the hurdles imposed by the state. That is, all legal marriages involving European men during Rodríguez de Francia's reign were of mixed couples, but not all couples were legally married. Although this resulted in many children being born, so to speak "out of wedlock", there was no stigma attached to it. It was also common for mothers and their children to live apart from the father of the children, due in part to the fact that many men also had one or more other families living elsewhere. As a consequence, women heads of households became the norm (Ganson 1990; Potthast-Jutkeit 1991; Potthast 2015). Although some earlier scholars described Paraguay as a matriarchal society, Potthast (2015; see also references therein) argues that even though women were of vital importance to the development of Paraguay as a country and Paraguayan culture – being responsible for household duties, childcare, and agricultural and, increasingly, all other types of labor – they formed and still form part of a patriarchal society.

The period of isolationism ended in 1841 when Carlos Antonio López took over as Paraguay's leader. He is credited with modernizing Paraguay's infrastructure and culture (Potthast-Jutkeit 1991), including ending the pro-miscegenation laws. Francisco Solano López, López's son, took over after his death, ruling for the following eight years (1862–1870). During his term, the War of the Triple Alliance (1864–1870) against the combined forces of Uruguay, Argentina, and Brazil took place. Paraguay suffered great losses during the war, including the loss of

---

1 *Mestizo* refers to a person born of one European parent and one Indigenous parent.

many men (Klee and Lynch 2009) with the result, according to post-war statistics, that adult women outnumbered men three to one (Ganson 1990).

As a result of the devastating human and material costs (Nickson 2009), the war and the use of Guarani were linked with the Solano López regime, with the result that both the regime and the language were increasingly seen in a negative light. Guarani became prohibited by the Triumverate of 1869, a puppet government set up by Brazil during the war. Post-war political struggles yielded the formation of a two-party system of governance (the Colorado and the Liberal parties). Because of Paraguay's debt burden, the Colorado Party, in power at that time, started selling off the country's vast land holdings, lands largely held by monolingual Indigenous Guarani. The Liberal Party, while supporting the same policy in principle, objected to the corruption involved in the land sales and the land sell-off became linked to anti-Guarani policies that were enacted country-wide. It was just a matter of time before the Guarani language fell in prestige and status. Nickson (2009) argues that a direct connection developed and continues to exist between the use of Guarani on the one hand, and poverty and education level on the other.

With the advent of the 20th century, calls for land reform in 1920 renewed positive interest in Guarani, as did the invention of the still-very-popular music style called Guarania. After ruling for 33 years, the Liberal Party lost the presidential election of 1937 to the Colorado party, which for its part promoted the Guarani language although it still served the elite classes. In 1954, Alfredo Stroessner, also of the Colorado party, took over the country's leadership and ruled until ousted in 1989. Stroessner used the concept of Guarani to unify its speakers around a national identity, while at the same time ruling over a government that turned a blind eye to rampant corruption and an ever-increasing income and wealth gap in the country (Nickson 2009: 7). Although he never gave a public speech in Guarani, and even rejected efforts to introduce Guarani education, Stroessner did make political use of Guarani – thus symbolizing his support of the people – by signing legislation that made Guarani the national language (Nickson 2009).

As evidence of the success of his strategy, a study carried out during the Stroessner regime found pride in and a very high loyalty to Guarani as the language of Paraguay (Garvin and Mathiot 1960). Garvin and Mathiot also point out, however, that it is the language rather than the Indigenous ancestry that resonates with Paraguayan pride. In addition, their study also revealed that for Paraguayans, Paraguayan Spanish, a variety that contains many Guarani loan words, is considered "sloppy" (1960: 789).

Since 1989, laws have been passed that have introduced schooling in Guarani, but they have rarely been enforced (Nickson 2009). In 1992, a law was enacted, and re-stipulated in 1998, that required primary education to be carried out in the first language of the student. However, only 5% of Paraguayan schools conducted classes in Guarani around that time, in spite of the fact that, as revealed in the census data of 2002, 59.2% of the population preferred Guarani while only 35.7% preferred Spanish.

The reasons for this failure to implement education in Guarani are complex. One hypothesis Nickson (2009) lays out is that, contrary to the data in the census, the general population has a preference for Spanish-language schooling, even among the native monolingual Guarani speakers. Another hypothesis involves the variety of Guarani taught in schools, known as Guaraniete. This standard for Guarani-medium schooling is considered the pure variety of Guarani, containing little to no Spanish and many Guarani-derived neologisms, constructed by language experts but not used natively by the general Guarani-speaking population. As a consequence, native monolingual Guarani speakers often do not understand it and cannot relate to Guaraniete as it is used in school. In other words, in the Guarani-medium education system there exists a kind of diglossia in which the language of instruction (Guaraniete) is not used or well understood by the students, who among themselves use Jopara, a variably conventionalized Spanish-Guarani mixed language. Nickson (2009) refers to students caught in this diglossic situation as "Hispanicized" Guarani children.

Although the attempt to introduce Guarani into the education system has enjoyed limited success, language attitudes towards Guarani have improved since the 1992 law came into effect. Between 1995 and 2001, education professionals increasingly opted not to use monolingual varieties of either Spanish or Guarani in the classroom. In the 1990s and into the early 2000s, Guarani and Jopara increasingly appeared as the language of choice in newspapers and political speech, on radio and television, and in advertisements and updated place names. Mortimer (2006) finds that, rather than being indicative of a divide between Indigenous and European populations, as it is in many language contact situations in the Americas, the distinction between Jopara and Guaraniete boils down to a rural versus urban divide. He also notes that those who prefer the use of Jopara as the language of instruction tend to be those who use it most often, that is, urban families who encounter both languages more regularly. Monolingual Guarani speakers from rural populations prefer Guaraniete as the language of instruction, as it is not as distant from their native variety of language use. However, this does not mean that native monolingual Guarani speakers speak Guaraniete outside of school. Our data, collected in an urban area (Asunción), are consistent with Mortimer's (2006) findings that Jopara is largely an urban variety. This stands in contrast to Lustig's (1996) finding that Jopara is used primarily by those on the margins of society. It is relevant to note that Lustig's (1996) and Estigarribia's (2015) findings are based on a literary text, and not on oral discourse (as in our case). This distinction could account for the difference in their findings, as compared to ours.

In spite of its increased usage, Guarani has continued to be linked to poverty, such that the bottom of the income pyramid consists almost entirely of Guarani speakers (Nickson 2009). Working women make around half as much as working men with the same job responsibilities (Patrinos, Velez, and Psacharopoulos 1994), and thus the poorest Paraguayans turn out to be women who speak Guarani monolingually.

Due to this situation, and given that historically native Guarani-speaking women played a dominant role in Paraguayan society, one might expect that they would display a greater proficiency in Guarani in quantitative studies. Recent research, however, does not seem to support this hypothesis unambiguously. Some sources (Ganson 1990; Gynan 2005) suggest that men are more proficient at Guarani, while women are more likely to be Spanish-dominant. Solé (1996), however, finds that men are more likely to claim Guarani proficiency, implying that although women may be proficient in Guarani, they are more reluctant to reveal their knowledge. Moreover, Solé emphasizes that looking at the sex of a participant complicates the understanding of the variable of language proficiency, and cautions against direct comparisons when analyzing Paraguayan culture and language use among different socially defined groups. In a similar vein, Gynan (2005) notes that proficiency in Guarani is currently not linked to the sex of the person, and that women's instrumental role in maintaining Guarani is no longer the case in Paraguay. Be this as it may, although the language dynamics are currently different from the 19th century, the existence of Jopara is traceable, we maintain, back to mixed marriages, a practice that went on in Paraguay for hundreds of years. Because of this social history, we argue that Jopara can reasonably be considered a mixed-marriage type of language mixture. In the next subsection, we present our arguments.

2.2 Jopara as a mixed-marriage language

In this paper, we adopt the evolutionary, population-genetic perspective on mixed languages developed by Croft (2000). In discussing types of language mixtures, Croft (2000: 209–221) considers mixed languages as instantiations of language hybridization of which he distinguishes three types. The first type is instantiated by code-switching and code-mixing (hybrid utterances). The second type is illustrated by varieties that form in language contact situations in which the languages are closely related (for example, the community of Uruguayans near/on the Uruguay-Brazil border who speak a Portuguese-Spanish mixed variety, see Waltermire 2006). In such cases, it is often difficult to tease apart which features come from one or the other language in contact, and sometimes it is impossible to do so. The third type distinguished by Croft are *mixed languages*, for which he offers a brief discussion while also noting that the social and linguistic facts in such contact situations are complex (2000: 214).

Based on the social situations that give way to mixed languages, Croft distinguishes three types of mixed languages: 1) languages resulting from death by borrowing, 2) languages resulting from semi-shift, and 3) mixed-marriage languages.

With regard to languages that develop due to death by borrowing, Croft (2000) cites cases in which extensive borrowing has occurred, such as in Asia Minor Greek (citing Thomason and Kaufman 1988: 215–222). Following Matras (2000), Croft adopts the term *functional turnover*, whereby "the basic vocabulary and sometimes some grammatical affixes of the original are restricted to a secret or in-group register of the now-acquired language of the external group" (Croft 2000: 217). One such case of this is Spanish Romani. It possesses a lexicon and certain grammatical features from Romani, but has its grammatical system borrowed from the external (host) country language (Spanish). An illustrative example is shown in (1), from González Caballero (1998: 12–13), in which the italicized lexical items are Romani, and the bolded function words *y* 'and', *su* 'his/her/their', the verbal suffixes *–aba* and *–s*, and the nominal pluralization marker *-s* (including the Spanish plural allomorphs *–s* and *-es*) are Spanish.

(1)   **Y**   na   teler-**aba-n**   *chaboró, presas,*   *Isabel* sin-**aba** *nanguí*
     and   NEG   have-PST-3PL   child   because   Isabel be-PST   barren
     y   **lo-s**   *dui chalado*-**s**   *dur andré* **su-s**   *chibés*-**es**
     and   the-PL   two advanced-PL   far in   their-PL day-PL
     'And they had no child because Isabel was barren and both were very advanced in age.'

Based on the study of the Spanish Romani text provided by González Caballero (1998), it is notable that it has only one copula, *sinar*, where Spanish has *ser* and *estar*. It also has only one verb class (*–a*) instead of the three from Spanish (*-a, -e, -i*), whereby all Romani verbs have the suffixal morphology of the Spanish *–a* verb class, the most common of three. This first type of language mixture does not apply to the Paraguayan context because Jopara is not associated with a secret register or in-group use, as was/is the case in with Spanish Romani.

The second situation in which a mixed language may form is called, following Croft, semi-shift. In SEMI-SHIFT, the speakers in a society appear to shift only part way to the external society's language. The semi-shift may be due to lack of full access to the external society's language, or may be a marker of a distinct social identity. The linguistic result of semi-shift is the minor image of functional turnover: the vocabulary is that of the external society's language, while many grammatical inflections . . . and most grammatical constructions . . . are at least in part those of the native-language society (Croft 2000: 219).

We can rule out Jopara as a situation of semi-shift because Jopara does not fit this description largely because of the stipulation that both languages be closely related, genetically.

The third situation in which a mixed language may form is in mixed marriages. Croft (2000: 214–217) states that mixed-marriage languages have emerged in communities where there are mixed marriages in which spouses speak genetically unrelated languages. As examples, Croft cites Mednyj Aleut (Russian finite VP morphosyntax, 90% Aleut lexicon) and Michif (Cree verbs and VP morphology, French nouns and NP morphology) (see also Meakins 2013: 163). We argue Jopara fits squarely into this category of mixed-marriage mixed language.

While Jopara is not as clear cut as the examples of Michif and Mednyj Aleut, it shows some clear features that suggest that it is a mixed-marriage language, albeit a variable one. As we shall see below, Jopara is also spoken by Paraguayans who are not bilingual in Spanish and Guarani. Following Herring (2015), we assume that conventionalization has taken place not on a national scale, but rather on a community-by-community basis. As such, we find different degrees of conventionalized mixtures depending on the community. One of the easily definable distinctions among communities the rural-urban division. An example of rural, Guarani-heavy Jopara is given in (2).[2]

(2) **Si** re-ñe'e   guarani-me n-o-japo-i   **caso.**
     if   you-speak guarani-in NEG-3-make-NEG attention
     'If you speak to them in Guaraní, they won't pay attention to you.'

The Spanish lexical elements are the conditional conjunction *si* 'if' and the noun *caso* 'attention'. In Jopara, as well as in Guarani, the pronominal expressions 'to them' in the conditional clause and 'to you' in the main clause are null, but must be overtly expressed in more standard forms of Spanish. Illustrative examples of

---

[2] The example is taken from the recordings provided to us by Kerry Steinberg. The speaker is a 42-year-old female, born in a rural town, who has lived there her whole life. She occasionally speaks Spanish when required when shopping, but does most of her shopping in the market, where she speaks Guarani. She speaks Guarani at home, exclusively.

urban, differently conventionalized Jopara are shown in (3)–(4), both from the Twitter urban corpus collected by and used in Herring (2015).

(3) *Mba'e la   nde **problema mi hija**?   rei-po'o-se   pio?*
    what EMPH your problem my daughter 2.SG-take-want   Q
    'What's your problem my dear? Do you want to take it?'

(4) ***No   soy   chismoso pero que** pa **pasa   de nuevo con***
    NEG be.1SG gossipy   but what Q happen.3SG of new   with
    Antho no   quiero   estar mal con ella nomas
    Antho NEG want.1SG to.be bad with her only
    'I don't want to be gossipy but what is going on with Antho. I just don't want to be on her bad side.'

Example (3) is a Spanish-Guarani-balanced sentence tweeted by an Asunción-area speaker in which the pronouns, functional elements, and verbs are expressed in Guarani and the NPs *el problema* 'the problem' and *mi hija* 'my daughter/dear' in Spanish. (4) is from a different Asunción-area speaker, a Spanish-heavy example in which the question particle *pa* is Guarani and the remainder of the utterance is Spanish.

This degree of variation notwithstanding, typical traits of Jopara are identifiable, as follows:
- The Spanish nominal and verbal agreement systems (Det-N, N-Adj, NPl-V) are variable.
- Guarani lexicon is part and parcel of Jopara, as are some of the determiner and pronominal paradigms, as well as inflectional affixes.
- Guarani inflectional and derivational affixes appear on Spanish-origin lexical items, but Spanish inflectional and derivational affixes never appear on Guarani lexical items.

Based on this evidence, we argue that Jopara is a variably conventionalized mixed-marriage language. Other scholars have not considered Jopara from this perspective. The views of Jopara as a mixed variety or Guarani-influenced Spanish are heterogenous. In the next subsection, we discuss some of them.

2.3 Views on Jopara and the various degrees of language mixture in Paraguay

The first passing mention of mixed Spanish/Guarani language is found in 1871, by an American dignitary Charles Washburn during the War of the Triple Alliance. He describes that outside of the home, women would use Spanish in the 1800s, while Guarani was used at home. Washburn clarifies that at that time, Guarani was the preferred language in spite of the status of Guarani Indigenous women possessing the lowest social status of any social group.

While there is general agreement in Paraguay and among scholars that Spanish and Guarani have impacted each other, linguistically and socially, there is less unanimity about how to identify and define the language used. The language mixture containing varying degrees of Guarani and Spanish influence has been alternatively called "Guarani Criollo" (Granda 1995a) and Jopara (Dietrich 2002, 2010). According to Dietrich (2010), it constitutes the default variety spoken in certain communities throughout Paraguay. The influence of each language on the other is seen at all linguistic levels: phonetic, phonological, morphosyntactic, semantic, and pragmatic.

Granda (1995b: 169–174) finds that Spanish borrows the morphosyntax and pragmatics of Guarani command structure. He argues that the form is not the only part of the Guarani linguistic system borrowed into Spanish, but that the pragmatic values of the borrowed morphemes are also found in Paraguayan Spanish. Granda points out that the act of giving a command to someone in Spanish is syntactically simple, yet pragmatically complex. The opposite is true for Guarani. Morphosyntactically, the Guarani imperative system is rather extensive. The differences between the Spanish and Guarani imperative systems are exemplified in (5) and (6), respectively (Granda 1995b: 166, 170).

(5) Paraguayan Spanish informal command
     ¡Ve-te!
     'go-INFORMAL'

(6) Guarani informal command structure
     e-guata-mi/-na/-ke/-katu/-kena/-mina/-katuke
     COMMAND-walk-COMMAND

Each suffix in (6) corresponds to a different degree of formality and/or urgency. Note the multiple possibilities and combinations of suffixes present in (6) is entirely absent in (5). In Guarani, there are many command morphemes, and these can also be combined in different ways, which leads to an even greater degree of complexity in expressing commands or imperatives. This complexity results in a smaller pragmatic inventory, as the various pragmatic meanings that can exist in a command situation are marked morphosyntactically on the verb produced. Granda concludes that ways for expressing commands are completely transferred into Paraguayan Spanish. He also states that Spanish strategies for expressing commands "have been completely eliminated" (1995b:172) in favor of the more explicit Guarani strategies.

However, Choi (2001) presents evidence to argue that characteristics of Paraguayan Spanish are only partially explained by contact with Guarani. As an example, Choi (2001) discusses the use of the stative preposition *en* with motion verbs, as in *voy en el mercado*, concluding that the use of the stative preposition *en* with verbs of direction or motion can be partially attributed to the existence of one Guarani postposition (*-pe/-me*)[3] that is equivalent to the two Spanish prepositions *en* and *a*. Directional *en* is also found in Old and Medieval Spanish, which could explain its presence in Paraguayan Spanish. Choi (2001) also points out the presence of the construction in other dialects of Spanish. She uses these considerations to rule out contact as the sole reason for the use of this construction in Paraguay presently.

Choi (2000) also argues that null pronominalization in Paraguay is accounted for by multiple causation, appealing to both internal and external language change, as described above for the directional preposition. Choi (2000) shows that Guarani's influence is only partly responsible for the existence of null pronominalization in Paraguayan Spanish. She argues that language-internal processes must also be at work given the presence of the phenomenon in other parts of the Americas. The repetitive nature of Spanish clitic use, combined with the fact that Guarani does not have a similarly redundant structure, can however account for the prevalence of null pronominalization in Paraguayan Spanish, found in the speech of all socioeconomic classes (Choi 2000).

Palacios Alcaine (2000) also looks at null pronominalization as well as *leísmo* and *loísmo* in Paraguayan Spanish with focus on sociolectal differences. She finds that Paraguayans in the middle to upper middle class in urban locations use *le* to pronominalize masculine and feminine singular animate direct and indirect objects as well as masculine plural inanimate direct and indirect objects. In this population, *le* is not used to refer to feminine plural objects of either accusative or dative case. In contrast with the urban communities, *loísmo* is more common in rural communities. Palacios Alcaine finds that Paraguayan *loísmo*

---

[3] The distinction between Guarani postpositions *-pe* and *-me* is phonologically determined, based on the nasality of the verb to which it is attached.

refers only to direct objects but neutralizes animacy, gender, number, and definiteness. The author notes that null pronominalization in inanimate contexts is generalized to all sociolects in Paraguayan society (see also Choi 2000).

In addition to the sources just discussed, there are many sources that describe the effects of Spanish on Guarani. Granda (1979) describes the use of Spanish *la* and *lo* in Paraguayan Guarani, pointing out that though *la* and *lo* are borrowed from Spanish, they do not function grammatically as in Spanish: *la* is used for singular nouns, both masculine and feminine, while *lo* marks plural nouns of both grammatical genders. In their study on the distribution of Spanish borrowings in Paraguayan Guarani, Bakker, Gómez-Rendón, and Hekking (2008: 195) caution, as Granda (1979) does, that *lo* and *la* do not have the same function as they do in standard varieties of Spanish and have a different distribution, as well. Specifically, *la* and *lo* can mark independent anaphora, cataphora, and ellipsis. They can also have a deictic function in a dimension that Guarani does not traditionally have: distant and not visible (Gutman and Avanzati, 2013). Thun (2006) shows that Guarani *la* also functions as a nominalizer, an emphasizer, and can co-occur with demonstratives. Overall, Bakker, Gómez-Rendón, and Hekking (2008: 195) point out the great number of borrowings of definite articles in Guarani.

Turning to how researchers have attempted to define Jopara, it is not as straightforward as characterizing an entirely conventionalized mixed-marriage language such as Michif (Bakker 2013). As already alluded to, in Jopara there is no established conventionalized delineation where Spanish ends and where Guarani begins. Despite this lack of consensus, the speakers of Jopara do agree that it falls somewhere in the middle, utilizing characteristics of both languages. The term *Jopara* refers to a dish prepared in Paraguay that combines many different ingredients (meat, corn, beans, manioc, and many kinds of vegetables). In its metaphorical extension, it is used by scholars and its speakers to refer to a Guarani-Spanish linguistic mixture, to a set of variably conventionalized varieties.

While it is not generally considered its own variety, Dietrich (2010), for example, acknowledges that Jopara is the only variety of Guarani (not Spanish) that has native speakers. As already mentioned, in school students learn Guaraniete, a Guarani variety that purports to have no Spanish influence. However, no postcolonial native speaker of any dialect of Guarani in Paraguay, or its linguistic relatives, speaks a Guarani that does not have at least some characteristics resulting from Guarani-Spanish contact. There is evidence of Spanish influence in monolingual Guarani phonology, morphosyntax, and semantics, due to which Dietrich (2010: 44) concludes that "Jopara is the only existing form of modern spoken Guarani". Somewhat contradictorily, he also remarks that "Jopara is much more a style of speaking than a proper language" (2010: 40).

Another way of describing Jopara, from the perspective of Guarani, would be: depending on the context, a speaker incorporates more or less Spanish into Guarani The more Spanish is incorporated into Guarani, the more Jopara-like their speech is. The less Spanish is incorporated into Guarani, the more it approaches Guaraniete. Given that for Dietrich (2010) Jopara is another way to refer to Modern Guarani, he states that the linguistic situation in Paraguay does not exemplify either linguistic borrowing or shift. Rather, it is a dialect based on two languages. He agrees with Fasoli-Wörmann (2002) that Jopara does not require a person to be bilingual in Guarani and Spanish in order to speak it, though many of its speakers are. This supports the observation Dietrich makes that Jopara has native speakers who are proficient in their variety but who do not speak Spanish or Guarani with the same proficiency.

Some of these claims seem contradictory. For example, although Dietrich (2010) writes that Jopara is not a language in and of itself, he also states that Jopara as a variety has native speakers. Furthermore, he states that it is the only native Guarani dialect that remains, and that there no longer are native Guarani speakers whose speech has no influence from Spanish. Taking these contradictory statements to their logical extreme, if we assume the characterization proposed by Dietrich (namely that Jopara is not a language), then monolingual speakers of what Dietrich would call Modern Guarani or Jopara could logically not exist.

For his part, Estigarribia (2015) argues that Jopara is explicitly not a mixed language in large part due to its lack of conventionalization as well as the lack of a clear split in linguistic responsibilities between Spanish and Guarani. While Estigarribia's written data source is held in high esteem by authors and the Paraguayan public, it was shown not to be representative in its use of Guarani interrogative markers present in spoken and computer-mediated modes (Herring 2015). Additionally, Estigarribia's data yields a number of examples of Guarani as a lexifier language accompanied by Spanish verbal morphology. However, our data produced zero examples of Spanish verbal morphology appearing on Guarani lexicon, but rather always Guarani grammar appearing often and easily with a Spanish lexicon. Below, we further argue that Jopara does in fact demonstrate variable conventionalization.

Extensive research into the historical background and roles of women in the history of colonial and post-colonial Paraguay, fieldwork and study, and interactions one of the authors of this study (Herring Dudek) has had with speakers of these varieties over the years bolster the claim that the variety of Spanish or Guarani spoken in Paraguay today, especially in urban areas, represents a case of a variably conventionalized mixed-marriage mixed language. Jopara's native speakers demonstrate that it is established within its community and that it possesses a degree of conventionalization that differs according to sociolinguistic factors, such as community of practice, register, and style.

It is also important to note that the well-known mixed languages, such as Media Lengua, Ma'a/Mbugu and Michif, are usually found within relatively small communities that number in the hundreds or thousands (Bakker 2013; Mous 2013; Muysken 2013). By contrast, Jopara is found in the whole of Paraguay, with a population of approximately 7 million. As Herring (2015) observes, it is not uniformly conventionalized at the country level, but rather at the level of individual communities.

Another paradox presented by Dietrich (2010) is that bilingualism is not a necessary requirement to speak Jopara natively but that different speech styles require more or less incorporation of Spanish. He goes on to state that "speakers of Jopara have a more or less active and passive command of both Guarani and Spanish" (2010: 49), and that it is a dialect based on two languages. Our interpretation of Dietrich's (2010) intent is that the dialect of Modern Guarani (aka Jopara) that a Paraguayan child acquires may already be a mixed variety, and the child acquiring it does not know which parts of their speech come from Guarani, and which from Spanish. In this way, such children are not bilingual in one language over the other, but rather have one native language that, in itself, is composed of more than one language. If this interpretation is correct, then Jopara is a mixed language, with its original sources developing out of mixed marriages.

2.4 Some specific examples of Jopara as a mixed language

As mentioned previously, there are three characteristics of Jopara that contribute to our classification of it as a mixed language: variable agreement in the noun phrase (Det-N, N-Adj) and between subjects and verbs (NP1-V), variably conventionalized Guarani lexicon determiners, pronouns, and inflectional affixes, and the variably conventionalized use of Guarani affixes on Spanish-origin lexical items, and the absence of Spanish affixal use on Guarani-origin lexicon. This section provides examples of all these features.

The example in (7), from a female bilingual speaker in Asunción, shows the mixed nature of Jopara's agreement paradigm as well as its lack of determiners.

(7) ***Paciencia!*** *Tené que ir, campaña* ndo-***vale***-i
patience have-2 COMP go countryside NEG-is.worthwhile-NEG
todo *tu prima etá todo en ciudá*
all-SG your-SG cousin-F-SG be-SG all-SG in city
o-***trabaj***-a *porã*
3-work-3SG well

Idiomatic Spanish: *Paciencia! Tenés que ir, el campo ya no vale. Todas tus primas están en la ciudad y todas trabajan bien.*
'Patience! You have to go [to the city]; the countryside is no longer worth it [for finding a job]. All your cousins are in the city and they all work well [i.e., have nice jobs].'

Agreement in Jopara is variable within and across phrases, illustrated in (7) by the lack of Subject-Verb agreement. The phrase stating that all of the speaker's cousins are in the city contains the 3SG form of *estar* 'be (located)', in spite of its reference to a plural subject. It also shows a lack of both gender and number agreement within the NP, as the portion of the text pertaining to 'all of your (female) cousins' contains no plural morphology and variable masculine/feminine affixation. Moreover, definite determiners are missing in the environments where they would be expected, even though both Spanish and Guarani have definite determiners, although the use of determiners in these languages differs significantly. Specifically, were the sentence to have been produced in Guaraniete, the nouns *campaña* and *ciudá* would have no definite articles while in Spanish definite articles would traditionally be used. Finally, the example clearly exemplifies the extent of Spanish-Guarani lexical and morphological mixture. In this example, the only Guarani lexical item is *porã* 'well', used instead of Spanish *bien* 'well'. What is remarkable is that Guarani negators and tense-aspect affixes appear attached to the Spanish verb, demonstrating Guarani affixal use with Spanish-origin roots.

Also common in Jopara of Asunción is the use of Guarani subject pronouns as definite determiners that replace, or are used in addition to, their Spanish counterparts. (8) shows the subject pronoun system most commonly found, with an example of the use of 1SG pronoun in (9), taken from a balanced bilingual 50-year-old woman from Asunción who grew up in a rural area. This example demonstrates that use of Guarani definite determiners, such as subject pronouns, in conjunction with verbal morphological agreement, is integral to Jopara.

(8) Subject pronouns (Commonly used system in Asunción Jopara):
    Singular   Plural
1   che (G)   ñande (G, inclusive), ore (G, exclusive)
2   nde (G), or vos (S)   N/A
3   él/ella (S) or ha'e   ellos/ellas (S) or ha'ekuéra
    (G, uncommon)   (G, uncommon)

(9) Che   a-ha-se   **porque la   tía**   oi-mé-ne
    1SG   1.SG-go-want   because FOCUS   aunt   3.SG-be-FUT
    muy delicada
    very delicate/frail
    Idiomatic Spanish: *Quiero ir porque mi tía está muy delicada de salud.*
    English: 'I want to go because my aunt is very frail.'

Above, we discussed previous literature that concludes that null pronominalization is common in Paraguay. It is not, however, used uniformly nor is it mandatory. In order to express objects of the verb pronominally, if the verb is Spanish, the object pronouns are more commonly Spanish clitics than Guarani pronouns, and the most commonly used clitic is the singular indirect object clitic *le*, independently of case or number. That is, Paraguay makes frequent use of *leísmo*. However, Guarani object pronouns are not uncommon. If the morphology attached to the verb is from Guarani, the object pronouns in the predicate are almost exclusively also from Guarani, even if the origin of the verb is Spanish. An example is given in (10), with each morpheme's language of origin indicated with either G (Guarani) or S (Spanish).

(10) G-**S**-**S**   S/G   G-**S**-G
     ai-**me**-**conforme** la   a-**grabá**-vo
     1.SG-be-satisfied FOCUS   1.SG-record-COMP
     G   S/G   G-G
     ndeve   **la**   che-ñe'ê.
     2.SG.OBJ   FOCUS   1.SG- word/story/language
     Idiomatic Spanish: *Me conformo con que me grabes la historia.*
     'I agree to record (for) you my words/story/language.'

In Jopara, it is exceedingly common that speakers use Guarani deictic determiners/pronouns, which code evidentiality, rather than Spanish deictic determiners. (11) contains the Guarani deictic determiner/pronoun paradigm from Asunción, and (12) is an illustrative example spoken by a 50-year-old female. Interestingly, the Spanish-origin content of the utterance, *este día*, consists of what we consider to be a fossilized expression calqued from the translation of Guarani *ko'ãga* 'this day' or, more colloquially, 'today'. Guarani deictic determiner use alongside Spanish deictic determiner use is yet another example of clear morphological mixing of Jopara's two parent languages.

(11) Guarani deictic determiners/pronouns
Proximal   ko, ko'ã 'this'
Evidentiality   in visual range in auditory range
Features
Distal 1   pe 'that' (Det)   +   +
Distal 2   péva 'that' (Pro)   −   +
Distal 3   amo 'that' (Det)   +   −
Distal 4   amóva 'that' (Pro)   −   +

(12) O-hecha-uká -ma   ko   este diá.
     3SG-hear-PST PERF this this day
     'He heard it just today.'

To sum up this subsection, what we showed with these examples is that the mixtures of Spanish and Guarani in Jopara are variable in four important ways:
1. Syntagmatic phenomena such as Spanish agreement within and across phrases is often absent. When present, however, Spanish agreement is variable, illustrated by (7).
2. There are, at least in Asunción, pronominal subsystems that are clearly a mixture of both languages. This is demonstrated in (10).
3. Guarani functional elements are found with Guarani and Spanish lexicon, but Spanish morphology does not operate this way. In this paper there are no examples of Spanish morphology on Guarani lexicon, because, we argue, it does not exist in Jopara.
4. Finally, in all the variability, there seems to be a general pattern where Guarani morphology is favored more so than Spanish morphology.

3 Concluding remarks

In spite of a history of patriarchal social structures, the importance of women in colonial and post-colonial economic and domestic realms has contributed to the continued strength of Guarani influence in modern day language use in Paraguay. In this paper, we have proposed that Jopara constitutes a variably conventionalized mixed-marriage mixed language, following the evolutionary, population-genetics model advanced by Croft (2000). Indeed, the historical developments of colonial and post-colonial Paraguay support this proposal. From very early on in Paraguay's colonial history, Guarani-speaking women had children with Spanish-speaking men. This was a consequence of the colonization process, first as a tradition of gifting women as agricultural laborers and household objects, and later made into policy during the 28-years of Paraguay's first leader José Gaspar Rodríguez de Francia. Although the policy was discontinued, the practice of language mixing continues today, borne out of a culture of mixed-marriages. Because of the consistent input and presence of monolingual and Guarani-dominant bilingual speech, many Paraguayans in Asunción now speak Jopara.

We have presented some of the researchers' views, and contradictions, in the conceptualization of Jopara, and have given some poignant illustrative examples of Jopara. It is clear that Guarani lexical items with Spanish-language morphology do not appear in the Jopara data. In Herring Dudek's corpus, in other instantiations of Jopara, and in Herring's other data collections (Herring 2015) there appear utterances with Spanish and/or Guarani lexical items, together with Guarani functional elements, be they function words or affixal material. It is also clear that there is a considerable amount of variation in Jopara, which depends on context, style, and birthplace and education level of the speaker, among other things. While it cannot be claimed that Jopara displays a degree of uniformity and conventionalization at the level of the country, we can conclude that among various communities of practice there is a significant degree of conventionalization, that Jopara has native speakers, and that there are speakers of Jopara who are not bilingual in Guarani and Spanish. In this way, Jopara exists as its own variety.

Abbreviations

COMP	complementizer
EMPH	emphatic
F	feminine
FUT	future
G	Guarani
NEG	negation
OBJ	object
PERF	perfect
PL	plural
PST	past
Q	question marker
S	Spanish
SG	singular

References

Bakker, Peter. 2013. Michif. In Susanne Maria Michaelis, Philippe Maurer, Martin Haspelmath & Magnus Huber (eds.), *The survey of pidgin & creole languages. Volume 2: Portuguese-based, Spanish-based, and French-based languages*, 158–173. Oxford: Oxford University Press.

Bakker, Dik., Jorge Gómez-Rendón & Ewald Hekking. 2008. Spanish meets Guaraní, Otomí, and Quechua: A multilingual confrontation. In Thomas Stolz, Dik Bakker, & Rosa Salas Palomo (eds.), *Aspects of language contact: New theoretical, methodological and empirical findings with special focus on Romancisation processes*, 165–238. Berlin: Moutin de Gruyter.

Caraman, Philip. 1976. *The lost paradise: the Jesuit Republic in South America*. New York: Seabury Press.

Choi, Jinny. 2000. [-Person] direct object drop: The genetic cause of a syntactic feature in Paraguayan Spanish. *Hispanic* 83(3). 531–543.

Choi, Jinny. 2001. The genesis of *voy en el mercado*: The preposition *en* with directional verbs in Paraguayan Spanish. *Word* 52(2). 181–196.

Croft, William. 2000. *Explaining language change: an evolutionary approach*. Essex: Longman.

Dietrich, Wolf. 2002. Guarani criollo y Guarani étnico en Paraguay, Argentina y Brasil. In Dorota Olejniczak & Andrzej Dembicz (eds.), *Current studies on South American languages: Selected papers from the 50th International Congress of Americanists in Warsaw and the Spinoza Workshop*, 31–41.

Dietrich, Wolf. 2010. Lexical evidence for a redefinition of Paraguayan 'Jopara'. *Sprachtypologie und Universalienforschung (STUF)* 63(1). 39–51.

Estigarribia, Bruno. 2015. Guaraní-Spanish Jopara mixing in a Paraguayan novel. *Journal of Language Contact* 8. 183–222.

Fasoli-Wörmann, Daniela. 2002. *Sprachkontakt und Sprachkonflikt in Paraguay: Mythos und Realität der Bilinguismussituation* (8). New York: Peter Lang.

Ganson, Barbara. 1990. Following Their Children into Battle: Women at War in Paraguay, 1864–1870. *The Americas* 46(3). 335–371.

Garvin, Paul L. & Madeleine Mathiot. 1960. The Urbanization of Guarani Language. A Problem in Language and Culture. In Anthony F. C. Wallace (ed.), *Men and cultures: Selected papers of the Fifth International Congress of Anthropological and Ethnological Sciences*, 783–794. Philadelphia: University of Pennsylvania Press.

González Caballero, Alberto. 1998. *El evangelio de San Lucas en Caló*. Annotated edition. Cordoba: Ediciones El Almendro de Cordoba, S. L.

Granda, Germán de. 1979. Un caso complejo de interferencia morfológica recíproca en situación de bilingüismo amplio (español y guaraní en el Paraguay). *Studii si cercetari lingvístice* 30(4). 379–382.

Granda, Germán de. 1995a. Español paraguayo y guaraní criollo. Un espacio para la convergencia lingüística. *Lenguaje* 23(Dec.). 36–48.

Granda, Germán de. 1995b. Un proceso bidireccional de transferencia lingüística por contacto. El imperativo en guaraní criollo y en español paraguayo. *Boletín de filología* 35. 163–175.

Gutman, Alejandro & Beatriz Avanzati. 2013. *The Language Gulper: Guaraní*. http://www.languagesgulper.com/eng/Guarani.html (accessed 23 July 2018).

Gynan, Shaw N. 2005. Official bilingualism in Paraguay, 1995–2001: an analysis of the impact of language policy on attitudinal change. In Lofti Sayahi & Maurice Westmoreland (eds.), *Selected Proceedings of the Second Workshop on Spanish Sociolinguistics*, 24–40. Somerville: Cascadilla Proceedings Project.

Herring, Elizabeth M. 2015. *Guarani question markers pa, pio, and piko in Paraguayan tweets, texts, and talk*. Bloomington, Indiana: Indiana University unpublished Ph.D dissertation.

Klee, Carol & Andrew Lynch. 2009. *El español en contacto con otras lenguas*. Washington, D.C.: Georgetown University Press.

Lustig, Wolf. 1996. Mba'éichapa oiko la guarani? Guarani y Jopara en el Paraguay. *Papia* 4(2). 19–43.

Matras, Yaron. 2000. Mixed languages: a functional-communicative approach. *Bilingualism: Language and Cognition* 3(2).79–99.

Meakins, Felicity. 2013. Mixed languages. In Peter Bakker & Yaron Matras (eds.) *Contact languages: A comprehensive guide*, 159–228. Berlin, Germany: De Gruyter Mouton.

Mortimer, Katherine S. 2006. Guaraní académico or Jopará? Educator perspective and ideological debate in Paraguayan bilingual education. *Working Papers in Educational Linguistics* 21(2). 45–71.

Mous, Martin. 2013. Mixed Ma'a/Mbugu. In Susanne Maria Michaelis, Philippe Maurer, Martin Haspelmath & Magnus Huber (eds.), *The survey of pidgin & creole languages. Volume 2: Portuguese-based, Spanish-based, and French-based languages*, 42–49. Oxford: Oxford University Press.

Muysken, Pieter. 2013. Media Lengua. In Susanne Maria Michaelis, Philippe Maurer, Martin Haspelmath & Magnus Huber (eds.), *The survey of pidgin & creole languages. Volume 2: Portuguese-based, Spanish-based, and French-based languages*, 143–148. Oxford: Oxford University Press.

Nickson, Robert Andrew. 2009. Governance and the revitalization of the Guarani language in Paraguay. *Latin American Research Review* 44(3). 3–26.

Palacios Alcaine, Azucena. 2000. El sistema pronominal del español paraguayo: un caso de contacto de lenguas. In Julio Calvo Pérez (ed.), *Teoría y práctica del contacto; el español en el candelero*, 123–143. Vervuert: Iberoamericana.

Patrinos, Harry Anthony, Eduardo Velez & George Psacharopoulos. 1994. language, education, and earnings in Asunción, Paraguay. *The Journal of Developing Areas* 29. 57–68.

Potthast-Jutkeit, Barbara. 1991. The ass of a mare and other scandals: marriage and extramarital relations in nineteenth-century Paraguay. *Journal of Family History* 16(3). 215–239.

Potthast, Barbara. 2015. Mujeres cabeza de hogar y relaciones de género en Paraguay, Siglo XIX y XX. In Mónica Ghirardi, Volpi Scott & Ana Silvia (eds.), *Familias históricas: interpelaciones desde perspectivas Iberoamericanas a través de los casos de Argentina, Brasil, Costa Rica, España, Paraguay y Uruguay*, 157–192. São Leopoldo: Oikos Editora/Editoria Unisinos.

Solé, Yolanda Russinovich. 1996. Language, affect and nationalism in Paraguay. In Ana Roca & John B. Jensen (eds.), *Spanish in contact: Issues in bilingualism*, 93–111. Somerville: Cascadilla Press.

Thomason, Sarah G. & Terrence Kaufman. 1988. *Language contact, creolization, and genetic linguistics*. Berkeley: University of California Press.

Thun, Harald. 2006. 'A dos mil la uva, a mil la limón.' Historia, función y extensión de los artículos definidos del castellano en el guaraní jesuítico y paraguayo. In Wolf Dietrich &

Haralambos Symeonidis (ed.), *Guaraní y Maweti-Tupi-Guarani: Estudios históricos y descriptivos sobre una familia lingüística de América del Sur*, 357–414. Münster: LIT-Verlag.

Waltermire, Mark. 2006. *Social and linguistic correlates of Spanish-Portuguese bilingualism on the Uruguayan-Brazilian border*. Albuquerque, New Mexico: University of New Mexico unpublished Ph.D. dissertation.

Washburn, Charles. 1871. *The history of Paraguay, with notes of personal observations, and reminiscences of diplomacy under difficulties*. Boston: Lee and Shepard.

Zajícová, Lenka. 2009. *El bilingüísmo paraguayo*. Madrid: Iberoamericana.

Nantke Pecht
Pronominal usage in *Cité Duits*, a Dutch-German-Limburgish contact variety

1 Introduction

While typical examples of mixed languages show a "split ancestry" and have arisen in settings where two unrelated languages came in contact (Bakker and Mous 1994; Matras 2000), it remains debatable how to deal with "mixed varieties" that show several grammatical features of closely related language varieties. Such new varieties, with regular grammatical patterns on a mixed language basis evolve only under certain sociolinguistic conditions, but appear to be rare in Europe. An exceptional case in this regard is *Cité Duits* ('mining district German'), "discovered" only recently. This contact variety developed among second-generation immigrants in a socially isolated mining district in Belgian-Limburg in the 1930s. While speakers perceive it as a variety of German (*Duits*), closer linguistic analysis suggests that it is composed of features of Belgian Dutch, German and the Limburgish dialect Maaslands spoken in this area (Auer and Cornips 2018; Pecht 2019).

This article aims to contribute to the debate on mixed languages by discussing the use of subject pronouns in Cité Duits.[1] Although much literature has been devoted to the analysis of pronominal elements (e.g. Lenerz 1993, 1994; Corver and Delfitto 1999; Cardinaletti and Starke 1999; Riemsdijk 1999; Simon and Wiese 2002; Bhat 2004; Benincà and Poletto 2005; de Vogelaer 2007; Audring 2009), scholars have yet to pay attention to pronouns in Cité Duits. The behavior of pronominal forms in contexts of language contact is interesting because it elucidates the stability of linguistic features. In language contact situations that are mainly characterized by code-switching, we expect to identify pronominal forms from variety A and B and possibly C. Speakers who switch

---

[1] Parts of this paper have appeared in the doctoral dissertation of the author (Pecht 2021).

Acknowledgements: I wish to thank the editors of this volume, Maria Mazzoli and Eeva Sippola, as well as two anonymous reviewers for valuable feedback. Special thanks go to Hans van de Velde for his detailed comments on Belgian Dutch, and to Rob Belemans for his support with the Maaslands dialect. Furthermore, I would like to thank all participants of the conference Mixed Languages (Bremen, Sep. 28 & 29, 2017) for fruitful discussions.

Nantke Pecht, Maastricht University, n.pecht@maastrichtuniversity.nl

https://doi.org/10.1515/9781501511257-011

between two or more varieties make use of more than one system. Yet once these systems fuse and become a stabilized variety, we can assume that certain features lose ground whereas others take over. While situations of code-switching allow for much more variation when several grammatical systems exist side by side, stabilized varieties show a high degree of homogeneity within the system itself (Auer 1998, 2014). In this chapter, I will assess which varieties are represented in the pronominal paradigm of Cité Duits, and I examine whether the resulting forms are employed in consistent and homogenous ways by its speakers. In a similar vein, I will pursue the question of whether pronominal forms have arisen that are not found in spoken Belgian Dutch, Maaslands or German. Directly related to this is the question as to whether the position of a pronoun affects its form, as it is often the syntactic position of a pronominal element that gives rise to form variation (Benincà and Poletto 2005; de Vogelaer 2007: 145).

This chapter is organized as follows. After a brief outline of the sociohistory, data and methodology (section 2), I provide a review of personal pronouns in Belgian Dutch (section 3.1), the Limburgish dialect Maaslands (section 3.2) and German (section 3.3). Next, the ensuing sections will discuss pronominal usage in Cité Duits by focusing on subject pronouns. While section 4 is devoted to frequency of occurrence and phonological variation, section 5 tries to explain form variation in relation to the position of the finite verb and complementizer. The final section (6) discusses the findings in the context of the debate of language contact and mixed varieties.

2 Cité Duits

2.1 Brief sociohistory

Cité Duits developed as an in-group variety among locally-born children of immigrant miners of European descent in the coalmining district of Eisden (*cité*) in the 1930s. Today it is on the verge of disappearing, with fewer than a dozen speakers left. Crucially, all of the speakers grew up speaking Belgian Dutch, which means that Cité Duits did not emerge out of communicative necessity but in addition to already available languages.

Located in Belgian-Limburg in the Dutch border region, the *cité* was built to provide accommodation for miners and their family members, and only employees of the mine were granted housing. While accommodating speakers of numerous European languages, such as Polish, Hungarian, Italian and Czech, there was little contact with the local Belgian population and the *cité* remained quite segregated. The following generation of speakers grew up speaking Belgian

Dutch, some French, the respective languages spoken in the home context and sometimes the Limburgish dialect Maaslands (Pecht 2019). Many of the first immigrants – the parents of the speakers – actually lived in more than one place before moving to Eisden, migrating for instance from Hungary to France to Eisden and sometimes back and forth. This multi-directional movement of people (see Mazzucato et al. 2004 for transnationalism) and the resulting "symbolic capital" (Bourdieu 1991) imply that speakers picked up numerous languages along their way, including different varieties of German, the latter being widely used in the former Habsburg Empire. Some miners had also worked in the Ruhr-area. As such, it can be assumed that a substantial number of languages and dialects as spoken in the early 20th century provided the input for Cité Duits. Against the background of this multilingual environment and the closed social setting of the district, Cité Duits emerged as contact variety among the multilingual sons of the miners. Over the decades, it seems that their language use stabilized. For instance, the order of verbal elements in the two-verb cluster almost invariably follows Dutch/Maaslands and therefore clearly differs from German, whereas the determiner system constitutes a fusion of Dutch, Maaslands and German with some structural simplifications (Auer and Cornips 2018; Pecht 2019).

2.2 Methods and data

The analyzed data, collected in 2012/13 and 2015/16, is based on 340 minutes of audio recordings from 14 male speakers (aged around 80 at the time of recording) collected through a particular sociolinguistic interview method (Labov 1972). In this context, I conducted in-group recordings with three groups of well-acquainted former miners, all of them born and raised in Eisden in the 1930s.[2] The goal was to obtain speech data that is produced when speakers feel not being observed. As a field worker, I tried not to intervene, so that the speech of the group was influenced as little as possible. To circumvent the effect of observation, the "observer's paradox" (Labov 1972), a small number of speakers (usually four to eight speakers per group) with a dense network was recorded in an informal setting. The data has been transcribed with the program ELAN and annotated with MOCA (Multimodal Oral Corpus Administration). Since transcriptions always involve a certain degree of interpretation (Bucholtz 2000), I carried out perception tests with listeners of different home

---

[2] Data in 2012/13 was collected by Leonie Cornips.

languages (German, Dutch only and Dutch/Limburgish) for pronominal forms that turned out to be phonologically extremely close.

Empirically, my concern is in particular with three issues: (1) Frequency: What does the distribution of pronominal forms look like? (2) Internal properties: Do we encounter phonological or lexical variation for a given pronoun? (3) Position: To what extent is variation of a given pronoun tied to its position in relation to the finite verb and complementizer? For the following analysis, I included all pronominal forms of Cité Duits for a given pronoun in the data set, i.e. the total number of tokens is based on the forms found across all speakers. The few utterances directed towards the fieldworker, generally at the beginning of a recorded session, were excluded since speakers would switch to the respective standard variety. My analysis here is limited to subject pronouns because of space limitations (object pronouns will be discussed in future reports). For the same reason, I excluded the third person singular feminine, neuter and masculine non-human, i.e. with a non-human antecedent. Grammatical gender is complex because it differs substantially in the source varieties and deserves to be discussed more in-depth elsewhere.

3 An overview of personal pronouns in Cité Duits' source varieties

Since the analyzed data consists of informal spoken language, this overview is primarily concerned with the behavior of pronouns in their spoken form. Naturally, Maaslands is mainly used in its spoken form.

3.1 Belgian Dutch

The pronominal paradigm for Belgian Dutch for both full and weak forms is represented in Table 1. In colloquial Belgian Dutch, much more phonological and morphological variation is found, but this is beyond the scope of this survey (for an overview, see Vandekerckhove 2004, 2005; Plevoets, Speelman, and Geeraerts 2008; Plevoets 2008; Velde and Geeraerts 2013; Mieroop, Zenner, and Marzo 2016; for variation across dialects, see de Vogelaer 2007; for clitics, see Schutter 1989).

Probably the most eye-catching fact is that Dutch – this holds for southern and northern varieties and most dialect groups – displays an opposition between full and weak pronominal forms containing a full vowel and a schwa,

Table 1: Full and weak subject pronouns in Belgian Dutch.

		full forms	IPA	weak forms	IPA
SG	1	ik	[ɪk]	'k	[ək] [k]
	2	gij/jij	[ɣɛɪ] [jɛɪ]	ge/je	[ɣə] [jə]
	3M	hij/die	[hɛɪ] [d iː]	'm	[əm]
	V/T	u	[y]	u	[y]
PL	1	wij	[wɛɪ]	we	[wə]
	2	jullie	[ˈjyli]	ge	[ɣə]
	3	zij/die	[zɛɪ] [ciː]	ze	[zə]

respectively (de Vogelaer 2007). The only exception is the second person plural, which has no weak form (although *ge* is possible). The first person singular is *ik* [ɪk] and reduced *'k* [ək]/[k]. The latter may occur both in pre- and postverbal position. There is an additional emphatic form, *ikke* [ɪkə],³ which is normally used in isolation and not with a finite verb (Broekhuis and den Dikken 2012: 789; Audring 2018). For the second person singular, *gij* [ɣɛɪ] or reduced *ge* [ɣə] are employed.⁴ The *jij/je*-paradigm, typical of Netherlandic Dutch, is mainly found in the domains of education, media and written language in Belgium (Vandekerckhove 2005: 386). For the third person masculine holds that next to *hij* [hɛɪ] or reduced *em* [əm], the demonstrative pronoun *die* [diː] is used. In Dutch, *die* is not specified for biological gender (cf. Broekhuis and den Dikken 2012: 773–774). The pronoun *u* ('you'), which is the polite form in Netherlandic Dutch, is used in Belgian varieties for both formal (V) and informal (T) addressees (Vandekerckhove 2005: 383; Geeraerts 2010: 250). For plural forms, the most common pronouns are the full form *wij* [wɛɪ] and reduced *we* [wə] for the first person, *jullie* [ˈjyli] and *ge* [ɣə] for the second person and *zij* [zɛɪ], reduced *ze* and the demonstrative pronoun *die* [diː] for the third person.

Regarding the behavior of weak versus strong pronouns, several additional notes on their grammatical properties are relevant. From a strictly grammatical

---

3 The emphatic form *ikke* occurs usually in question-answer pairs such as *Wie gaat er met me mee? Ikke!* 'Who is coming with me? I will!', or to express indignation or surprise on a preceding utterance (Broekhuis and den Dikken 2012: 789). There is, however, dissention on the emphatic status of *ikke* (see the discussion between Hoeksema [2000] and Zwart [2000]).
4 Some authors also mention the clitics *-de* and *-degij* for casual speech (Mieroop, Zenner and Marzo 2016: 40).

perspective, weak and strong forms may be used interchangeably (de Vogelaer 2007: 153):

(1) **Ge/gij** bent op tijd.
     2SG   are on time
     'You are on time.'

In (1), although yielding constructions that slightly differ in terms of their semantics, both *ge* ('you', weak) and *gij* ('you', strong) may be employed. However, this is not always possible. Some idiomatic expressions require a phonologically reduced form (Linke and Kirstein 2018). The full form, in turn, is the only grammatical option in finite imperatives with overt subject pronouns, whereas the phonetically reduced form would lead to an impossible construction (Broekhuis, Corver, and Vos 2015: 92). For instance, the strong form *wij* ('we') is usually obligatory in oppositions, comparisons, reactions to a previous utterance and with attributes like *ook* ('also') and *zelfs* ('even') (Temmerman 2014: 248).

3.2 The Maaslands dialect

Similar to Belgian Dutch, Maaslands has a set of full and weak personal pronouns (Table 2, see Goeman, Taeldeman, and Van Reenen 2014; for grammatical properties of Limburgish, see De Schutter and Hermans 2013: 364; further Stevens [1949] 1985; Goossens 1996).

Table 2: Full and weak subject pronouns in Maaslands.

		full forms	IPA	weak forms	IPA
SG	1	i:ch	[i:ç]	'ch	[ç]
	2	di:ch	[di:ç]	de/'te	[də][tə]
	3M	(h)eeë(r)/dè	[e:ɐ] [də]	er	[e:]
	V	geer	[ˈyeːʀ]	ger	[yeʀ]
PL	1	weer	[veːʀ]	wer	[veʀ]
	2	geer	[ˈyeːʀ]	ger	[yeʀ]
	3	zi-j/dièj	[ze̝ʲ] [di:ʲ]	ze/'se	[zə]

Table 2 shows that all pronouns are available as full and weak forms, with the main difference often being one of vowel length (for example [ˈyeːʀ] vs. [yeʀ]).

Importantly, the phonological development known as the "High German consonant shift" affected central and southern German dialects, but usually not the dialects of Dutch, except in parts of Limburg where the stop-sound /k/ in *ik, ook, -lijk* and *maken* developed into the fricative /x/, as in German *ich, auch, -lich, machen* (Marynissen and Janssen 2013: 85). In Maaslands, this is visible in the first person singular, which is *i:ch* [iːç] and reduced *'ch* [ç] with a voiceless post-palatal fricative, articulated in the back. Similar to Dutch, the latter form may occur both in pre- and postverbal position.

For the second person singular, the full form is *di:ch* [diːç], which seems to have developed out of the accusative object form, replacing *du* (Stevens [1949] 1985: 5). Although *du* has been retained in a few fixed expressions, it disappeared in most places. Furthermore, Maaslands has two weak forms that differ slightly as to their behavior as clitics: While *de* [də] mainly occurs before, *te* [tə] is confined to the position after the finite verb and complementizer (Goeman, Taeldeman, and Van Reenen 2014), in line with a number of Limburgish dialects (De Schutter and Hermans 2013: 364). The third person singular masculine is *(h)eeë(r)* [eːɐ] or reduced *er* [ɛː], sometimes realized as schwa [ə]. For plural forms, *weer* [veːʀ] and weak *wer* [vɐʀ] are used for the first person, while *geer* [ˈɣeːʀ] and weak *ger* [ɣɐʀ] are used for the second person and *zi-j* [zeʲ], weak *ze* and the demonstrative pronoun *dièj* [diːʲ] for the third person. Unlike Belgian Dutch, Maaslands has maintained the V-T distinction on personal pronouns: Whereas *di:ch* [diːç] functions as informal pronoun, the form *geer* [ˈɣeːʀ]/*ger* [ɣɐʀ] is used for formal addressees.

3.3 German

As pointed out above, the German input of Cité Duits cannot be traced back to one particular variety of German because the parents of the speakers immigrated from several countries where German was used around 1900. What is more, German was generally not the language spoken at home. The paradigm for personal pronouns in colloquial standard German is provided below (Nübling 1992: 303; Howe 1996: 263; Zifonun, Hoffmann, and Strecker 1997: 316–320). While there are regional differences, these are too extensive to be discussed here.

From Table 3, it can be observed that all pronouns have a full and a reduced form, except for *ich* 'I' (see below for a discussion). Vowel reduction is typical, especially in allegro speech (Nübling 1992: 303). From a phonological perspective but not indicated in Table 3, it appears that the near-open central vowel [ɐ] is often not fully articulated after another vowel, which means that the pronunciations

Table 3: Full and reduced subject pronouns in spoken German.

		full forms	IPA	clitic forms	IPA
SG	1	ich	[ɪç]	–	–
	2	du	[duː]	'te/'de	[tə] [də]
	3M	er/der	[eːɐ̯] [deːɐ̯]	'a	[ɐ]
	V	Sie	[ziː]	'se	[zə]
PL	1	wir	[viːɐ̯]	'wa/'ma	[vɐ] [mɐ]
	2	ihr	[ʔiːɐ̯]	'a	[ɐ]
	3	sie/die	[ziː] [diː]	'se	[zə]

[viːɐ̯] 'we' and [iːɐ̯] 'you', as well as the pronunciation without final [ɐ] are also possible (Howe 1996: 263).

The first person singular is *ich* [ɪç]. Generally, a clitic form is not found (*ch* exists as proclitic but occurs seldom and only in particular regions, cf. Zifonun, Hoffmann, and Strecker 1997: 318). For the second person singular holds that the full form is *du* [duː] – also realized as [dʊ] or [du] (Howe 1996: 263) – while the reduced forms are *de* [də] and *te* [tə], both confined to enclitic position (Nübling 1992: 22, 307; Zifonun, Hoffmann, and Strecker 1997: 317–318). Cliticization is frequent here: usually, the full form *du* ('you') is attached to the verb while the consonant is omitted, and the vowel becomes a schwa (e.g. /hastduː/ >/hastə/) (Nübling 1992: 15). For the third person singular masculine, the full form *er* [eːɐ̯], the clitic *'a* [ɐ] or the demonstrative pronoun *der* [deːɐ̯] is employed. For plural forms, the full pronoun *wir* [viːɐ̯] and both the reduced forms *'wa* [vɐ] and *'ma* [mɐ] may be used for the first person (Zifonun, Hoffmann, and Strecker 1997: 319), whereas *ihr* [ʔiːɐ̯] and reduced *'a* [ɐ] are used for the second person. For the third person plural, *sie* [ziː], reduced *'se* [zə] and the demonstrative pronoun *die* [diː] are used. Importantly, all reduced forms are usually enclitics (Nübling 1992: 304) and must attach phonologically to a host such as a verbal element. Unlike in Dutch, reduced and full pronominal forms may not be used interchangeably (Nübling 1992: 1–2).[5] Finally, German has maintained the T-V distinction between formal (*Sie* [ziː]) and informal pronouns (*du* [duː]/*ihr* [ʔiːɐ̯]) of address (Howe 1996: 266).

---

5 German dialects may differ. In Bavarian and Alemannic, personal pronouns seem to occur exclusively as clitics (Abraham and Wiegel 1993: 3–4; Howe 1996: 262–282).

3.4 Summary

In spite of the close typological relationship between the three source varieties, the pronominal paradigms of Belgian Dutch, Maaslands and German differ in some respects. Little overlap can be observed between Belgian Dutch and German. While the paradigm of Belgian Dutch and Maaslands consists of strong and weak forms, German does not have a set of weak personal pronouns that may occur both before and after the finite verb. In the latter, weak forms always occur as enclitics. While weak forms are grammaticalized in Dutch, clitics in German are confined to spoken language. For the full form of the first person singular holds that it carries a long vowel and is pronounced with a voiceless post-palatal fricative in Maaslands ([iːç] 'I'), articulated slightly more back compared to German, whereas German *ich* [ɪç] is pronounced with a voiceless palatal fricative and a short vowel. In Dutch, both the full and weak form have a final /k/. In addition, Maaslands shows overlap with German in the weak forms *de* [də] and *te* [tə] 'you' of the second person singular. While *de* [də] mainly occurs before the finite verb in Maaslands but after it in German, *te* [tə] is confined to the position after the finite verb and complementizer in both varieties. Regarding the Maaslands paradigm of personal pronouns vis-à-vis Belgian Dutch, the phonological realization differs for all forms from Belgian Dutch except for the third person plural. Finally, the three varieties exhibit some differences in usage. In Belgian Dutch, the form *ge* 'you' serves for both singular and plural (see Mieroop 2014: 314). In a similar way, in Maaslands, the form *geer* 'you' functions both as V-pronoun and as second person plural form. German has distinct pronominal forms here: While *ihr* 'you' serves as second person plural pronoun (informal), the V-pronoun *Sie* 'you' is the polite pronoun of address (singular and plural). Finally, there are some restrictions as to the use of certain strong forms. In Dutch, the strong pronoun *zij* 'they' must be animate whereas in German, the full pronoun *sie* 'they' may be employed for both animate and non-animate referees.

4 Subject pronouns in Cité Duits: Frequency and phonological properties

4.1 First person singular

Table 4 presents the total number of first person singular subject forms in the data and their percentages.

Table 4: Frequency in absolute numbers and percentages of all first person singular subject pronoun forms in Cité Duits.

1SG	[ɪç]	[ɪk]	[iːç]	[i]	[iː]	[ɪkə]	Total
n	1282	11	4	22	11	1	1331
%	96,4	0,8	0,3	1,7	0,8	0,1	100

The speakers produce in total 1331 tokens of the first person singular pronoun, which exhibits six different realizations. Yet, the overwhelming majority of these forms is realized as *ich* [ɪç], pronounced with a voiceless post-palatal fricative as in Maaslands, articulated slightly more back compared to German, but with a short vowel as in German/Dutch. That is, speakers use an intermediate form here. This form accounts for 96.4 percent (n = 1282), which means that there is hardly any variation.

Other attested forms are *ie* [iː] (n = 11 or 0.8%), and *i:ch* [iːç] pronounced as in Maaslands (n = 4 or 0.3%). The most frequent form following *ich* [ɪç] is the short form *i* [i], representing 22 tokens or 1.7 percent. While the short form *i* [i] has also been attested in Ruhr-German in allegro-speech (Schiering 2002: 19), it is difficult to say whether it may be a type of weak pronoun, as it occurs seldom in the data. Rather, it shows that the full form *ich* [ɪç] is preferred by the speakers over possible weak or other strong forms. There is no indication that speakers make use of the Belgian Dutch weak pronoun 'k [ək]/[k]. Likewise, its strong counterpart *ik* [ɪk] is hardly represented (n = 11 or 0.8%). The strong form common in Belgian Dutch for emphasis, *ikke* [ɪkə], was used only once (0.1%). These realizations of the final and word-internal /k/, considering the low number of tokens, probably occur because speakers sometimes switch to Belgian Dutch for quotations. What we potentially observe here, in other words, are a few examples of transition effects at clause boundaries when speakers switch to another variety.

4.2 Second person singular

Table 5 provides the same information in terms of percentages and absolute numbers for the second person singular pronoun in Cité Duits (n = 730).

At first sight, the picture appears to be less homogenous, with two forms scoring the highest, namely *du* [duː] (78.3% or n = 573) and *te* [tə] (19.8% or n = 145). Yet, these forms make up together 98.1 percent, whereas hardly two percent of the tokens go back to other forms. Phonetically, both *du* [duː] and *te* [tə] are in line with the pronunciation of second person singular

Table 5: Frequency in absolute numbers and percentages of all second person singular subject pronoun forms in Cité Duits.

2SG	[du:]	[də]	[tə]	[ə]	[ɣə]	[ɣɛɪ]	Total
n	573	4	145	2	6	2	730
%	78,3	0,5	19,8	0,3	0,8	0,3	100

pronouns in German, where *du* [du:] is the full and *te* [tə] the reduced form confined to enclitic position (section 3.3). In addition, *te* [tə] is the respective enclitic pronoun in Maaslands (section 3.2). For Dutch, it holds that neither *du* nor *te* are used (section 3.1). The form *di:ch* [di:ç] with a voiceless velar fricative as in Maaslands, in turn, does not occur in Cité Duits. The Maaslands/German weak form *de* [də] appears only in four tokens. Additionally, eight of the 730 tokens resemble Belgian Dutch, i.e. *gij* [ɣɛɪ] (0.3%) and *ge* [ɣə] (0.8%), whereas *je* [jə] (n = 2) and *jij* [jɛɪ] (n = 0) are almost absent. The absence of the *je/jij*-paradigm is not surprising, since it is more typical of formal registers in Belgian Dutch (Vandekerckhove 2005).

4.3 Third person singular masculine + human

The third person singular masculine pronoun + human is with 1301 tokens extremely frequent in the data (Table 6). For methodological reasons, pronouns with a non-human antecedent have been excluded here (see section 2.2).

Table 6: Frequency in absolute numbers and percentages of all third person singular masculine subject pronoun forms + human in Cité Duits.

3SG.M	[hɛɪ]	[i]	[e:ʁ]	[de:(ʁ)]	die[di:]	Total
n	2	2	232	1047	18	1301
%	0.2	0.2	17.8	80.5	1.3	100

Again, two forms make up the lion's share. The dominant form is *de(r)* [de:]/[de:ʁ] with 80.5 percent of the tokens (n = 1047), followed by *er* [e:ʁ] (n = 232) with 17.8 percent, which sometimes seems to be realized as [e:]/[ɐ].[6] Together,

---

[6] Due to voice overlap in the data, these are extremely difficult to distinguish.

there is a chance of 98.3 percent that either *er* [eːɐ̯] or *de(r)* [deː]/[deːɐ̯] are produced for the third person singular masculine. Phonetically, *er* [eːɐ̯] shows much overlap with the strong form *(h)eeë(r)* [eːɐ̯] in Maaslands and *er* [eːɐ̯] in German, while *der* [deː] resembles the respective demonstrative pronoun *der* [deːɐ̯] in German and *dè* [də] in Maaslands. These forms do not exist in Dutch, but *hij* [hɛɪ] and *die* [diː] are used instead. The remaining three percent are spread among the forms *die* [diː] (n = 18 or 1.3%), resembling the Belgian Dutch (feminine, masculine, plural) and the German (feminine, plural) demonstrative pronoun, *hij* [hɛɪ] (n = 2 or 0.2%), in line with the Belgian Dutch strong pronoun, and *ie* [i] (n = 2 or 0.2%), similar to the Netherlandic Dutch weak pronoun.

4.4 First person plural

There is quite some variation in the use of the first person plural (n = 556). Six different forms re-occur, with four of them being frequently produced (>10%) (Table 7).

Table 7: Frequency in absolute numbers and percentages of all first person plural subject pronoun forms in Cité Duits.

1PL	[wə]	[viːɐ̯]	[viː]	[mɐ]	[vɐ]	[vɐʀ]	Total
n	81	203	81	149	38	4	556
%	14,6	36,5	14,6	26,8	6,8	0,7	100

The two most frequent forms, *wir* [viːɐ̯] (n = 203 or 36.5%) and *ma* [mɐ] (n = 149 or 26.8%), are pronounced according to German phonology. While *wir* is the full pronoun in German, *ma* is confined to the enclitic position. The form *wa* [vɐ] (n = 38 or 6.8%), occurring less often, is also similar to the German enclitic. As outlined in section 3.3, spoken German has a number of enclitic forms for the first person plural. These findings strongly suggest that it is worth taking a closer look at the behavior of these forms before and after the finite verb and complementizer.

A noticeable variant that cannot be analyzed as being homophonous to one of the available forms in the source varieties is *wie* [viː], a form that accounts for 14.6 percent of the tokens (n = 81). Although this form is neither Dutch, German nor Maaslands, it shows overlap regarding the phonetic realization. The /w/ is generally realized as a voiced labiodental fricative [v] as in German/ Maaslands, and not as a voiced velar approximant [w]. It is followed by a long vowel [iː], the final /r/ is not realized. Furthermore, there are 81 examples realized as *we* [wə] (14.6%), matching the Belgian Dutch weak pronoun *we* [wə]. *Wer* [vɐʀ], resembling Maaslands' weak form, was produced in merely four examples.

4.5 Second person plural

The forms for the second person plural in Cité Duits are given below (Table 8).

Table 8: Frequency in absolute numbers and percentages of all second person plural subject pronoun forms in Cité Duits.

2PL	[ʔɔɪç]	Total
n	6	6
%	100	100

It was possible to establish only six tokens, all of which realized as *euch* [ʔɔɪç], in line with the second person plural object form in German and phonologically fairly close to the Maaslands object pronoun *uuch* [yːx]. Neither the German *ihr* [ʔiːɐ̯]/*'a* [ɐ], the Dutch *jullie* [ˈjyli]/ *ge* [ɣə] or the Maaslands *geer* [ɣeːʀ]/*ger* [ɣeʀ] are used. Such forms appear only in a few quotes. *Ihr* [ʔiːɐ̯], for instance, occurred in a German quote, suggesting that speakers are aware of this pronoun and perfectly able to switch between different varieties, as illustrated in example 2 (the speaker quotes a cabdriver):

(2) wenn **ihr** zurück wollt eh,
 when 2PL back want Q
 'When you want to return'
 (171115_4:1029.497–1035.802)

German quotes, however, are the only instances where speakers use the "standard" German pronoun *ihr* [ʔiːɐ̯]. Normally, *euch* [ʔɔɪç] is used (incidentally, it is also the object form in Cité Duits, attested in all tokens). An example is given below (3).

(3) sin **euch** auch gehn biechte?
 are 2PL also go pray
 'Did you also go to confession?'
 (231115_4:1649.742–1653.566)

The development from an object to a subject pronoun has been observed in several varieties of Dutch, including in Limburgish (for Netherlandic Dutch, see Broekhuis and den Dikken 2012: 783; Audring 2018; for southwestern Dutch dialects, Vos 2013: 181; for Limburgish, de Vogelaer 2007: 209–211; De Schutter and Hermans 2013: 363). In northern varieties, the pronoun *hun* 'them' is currently developing more and more into an "omnipurpose" pronoun for the third person plural (Broekhuis and den Dikken 2012: 783). Moreover, in colloquial Belgian Dutch, the third person singular masculine object form *hem* 'him' seems to be spreading towards the subject position. While the number of tokens in the data is too small to draw evidence-based conclusions, it may be the case that a similar process can be observed in Cité Duits, with language contact having accelerated these processes. Note that whereas the respective object and subject forms currently exist side-by-side in Dutch, the findings suggest that this use is no longer optional in Cité Duits but that the form *euch* [ʔɔɪç] has become the only possible option.

4.6 Third person plural

The distribution of all third person plural subject forms is illustrated in Table 9.

Table 9: Frequency in absolute numbers and percentages of all third person plural subject pronoun forms in Cité Duits.

3PL	[zɛɪ]	[ziː]	[zə]	[diː]	Total
n	2	26	168	421	617
%	0,3	4,2	27,2	68,2	100

The most frequent form is *die* [diː], accounting for 68.2 percent, which is homophonous with the Dutch/German demonstrative pronoun, and close to Maaslands *dièj* [diːʲ]. Additionally, speakers use *ze* [zə] (27.2%), resembling the respective German enclitic and the Dutch/Maaslands weak pronoun. These two forms account together for 95.4 percent. Note that the three source varieties provide very similar forms. In turn, the Belgian Dutch full form *zij* [zɛɪ] is almost absent from the data (n = 2 or 0.3%), whereas *sie* [ziː] as in German is used in 4.2 percent (n = 26).

4.7 Summary: Distribution of personal pronouns in Cité Duits

I conclude this section by providing the paradigm of subject pronouns in Cité Duits based on the forms with the highest distribution in the data.

As visible from Table 10, usually not more than two variants are encountered frequently for a given pronoun, except in the case of the first person plural. V-pronouns are completely absent, which is unsurprising as Cité Duits emerged as in-group variety in informal contexts. A pronoun that is extremely frequent and shows particularly little internal variation is the first person singular (n = 1331), which is realized in roughly 96 percent of the tokens as *ich* [ıç]. Interestingly, this form seems to be a Dutch-Maaslands-German intermediate form. As to the second person singular, the most frequent form is *du* [duː] (78%), phonologically in line with German but not with Dutch/Maaslands. In addition, speakers use *te* [tə], which can be analyzed as a Maaslands/German component of the speech. For the third person singular masculine + human, speakers use again two forms that resemble German/Maaslands but differ from Belgian Dutch.

Table 10: Most frequent subject pronoun forms in Cité Duits compared to the source varieties.

		Cité Duits	German	Maaslands	Belgian Dutch
SG	1	[ıç]	[ıç]	[iːç̝] [ç̝]	[ɪk] [ək] [k]
	2	[duː] [tə]	[duː] [də] [tə]	[diːç̝] [də] [tə]	[ɣɛɪ] [ɣə] ([jɛɪ] [jə])
	3M	[deː(ɐ̯)] [eːɐ̯]	[eːɐ̯] [deːɐ̯] [e]	[eːɐ̯] [də] [eː]	[hɛɪ] [diː] [əm]
	V	–	[ziː] [zə]	[ˈɣeːʀ] [ɣeʀ]	[y]
PL	1	[viːɐ̯] [viː] [wə] [mɐ] ([vɐ])	[viːɐ̯] [vɐ] [mɐ]	[veːʀ] [veʀ]	[wɛɪ] [wə]
	2	[ʔɔɪç]	[ʔiːɐ̯] [ɐ]	[ˈɣeːʀ] [ɣeʀ]	[ˈjyli] [ɣɛɪ][ɣə]
	3	[diː] [zə]	[ziː] [diː] [zə]	[zeː] [diːj] [zə]	[zɛɪ] [diː] [zə]

The first person plural shows an exceptional range of internal variation, with four frequently-attested variants, namely *wir* [viːɐ̯], *wie* [viː], *we* [wə] and *ma* [mɐ] 'we' (and seldom *wa* [vɐ]). Three of these variants are realized according to one of the available forms in the source varieties: *wir* [viːɐ̯] is homophonous to the German strong form and *ma* [mɐ] to the weak one, while *we* [wə] resembles the weak form in Dutch. But the form *wie* [viː] is neither Dutch, Maaslands nor German. The most obvious explanation, given the phonetic closeness of the German full pronoun *wir* [viːɐ̯] and the Belgian Dutch weak pronoun *we* [wə], is that *wie* [viː] developed as an intermediate form. The second person plural, in turn, is consistently realized as *euch* [ʔɔɪç] 'you' in line with the respective object pronoun in German. The third person plural forms *die* [diː] and *ze* [zə] 'they' can be associated with all three source varieties.

In sum, the overall picture is that many pronouns phonetically resemble German and partly Maaslands. Additionally, two forms, namely [ɪç] *ich* 'I' and *wie* [viː] 'we', look like a fusion of the source varieties.

5 Explaining variation in the data: Position of pronominal forms

This section discusses the findings in terms of internal variation of pronominal forms in relation to their position. Studies devoted to the pronominal domain already point to the syntactic position of the verb as a pivotal factor for determining form variation of a pronoun (Benincà and Poletto 2005: 278; de Vogelaer 2007: 145). For the subsequent analysis, I identified three patterns: i) the pronoun occurs in verb-initial position in the main clause, the V2-straight order (subject-verb order or S-V), ii) the pronoun follows the finite verb in the main clause, the V2-inverted order (verb-subject order or V-S) and iii) the pronoun occurs after a complementizer (COMP-S). To explain variation in the data, I will concentrate on the most frequent forms as illustrated in Table 10. As we have seen, most of the other forms do not exceed two percent. I will disregard the first person singular and the second person plural because they are consistently employed in the same way.

5.1 Second person singular

Table 11 illustrates the distribution of second person singular forms before the finite verb (S-V), after the finite verb (V-S) and after the complementizer (COMP-S).

Table 11: Comparison of second person singular subject forms according to position.

	[duː]	[tə]	n-total
S-V	203	0	203
V-S	313	143	456
COMP-S	57	2	59
n-total	573	145	718

Comparing the forms preceding the finite verb, *du* [duː] accounts for 100 percent (n = 203) of the tokens (S-V). In contrast, *te* is clearly confined to the position after the finite verb (V-S=143). Given that this form is an enclitic in Maaslands and German, it comes as no surprise that *te* [tə] is exclusively found after the finite verb in Cité Duits (plus two tokens after the complementizer). Yet, both forms equally occur in postverbal position, as depicted below (4), (5):

(4) dat däbs **du** normal nich sagen
    that may ₂SG normally not say_INF
    'You should normally not say that.'
    (231115_4: 365.597–369.803)

(5) un da dachs-**te** in dein eigen, wie?
    and there thought-₂SG in your own how
    'And you thought by yourself, how?'
    (0313_144739: 199.513–203 725)

This use is in line with German (Nübling 1992: 23). The reduction of *du* to *te* can be explained by phonetic rules of German: While weakening of the vowel (*u* > *e*) goes back to the tendency of centralization, the elision of the alveolar plosive (*d* > *t*) derives from assimilation with [s] after the finite verb (Schiering 2002: 21).

While a tremendous scope of variation has been observed across dialects of Dutch in the second person singular (de Vogelaer 2007: 170–179), in Cité Duits, this pronoun behaves in a consistent way, which resembles German (Nübling 1992: 303–307) and to a lesser degree Maaslands. Clearly, *du* [duː] is the most frequent form in Cité Duits. Compared to *te* [tə], there is a probability of 96.6 percent that *du* occurs after the complementizer; of 100 percent before the finite verb (S-V), and to almost seventy percent after the finite verb (V-S). Despite the variation that appeared at first sight, there is strong evidence that the two pronominal forms appear in different positions.

5.2 Third person singular masculine + human

For the third person masculine, speakers almost exclusively employ *de(r)* [deː(ɐ)] and *er* [eːɐ]. The distribution of both variants is given below (Table 12).

With very few exceptions (n = 11 or 1.5%), the form *er* [eːɐ] is preferred in the position after the finite verb, whereas *de(r)* [deː(ɐ)] may occur both before and after, with a clear preference for the position before the verb. In all three source varieties, demonstrative pronouns may replace third person pronouns

Table 12: Comparison of third person singular masculine + human forms according to position.

	[deː(ɐ)]	[eːɐ]	n-total
S-V	703	11	714
V-S	315	215	530
COM-S	29	6	35
n-total	1047	232	1279

(cf. Ehlich 1982; Bosch, Katz, and Umbach 2007; de Vogelaer 2007: 189; Plevoets 2008; Rozendaal 2008; Eisenberg 2016: 158), and particularly speakers of Dutch in Belgian Limburg are inclined to choosing the demonstrative pronoun (i.e. *die*) as a general third person pronominal form (cf. de Vogelaer 2007: 189). According to Rozendaal (2008: 29), the "use of demonstrative pronouns is, as with personal pronouns, in part determined by topic continuity". The frequent use of *de(r)* [deː(ɐ)] is thus unsurprising. In turn, it is striking that *er* [eːɐ] seems to behave as enclitic in Cité Duits, in contrast to German, where both positions are principally possible.

5.3 First person plural

Table 13 compares the five most frequent first person plural forms according to their position.

Table 13: Comparison of first person plural forms according to position.

	[viː]	[viːɐ]	[wə]	[mɛ]	[vɛ]	n-total
S-V	65	154	30	0	0	249
V-S	15	34	41	149	37	276
COMP-S	1	15	10	0	1	27
n-total	81	203	81	149	38	552

As this table reveals, all variants may occur after the finite verb (V-S), but only three variants occur before the finite verb ([viː] [viːɐ], [wə]). Yet, *wie* [viː] occurs more than four times as often before the finite verb than after it (n = 65 vs. 15) and *wir* [viːɐ̯] occurs almost five times as often (n = 154 vs. 34). *We* [wə] shows almost the reverse picture, being produced 41 times after the finite verb and 30 times before it. In contrast, *ma* [mɐ] and *wa* [vɐ] behave as enclitics, which corresponds to German (section 3.3). Two examples are provided below (6, 7).

(6) de(r)   ham   **ma**, de(r)   ham   **ma**   dat   lasse   leze,
    3SG-OBJ have 1PL   3SG-OBJ have 1PL   that let   read$_{INF}$
    'We had him read that.'
    (0314_134351: 1444.105–1445.995)

(7) dann   ham   **wa**   gebaut   un   ich   ging   wohnen,
    then   have 1PL   built   and   1SG   went   live$_{INF}$
    'Then we built a house and I started living there.'
    (231115_5: 1469.366–1471.797)

While the first person plural exhibits more variation than other pronouns, this type of variation can only be explained to some extent by the position of the pronominal form. It is clear that *ma* [mɐ] and *wa* [vɐ] are enclitics, but unlike in the source varieties, Cité Duits has three full forms. At this point, it remains unclear whether inter-speaker variation is involved, an aspect still in need of closer analysis.

5.4 Third person plural

The distribution of the third person plural variants is the following (Table 14):

Table 14: Comparison of third person plural subject forms according to position.

	[zə]	[diː]	n-total
S-V	3	289	292
V-S	151	89	240
COMP-S	14	25	39
n-total	168	403	571

It can be observed that one form, namely *ze* [zə], is confined to the position after the finite verb and complementizer, whereas the more frequently used form, *die* [diː], shows a strong tendency towards the position before the finite verb. Accordingly, *ze* [zə] behaves in line with German/Maaslands but does not seem to share the grammatical properties of Dutch, where it may occur both before and after the finite verb.

6 Cité Duits – a mixed variety?

6.1 Discussion

Mixed languages are a type of contact language that exhibit extensive diversity in terms of linguistic structure, sociohistorical origin and function. While most languages that are regarded as "mixed" originate from two unrelated languages that came in contact, often with a split between the grammar and lexicon (Bakker and Mous 1994; Matras 2000; Mous 2003; Meakins 2018), Cité Duits consists of features of structurally similar varieties. Likewise, although usually regarded as a manifestation of cross-dialectal convergence, work on koineization has pointed to similar processes (Kerswill 2002; Kerswill and Trudgill 2005; Trudgill 2010). Such structural convergence between closely related linguistic systems may result in a compromise variety with stable features, a koiné. As established by the analysis of personal pronouns, the resulting forms are employed in a notable consistent way, which means that speakers do not simply mix languages by choosing pronominal forms from variety A and B or C, but that the use of these forms has become obligatory. These observations support the assumption that Cité Duits exhibits stable features, similar to some koinés. Yet, unlike in the case at hand, the formation of a koiné requires several generations (Trudgill 2010). Apart from that, both dialect and language contact are involved here. While I have shown that pronouns rather resemble German and partly Maaslands, Cité Duits mostly follows the syntactic structures of Dutch (Auer and Cornips 2018), placing Cité Duits closer to a contact variety on a mixed basis.

Beyond that, in terms of the sociolinguistic situation, Cité Duits does not differ from varieties that have been classified as "mixed" in the literature. What these have in common is the fact that they all emerged in settings of multilingualism where speakers already share a common language. Their function is not to ensure communication but rather to mark an in-group identity (Meakins 2018). Also, Cité Duits developed in a very short time span, and functioned for a long time as a vehicle for identifying with one particular group (miners and family members) and dis-identifying with others (local population). While not a prototypical "mixed language" as described in the literature (e.g. Bakker and Mous 1994; Mous 2003), its history of emergence and its additional status in the mining district are similar to those of many mixed languages.

6.2 Conclusions

This chapter provided a first analysis of the use of subject pronouns in Cité Duits, a contact variety composed of German, Belgian Dutch and the Limburgish dialect Maaslands, three closely related varieties. While Cité Duits differs from prototypical cases of mixed languages in having no "split ancestry" (Bakker and Mous 1994; Matras 2000), my argument revealed that it exhibits a regular pattern of language mixing in pronouns. The analysis focused on frequency distribution, phonological-lexical variation and the position of the pronoun to the finite verb and complementizer. By drawing on data of informal conversations of 14 speakers (340 minutes), the results indicate that pronominal forms exhibit a remarkable degree of homogeneity. While most pronouns phonetically resemble German and to a certain degree Maaslands (section 4), Cité Duits has developed one "new" form, *euch* [ʔɔɪç], and two mixed forms, *wie* [viː] and *ich* [ɪç], apparently a fusion of the three source varieties. Furthermore, I have shown that the position of the pronoun affects its form, similar to most varieties of Dutch and German. A large number of forms – specifically *te* [tə], *ma* [mɐ], *wa* [vɐ], *er* [eːɐ] and *ze* [zə] – occurs almost exclusively after the finite verb and complementizer. I have argued that what looked like free variation at first sight turns out to be structured language use, with the use of a phonological form being predictable to a high degree.

Apparently, personal pronouns in Cité Duits became conventionalized over the decades, yielding a rather stable paradigm. This suggests that, unlike in contexts of code-switching, speakers use a single pronominal system. The only pronoun that stands out in this regard is the first person plural, which has three full and two clitic forms. In a follow-up analysis, it will be worthwhile to consider inter-speaker variation to verify to what extent individual preferences play a role. Furthermore, additional analyses of some third-person singular forms and object pronouns, which I ignored here due to limits of space, may well substantiate the findings.

Abbreviations

1	first person
2	second person
3	third person
COMP-S	complementizer-subject order
INF	infinitive
M	masculine
OBJ	object pronoun
PL	plural
Q	question marker
S-V	subject-verb order
SG	singular
T	informal pronoun of address
V	formal pronoun of address
V-S	verb-subject order

References

Abraham, Werner & Anko Wiegel. 1993. Reduktionsformen und Kasussynkretismus bei deutschen und niederländischen Pronomina. In Werner Abraham & Josef Bayer (eds.), *Dialektsyntax*, 12–49. Opladen: Westdeutscher Verlag.

Audring, Jenny. 2009. *Reinventing Pronoun Gender*. Utrecht: LOT.

Audring, Jenny. 2018. Personal pronouns. *Taalportaal*. http://www.taalportaal/topic/pid/topic-13998813298162864 (accessed 17 April 2018).

Auer, Peter. 1998. From code-switching via language mixing to fused lects: Toward a dynamic typology of bilingual speech. *InLiSt – Interaction and Linguistic Structures* 6.1–28.

Auer, Peter. 2014. Language mixing and language fusion: when bilingual talk becomes monolingual. In J. Besters-Dilger, C. Dermarkar, S. Pfänder & A. Rabus (eds.), *Congruence in contact-induced language change: Language families, typological resemblance, and perceived similarity*, 294–336. Berlin: De Gruyter.

Auer, Peter & Leonie Cornips. 2018. Cité Duits – a polyethnic miners' variety. In Leonie Cornips & Vincent de Rooij (eds.), *The sociolinguistics of place and belonging. Perspectives from the margins*. 55–88. Amsterdam: John Benjamins.

Bakker, Peter & Marteen Mous. 1994. *Mixed languages: 15 case studies in language intertwining*. Amsterdam: Institute for Functional Research into Language and Language Use.

Benincà, Paola & Cecilia Poletto. 2005. The third dimension of person features. In Leonie Cornips & Karen P. Corrigan (eds.), *Syntax and variation: Reconciling the biological and the social*, 265–299. Amsterdam: John Benjamins.

Bhat, D.N. Shankara. 2004. *Pronouns*. Oxford: Oxford University Press.

Bosch, Peter, Graham Katz & Carla Umbach. 2007. The non-subject bias of German demonstrative pronouns. In Monika Schwarz-Friesel, Manfred Consten & Mareile Knees (eds.), *Anaphors in text: Cognitive, formal and applied approaches to anaphoric reference*, 145–164. Amsterdam: John Benjamins

Bourdieu, Pierre. 1991. The production and reproduction of legitimate language. In Pierre Bourdieu & J. B. Thompson (eds.), *Language and symbolic power*, 37–43. Cambridge: Polity Press.
Broekhuis, Hans, Norbert Corver & Riet Vos (eds.). 2015. *Syntax of Dutch: Verbs and verb phrases*, vol. 1. Amsterdam: Amsterdam University Press.
Broekhuis, Hans & Marcel den Dikken. 2012. *Syntax of Dutch: Nouns and noun phrases*, vol. 2. Amsterdam: Amsterdam University Press.
Bucholtz, Mary. 2000. The politics of transcription. *Journal of Pragmatics* 32. 1439–1465.
Cardinaletti, Anna & Michal Starke. 1999. The typology of structural deficiency: A case study of the three classes of pronouns. In Henk C. van Riemsdijk (ed.), *Clitics in the languages of Europe*, 145–234. Berlin & New York: Mouton de Gruyter.
Corver, Norbert & Denis Delfitto. 1999. On the nature of pronoun movement. In Henk C. van Riemsdijk (ed.), *Clitics in the languages of Europe*, 799–864. Berlin & New York: Mouton de Gruyter.
Ehlich, Konrad. 1982. Anaphora and deixis: Same, similar, or different? In R. J. Jarvella & W. Klein (eds.), *Speech, place and action*, 315–338. Chichester: John Wiley & Sons.
Eisenberg, Peter. 2016. *Grundriss der deutschen Grammatik: Band 2: Der Satz*. Stuttgart: J. B. Metzler.
Geeraerts, Dirk. 2010. Schmidt redux. How systematic is the linguistic system if variation is rampant? In Kasper Boye & Elisabeth Engberg-Pedersen (eds.), *Language usage and language structure*, 237–262. Berlin & New York: Walter de Gruyter.
Goeman, Ton, J. Taeldeman & P. Th. Van Reenen. 2014. MAND (Morfologische Atlas van de Nederlandse Dialecten) [morphological atlas of the Dutch dialects] database. Amsterdam: Goeman-Taeldeman-Van Reenen-project. http://www.meertens.knaw.nl/mand/data base/ (accessed 10 June 2018).
Goossens, Jan. 1996. Een geïsoleerd voornaamwoord: Limburgs doe, dich, dijn [An isolated pronoun: Limburgish you, you, your]. *Mededelingen van de Vereniging voor Limburgse Dialect- en Naamkunde* 88.
Hoeksema, Jack. 2000. Ikke als default-nominatief [I as default case]. *Tabu* 30. 27–46.
Howe, Stephen. 1996. *The personal pronouns in the Germanic languages. A study of personal pronoun morphology and change in the Germanic languages from the first records to the present day*. Berlin & New York: Walter de Gruyter.
Kerswill, Paul. 2002. Koineization and accommodation. In J. K. Chambers, P. Trudgill & N. Schilling-Estes (eds.), *The handbook of language variation and change*, 669–702. Oxford: Blackwell.
Kerswill, Paul and Peter Trudgill. 2005. The birth of new dialects. In P. Auer, F. Hinskens & P. Kerswill (eds.), *Dialect change: convergence and divergence in European languages*, 196–220. Cambridge: Cambridge University Press.
Labov, William. 1972. *Sociolinguistic patterns*. Philadelphia: University of Pennsylvania Press.
Lenerz, Jürgen. 1993. Zu Syntax und Semantik deutscher Personalpronomina. In Marga Reis (ed.), *Wortstellung und Informationsstruktur*, 117–154. Tübingen: Niemeyer.
Lenerz, Jürgen. 1994. Pronomenprobleme. In Brigitta Haftka (ed.), *Was determiniert Wortstellungsvariation?: Studien zu einem Interaktionsfeld von Grammatik, Pragmatik und Sprachtypologie*, 161–174. Opladen: Westdeutscher Verlag.
Linke, Kathrin & Anna Kirstein. 2018. Clitics. *Taalportaal*. http://www.taalportaal.org/taalpor taal/topic/pid/topic-14020545821582167 (accessed 25 September 2018).

Marynissen, Ann & Guy Janssen. 2013. A regional history of Dutch. In Frans Hinskens & Johan Taeldeman (eds.), *Language and space. An international handbook of linguistic variation. Volume 3: Dutch*, 81–100. Berlin & Boston: Mouton de Gruyter.

Matras, Yaron. 2000. Mixed languages: a functional-communicative approach. *Bilingualism: Language and Cognition* 3. 79–99.

Mazzucato, Valentina, Rijk van Dijk, Cindy Horst & Pieter de Vries. 2004. Transcending the nation. Explorations of transnationalism as a concept and phenomenon. In D. Kalb, W. Pansters & H. Siebers (eds.), *Globalization and development: Themes and concepts in current research*, 131–162. Dordrecht: Kluwer Academic Publishers.

Meakins, Felicity. 2018. Mixed languages. In Mark Aronoff (ed.), *Oxford Research Encyclopedia of Linguistics*, 1–29. Oxford: Oxford University Press.

Mieroop, Dorien van de. 2014. On the use of 'we' in Flemish World War II interviews. In Theodossia-Soula Pavlidou (ed.), *Constructing collectivity. 'We' across languages and contexts*, 309–330. Amsterdam & Philadelphia: John Benjamins.

Mieroop, Dorien van de, Eline Zenner & Stefania Marzo. 2016. Standard and Colloquial Belgian Dutch pronouns of address: A variationist-interactional study of child-directed speech in dinner table interactions. *Folia Linguistica* 50(1). 31–64.

Mous, Marteen. 2003. The linguistic properties of lexical manipulation and its relevance for Ma'a. In Yaron Matras & Peter Bakker (eds.), *The mixed language debate: Theoretical and empirical advances*, 209–235. Berlin & New York: Mouton de Gruyter.

Nübling, Damaris. 1992. *Klitika im Deutschen: Schriftsprache, Umgangssprache, alemannische Dialekte*. Tübingen: Gunter Narr Verlag.

Pecht, Nantke. 2019. Grammatical features of a moribund coalminers' language in a Belgian cité. In Leonie Cornips & Pieter Muysken (eds.), *International Journal of the Sociology of Language (IJSL)*, 71–98. New York: de Gruyter.

Pecht, Nantke. 2021. Language contact in a mining community. A study of variation in personal pronouns and progressive aspect in *Cité Duits*. Amsterdam: LOT.

Plevoets, Koen. 2008. Tussen spreek- en standaardtaal. Een corpusgebaseerd onderzoek naar de situationele, regionale en sociale verspreiding van enkele morfosyntactische verschijnselen uit het gesproken Belgisch-Nederlands [Between spoken- and standard language. A corpus-based study of the situational, regional and social distribution of some morphosyntactic phenomena of spoken Belgian-Dutch]. Leuven: KU Leuven PhD thesis.

Plevoets, Koen, Dirk Speelman, and Dirk Geeraerts. 2008. The distribution of T/V pronouns in Netherlandic and Belgian Dutch. In Klaus Schneider & Anne Barron (eds.), *Variational pragmatics: a focus on regional varieties in pluricentric languages*, 181–209. Amsterdam: John Benjamins.

Riemsdijk, Henk C. van. 1999. Clitics: a state-of-the-art report. In Henk C. van Riemsdijk (ed.), *Clitics in the Languages of Europe*, 1–30. Berlin & New York: Mouton de Gruyter.

Rozendaal, Margaretha Isabella. 2008. *The acquisition of reference: A cross-linguistic study*. Utrecht: LOT.

Schiering, René. 2002. Klitisierung von Pronomina und Artikelformen. Eine empirische Untersuchung am Beispiel des Ruhrdeutschen. In *Arbeitspapier (Neue Folge)*, 1–62. Köln: Universität zu Köln.

Schutter, Georges de. 1989. *Pronominale clitica in de Nederlandse dialecten* [Pronominal clitics in the Dutch dialects]. Antwerpen: Antwerp Papers in Linguistics.

Schutter, Georges de & Ben Hermans. 2013. The Limburg dialects: Grammatical properties. In Frans Hinskens & Johan Taeldeman (eds.), *Language and space. An international handbook of linguistic variation. Volume 3: Dutch*, 356–377. Berlin: Mouton de Gruyter.

Simon, Horst J. & Heike Wiese. 2002. Grammatical properties of pronouns and their representation: An exposition. In Horst J. Simon & Heike Wiese (eds.), *Pronouns: Grammar and representation*, 1–22. Amsterdam & Philadelphia: John Benjamins.

Stevens, A. 1985 [1949]. Pronominale isomorfen in Belgisch-Limburg. *Taal en Tongval* 1(1949), 132–154 & *Mededelingen van de Vereniging voor Limburgse Dialect- en Naamkunde* 34 (1985). Hasselt.

Temmerman, Martina. 2014. "Nail polish – We've chosen the nicest shades for you!" Editorial voice and 'we' in a Flemish women's magazine. In Theodossia-Soula Pavlidou (ed.), *Constructing collectivity. 'We' across languages and contexts*, 247–264. Amsterdam & Philadelphia: John Benjamins.

Trudgill, Peter. 2010. *Investigations in sociohistorical linguistics*. Cambridge: Cambridge University Press.

Vandekerckhove, Reinhild. 2004. Waar zijn je, jij en jou(w) gebleven? Pronominale aanspreekvormen in het gesproken Nederlands van Vlamingen [Where are you, you and your? Pronominal forms of address in the spoken Dutch of Flanders]. In Johan De Caluwe, Magdalena Devos, Jacques Van Keymeulen & Georges De Schutter (eds.), *Taeldeman, man van de taal, schatbewaarder van de taal: Liber amicorum Johan Taeldeman*, 981–994. Gent: Academia Press.

Vandekerckhove, Reinhild. 2005. Belgian Dutch versus Netherlandic Dutch: New patterns of divergence? On pronouns of address and diminutives. *Multilingua* 24. 379–397.

Velde, Hans van de & Dirk Geeraerts. 2013. Supra-regional characteristics of colloquial Dutch. In Frans Hinskens & Johan Taeldeman (eds.), *Language and space. An international handbook of linguistic variation. Volume 3. Dutch*, 532–555. Berlin & Boston: Mouton de Gruyter.

Vogelaer, Gunther de. 2007. *De Nederlandse en Friese subjectsmarkeerders: geografie, typologie en diachronie*. Gent: Koninklijke Academie voor Nederlandse Taal- en Letterkunde.

Vos, Magda de. 2013. The grammar of the southwestern dialects. In Frans Hinskens & Johan Taeldeman (eds.), *Language and space. An international handbook of linguistic variation. Volume 3: Dutch*, 174–193. Berlin & Boston: Mouton de Gruyter.

Zifonun, Gisela, Ludger Hoffmann & Bruno Strecker. 1997. *Grammatik der deutschen Sprache*. Berlin: De Gruyter.

Zwart, Jan Wouter. 2000. 'Ikke' en de default-naamval. Een reactie op Hoeksema ['I and the default case. A reaction to Hoeksema]. *Tabu* 30. 175–182.

Erika Sandman
Wutun as a mixed language

1 Introduction

1.1 The Wutun language and the Amdo Sprachbund

The Wutun language is spoken by ca. 4000 people in Wutun, a rural locality consisting of the three villages of Upper Wutun, Lower Wutun and Jiacangma located in Tongren County, Huangnan Autonomous Prefecture, Qinghai Province, P.R. China. In spite of the small number of speakers, it remains a vigorous language actively used by all generations of its speech community. Wutun represents a high degree of both lexical and grammatical mixing. While most of its basic vocabulary and grammatical forms are of Sinitic (more precisely, Northwest Mandarin) origin, its morphology and syntax show heavy influence from neighboring Tibetic and Mongolic languages. Both non-Sinitic and Sinitic source languages contribute significant amounts of grammar (Sandman 2016). Unlike most of the Sinitic varieties that are predominantly isolating languages, Wutun has an agglutinative morphology with an elaborate system of number and case marking, aspect marking, egophoric marking and converbal constructions used for clause combining. The most prominent contact language of Wutun is Amdo Tibetan, a local lingua franca and the second language for almost all the Wutun speakers. Wutun has also interacted with Bonan, a Mongolic language spoken by ca. 4000 people in four villages located near three Wutun-speaking villages.[1] The contact situation of Wutun is further complicated by the fact that Wutun and its contact languages are part of a larger linguistic area, the Amdo Sprachbund. Many contact features of Wutun are also observed in other Sinitic languages of the region, such as Huangshui (previously known as Xining Chinese, Dede 2007), Xunhua (Dwyer 1995), Linxia (Dwyer 1992; Lee-Smith 1996a), Gangou (Zhu et al. 1997) and Tangwang (Ibrahim 1985; Lee-Smith 1996b; Xu 2017), and it is not always obvious whether the source language for these features is Tibetic or Mongolic,

---

[1] A variety of Bonan is also spoken in Gansu province. While Qinghai Bonan speakers are Buddhists like Wutun speakers, Gansu Bonan speakers are Moslems. The exact number of Gansu Bonan speakers, as well as lexical and grammatical differences between Qinghai Bonan and Gansu Bonan remain unclear.

Erika Sandman, University of Helsinki, erika.sandman@helsinki.fi

https://doi.org/10.1515/9781501511257-012

since Tibetic and Mongolic languages share a number of morpho-syntactic features (such as basic word order, agglutinative morphology, differential object marking and lack of numeral classifiers).

The Amdo Sprachbund[2] (also known in the literature as the Qinghai-Gansu Sprachbund) comprises some 15–19 languages spoken in the Upper Yellow River Basin of Western China, in Eastern Qinghai and Southern Gansu Provinces (Janhunen 2007, 2012, 2015). Historically the area has been part of Tibet and it has been known by the name Amdo. Genealogically, the languages of the Amdo Sprachbund represent four language families: Sinitic, Tibetic, Mongolic and Turkic. In the course of its history, the Amdo region has been dominated by all these linguistic groups, which have left linguistic traces. The Tibetans represent the oldest population in the area, their arrival connected to the expansion of the Tibetan empire between the 7th and 9th centuries. The Mongol empire and its representative in China, the Yuan dynasty (1279–1368) contributed to the migration of both Mongolic-speaking populations as well as for Turkic and Sinitic speakers to the area. Since the Ming dynasty (1368–1644), the Amdo Sprachbund has been politically dominated by the Chinese, although the number of Sinitic speakers in many parts of the area has remained low until very recently. Due to centuries of intense contact, languages of the Amdo Sprachbund have developed shared grammatical features not found in their genetic relatives spoken elsewhere. While varieties of Northwest Mandarin and Amdo Tibetan are generally used as dominant regional languages and lingua francas in the area, Mongolic and Turkic languages are mainly spoken at a more local level. Besides, some typologically transformed Sinitic varieties with a small number of speakers (such as Ganou and Tangwang) exist, but their use is restricted to individual villages.

Before the 1980s, Wutun was a completely undocumented language. The first publications written by professional linguists were published in the 1980s by Chen (1982, 1986, 1988, 1989, in Chinese) and Li (1983, 1984, 1986, in English). An entirely secondary treatise based on Li's and Chen's materials is Lee-Smith and Wurm (1996). Acuo (2004, in Chinese) discusses Wutun in his book on Daohua, another mixed language with Chinese lexicon and Amdo Tibetan grammar spoken in Sichuan Province. Janhunen et al. 2008 is a brief grammar sketch that discusses aspects of Wutun phonology, morphology and syntax, as well as its areal context as a member of the Amdo Sprachbund. The first comprehensive reference grammar is Sandman (2016).

---

[2] 'Amdo' is the historical name of Tibetan areas that today cover parts of Qinghai, Gansu and Sichuan provinces of China.

1.2 Sociohistorical background of the Wutun people

Our current understanding posits the genesis of the Wutun language as a product of both mixed marriages between partners from different linguistic groups, and long-term community bilingualism. Interestingly, the Wutun people's historical sources and local narratives have an opposite view on whether the mixed marriages took place between Chinese men and Tibetan women or vice versa. According to Chen (1986) and Janhunen et al. (2008), the history of the Wutun language dates back to the 14th century, when the Upper Yellow River region formed a borderland between Chinese and Tibetan territory. During the Ming (1368–1644) and Qing (1644–1911) dynasties, inhabitants of certain local villages were organized into hereditary border guard units based on various parts of the Amdo area. The Wutun villages in the Tongren area were part of this border guard system and in this account, the Wutun language most probably emerged due to marriages between Chinese soldiers sent to the area from other parts of China and local Tibetan and Mongolian women. Chen (1986) claims that some of the ancestors of the Wutun people were Chinese soldiers sent from the Nanjing area. He justifies his claim by observing the similarities between the vowel systems of Wutun and the Old Nanjing dialect.

However, the Wutun speakers themselves have a different view about the origins of their language. This is evident from local folktale narratives that deal with the ethnogenesis of the Wutun population. According to local narratives, the creation of the Wutun language was linked to the expansion of Tibetan empire during King Songtsen Gampo (605–650), whose troops came to the area to fight the Tang dynasty (618–907). Some of the Tibetan soldiers settled in the Tongren area and married local Chinese and Mongolian women, and the Wutun language was created in these bilingual families (Cabras forthcoming). The Wutun speakers adopted Tibetan Buddhism and continued to use Amdo Tibetan as their lingua franca in communicating with neighboring linguistic groups. This community bilingualism has contributed to the development and preservation of Tibetan features in Wutun. The number of Sinitic speakers in Tongren remained very low until recent political developments such as the Cultural Revolution (1966–1976) and the Western Regions Development Campaign (since 2000) that have attracted an increasing number of Chinese to the area. Amdo Tibetan continues to be used as the dominant regional language in the present day.

Today's Wutun speakers, except certain older women, are all bilingual in Amdo Tibetan. The children usually attend Tibetan schools and Tibetan is the working language in local monasteries. Knowledge of Tibetan is also needed in painting and selling *thangkas* (traditional Tibetan religious paintings made on canvas), which is, besides agriculture, the most important means of livelihood for the Wutun people. This tradition is known as *Rekong School of Tibetan Art*. Chen (1982, 1986) who did fieldwork in the 1980s, notes that at that time the Wutun people did not speak Chinese. This situation has changed due to education, mass media, migration of Chinese to Tongren. At the time of my fieldwork between 2007 and 2018 knowledge of both local Northwest Mandarin and Modern Standard Chinese has become common among the younger generation. Most present-day Wutun speakers do not speak Bonan, a Mongolic language spoken nearby, except some bilingual individuals who have moved from Bonan to Wutun due to mixed marriages. However, based on some shared grammatical features between Wutun and Bonan that do not exist in Amdo Tibetan and other Sinitic languages of the Amdo Sprachbund (see section 3.4), it can be concluded that historically, the interaction between the two languages is likely to have been more intense in the past than it is today.

Whether Wutun people constitute a separate ethnic group is a matter of debate. The Wutun language lacks official recognition in China and its speakers have been classified as the Tu (Monguor) nationality or Tibetans in the Chinese system of officially recognized "nationalities" (Janhunen et al. 2008). The Wutun people tend to identify as Tibetans, often emphasizing the importance of Tibetan Buddhism in their identity. They have no actual name for their ethnic group and language. The language is usually referred to as *ngan-de-hua*, 'our speech'.

On the other hand, people are well aware that their mother tongue is a mixture of Mandarin Chinese and Amdo Tibetan, and they appreciate it as a "secret" language that neighboring linguistic groups do not understand. While almost all its speakers are bilingual or multilingual, Wutun retains a strong position as an in-group language. It is actively used by all generations in the community, and children acquire it as a first language before attending school.

1.3 Typological characteristics of Sinitic and Tibetic languages

Most Sinitic languages are morpho-syllabic tonal languages. Their morphosyntactic structure is analytic with very little inflectional morphology and grammatical relations are primarily expressed by word order or by independent grammatical particles. The basic, unmarked word order generally appears to be Agent-Verb-Patient (Norman 1988: 8–10). However, it is important to note that sentences are characteristically organized based on a topic-comment structure rather than an argument structure (Li and Thompson 1981 for Mandarin). In noun phrases, numerals, demonstratives and adjective attributes precede the noun. Most of the Sinitic languages have a rich system of numeral classifiers, which are used with numerals and demonstratives. Verbs are marked for aspect, but not for tense and person. Clause combining is achieved through serial verb constructions where verbs occur in chains without any morphology specifying their relationships.

Tibetic languages are characterized by Agent-Patient-Verb word order and polysyllabic words derive from monosyllabic roots. The noun phrase comprises an optional dual and plural marker, as well as case marking. Definiteness is optionally marked by demonstratives or by more specific definiteness markers that are morphologically enclitics. The Tibetic languages are generally classified as ergative languages with ergativity marked by cases on the noun phrase, although other alignment types coexist besides this predominant type (Tournadre 1996: 73; Zeisler 2007: 400). Modern Tibetic languages have rich systems of grammaticalized evidentials and other knowledge-related grammatical categories, such as egophoric marking that is due to speech act participants' access to the instigation of the events or states.

In summary, Sinitic and Tibetic languages show marked differences in typological profile. However, due to long-term language contact, Wutun combines structural properties from both language groups.

2 Sociohistorical and structural approaches to mixed languages

In this section, I will refer to both sociohistorical and structural approaches to mixed languages. From a sociohistorical perspective, mixed languages have been distinguished from other types of contact languages by their genesis. While creole languages have arisen from a language contact situation in which the speakers of different languages need to acquire means of interethnic communication (Bartens 2013: 65), mixed languages have arisen in contexts in which a common language already exists, and they have been created for expressing acts of identity rather than for communicative functions (Bakker 1997: 375). They often serve as markers of group identity. Mixed languages have further been classified according to mechanisms that contributed to their genesis, such as mixed marriages, incomplete shift from an ancestral language to newly introduced language and attempts to reverse the language shift and maintain the ancestral language. Other sociolinguistic features discussed in relation to mixed languages are whether speakers of a mixed language constitute a separate ethnic group and if mixed languages are used as native languages (see Meakins 2013, 2018; Bakker

2017; Meakins and Stewart forthcoming). The existence of mixed languages as a separate type of contact languages has also been questioned by some authors (see e.g. Versteegh 2017).

From a structural perspective, mixed languages are often defined based on genetic ambiguity (Thomason and Kaufman 1988). They are typically defined as the result of the fusion of two identifiable contact languages. Most mixed languages exhibit a split between lexicon and grammar; Bakker (2003: 135) calls them Grammar-Lexicon mixed languages (2003: 135). Examples of Grammar-Lexicon mixed languages include e.g., Angloromani with a restricted set of Romani lexicon within an English grammatical frame and Media Lengua with predominantly Spanish lexicon and Quechua grammar. Also, a number of mixed languages exist in which both contact languages contribute a significant amount of grammar. These include, for example, Michif, in which the nominal system is mainly based on French and the verbal system on Cree. It is common in mixed languages with a significant amount of grammatical mixing that there is some split between different grammatical systems, e.g., nominal and verbal systems are based on different contact languages. Bakker (2003: 122) calls these Noun-Verb mixed languages. Other examples of mixed languages with a significant amount of structural mixing are Australian languages Gurindji Kriol, based on the Pama-Nyungan language Gurindji and English-lexifier creole Kriol, as well as Light Warlpiri based on Warlpiri and Aboriginal English/Kriol. In these mixed languages, both contact languages contribute to the lexicon and grammar, and the grammatical forms are used in a unique system that is not a mere replication of contact languages (see Meakins 2013: 175).

From a sociohistorical perspective, Wutun shares many features with mixed languages, since it is an in-group language rather than a language of interethnic communication and it has developed as the result of mixed marriages and community bilingualism. We will see in section 3 that Wutun exhibits a significant amount of structural mixing and there is no clear split between different grammatical systems; both its nominal and verbal systems are a blend of Sinitic, Tibetic and Mongolic features. Despite being a relatively little-documented language, Wutun has received some attention in language contact literature, and it has been mentioned as a potential example of a mixed language (Meakins 2013; Dede 2015; Xu 2017), as well as a creole (Ansaldo 2015). While earlier accounts on contact features of Wutun are based on entirely secondary sources, this study aims to give a systematic overview of grammatical mixing in Wutun based on first-hand field data.[3]

---

[3] The Wutun examples cited in this article are based on author's field work among the Wutun speech community in between 2007 and 2018 and they include elicited examples, narrative

3 Overview of structural features of Wutun

In this section, I will give an overview of the structural features of Wutun. In section 3.1, I will discuss features that are of Sinitic origin. In section 3.2, I will give an overview of the features that can be attributed to either Tibetic or Mongolic influence and they are shared by other high-contact varieties of Northwest Mandarin spoken in the context of the Amdo Sprachbund. In section 3.3, I will discuss the features that are unambiguously the result of contact with Amdo Tibetan, and in 3.4, I will summarize the features whose source language is Bonan.

3.1 Lexical and grammatical features shared with other varieties of Mandarin

Certain of the Wutun lexical and grammatical features are shared by varieties of Mandarin spoken outside the Amdo Sprachbund. They are unambiguously of Sinitic origin. These include basic vocabulary and grammatical forms (section 3.1.1), standard negation (section 3.1.2) and complement verbs (3.1.3).

3.1.1 Basic vocabulary and grammatical forms

Most of the Wutun basic vocabulary is of Sinitic origin and has unambiguous cognates in other varieties of Mandarin. Janhunen et al. (2008: 118) contains a modified Swadesh 200-word list with some additions for numerals and culture-specific terms (altogether 235 words). In total, 205 words from the wordlist (ca. 87 percent) are always expressed by using a word of Sinitic origin. Personal and demonstrative pronouns, the lower numerals, color terms and many basic verbs such as motion verbs remain consistently Sinitic. Twenty-one words (ca. 9 percent) are always expressed by the word of Tibetan origin. These include some body parts (e.g., *la*, 'leg' and *hongba*, 'arm'), two higher numerals (*dong*, 'thousand' and *che*, 'ten thousand'), some concepts referring to environment (e.g., *co*, 'lake'), some verbs related to physiology (e.g., *jje*, 'to breathe' and '*tai*', 'to spit'), cognition (e.g., *ddang*, 'to think') and interaction (e.g., *zho*, 'to dance') and two adjectives for qualities (*loqong*, 'young' and

---

texts and conversations. When citing examples, I have indicated whether they come from naturally-occurring data or elicitation.

tama, 'bad'). Some items in basic vocabulary have both a Sinitic and Tibetic equivalent. This category includes many verbs for qualities (e.g., *rai/zho*, 'warm', *lo/ggi*, 'old' and *xen/soma*, 'new'). Finally, 4–5 words on the list have no obvious cognates on either Chinese or Tibetan side. These include, for example, *wuwa*, 'mountain' and *galamala*, 'child'.

It must be noted that the proportion of Tibetan vocabulary is higher among cultural vocabulary items (such as vocabulary related to religion, food and local festivals) than basic vocabulary. This is to be expected for people who are part of Tibetan culture. However, the basic vocabulary of Wutun clearly represents the Sinitic component of the language. In addition to basic vocabulary, most of the grammatical morphemes of Wutun have their origins in Mandarin Chinese. It is important to note that while actual grammatical forms usually come from Mandarin Chinese, their underlying syntactic function often represents influence from non-Sinitic languages. This will be evident from sections 3.2–3.5, which focus on Tibetic and Mongolic features of Wutun grammar.

3.1.2 Standard negation

Standard negation in Wutun resembles standard negation in other varieties of Mandarin in terms of both grammatical forms, their semantics and the underlying morphosyntactic structure. By standard negation, I refer to the basic ways a language has for negating declarative verbal main clauses (Miestamo 2005: 39). Wutun has the negative prefixes, *be-* (MSC negative particle *bù* 不) and *mi-* (MSC negative particle *méi* 没) that are equivalent to negative morphemes in Modern Standard Chinese. The negative prefix *be-* negates the existence of an event or a state (as in 1), while the negative prefix *mi-* negates the completion of an event and is typically used in clauses expressing a change of state (as in 2):

(1) *laizha*   ***be****-do-li*
 homework   NEG-much-SEN.INF
 '(There) is not much homework (to do).'
 (Wutun conversation 1_School)

(2) da **mi-**lai-lio⁴ ze-li
    then **NEG-**come-PFV EXEC-SEN.INF
    'Then (the disciple) did not come (anymore).'
    (Wutun narrative 1_Pilgrimage)

Functions of Wutun negative morphemes resemble the functions of negative morphemes in Modern Standard Chinese, in which *bù* is used for negating the existence of events or states and *méi* is used for negating the completion of events. In addition to standard negation, the negation of imperatives resembles other varieties of Mandarin. The negative prefix *bai-* (SM prohibitive particle *biè* 别) functions as a prohibitive and it is used to negate imperatives (as in 3):

(3) ni **bai-**man-da
    2SG **PROH-**(be) busy-IMP
    'You, do not hurry!'
    (Wutun narrative 3_Bike)

As in the case of standard negation, negative imperatives in Wutun resemble negative imperatives in Modern Standard Chinese in terms of both grammatical form and the underlying morphosyntactic structure.

3.1.3 Verb-complement constructions

Another grammatical feature that Mandarin contributes to Wutun grammar is an elaborate system of complement verbs. Complement verbs are partly grammaticalized verbs that have lost some of their semantic properties, as well as syntactic and phonological independence, and they are used as suffixes in combination with the main verb. They add both lexical and aspectual/modal meaning of the main verb. Complement verbs are common in all Sinitic languages (Yue 2003: 116), and they play an important role in TAME⁵ systems of Sinitic languages.

In Wutun, many regular verbs (such as *do*, 'to get done', *se*, 'to die', *jhan*, 'to see', *qhi*, 'to go', *pe*, 'to get broken') can be employed as complement verbs.

---

4 Wutun aspect marker -lio can express both perfective and change of state. In (2), -lio is used as a change of state- marker and its occurrence of *mi-* resembles Mandarin, in which the negative marker *méi* is often used with change of state-markers.
5 Tense-aspect-modality-evidentiality.

In (4) the main verb *da*, 'to hit' is used without a complement verb, while in (5) it is used together with the complement verb *pe*, 'to get broken':

(4) ni   nga   da-lio
    2SG   1SG.OBL   hit-PFV
    'You hit me. / You have beaten me.'
    (Elicited)

(5) ni   zhaze   da-**pe**-lio   ze-li
    2SG   window   hit-**get broken**-PFV   EXEC-SEN.INF
    'You have broken (lit. hit and broken) the window.'
    (Elicited)

In (5), the main activity 'hit' is expressed by the verb *da* and the complement verb *pe*, 'to get broken' specifies the outcome of the main activity and its effect to the Patient. In addition to this lexical meaning, the complement verb *pe* adds an aspectual meaning of completion and punctuality to the main verb. Complement verbs in Wutun are a part of the TAME system together with highly grammaticalized aspect and evidential markers and various auxiliary constructions. The TAME system in Wutun is a complex blend of Chinese and Tibetan grammatical elements and morphosyntactic structures. While a system of complement verbs clearly represents the/a Sinitic component in Wutun TAME system, Tibetan influence is considerable in aspect marking (section 3.3.2) and in egophoric marking (section 3.4.1).

3.2 Grammatical features shared with other 'Altaicized' varieties of Mandarin

Several scholars have noted since the 1970s that varieties of Northern Chinese have been influenced by "Altaic" (Mongolic, Turkic and Tungusic) languages (Hashimoto 1976; Janhunen 2007, 2012, 2015; Szeto, Ansaldo, and Matthews 2018), while varieties of Southern Chinese have been oriented towards Mainland Southeast Asian languages. This impact of language contact explains some of the typological differences between northern and southern varieties of Chinese. Frequently observed typological changes in Northern Chinese varieties that can be attributed to the interference from 'Altaic' languages include the emergence of agglutinative morphological patterns, the development of stress-accent dominance over tone, as well as word order changes and loss of numeral classifiers (Chappell 2001: 335–337). In Gansu and Qinghai that have been primarily populated by non-Sinitic speakers, Sinitic languages have until the present day remained minority languages nested between Tibetic, Mongolic or Turkic speakers. This areal interference has led to a number of Sinitic varieties whose morphosyntactic structure resembles the "Altaic" type of languages. In this section, I will discuss some non-Sinitic features of Wutun that are shared by several other "Altaicized" Sinitic varieties of Amdo Tibetan. These features are common to both Amdo Tibetan and Mongolic languages, and they can be attributed to either Mongolic or Tibetan influence. They include loss of tonal distinctions (section 3.2.1), basic word order (section 3.2.2), agglutinative morphology (section 3.2.3), loss of numeral classifiers (section 3.2.4) and differential object marking (section 3.2.5).

3.2.1 Loss of tonal distinctions

A striking feature in Wutun phonology is that the lack of tones. Many minimal pairs based on tonal differences in Modern Standard Chinese have been neutralized in Wutun. Consider:

(6) a. *da* [ta], 'to hit, big' (= MSC *dǎ*, 'to hit' vs. *dà*, 'big')
     b. *tu* [tʰu], 'earth, to vomit' (= MSC *tǔ*, 'earth' vs. *tù*, 'to vomit')
     c. *se* [sʰə], 'to die, four' (= MSC *sǐ*, 'to die' vs. *sì*, 'four')
     (Elicited)

The present-day Wutun is best described as a language with no phonologically relevant suprasegmental distinctions at the level of isolated words. However, the contrast between regular vowels /i/ and /u/ and their long and tense counter parts /ii/ and /uu/ might contain traces of earlier tonological opposition (see Sandman 2016: 53). The simplification of tonal systems has been reported in many varieties of Northwest Mandarin spoken in Western China (see Lee-Smith 1996a) and it is obviously due to language contact with non-tonal languages such as Mongolic and Turkic languages, as well as Amdo Tibetan.

3.2.2 Basic word order

In Mongolic and Tibetic languages the basic word order is APV, unlike in Sinitic languages which are usually AVP languages. Examples (7) and (8) illustrate the basic word order in Wutun:

(7) gu   pigo-ge   qe-she-lio
    3SG apple-REF eat-RES.AO-PFV
    'S/he ate an apple.'
    (Elicited)

(8) londonwa-jhege tian   zhun-she-lio   ze-li
    farmer-PAUC   field till-RES.AO-PFV   EXEC-SEN.INF
    'The farmers have tilled the land.'
    (Elicited)

As illustrated by the examples (7) and (8), Wutun basic word order is APV as in Tibetic and Mongolic languages, while in Modern Standard Chinese, the basic word order is AVP. APV word order similar to Wutun has also been reported in other varieties of Northwest Mandarin with long-term contact with non-Sinitic languages.

3.2.3 Agglutinative morphology

Another non-Sinitic feature present in Wutun and other varieties of Northwest Mandarin is agglutinative morphology. While most of the Sinitic languages are predominantly isolating with very little inflectional morphology, Wutun has a rich system of suffixes and clitics. Etymologically, most of the suffixes in Wutun are derived from Northern Chinese. However, in Northern Chinese many of the cognates of these suffixes function as independent words, and their grammaticalization towards suffixes in Wutun has been triggered by language contact with Amdo Tibetan and Bonan that are predominantly agglutinating languages. Example (9) illustrates the agglutinative nature of the Wutun language:

(9) gu-n-de   awu-ha huaiqa-ge **yek**-li
    3-COLL-ATTR boy-OD book-REF   **EXIST**-SEN.INF
    'Their boy has a book.'
    (Elicited)

Wutun nouns have an elaborate system of marking of number, case and referentiality, while verbs are inflected for aspect and egophoric marking. In terms of morphological typology, Wutun is closer to Tibetic and Mongolic languages than to Sinitic languages.

3.2.4 Loss of numeral classifiers

Classifiers are grammatical noun categorization devices that classify objects expressed by nouns according to various semantic parameters (Aikhenvald 2000: 271). Most common semantic parameters employed for categorization include humanness, animacy, physical properties (shape, size) and functional properties. While most of the southern Sinitic varieties are known for their extremely rich systems of numeral classifiers,[6] reduction of numeral classifier systems is common in northern Sinitic (Norman 1988; Yue 2003). There are generally two sets of classifiers in Sinitic languages: sortal classifiers that occur with concrete, discrete units (such as a man, a stick and a book), and mensural classifiers that can be used to quantify both nouns naturally occurring in discrete units and nouns that do not naturally occur in discrete units (such as water and flour). In most Sinitic languages, including Modern Standard Chinese numeral classifiers are obligatorily used with number and/or demonstrative, or with certain quantifiers before a noun. Example (10) illustrates numeral classifiers in Modern Standard Chinese:

(10) Modern Standard Chinese
    a. *liǎng-**běn**   shū*
       two-CLF-BOOK book
       'two books'
       (Zhang 2007: 45)
    b. *liǎng-**xiāng**   shū*
       two-CLF-BOX book
       'two boxes of books'
       (Zhang 2007: 45)

---

6 *Hanyu Liangci Cidian* (*A Dictionary of Chinese Classifiers*, 1988) lists altogether 902 classifiers, including nominal classifiers, verbal classifiers and other measurement units. In practice, speakers of modern Sinitic languages do not actively use such a high number of classifiers (see Zhang 2007: 44).

c. liǎng-**píng** jiǔ
two-**CLF-BOTTLE** wine
'two bottles of liquor'
(Zhang 2007: 45)

A striking feature of the Wutun noun phrase is a radically reduced system of numeral classifiers. Wutun lacks sortal classifiers that assign nouns into specific semantic classes. Only the suffix -ge[7] based on the Mandarin Chinese generic classifier is retained. It is used with numerals, demonstratives, nominal quantifiers and indefinite singular nouns. Example (11) illustrates the use of -ge with demonstratives and numerals:

(11) a. je-**ge** joze
 this-**CLF-GENERIC** table
 'this table'
 (Elicited)
 b. awo liang-**ge** yida zhan-she-ma-li
 man two-**CLF-GENERIC** together stand-RES.AO-RES.PO-SEN.INF
 'Two men were standing together.'
 (Wutun narrative 4_Beach)
 c. nga ma liang-**ge** yek
 1SG.OBL horse two-**CLF-GENERIC** EXIST
 'I have two horses.'
 (Elicited)
 d. qhichai liang-**ge**
 car two-**CLF-GENERIC**
 'two cars'
 (Wutun conversation 2_Thangkas, smoking and car)

Tibetic and Mongolic languages lack numeral classifiers, as illustrated by the examples (12) and (13) from Amdo Tibetan and Bonan:

(12) Amdo Tibetan
 ɕajə tʃʰuŋtʃʰuŋ səq xsəm
 child small INDEF three
 'three small children'
 (Sandman and Simon 2016: 102)

---

[7] One of the main reasons of treating -ge as a suffix is that it forms a single prosodic entity with the preceding word.

(13) Bonan
 tʰər gər ədəpkə-tɕo
 that.out-of-sight house collapse-IMPF.OBJ
 'That house collapsed.'
 (Fried 2010: 127)

Classifiers in Sinitic languages are typically used with referential nouns. Referential nouns can be defined as nouns that refer to already identified entities, which can be indefinite (identified by the speaker) or definite (identified by the speaker and the addressee), while non-referential nouns denote arbitrary members of the class of entities described by the noun phrase. Unlike the use of classifiers in elaborate classifier systems, the use of -ge in Wutun is not determined by the semantics of its noun referent. However, it still retains its referential meaning. Therefore, it could be analyzed as a referential marker. In (14) the referential noun *qhichai*, 'a car' refers to a particular, identified entity, while in (15) the non-referential noun *lhoma* 'a student' is a property-denoting nominal that refers to an arbitrary member of the class of entities, and not to any particular student:

(14) je nian nga-n-de dojjai qhichai-**ge** mai-she-lio
 this year 1-COLL-ATTR PN car-**REF** buy-RES.AO-PFV
 'This year our Dojjai bought a car.'
 (Wutun conversation 2_Thangkas, smoking and car)

(15) gu lhoma hai-li
 3SG student EQU-SEN.INF
 'S/he is a student.'
 (Elicited)

Sinitic languages with radically reduced classifier systems include several varieties of Northwest Mandarin spoken in the Western provinces of China, such as Gansu and Qinghai, as well as some dialects spoken in Shanxi and Shandong. These Sinitic varieties have generally lost all of their sortal classifiers with a more specific meaning, and they retain only the generic classifier -ge. (Yue 2003: 85). Therefore, the loss of numeral classifiers in Wutun is part of a more general typological change affecting Sinitic languages of Northwest China.

3.2.5 Differential object marking

Languages with differential object marking (DOM) mark overtly some of their O arguments, but not others, according to semantic or pragmatic factors (Aissen 2003: 436). DOM is often based on a hierarchy of animacy or definiteness. It can also be based on exclusively pragmatic factors, such as topicality. This type of pragmatically conditioned DOM is particularly common in Sino-Tibetan languages (Iemmolo 2011: 81, 134, 210). Differential object marking in Wutun is expressed by the optional dative marker *-ha*, which has cognates in several varieties of Northwest Mandarin spoken in the Amdo Sprachbund, such as Linxia, Gangou, Tangwang, Xunhua and Huangshui (see Dwyer 1995: 153; Lee-Smith 1996a: 866, 1996b: 876; Zhu et al. 1997: 444; Dede 2007).

The optional dative marker *-ha* is employed with highly affected participants that have a semantic role other than intentional Agent. It is most commonly used with Recipients of ditransitive clauses and Patients of transitive clauses,[8] as in (16) and (17):

(16) *ana   enian-**ha**   huaiqa-ge ka-lio*
     mother child-DOM   book-REF   give-PFV
     'The mother gave the child a book.'
     (Elicited)

(17) *bianshe-**ha**   gek   qe-she-lio   ze-li*
     dumpling-DOM   dog   eat-RES.AO-PFV   EXEC-SEN.INF
     'The dumplings were eaten by a dog.'
     (Elicited)

The use of *-ha* in Wutun is optional, and it is often conditioned by definiteness and identifiability.[9] An argument that has been introduced and integrated into discourse, and is therefore definite and easily identifiable, is more likely to be marked by *-ha* than an argument that is newly introduced. On the first line of (18), the argument *zhawa*, 'disciple' is first introduced to the discourse. After it has been introduced and it is therefore definite and identifiable for both the

---

8 In addition, *-ha* can be used with Experiencers, Possessors, locative phrases and even with involuntary Agents.
9 Iemmolo and Arcodia (2014) have argued that these factors also play an important role in Differential Object Marking in Modern Standard Chinese.

speaker and the addressee, it occurs with the optional dative marker -*ha*, as on the second line of (18):

(18) *zhawa   ta   ra   qhi-zhe   sho-de   kuli   zhawa-**ha**   ra*
disciple 3SG also go-PROSP say-ATTR time disciple-DOM also
nia   xakmo-ge ssek-la-ge   ze-ma
2SG.OBL pearl-REF see-INCOMPL-CAUS do-COORD
'When the disciple said that he would also go, they asked (the lama) to also look at the divination ball for him . . . '
(Wutun narrative 1_Pilgrimage)

The cognates of -*ha* in Sinitic languages of the Amdo Sprachbund may have their origins in topic marking, whose grammaticalization towards optional case marker has been further triggered by DOM in Amdo Tibetan. On the other hand, DOM is also present in Mongolic languages, including Bonan and Mangghuer from the Amdo Sprachbund (see Slater 2003; Fried 2010). Dede (2007) has suggested that -*ha* ~*xa* is connected to the Mandarin Chinese *bǎ*-sentence. Mandarin Chinese *bǎ*-sentences are based on serial verb constructions with the verb *bǎ* originally meaning 'take' and also used for topic. The core meaning of this construction is to highlight a highly affected Patient that is usually handled or manipulated in some way (see e.g., Li and Thompson 1981: 465). The occurrence of *bǎ* has later been explained by being due to topicality (Iemmolo 2011: 222–223), as well as definiteness and identifiability of referents in the discourse (Iemmolo and Arcodia 2014). Example (19) illustrates the use of the *bǎ*-sentence in Modern Standard Chinese. In (19 b) *bǎ* marks a topical Patient:

(19) Modern Standard Chinese
    a. *wo   bo-le   juzi*
       1SG peel-PFV orange
       'I peeled an orange.'
       (Li 2006: 418)
    b. *wo   **ba**   juzi   bo-le*
       1SG DOM orange peel-PFV
       'I peeled that orange.'
       (Li 2006: 418)

Examples (20) illustrates the Amdo Tibetan dative case *ra*, which expresses differential object marking. Amdo Tibetan marks animate participants that are not Agents, and it is used with both Recipients of ditransitive clauses (as in 20 a) and Patients of transitive clauses (as in 20 b) (Dede 2007: 872–873).

(20) Amdo Tibetan
    a. *nor* **ra** *rtsva byin*
       cow DAT grass give
       'Give the grass to the cattle.'
       (Wang 1995: 16–17)
    b. *nor* **ra** *rdo gis ma rgyag*
       cow DAT stone INSTR NEG hit
       'Don't hit the cattle with a stone.'
       (Wang 1995: 16–17)

The origins of *-ha* as a topic marker in Wutun is evident from the fact that it is still used in topic-comment constructions, as in (21):

(21) *gu-jhege-**ha** yanza-la-di-li*
     3-PAUC-**DOM** surprise-INCOMPL-PROGR-SEN.INF
     '(She) is surprised (because of seeing) them (lit. Them, surprised).'
     (Wutun conversation 3_Babies)

My data suggests that the analysis of *-ha* as a topic marker that is on its way towards a grammaticalized case marker, seems plausible. However, several Sinitic languages of the Amdo Sprachbund share the same marker, and the exact source language of this pattern remains unclear.

3.3 Grammatical systems that display a blend of Chinese and Tibetan strategies

In this section, I will discuss some grammatical systems whose compositions cannot be attributed to a single contact language, but rather represent a blend of Sinitic and Tibetic influence. The most obvious examples of this type include the word order of the noun phrase (section 3.3.1) and aspect marking (section 3.3.2).

3.3.1 Word order of the noun phrase

Word order of the noun phrase in Wutun is not based exclusively on either Sinitic or Tibetic languages. Instead, it is a blend of strategies from the two language groups. Demonstratives in Wutun can either precede the noun as in Sinitic languages or follow the noun as in Tibetic languages. Consider:

(22) Wutun
je-ge   *joze*   ~   *joze*   *je-ge*
this-CLF   table   table   this-CLF
'this table'   'this table'
(Sandman 2016: 43–44, 47)

Numerals consistently follow the noun as in Tibetic languages:

(23) *awo liang-ge yida zhan-she-ma-li*
man two-CLF together stand-RES.AO-RES.PO-SEN.INF
'Two men were standing together.'
(Wutun narratives 4_Beach)

(24) *qhichai liang-ge*
car two-CLF
'two cars'
(Wutun conversation 2_Thangkas, smoking and car)

Adjectives can occur either in attributive phrases that precede the noun (as in 25) or as derived adjectives that follow the noun (as in 26). The first strategy is typical for Sinitic languages, while the second strategy is found in Tibetic languages:

(25) *da je kan-la* **yak-la-de**
then this look-COND **beautiful-INCOMPL-ATTR**
ti she-li qhi-lai
place on-LOC go-1.IMP
'Let's go to a more beautiful place than this one!'[10]
(Wutun narratives 3_Picnic)

---

[10] In this sentence, the construction *kan-la* indicates the comparative. Wutun has a construction *kan-la ~ kan-ra*, which is a compound of the verb *kan* (SM *kàn* 看, 'to look, to watch') and the conditional converb *-la ~ -ra*. This construction means literally 'looking at' and is used to express one's point of view.

(26) ngu   hu   **yak-la~la-de-ge**   mai-lio
    1SG flower **beautiful-INCOMPL~INCOMPL-NMLZ-REF** buy-PFV
    'I bought a very beautiful flower.'[11]
    (Elicited)

In Amdo Tibetan, as in all Tibetic languages, demonstratives, adjectives and numerals follow the noun, as in (27):

(27) Amdo Tibetan
    ɕajə   tʃʰuŋtʃʰuŋ   səq   xsəm
    child small   INDEF   three
    'three small children'
    (Sandman and Simon 2016: 102)

To sum up, word order of the noun phrase in Wutun clearly illustrates how both Sinitic and Tibetic languages have contributed to Wutun grammar.

3.3.2 Aspect marking

Another grammatical system that is a blend of Chinese and Tibetan is aspect marking. In Wutun, aspect is a very complex category. It is possible to use more than one aspect marker with the same verb (multiple aspect marking). There are two sets of aspect markers: primary aspect markers and secondary aspect markers. Morphologically zero-marked verbs always entail imperfectivity, as in (28):

(28) nga   tin-li
    1SG.OBL (be) sick-SEN.INF
    'I am sick.'
    (Elicited)

---

[11] In Sino-Tibetan languages, attributive markers are often based on nominalizations (for introduction to grammaticalization paths from nominalizer to attributive, see Yap, Grunow-Hårsta, and Wrona 2011). This is also true for Wutun -de. I will gloss -de as ATTR=ATTRIBUTIVE when it is used to connect attributive phrases (genitive attributes and relative clauses) to the head noun (as in 25) and the label NMLZ=NOMINALIZER is reserved for cases in which -de marks nominalizations occurring as arguments of the clause, derived adjectives (as in 26), subordinate clauses or non-embedded nominalization constructions. Similar glossing is used in many other descriptions of Sino-Tibetan languages (see e.g. Hargreaves 2003: 379 for Kathmandu Newar).

In addition, there are four primary aspect markers: perfective -*lio* (as in 29), progressive -*di* (as in 30), patient-oriented resultative -*ma* (as in 31) and prospective -*zhe* (as in 32):

(29) *ngu-jhege guda wa-ge she zhek-**lio** ze-li*
 1-PAUC there hill-REF on go-**PFV** EXEC-SEN.INF
 'We climbed up a hill.'
 (Wutun narratives 3_Picnic)

(30) *gu-jhege zang-li wanlan-**di**-li*
 3-PAUC Tibet-LOC do-**PROGR**-SEN.INF
 'They are (currently) working in Tibet.'
 (Wutun conversation 2_Thangkas, smoking and car)

(31) *hura-li hu dodode zhun-**ma**-li*
 garden-LOC flower many plant-**RES.PO**-SEN.INF
 '(Somebody) planted a lot of flowers in the garden.'
 (Elicited)

(32) *ngu rongbo-li qhi-**zhe***
 1SG Longwu-LOC go-**PROSP**
 'I am going to Longwu.'
 (Elicited)

In addition to the four primary aspect markers, Wutun has three secondary aspect markers: incompletive -*la* (as in 33), completive -*gu* (as in 34) and agent-oriented resultative -*she* (as in 35):

(33) *ngu ni lai be-ji-li ddo-**la**-lio*
 1SG 2SG come NEG-reach-SEN.INF think-**INCOMPL**-PFV
 'I thought you will not come in time.'
 (Elicited)

(34) *gu she zha-**gu**-lio ze-li*
 that house explode-**COMPL**-PFV EXEC SEN.INF
 'That house has exploded.'
 (Elicited)

(35) je   nian nga-n-de   jashe qhichai-ge mai-**she**-lio
     this year 1-COLL-ATTR   PN   car-REF   buy-**RES.AO**-PFV
     'This year our Jashe bought a car.'
     (Wutun conversation 2_Thangkas, smoking and car)

When secondary aspect markers are used with the primary aspect markers, they are always based in between the verbal stem and the primary aspect marker. The primary aspect marker, which occurs as the last aspect marking element on the verb, sets the main framework for the temporal structure of the situation, while the secondary aspect marker offers further specification of the temporal structure of the situation within the main framework. Examples (33)–(35) all express terminated situations, which is indicated by the primary aspect marker, perfective -*lio*. However, the terminated situations have different internal structures, which is indicated by the secondary aspect markers, incompletive -*la*, completive -*gu* and agent-oriented resultative -*she*. In (33) the terminated situation has an internal structure of a state that has not led to any results, while in (34) the terminated situation is viewed as a completed event that totally affects the Patient. In (35), the terminated situation has led to some results due to the past actions of the Agent.

The perfective, prospective, completive and agent-oriented resultative aspect markers have their origins in Mandarin Chinese and show resemblance to their Mandarin counterparts both in meaning and function, while incompletive -*la* is a borrowing from Amdo Tibetan. The origin of the patient-oriented resultative aspect marker -*ma* is unknown. The progressive aspect marker -*di* is derived from a combination of the nominalizer -*de* (SM *de* 的) and the existential copula *yek* (SM *yǒu* 有). This construction is built on Chinese grammatical forms that have been reanalyzed to replicate Amdo Tibetan morphosyntactic structure. Amdo Tibetan has a progressive aspect marker based on nominalizer and existential copula, which does not exist in Mandarin varieties (see Sandman and Simon 2016: 118). The origin of the progressive aspect marker is evident from the fact that progressive meaning can still be expressed by the periphrastic construction -*de yek*, and in negating the progressive aspect marker -*di*, the negative counterpart *mi* of the existential copula *yek* is used, as in (36):

(36) a. ni   chuang she za-**de**   **yek**   ya
        2SG bed   on   smoke-**NMLZ**   **EXIST** **EMPH**
        'Do you smoke in bed?'

b. *ngu za-**di**   **mi**-yek*
   1SG smoke-PROGR NEG.EQU-EGO
   'No, I don't.'
   (Wutun conversation 2_Thangkas, smoking and car)

In (36) speaker A uses periphrastic construction -*de yek* in asking a question about speaker B's smoking habits, and speaker B gives a negative reply using the progressive suffix -*di* and the existential copula *mi*. The use of the copular verb in negative clauses with progressive aspect represents traces of periphrastic construction based on a nominalizer and an existential copula.

3.4 Grammatical features borrowed from Amdo Tibetan

In this section, I will discuss grammatical features that have unambiguous equivalents in Amdo Tibetan and are therefore, the result of contact with Amdo Tibetan. The Amdo Tibetan features in Wutun include egophoric marking (section 3.4.1) and the causal subordination structure (section 3.4.2)

3.4.1 Egophoric marking

Egophoric marking refers to a grammatical pattern that marks the speaker's involvement in events or states (ego), in contrast to non-involvement (non-ego) (see Floyd et al 2018). This category is found in all Tibetic languages, including Amdo Tibetan. As in Tibetic languages, Wutun egophoric marking is a tripartite system intertwined with the more familiar category of evidentiality (source of information). Wutun has one ego evidential -*yek* (as in 37 and 41) and two non-ego evidentials, sensory-inferential evidential -*li* (as in 38 and 39) and factual evidential *re* (as in 40):

(37) *ngu huan xhe-di-**yek***
    1SG food drink-PROGR-EGO
    'I am eating (personal involvement).'
    (Elicited)

(38) *ni huan xhe-di-**li***
    2SG food drink-PROGR-SEN.INF
    'You are eating (as I see/infer).'
    (Elicited)

(39) gu   huan xhe-di-**li**
     3SG   food drink-PROGR-**SEN.INF**
     'S/he is eating (as I see/infer).'
     (Elicited)

(40) nianha   she-wu   tian **yek-de**   **re**
     blind eye   ten-five day   EXIST-NMLZ   FACT
     'The Losar festival lasts for fifteen days.' (as we all know)
     (Wutun narratives 5_Festivals)

(41) ni   ma-ge   nian-di-**yek**
     2SG   what-REF   read-PROGR-**EGO**
     'What are you reading?' (addressee's personal involvement)
     (Elicited)

While the ego and sensory-inferential evidentials are suffixes, the factual evidential is grammatically an auxiliary connected to the preceding verb with the nominalizer *-de*. Ego evidential is typically used with the first person in statements when the action is volitional and allows the speaker's control (as in 37), as well as in second person statements when the perspective shifts to the addressee (as in 41). Sensory-inferential and factual evidentials are typically used with the second and third person in statements (as in 38–40). The sensory-inferential evidential indicates information based on the speaker's sensory perception or inference, while the factual evidential is used for generic, unspecific knowledge that the speaker has accumulated from various sources.

The Wutun ego evidential *-yek* is most probably based on either the Mandarin Chinese existential copula *yǒu* 有 or the Amdo Tibetan existential copula *yod* that also expresses ego evidentiality. The sensory-inferential evidential *-li* can be connected to the Mandarin Chinese modal particle *le* 了, which indicates a change of state. The factual auxiliary *re* resembles the Amdo Tibetan factual equative copula *re* in both meaning and form, and it is one of the most obvious examples of grammatical morphemes borrowed directly from Amdo Tibetan to Wutun.

In addition to ego, sensory-inferential and factual evidentials, Wutun has a distinct evidential for reported information. It indicates that the speaker bases his/her statement on hearsay. The reported information evidential in Wutun is based on the auxiliary *sho*, which is a grammaticalized form of the full lexical verb *sho* 'to say, to speak' and a cognate of the Standard Mandarin verb *shuō* (说) 'to say, to speak'. The use of this speech act verb has a reported evidential in Wutun based on the Amdo Tibetan quotative marker *se*, which is based on the verb 'to say, to speak'. It is used in combination with egophoric marking as in Wutun (see Sun 1993: 956). When used as reported information evidential, this auxiliary is used in combination with the sensory-inferential marker -*li*, resulting in the form *sho-li* 'they say'.

(42) *gu she zha-gu-lio* **ze-li**
that house explode-COMPL-PFV EXEC SEN.INF
'That house has exploded (I saw it).'
(Elicited)

(43) *gu she zha-gu-lio* **ze-li sho-li**
that house explode-COMPL-PFV EXEC-SEN.INF REP-SEN.INF
'That house has exploded, they say (I heard it from other people who saw it).'
(Elicited)

The egophoric marking system in Wutun shows clear resemblance to that of Amdo Tibetan, which distinguishes speaker's volitionally instigated events (ego) from events that the speaker is not part of (non-ego). In non-ego contexts, there is a distinction between plain facts, direct sensory evidence and indirect evidence, such as inference. Also, there is a reported evidential combined with egophoric marking morphemes (Sun 1993: 965). Egophoric marking is an example of a category that is built on partly Sinitic and partly Tibetan grammatical forms, but the underlying syntactic structure and semantic distinctions clearly come from Amdo Tibetan. In addition to Amdo Tibetan and Wutun, egophoricity has been documented in several Mongolic languages of the Amdo Sprachbund, such as Mongghul (Georg 2003), Mangghuer (Slater 2003) and Bonan (Wu 2003; Fried 2010), as well as in Turkic Salar (Dwyer 2000). While Sinitic, Mongolic and Turkic languages generally lack egophoric marking, whereas the category is present in Tibetic languages, it is obvious that the egophoric marking systems in the Amdo Sprachbund replicate the Amdo Tibetan grammatical pattern. While all the egophoric marking systems documented in Mongolic and Turkic languages in the area are binary and only make a distinction between ego and non-ego, the tripartite system of Wutun resembles more closely the elaborate system of Amdo Tibetan, which suggests that it has been acquired via direct contact with a Tibetic language.

3.4.2 Clause combining: The subordination structure

In Sinitic languages, the most important means of combining clauses are serial verb constructions that involve juxtaposed clauses without any intervening markers between them. However, Wutun makes extensive uses of converbs in clause combining as do Tibetic and Mongolic languages. The subordination structure of a causal proposition is one of the best examples of the influence of Amdo Tibetan on Wutun. In Amdo Tibetan, as in other Tibetic languages, the ergative-instrumental case marker suffixed to a nominalized verb is used to express a causal relation between two phrases (as in (44):

(44) Amdo Tibetan
teraŋ ^{ɦ}nam ^{m}bab-go-no-gi   ŋa ^{ɸ}ɕiloʁ -ga
today sky[ABS] fall-IPFV-NMZ-ERG 1SG[ABS] outside-DAT
mə-^{n}dʑo
NEG.IPFV-go
'Because it is raining, I will not go outside today.'
(Sandman and Simon 2016: 108)

In Wutun, a causal relation is expressed by a structure similar to that of Tibetic languages. The Wutun causal structure involves nominalization of the verb using the nominalizer -de (which has cognates in all varieties of Mandarin Chinese), together with the use of the comitative-instrumental case marker -liangge, as in (45):

(45) dak   jhan-lio-de-**liangge**   ren   yidaze haipa-gu-lio
     tiger see-PFV-NMLZ-**INSTR**   person   all   (be) afraid-COMPL-PFV
     ze-li
     EXEC-SEN.INF
     'Because of seeing a tiger, all the people were frightened.'
     (Elicited)

The influence of Tibetic manifests itself in the very existence of such converb structures, and in use of the comitative-instrumental case marker. It is interesting to note that while Wutun has not acquired ergativity from Amdo Tibetan, in causal subordination construction, the comitative-instrumental marker -*liangge* resembles the function of ergative marker -*gi* in Amdo Tibetan.

3.5 Grammatical features borrowed from Bonan

In this section, I will discuss the grammatical features that represent the influence of Bonan. Bonan grammatical features in Wutun include nominal number (section 3.5.1), comitative-instrumental case (section 3.5.2) and two borrowed grammatical morphemes (section 3.5.3).

3.5.1 Nominal number

One of the most obvious examples of a grammatical system influenced by Bonan in Wutun is nominal number. Wutun makes a distinction between paucal and plural. Paucal is marked by the suffix *-jhege*. It indicates small numbers, usually three to five entities. The plural marker *-dera*, which also has a variant *-duru*, indicates larger numbers than paucal marker *-jhege*. Consider:

(46) *jashe da   gu-de   adia da asak-**jhege**   bijin*
      PN   and 3SG-ATTR monk and sister-in-law-PAUC Beijing
      qhi-gu-ma-li
      go-COMPL-RES.PO-SEN.INF
      'Jashe and the monk and the sister-in-law (of his family) went to Beijing.'
      (Wutun conversation 2_Thangkas, smoking and car)

(47) *ren-**dera** xaige xho-li*
      person-PL   very   good-SEN.INF
      'The people (in this country) are very good.'
      (Elicited)

The origin of the paucal marker is the Mandarin Chinese quantifier *jǐ-ge* (几个), 'a few', 'several', which has been grammaticalized into a paucal marker due to the influence of Bonan. Bonan has a paucal enclitic =ʁula, which may be connected with number ʁuran 'three' + plural enclitic =la (Chen and Chinggeltei 1986: 85–86). However, Bonan paucal can be used to refer to larger units than just three referents (Fried 2010: 72–73) and the same is true for Wutun. The origin of Wutun plural marker *-dera ~ -duru* is unknown. In Bonan, the plural is marked by an enclitic =la which is functionally equivalent but etymologically unrelated to the Wutun plural marker. Examples (48a) and (48b) illustrate the paucal-plural distinction in Bonan:

(48) Bonan
    a. *au=ʁula   silaŋ=da   o-tɕo*
       man=PAU Xining=LOC go-IMPF.OBJ
       'A few men are going to Xining.'
    b. *au=la   silaŋ=da   o-tɕo*
       man=PL Xining=LOC go-IMPF.OBJ
       'The men are going to Xining.'
    (Fried 2010: 72)

Wutun and Bonan are the only languages of the Amdo Sprachbund that have been documented to have a paucal-plural distinction in their nominal system. While Sinitic languages usually lack an elaborate system of number marking, it is quite likely that Wutun has acquired its nominal number system due to influence from Bonan.

3.5.2 Comitative-instrumental case

The comitative-instrumental case offers another example of Bonan influence on Wutun grammar. The comitative-instrumental case is marked by a bisyllabic element *-liangge*, which is a compound of the Mandarin Chinese numeral *liǎng* (两), 'two' and the general classifier *ge* (个). It expresses both accompaniment (as in 49) and instrument (as in 50):

(49) *ya   lai   Lhamo Yangzhe lai   yayaya nini-**liangge***
     yeah come PN   come yayaya grandmother-COM
     qhi-lai
     go-1.IMP
     'Yeah, come, Lhamo Yangzhe, come. Yeah, yeah, yeah, come with the grandmother!'
     (Wutun conversation 3_Babies)

(50) *gu   agu shetek-**liangge** zhaze   da-pe-lio   ze-li*
     that girl rock-INSTR   window hit-get broken-PFV EXEC-SEN.INF
     'That girl smashed the window with a rock.'
     (Elicited)

The comitative-instrumental case marker in Wutun is a calque from Bonan. Bonan has a grammatical marker =ʁala (*ghwala*) based on the numeral ʁar (*ghwar*), 'two', which is functionally very similar to Wutun sociative marker -*liangge* and has probably served as a model of grammaticalization for the Wutun comitative-instrumental case. Consider:

(51) Bonan
    atɕaŋ jəɕə=la=ʁala   daŋ=nə   ne-tɕo
    3SG   key=PL=INST   door=ACC open-IMPF.OBJ
    'He used the keys to open the door.'
    (Fried 2010: 60)

It is interesting to note that the origin of the comitative-instrumental case marker in Wutun appears to be unusual from a cross-linguistic perspective. The number 'two' is not mentioned as a source for comitatives and instrumental in recent work on the grammaticalization of comitatives and related categories (e.g., Heine and Kuteva 2002: 329; Stolz, Stroh, and Urdze 2006: 357–361). Widely attested sources for comitatives include the verbs 'follow' and 'take' and the nouns 'friend' and 'comrade'. The numeral 'one' is also mentioned (Stolz, Stroh, and Urdze 2006: 357–361). However, comitative-instrumentals based on numeral 'two' are common in the languages of Amdo Sprachbund. They have been documented in Sinitic languages Linxia, Xining and Gangou (Dwyer 1992: 167; Zhu et al. 1997: 445) and Mongolic languages Bonan and Santa (Chen and Chinggeltei 1986: 121–122; Dwyer 1992: 166; Wu 2003: 334; Fried 2010: 60). It seems plausible that the Sinitic languages, which usually lack case, are replicating the Mongolic grammatical pattern. Several genetically unrelated languages spoken in the same geographical area have undergone similar grammaticalization process due to areal interference.

3.5.3 Borrowed grammatical morphemes

While Wutun nominal number and comitative-instrumental case represent grammatical categories built on Sinitic grammatical forms that replicate Mongolic morphosyntactic structure, there are at least two grammatical forms that have obviously been borrowed from Bonan into Wutun. The first one is the interrogative clitic =*mu*, which is used for forming polar questions. This marker represents a grammatical borrowing from Bonan, which has an interrogative marker =*mu* based on the interrogative suffix -*u* and the narrative suffix -*m* (Fried 2010: 259). Consider:

(52) gu   xan   ni   getan-lio=**mu**
     that cord 2SG cut-PFV=**INTERR**
     'That cord, did you cut it?'
     (Wutun narratives 1_Pilgrimage)

Another example is the terminative converb -*tala*. When connecting clauses -*tala* expresses the end point of the main action indicated by the final clause:

(53) dangma   zang do-**tala**   san-ge   yai-ma   shewu
     a long time ago Tibet arrive-**TERM** three-RE   month-COORD fifteen
     tian yo-de   re
     day   NEC-NMLZ   FACT
     'In those days, you needed three months and fifteen days to go to Tibet.'
     (Wutun narratives 1_Pilgrimage)

This converb has been borrowed from Bonan, which has an identical terminative suffix (Wu 2003: 338). The terminative -*tala* is of common Mongolic origin and it was present already in Middle Mongol (Rybatzki 2003: 77–78). Borrowed grammatical morphemes suggest that Wutun has interacted with Bonan in the past, although most of the present day Wutun speakers do not know Bonan.

4 Summary and discussion

In this chapter, I have discussed the sociohistorical origins of the Wutun people and the structural features of the Wutun language in relation to generally observed tendencies in mixed languages. From a sociohistorical perspective, the genesis of Wutun shows many similarities to the genesis of other mixed languages. While Wutun was created in bilingual families with Sinitic, Mongolic and Tibetic speakers, at the present day almost all the Wutun speakers are bilingual in local lingua franca, Amdo Tibetan. The communication with neighboring linguistic groups is not an issue, and the Wutun language is rather used as a community language which has important meaning for the group identity, than the language of interethnic communication. From a structural perspective, Wutun belongs to the type of mixed languages that exhibit a high degree of structural mixing. An interesting feature that distinguishes Wutun from many relatively well-documented mixed languages is that its grammar is the result of mixing of at least three languages, Northwest Mandarin, Amdo Tibetan and Bonan. All these languages contribute a significant amount of grammar. Sometimes it is difficult to identify which language is the source of a particular grammatical feature (as observed in section 3.2). This is because Wutun is spoken in the context of a Sprachbund and many non-Sinitic features of Wutun (such as word order, agglutinative morphology, lack of numeral classifiers and case marking) are found in both Amdo Tibetan and Mongolic languages. The bulk of Wutun morphemes are of Sinitic origin and many non-Sinitic grammatical categories are built on Sinitic grammatical forms that are reanalyzed to replicate Tibetic or Mongolic morphosyntactic structures. Hence both Amdo Tibetan and Bonan contribute a number of borrowed grammatical morphemes. Another important observation is that there is no clear split between different grammatical systems. All the contact languages contribute to nominal and verbal morphosyntax, clause structure and clause combining. Some of the grammatical systems, such as aspect marking, exhibit a particularly complex blend of Sinitic and Tibetic grammatical forms and strategies. The effect of a Sprachbund situation into mixed language genesis and blended grammatical systems arisen from language contact requires more research. Wutun is a unique result of language contact between Sinitic, Tibetan and Mongolic languages and can contribute to our understanding of mixed language genesis and structural features of mixed languages.

Abbreviations

1	first person
2	second person
3	third person
ATTR	attributive
CAUS	causative
CLF	classifier
COLL	collective
COM	comitative
COMPL	completive
COND	conditional
COORD	coordinative
DOM	differential object marking
EGO	ego
EQU	equative
EXEC	executive auxiliary
EXIST	existential

FACT	factual
IMP	imperative
INCOMPL	incompletive
INSTR	instrumental
INTERR	interrogative
LOC	locative
NEC	necessitative
NEG	negative
NMLZ	nominalizer
OBL	oblique
PAUC	paucal
PFV	perfective
PL	plural
PN	proper name
PROGR	progressive
PROH	prohibitive
PROSP	prospective
REF	referential
REP	reported
RES	resultative
RES.AO	agent-oriented resultative
RES.PO	patient-oriented resultative
SEN.INF	sensory-inferential
TERM	terminative

References

Acuo, Yixiweisa. 2004. *Daohua Yanjiu* 倒话研究 [Research on the Dao Vernacular]. Beijing: Minzu Chubanshe.

Aikhenvald, Alexandra Y. 2000. *Classifiers: A Typology of Noun Categorization Devices*. Oxford: Oxford University Press.

Aissen, Judith. 2003. Differential object marking: Iconicity vs. economy. *Natural Language & Linguistic Theory* 21. 435–483.

Ansaldo, Umberto. 2015. Pidgins and Creoles. In Rint Sybesma (ed.), *Encyclopedia of Chinese Language and Linguistics*. Brill. http://dx.doi.org/10.1163/2210-7363_ecll_COM_00000331 (accessed 10 February 2019).

Bakker, Peter. 1997. *A language of our own: The genesis of Michif, the mixed Cree-French language of the Canadian Métis*. New York: Oxford University Press.

Bakker, Peter. 2003. Mixed languages as autonomous systems. In Yaron Matras & Peter Bakker (eds.), *The mixed language debate: Theoretical and empirical advances*, 107–150. Berlin: Mouton de Gruyter.

Bakker, Peter. 2017. Typology of mixed languages. In Alexandra Y. Aikhenvald & R. M.W. Dixon (eds.), *The Cambridge handbook of linguistic typology*, 217–253. Cambridge: Cambridge University Press.

Bartens, Angela. 2013. Creole languages. In Peter Bakker & Yaron Matras (eds.), *Contact languages: A comprehensive guide*, 65–158. Berlin: De Gruyter Mouton.
Cabras, Giulia. (forthcoming). Ethnogenesis and language contact in Amdo Tibet: the oral narratives of the Wutun language community. www.academia.edu/34032528/Ethnogenesis_and_language_contact_in_Amdo_Tibet_the_oral_narratives_of_the_Wutun_language_community (accessed 10 January 2019).
Chappell, Hilary. 2001. Language contact and areal diffusion in Sinitic languages. In Alexandra Aikhenvald & R. M.W. Dixon (eds.), *Areal diffusion and genetic inheritance: Problems in comparative linguistics*, 328–357. Oxford: Oxford University Press.
Chen Naixiong. 1982. Wutunhua Chutan 五屯话初探 [A preliminary investigation on Wutun speech]. *Minzu Yuwen* 1. 10–18.
Chen Naixiong. 1986. Guanyu Wutunhua 关于五屯话 [An outline of Wutun linguistic structure]. *Journal of Asian and African Studies* 31. 33–52.
Chen Naixiong. 1988. Wutunhua yinxi 五屯话音系 [The sound system of the Wutun speech]. *Minzu Yuwen* 3. 1–10.
Chen Naixiong. 1989. Wutunhua de dongci xingtai 五屯话的动词形态 [Verb forms of the Wutun speech]. *Minzu Yuwen* 6. 26–37.
Chen, Naixiong & Chinggeltei. 1986. *Baoanyu he Mengguyu* 保安语和蒙古语 [The Bonan language and the Mongolian language]. Hohhot: Nei Menggu Renmin Chubanshe.
Dede, Keith. 2007. The origin of the anti-ergative [xa] in Huangshui Chinese. *Language and Linguistics* 8(4). 863–881.
Dede, Keith. 2015. Mixed Languages. In Rint Sybesma (ed.), *Encyclopedia of Chinese Language and Linguistics*. Brill. http://dx.doi.org/10.1163/2210-7363_ecll_COM_00000271 (accessed 10 February 2019).
Dwyer, Arienne M. 1992. Altaic elements in the Línxià Dialect: Contact-induced change on the Yellow River Plateau. *Journal of Chinese Linguistics* 20(1). 160–178.
Dwyer, Arienne M. 1995. From the Northwest China Sprachbund: Xúnhuà Chinese dialect data. *Yuan Ren Society Treasury of Chinese Dialect Data*, vol. 1. 148–182.
Dwyer, Arienne M. 2000. Direct and indirect experience in Salar. In Lars Johanson & Bo Utas (eds.), *Types of evidentiality in Turkic, Iranic and neighbouring languages*, 45–59. Berlin: Mouton de Gruyter.
Floyd, Simeon, Elisabeth Norcliffe & Lila San Roque (eds.). 2018. *Egophoricity*. Amsterdam: John Benjamins.
Fried, Robert Wayne. 2010. *A grammar of Bao'an Tu, a Mongolic language of Northwest China*. New York: The University of Buffalo, State University of New York PhD dissertation.
Georg, Stefan. 2003. Huzhu Mongghul. In Juha Janhunen (ed.), *The Mongolic languages*, 286–306. London & New York: Routledge.
Hanyu Liangci Cidian. 1988. *Hanyu Liangci Cidian* [A dictionary of Chinese classifiers]. Fuzhou: Fujian Renmin Chubanshe.
Hargreaves, David. 2003. Kathmandu Newar (Nepal Bhāṣā). In Graham Thurgood & Randy LaPolla (eds.), *The Sino-Tibetan languages*, 371–384. London & New York: Routledge.
Hashimoto, Mantaro. 1976. Language diffusion on the Asian continent: Problems of typological diversity in Sino-Tibetan. *Computational Analysis of Asian and African Languages* 3. 49–63.
Heine, Bernd & Tania Kuteva 2002. *World lexicon of grammaticalization*. Cambridge: Cambridge University Press.

Ibrahim (A. Yibulaheimei). 1985. Gansu jingnei Tangwanghua jilüe 甘肃境内唐旺话寄略. [Introduction to the Tangwang speech of Gansu province]. *Minzu Yuwen* 6. 33–47.
Iemmolo, Giorgio. 2011. *Differential object marking*. Pavia: University of Pavia PhD dissertation.
Iemmolo, Giorgio & G. F. Arcodia. 2014. Differential object marking and identifiability of the referent: a study of Mandarin Chinese. *Linguistics* 52(2). 315–354.
Janhunen, Juha. 2007. Typological interaction in the Qinghai linguistic complex. *Studia Orientalia* 101. 85–103.
Janhunen, Juha. 2012. On the hierarchy of structural convergence in the Amdo Sprachbund. In Pirkko Suihkonen, Bernard Comrie & P. Solovyev (eds.), *Argument structure and grammatical relations: A cross-linguistic typology*, 177–189. Amsterdam: John Benjamins.
Janhunen, Juha. 2015. Describing and transcribing the phonologies of the Amdo Sprachbund. In Gerald Roche, Keith Dede, Fernanda Pirie & Benedict Copps (eds.), Centering the local. A Festschrift for Dr. Charles Kevin Stuart on the occasion of his sixtieth birthday. *Asian Highlands Perspectives* 37. 122–137.
Janhunen, Juha, Marja Peltomaa, Erika Sandman & Xiawu Dongzhou. 2008. *Wutun*. Muenchen: Lincom Europa.
Lee-Smith, Mei W. 1996a. The Hezhou language. In Stephen A. Wurm, Peter Mühlhäusler & Darrell R. Tryon (eds.), *Atlas of languages of intercultural communication in the Pacific, Asia and the Americas*, 865–873. Berlin: Mouton de Gruyter.
Lee-Smith, Mei W. 1996b. The Tangwang language. In Stephen A. Wurm, Peter Mühlhäusler & Darrell R. Tryon (eds.), *Atlas of languages of intercultural communication in the Pacific, Asia and the Americas*, 875–882. Berlin: Mouton de Gruyter.
Lee-Smith, Mei W. & Stephen A. Wurm. 1996. The Wutun language. In Stephen A. Wurm, Peter Mühlhäusler & Darrell R. Tryon (eds.), *Atlas of languages of intercultural communication in the Pacific, Asia and the Americas*, 883–897. Berlin: Mouton de Gruyter.
Li, Charles N. & Sandra A. Thompson. 1981. *Mandarin Chinese. A functional reference grammar*. Berkeley, Los Angeles & London: University of California Press.
Li, Charles N. 1983. Languages in contact in Western China. *Papers in East Asian Languages* 1. 31–51.
Li, Charles N. 1984. From verb-medial analytic language to verb-final synthetic language: a case of typological change. In Claudia Brugman, Monica Macaulay & Amy Dahlstrom (eds.), *Proceedings of the Tenth Annual Meeting of the Berkeley Linguistics Society*, 307–323.
Li, Charles N. 1986. The rise and fall of tones through diffusion (1). *Proceedings of the Twelfth Annual Meeting of the Berkeley Linguistics Society*, 173–185. Berkeley.
Li, Yen-Hui Audrey. 2006. Chinese ba. In Martin Everaert & Henk van Riemsdijk (eds.), *The Blackwell companion to syntax*, vol. 1, 374–468. Oxford: Blackwell.
Miestamo, Matti. 2005. *Standard negation: The negation of declarative verbal main clauses in a typological perspective*. Berlin: Mouton de Gruyter.
Meakins, Felicity. 2013. Mixed languages. In Peter Bakker & Yaron Matras (eds.), *Contact languages: A comprehensive guide*, 159–228. Berlin: De Gruyter Mouton.
Meakins, Felicity. 2018. Mixed languages. In M. Aronoff (ed.), *Oxford Research Encyclopedia of Linguistics*. Oxford: Oxford University Press.
Meakins, Felicity & Jesse Stewart, (forthcoming). Mixed languages. In S. Mufwene & A.M. Escobar (eds.), *Cambridge handbook of language contact*. Cambridge: Cambridge University Press.

Norman, Jerry. 1988. *Chinese*. Cambridge: Cambridge University Press.
Rybatzki, Volker. 2003. Middle Mongol. In Juha Janhunen (ed.), *The Mongolic languages*, 57–82. London & New York: Routledge.
Sandman, Erika. 2016. *A grammar of Wutun*. Helsinki: University of Helsinki PhD dissertation.
Sandman, Erika & Camille Simon. 2016. Tibetan as a "model language" in Amdo Sprachbund: evidence from Salar and Wutun. *Journal of South Asian Languages and Linguistics (JSALL)* 3(1). 85–122.
Slater, Keith W. 2003. *A grammar of Mangghuer*. London & New York: Routledge Curzon.
Stolz, Thomas, Cornelia Stroh & Aina Urdze 2006. *On comitatives and related categories: A typological study with special focus on the languages of Europe*. Berlin: Mouton de Gruyter.
Sun, Jackson T. S. 1993. Evidentials in Amdo Tibetan. *Bulletin of the Institute of History and Philology, Academia Sinica* 63(4). 945–1001.
Szeto, Pui Yiu, Umberto Ansaldo & Stephen Matthews. 2018. Typological variation across Mandarin dialects: An areal perspective with a quantitative approach. *Linguistic Typology* 22(2). 233–275.
Thomason, Sarah G. & Terrence Kaufman 1988. *Language contact, creolization, and genetic linguistics*. Berkeley: University of California Press.
Tournadre, Nicolas. 1996. *L'ergativité en tibétain, approche morphosyntaxique de la langue parlée*. Louvain: Peeters.
Versteegh, Kees. 2017. The myth of the mixed languages. In Benjamin Saade & Mauro Tosco (eds.), *Advances in Maltese linguistics*, 245–266. Berlin: Mouton de Gruyter.
Wang, Qingshan. 1995. *A grammar of spoken Amdo Tibetan*. Chengdu: Sichuan Nationality Publishing House.
Wu, Hugjiltu. 2003. Bonan. In Juha Janhunen (ed.), *The Mongolic languages*, 325–345. London & New York: Routledge.
Xu, Dan. 2017. *The Tangwang language. An interdisciplinary case study in Northwest China*. Cham: Springer International Publishing.
Yap, Foong Ha, Karen Grunow-Hårsta & Janick Wrona. 2011. Introduction: Nominalization strategies in Asian languages. In Foong Ha Yap, Karen Grunow-Hårsta & Janick Wrona (eds.), *Nominalization in Asian languages: Diachronic and typological perspectives*, 1–57. Amsterdam: John Benjamins.
Yue, Anne O. 2003. Chinese dialects: grammar. In Graham Thurgood & Randy LaPolla (eds.), *The Sino-Tibetan languages*, 84–125. London & New York: Routledge.
Zeisler, Bettina. 2007. Sentence patterns and pattern variation in Ladakhi: A field report. In Roland Bielmeier & Felix Haller (eds.), *Linguistics of the Himalayas and beyond*, 399–425. Berlin: Mouton de Gruyter.
Zhang, Hong 2007. Numeral classifiers in Mandarin Chinese. *East Asian Linguist* 16. 43–59.
Zhu Yongzhong, Üjiyediin Chuluu, Keith W. Slater & Kevin Stuart. 1997. Gangou Chinese dialect: A comparative study of a strongly Altaicized Chinese dialect and its Mongolic neighbor. *Anthropos* 92. 433–450.

Yaron Matras
Repertoire management and the performative origin of Mixed Languages

1 Introduction

Mixed Languages (MLs) are usually defined in relation to their structural profile as well as the societal circumstances in which they emerge. Indicative structural profiles that have been associated with MLs include the split between the etymological sources of the bulk of the lexicon (including core lexicon) and grammar (grammatical inflection and clause structure), the split between the etymological sources of noun phrase and verb phrase grammars, as well as, more generally, the impression that the language resists straightforward language-genealogical classification (Matras and Bakker 2003; Thomason 2007; O'Shannessy 2020; Mazzoli & Sippola, this volume; Bakker, this volume). The latter usually rests on an implicit (rather than explicitly formulated) expectation that some structural admixtures are less likely to emerge through conventional processes of gradual contact-induced change, which are not regarded as interfering with continuity of classification. Whether or not the concept of structural borrowing can be applied to MLs is therefore controversial, a point to which I shall return below. More commonly, MLs are considered cases of broken transmission (Thomason & Kaufman 1988) where new languages emerge, though unlike pidgins and creoles there is greater equilibrium in the contribution of (at least) two source languages as well as continuation of grammatical inflection from at least one of those source languages and in some cases from both. Societal settings that have been associated with the birth of MLs include the emergence of new communities of ethnically mixed households, a process of acculturation while retaining community separateness in colonial settings, and the flagging of ethnic distinctness in itinerant or nomadic communities

The precise factors that determine the link between these societal processes, and the structural outcomes that characterise MLs, remain subject to debate and speculation. A key issue is whether MLs should be regarded as a distinct language type that owes its existence to a distinctive communicative purpose; or

---

Acknowledgements: I am grateful to the volume editors, to an anonymous reviewer, and to Evangelia Adamou for valuable and helpful comments on an earlier version of this chapter.

Yaron Matras, University of Manchester, yaron.matras@manchester.ac.uk

https://doi.org/10.1515/9781501511257-013

whether MLs should instead be placed at the far end of a continuum of structural borrowing, where social conditions merely facilitate outcomes that appear more extensive or dense and which therefore blur genetic classification. If we opt for the latter – the idea that MLs occupy an extreme position on a continuum of structural borrowing – then the category of 'ML' is likely to remain somewhat impressionistic and vague, denoting a conspicuous structural outcome without necessarily following any indicative threshold of structural mixing beyond which a language can be classified as 'ML'. Problematic in that regard is the fact that the notion of language-genetic classification rests on the assumption that some structures (notably inflectional paradigms and basic vocabulary) are less likely to be borrowed wholesale across languages and that therefore consistency in the source of inflectional paradigms, on the one hand, and of basic vocabulary, on the other, allows us to identify genetic classification, while inconsistency among the etymological sources of these structural components obscures such classification. Thus, if MLs are defined primarily through the fact that they resist straightforward genetic classification, then by implication they must be treated as idioms that contradict expectations on borrowing rather than as examples of extreme forms of borrowing. If, by contrast, we follow the former notion – the idea that MLs are qualitatively distinct from cases of borrowing – then we require a definition of the structural profile (or prototype) that would allow us to distinguish MLs from cases of contact-induced change that are not MLs. For an explanatory model we would also require an exposition of the link between such profile and the distinctive social settings that give rise to the ML language type.

In this chapter I argue that MLs should be treated as a distinct language type that is not situated at the far end of a continuum of structural borrowing. I begin by reviewing what we know so far about that continuum and the typical scope of structural borrowing, and argue that it can be explained in terms of users' motivations to manage their bilingual repertoire across an array of different though conventional communication routines. Next, I briefly review the kind of structural outcomes that have been associated with MLs and offer a structural definition of the ML prototype, one that distinguishes it from borrowing. Note that I will reserve the term 'borrowing' for cases of contact-induced language change that do not fall under the ML prototype and I will not use that term to account for processes that lead to the formation of MLs (while recognising that MLs, once formed, can of course come into contact with other languages and borrow from those in the normal way, as in the case of Michif, a French-Cree mixture, which is now in contact with English). I then turn to an explanatory model of the emergence of the ML prototype. Following up on tentative suggestions that MLs are the product of deliberate speech manipulation or structural moulding, I propose that MLs arise from the conventionalisation of performative speech acts. I argue that the performative effect is achieved by explicitly defying the conventions on language mixing (or everyday repertoire management in bilingual settings), giving rise to mixed utterances that stand out even in an environment that is already accustomed to language mixing. In that way, in addition to their content and illocutionary force, such utterances function as actions in their own right: They convey a message pertaining to social relations and bonding, enabling speakers to construct and reinforce a new identity and project and reaffirm a newly-shaped sense of belonging. The conventionalisation of such utterances may lead ultimately to a neutralisation of the performative function and to a 'normalisation' of the ML as an all-purpose mode of speech, though such cases are relatively rare and almost all attested MLs appear to retain at least some residual performativity and carry accordingly a very distinctive indexical meaning within users' multilingual repertoire.

Since the performative effect is achieved at the emergence stage through a communication routine that defies conventional patterns of language mixing, the structural outcome (once conventionalised) is distinct from patterns of borrowing that arise from everyday mixed utterances that are not explicitly performative but driven by other factors. My argument is thus that MLs arise from a particular form of communicative routine that is associated with the social settings named above, where identity is re-negotiated, typically in small population groups that are undergoing some form of socio-cultural transition. The performative nature of that communicative routine accounts for the kinds of structural mixture that stand out as exceptional, indeed as defying expectations and general observations on the outcomes of structural borrowing encountered in other settings. In the final section I briefly survey the case studies presented in this volume and discuss their relation to my hypotheses about the borrowing of structural categories, exceptionality, and the role of performativity in ML formation.

2 Repertoire management and motivations for borrowing

In this section I outline a functional model of contact-induced change that is anchored in an understanding of discourse interaction as the site of contact (for a full discussion see Matras 2020). Individuals have at their disposal a wholesale, integrated repertoire of linguistic resources. Experimental evidence suggests that the repertoire is not inherently compartmentalised by languages in the sense that bilinguals can activate or de-activate a 'language' on a wholesale basis (cf. Bialystok et al. 2009). Instead, the selection of items or features and sets of features from the repertoire for use in a given interaction, and the de-selection or inhibition of others, is an activity in which users of language constantly engage. Communication in multilingual settings can be seen as impacted by three distinct pull factors:

The first is the need to accommodate to the expectations of the setting or interlocutor by selecting those elements from the repertoire that are admissible, understandable, and thus purposeful in that particular setting or context, and de-selecting or inhibiting those that are not. I will call this the 'accommodation' factor, merely for the sake of referencing. That is what we mean by 'choosing the correct language' in an interaction context. The skill to do this relies on the ability to exercise mental control over selection and inhibition of structural elements from the repertoire by activating the executive control mechanism (Green 1998; Bialystok 2015). Effective control over selection and inhibition is subject to a variety of factors including social and sociolinguistic competence (which is gradually acquired in the early years of linguistic socialisation) but also cognitive factors such as distractions or interactional tension as well as pathological factors such as memory lapses, fatigue, injuries and so on.

The second pull factor is the urge to exploit the full expressive potential of the linguistic repertoire. This factor competes with the first – the accommodation factor – when repertoire items are deemed to be functional but do not meet the expectations of the interaction setting or context (i.e. they are not in the selected 'language'). Speakers exercise their judgement whether, in such cases, to override such constraints. In what Grosjean (2001) has termed the 'bilingual mode' speakers will more frequently override such inhibitions, and indeed there may be little or no friction between the two pull factors as all elements of the repertoire may equally be admissible. Where stricter constraints on accommodation apply, speakers may prioritise certain elements for de-inhibition, such as 'unique referents' (Matras 2020) or lexical items marked by 'specificity' (Backus 1996) that lack translatable equivalents (such as terms for institutions or procedures, or culture-specific items).

The final pull factor is what I call load reduction. Effective management of the discourse may compete with the effective management of (that part of) the executive control mechanism that regulates selection and inhibition of elements from the repertoire. Competition among items of similar meaning may be most pronounced where discourse management tasks require particularly high concentration or intensive processing and thus impose a high cognitive load on the speaker.[1] A pertinent indicator of high cognitive load is the apparent frequency of language selection errors or bilingual slips of the tongue showing

---

[1] For recent work using Event-Related Potential (ERP) experiments to measure processing cost in the comprehension (rather than production) of discourse markers see Rasenberg et al. (2020).

'loss of control' around such items, and the link to high susceptibility to long-term borrowing (see Matras 1998, 2000a): Speakers are more likely to show lapses in effective selection and inhibition around items that monitor and direct the listener's processing of content, and which anticipate gaps in shared presuppositional knowledge. Tasks of this kind typically involve language-processing operations where there is a potential clash of expectations or inferences between the speaker and the listener and therefore a risk to efficient and harmonious communication. They include, for instance, the linking of propositional units, processing unexpected or non-confirmed and non-presuppositional propositions such as those marked by contrast, discontinuity, modality, or indefiniteness ('somebody', 'anywhere', etc.), and general procedures of monitoring and directing turn structure. Generalising just a single item or set of items for a particular function can eliminate the need to choose between 'languages' around that functional operation and with it the need to engage the executive control in selection and inhibition. That reduces the cognitive load. Load reduction, like exploitation of expressive potential, can occur locally on a one-off basis (often unintentionally, as in bilingual slips or choice of 'wrong' language for the right item, which can be subject to self-repair), or be replicated and perpetuated, leading to long term change of communicative routines, i.e. eliminating the need to choose among items of equivalent or near-equivalent functions according to 'language' context; that is what we commonly call structural or grammatical borrowing. In Matras (1998) I coined the term 'fusion' to capture the non-separation of labelled languages around an entire set of operators for a particular operational domain (such as conjunctions, discourse markers, indefinites, aktionsart affixes, modals, and so on) and demonstrated that there is a link between one-off speech production errors involving such items, regularisation of 'mixing' involving the same, and long term structural change or borrowing. Load reduction, then, in a nutshell, is the use of only one item to reduce cognitive work needed to choose among different items of similar or equivalent function. Replication of the same process and its propagation among the community of speakers will lead to long-term language change where the item from one language is replaced by its equivalent from another. Invariably, the item that prevails is the one that is acceptable to the community of speakers, the one that carries with it fewest constraints on intelligibility in various interaction settings, and the one belonging to the language that enjoys greater power. When bilingualism is unidirectional, as with many minority languages, borrowing in such cases always targets the majority language.

Note that pull factors may interact and overlap. The generalisation of a word across the multilingual speaker's range of interaction settings – the borrowing of a lexical item from one language into another – allows the speaker to make use of the full expressive potential of the repertoire without regard to the constraints on accommodation toward setting or interlocutor, while at the same time eliminating the need to select between competing items of the same meaning. Load reduction is driven by the urge to ease processing and eliminate the need to select among competing forms with the same or similar function, while also resulting in a single expressive grid around certain functions or classes of functions. The difference between the two pull-factors is the initial trigger, with the first motivated by the need to equalise expressive means while the second aims to level differences in form.

Social conventions and relations among potential interlocutors dictate the extent to which selection and inhibition from the repertoire is strict or consistent. Taken in this perspective, contact-induced language change is the product of lines being re-drawn, as multilingual speakers balance the three pull factors in new ways around individual meanings and functions, giving rise to innovative usages. In extreme scenarios, some factors may override others: The ultimate drive toward full exploitation of the expressive potential would lead in theory to a completely random selection from the repertoire that is not governed by accommodation constraints. This would be the consistent bilingual mode, more recently understood as a 'translanguaging', 'heterolinguistic' or 'metrolinguistic' scenario that hesitates to distinguish language boundaries in practical usage yet acknowledges the presence of socially constructed, prescriptive notions of language separateness (cf. Jørgensen 2008, Blommaert & Backus 2013, Li Wei 2018, Pennycook & Otsuji 2015). The emergence of pidgins and creoles might be seen as a process by which users avail themselves of all features that are readily accessible in a shared feature pool of the surrounding language ecology (cf. Mufwene 2013), accommodation yielding to expressive potential rather than guided by pre-set considerations of well-formedness. By contrast, ultimate load-reduction would mean the complete abandonment of dual or multiple language options, resulting in effect in language shift and the abandonment of one of the languages.[2] Where load reduction is so prevalent that it exempts entire categories from accommodation-based selection constraints, the languages in effect fuse or converge wholesale around a number of functional categories.

The cumulative effect of these various motivations is well illustrated in languages that have experienced situations of intense contact, in particular where one language is socially, economically or politically dominant and where active

---

[2] Of course, even within a 'language' there are always stylistic variants, which are subject to selection and inhibition in a way that is similar to the management of multilingual repertoires.

bilingualism is widespread and often unidirectional. Consider the case of Nova Scotia Acadian French:

(1) Nova Scotia Acadian French (YouTube recording by Anna Pottier, published on Nov 8, 2008; available at: https://www.youtube.com/watch?v= WUrbdLnPkmE; last accessed 09.08.2018)
Well, chais-pas comment *useful* que ça/ ça va être, *but*, uhm, c'est pour parler en acadien, parce que i ny'a *no-one around* avec qui ce que je peux parler, *so*, je vas juste faire cett-i *recording* et *who knows*, quelque *someone* va me répondre *back, you know*, juste pour dire *Hi or something*, parce que, c'est comme ça que je parle/ qu'on parle chez nous, *which* que de Nova Scotia, et *I hope* que je vas *mover* à Austin Texas *which* qu'est *really* proche de Louisiana, est-ce le monde là bas/ *well* c'est mon monde *really, I mean*, quand que j'écoutes cela radio KB101 ah/ Louisiana Proud, des fois j'écoutes ce *radio station* là, *even though* qu'ils avoient un différent *áccent* comme moi, ils sont comme [ ] chez nous. *So*, ça sera *really nice*, ah *especially* j'aurais vous dire, *sorry*, j'aurais vous dire de Ménard, *really really nice*, je *watch* ça passe en chante dans son Youtube, il est *really good*, moi j'*enjoy* ça beaucoup.

The community is bilingual in Acadian French and in English. The use of particular English expressions is a permanent feature of this local style of Nova Scotia regional French. At a superficial glance the passage might be perceived as a random 'mixture' of French and English. At closer examination we can note that the diffusion of English loans across functional categories follows certain patterns. First, we find elements that belong to the class of discourse markers, fillers, conjunctions, focus particles and interjections: *well, but, even though, especially, sorry*. An extension of the same category are the expressions *who knows, you know, I mean*. They take the overt form of conjugated verbs accompanied by pronouns, and from a strictly formal perspective they might be viewed as short phrase insertions, or 'EL islands' in Myers-Scotton's (1993) terminology. However, from a functional perspective they act as self-contained fillers that allow the speaker to monitor and direct listener-sided participation (see Matras 1998). We are therefore not looking in such cases at the borrowing of English pronouns and inflected verbs but rather at the wholesale adoption of entire expressions.

Loosely related to the same category are the relativiser *which* (doubled in the expression *which que*), which initiates a procedure of information supplementation, and the utterance level modifiers *really, really nice, really good*; the latter are lexical content items that constitute discrete illocutionary units that convey an exclamatory evaluation of entire propositions. We then find the indefinite expressions *no-one, someone, something*, and the verbal augments *around, back* (which might be classified as aktionsart modifiers). A series of content-lexical borrowings includes the adjective *useful*, the nouns *accent, radio station*, and the integrated verbs *je watch, j'enjoy, mover*. Finally, there is one single example of the borrowing of a verb along with its inflection (in the form of the proclitic English pronoun), in the modal verb *I hope*. In regard to some of the categories identified above, a case can be made for the wholesale adoption of certain functional categories from English, or 'fusion'. However, with the exception of the modal *I hope*, there is no evidence of language mixing at the level of inflectional material. The modal *I hope* is a case in point: Here, I argue, the motivation to reduce processing load leads to a fusion (elimination of competing equivalent expressions) around a modal expression. That in turn carries with it as a kind of side effect the importation of English-derived inflection (manifested in this case through the use of the English proclitic *I*). We cannot, therefore, speak of borrowing of English verb inflection as such, and indeed we find other English-derived verbs – lexical content verbs, not modals – in this example that are integrated into French verb inflection. So the point here is that while there is no general motivation to borrow English verb inflection, such borrowing of English verb inflection accompanies the borrowing of an English modal verb, motivated by the search for load reduction around the production of modals. I shall return to some similar examples below.

Consider now an example from Domari, an Indo-Aryan language of the Middle East, as spoken in Jerusalem, a variety that was moribund in the 1990s and has since become all but extinct (Matras 2012). Here, structural borrowing from the contiguous dialect of Arabic appears in each and every utterance:

(2) Jerusalem Domari (from Matras 2012; Arabic-derived elements are italicised):
    a. *Lamma kunt* ama qašṭōṭ-ik, na nēr-ded-im
       when was.1SG I small-PRED.F.SG NEG send-PERF-3PL
      madāris-an-ka.
      schools-PL.OBL-DAT
    b. *ū baqēt* kury-a-ma *zayy xaddām*-ēk
      and stayed.1SG house.-F.SG.OBL-LOC like servant-PRED.F.SG
    c. *ū daʔiman yaʕnī* kunt ama kury-a-m-ēk
      and always that.is was.1SG I house-F.SG.OBL-LOC-PRED.F.SG
    d. *wala* kil-šam-i *wala* aw-am-i
      and.not exit-1.SG-PRES and.not come-1SG-PRES

e. *wala waddi*-ka-d-m-i *mahall*-ak.
and.not bring-LOAN.TR-3PL-1SG-PRES place-INDEF
a. *When* I *was* small, they didn't send me to [any] *school*.
b. *And* [so] I *stayed* at home *like* a *servant*
c. *And* I *was always* I *mean* at home,
d. *not* going out *nor* coming,
e. *nor* do they *take* me *anywhere*.

Arabic borrowings cover all conjunctions (e.g. *lamma* 'when', *ū* 'and', *wala* 'neither . . . nor'), most prepositions (e.g. *zayy* 'like'), most indefinite expressions (*daʔiman* 'always', *mahall-* 'some-*where*'), fillers (*yaʕni* 'that is'), as well as modal and aspectual auxiliaries, which also carry Arabic inflection (*kunt* 'I was', *baqēt* 'I remained').[3] Note that otherwise verb and nominal inflection belong consistently to the inherited Indo-Aryan component. We thus find a pattern that is somewhat similar to the Acadian French examples, where lexical verbs are integrated into French inflection but the English modal *I hope* carries its English inflection (such as it is).

We do not find a lexicon-grammar split in either Nova Scotia Acadian French, or in Jerusalem Domari. Nor is there a consistent split between the sources of nominal and verbal grammar, or any consistent split between the source language of the finite predication grammar and that of the core lexicon or major deictic categories (demonstratives and personal pronouns) that would match the profile that is typically associated with MLs (see below). Instead what we find in both cases is a tendency toward wholesale borrowing from the surrounding majority language of categories that help organise the discourse at the level of turn taking and clause combining, those that highlight gaps in presuppositions (e.g. indefinites), expressions of modality and modal auxiliaries, some expressions of local relations (metaphorical aktionsart modifiers in Acadian French, prepositions in Domari) as well as various lexical items, most of them arguably non-core. The density of borrowed items and their distribution across a range of functional categories might qualify as 'heavy' borrowing if we are to set a quantitative measure in terms of relative number of borrowed items and the number of distinct categories that absorb borrowing, as well as the tendency toward wholesale adoption of categories, or fusion. Note again that in both cases all speakers are bilingual and have active command of the respective

---

3 Both these verbs are used primarily as modals auxiliaries that modify other verbs (assigning remoteness tense, and iterativity, respectively) though here they modify a Domari nominal predication and are therefore rendered in the translation as lexical verbs.

contact language, English and Arabic, and bilingualism in the relevant communities tends to be unidirectional (most Anglophones in Nova Scotia do not learn Acadian French, though they study Standard French as a school subject; and no Arabic speakers learn Domari beyond just a handful of expressions).

We should at this point revisit the question whether there are any limitations on borrowing. Since Whitney (1881), studies of language contact have been postulating different kinds of generalisations on structural borrowing. Thomason & Kaufman's (1988) frequently cited borrowing hierarchy links the extent of borrowing to the duration and intensity of cultural contacts. It identifies structural categories that are more and less likely to require more intense contact in order to be subjected to borrowing, but it does not attempt to offer an explanation for the links between category function and ease of borrowing. Instead, the point is to show that no structure is completely immune to borrowing and that given sufficient intensity of contact, borrowing can bring about significant structural change. Campbell (1993) embarks on a similar argument. Surveying proposed constraints in detail, he shows that virtually none are absolute. Consequently, he concludes along with Thomason & Kaufman (1988) that proposed generalisations must be seen as tendencies rather than absolute constraints that categorically rule out the possibility of borrowing of particular structures.

In a way, this cautious approach toward constraints runs open doors: It treats 'constraint' as a limitation rather than a facilitating factor. In the functionalist oriented typological tradition, generalisations on borrowing have been presented as implicational hierarchies in an effort to identify a link between inherent properties of categories and their susceptibility to borrowing, introducing an element of causality and thereby an explanatory dimension into our understanding of structural borrowing. In her pioneering work in this area, Moravcsik (1978) identifies referential autonomy and semantic transparency as properties that facilitate borrowing, predicting the higher borrowability of lexical over non-lexical features, of nouns over other word classes, of free morphemes over bound ones and of derivation over inflection (see also Field 2002). Recent studies devoted to morphological borrowing (Gardani et al. 2015; Otsuka et al. 2012) have on the whole confirmed that while the borrowing of derivational morphemes is frequent, that of inflectional markers such as person, tense, or case is much more exceptional.

In the domain of lexicon, comparative studies (cf. Haspelmath and Tadmor 2009) have shown that activity domains that are more prone to the influence of external practice routine, such as the organisation of formal institutions and commerce, religion and belief, or fashion and domestic equipment, are also more prone to lexical borrowing than those that are stable, close and intimate, such as spatial relations, the body, and sense and perception. That gives an empirical foundation to the notion represented for many years by the Swadesh list of 'basic vocabulary' taken to represent words that are less likely to be borrowed across languages and therefore might serve as a reliable indicator of language-genetic relatedness. Haspelmath and Tadmor's 'Leipzig-Jakarta List' of basic vocabulary derived from the compilation of studies actually bears close similarities to the Swadesh list of just over two hundred lexical items.

The same kind of semantic hierarchy (close/intimate vs remote/formal) can also be represented within individual word categories: Borrowed kin terms are more likely to be designations for those who are less closely related, less frequently mentioned, and more likely to be named in the context of formal titles and genealogical inventories (e.g. English *uncle, aunt, grandparents, niece, nephew*, all from French; Maltese *nannu* 'grandfather', *ziju* 'uncle', *kugin* 'cousin', *neputi* 'nephew' from Italian/Sicilian) (cf. Matras 2020: 183–184). Languages that borrow numerals, such as Swahili and Domari (both from Arabic) and Romani (from Greek) are more likely to borrow numerals above than under '5'. The proneness to borrowing of higher numerals (as well as those associated strictly with formal mathematical routines rather than with everyday counting, namely 'zero' and fractions) reflects their association with non-casual, institutional procedures and transactions and therefore with the language that dominates such routines (see also Williams-Van Klinken and Hajek's (2018) study of the distribution of indigenous, Indonesian and Portuguese numerals in Tetun Dili). In both cases, everyday concepts that are simple, close, intimate, and more frequently used tend to be more resistant to borrowing whereas their paradigm counterparts that indicate greater complexity, remoteness, formality and tightly regulated routines are more borrowing-prone.

The few studies that have considered the borrowing of grammatical categories across language samples (cf. Stolz & Stolz 1996; Matras 1998; Elšík & Matras 2006; Matras 2007) together paint a fairly consistent picture of implicational hierarchies at the top of which are the highly borrowable semantic-pragmatic meanings such as contrast, subjunctive modality and conditionality, obligation and necessity, exceptionality and superlatives, and the structural categories that express them, namely conjunctions, discourse and focus particles, phasal adverbs (adverbs of change and continuation), indefinites, expressions of peripheral relations and metaphorical spatial relations (verbal augments or particles and aktionsart modifiers), to name but some. The different degrees of susceptibility to contact of such categories have been confirmed by other studies devoted to single contact situations even when emphasising the lack of absolute predictive power and the need to take into consideration particular structural-typological constraints (e.g. Melissaropoulou and Ralli 2019).

On the whole, then, borrowing appears to be driven by motivations of repertoire management as described above in relation to the three pull factors: The desire to maximise expressive potential (in the lexical domain as well as in nuanced semantic distinctions such as aktionsart) and to reduce processing load by allowing the fusion or partial fusion of structural categories around those functions that place a high demand on the management of interaction, clashes with presuppositions, unexpected inferences, and the chaining of propositions. Those are balanced against speakers' determination to manifest accommodation to context, setting, interlocutor and so on through the choice of what is perceived to be the appropriate 'language', meaning in the multilingual setting that there is a motivation for language maintenance and toward resisting language shift, hence the modifications to communication routines that we perceive as contact-induced structural change or borrowing.

While structures or individual items that belong to core lexicon, finite predication grammar, nominal inflection or personal pronouns are not categorically exempted from borrowing, there are, for the reasons explained above, comparatively few cases in which borrowing is attested in these domains. In other words, borrowing of finite inflection markers, of nominal case markers, and of entire sets of personal pronouns and demonstratives is relatively rare. I propose that this is not the product of a constraint as such but rather of the absence, relatively speaking, of a motivation to borrow in these functional domains. Taken from a semantic-pragmatic perspective, inflectional markers of person, tense, and nominal case (so-called contextual inflection) provide a system of navigating the relations between entities in an utterance that are derived from a presupposed, shared mapping of roles and perspectives (shared between speaker and listener, that is). Similarly, deictic and anaphoric expressions (demonstrative and personal pronouns) equally navigate a shared reference space that is either physically present or imagined through the shared verbalised context. In both cases – contextual inflection, and indexical expressions – we therefore do not find the typical prompts for load reduction, namely the need to navigate potential gaps and discrepancies between speaker's and listener's expectations and presupposed mapping of knowledge and information. Nor do we find the content-lexical drive to maximise expressive potential (though of course semantic categorisation of the real world is prone to convergence or pattern replication, and we find analogous re-mapping of semantic case, tense-aspect categories, inclusive-exclusive distinctions in pronouns, and so on, proving that where motivations for the borrowing of form-function mapping arise, such structural categories are not principally immune to contact-induced change). So what 'protects' inflectional paradigms and sets of demonstratives and personal pronouns, as well as core vocabulary, by and large, from direct borrowing (replication of matter, rather than pattern) is not an exemption constraint as such but rather the absence, relatively speaking, of motivation for borrowing.

The exceptions that prove the rule are cases where local motivations arise. Examples of the borrowing of nominal case markers have been documented by Heath (1984) for languages of Arnhem Land and appear to be part of a larger scale diffusion of nominal properties that include derivation markers and classifiers, but the background of social contacts is not well understood. Thomason and Everett (2001) make the case for the borrowability of personal pronouns but rely in their examples in part on cases of MLs (Chavacano and Mednyj Aleut), making the argument in effect circular (because, as alluded to above, if we accept that MLs are a distinct type of language because they defy generalisations on contact-induced structural change then we cannot at the same time use them to exemplify generalisations on contact-induced structural change). Their other examples are cases already discussed by Wallace (1983) for Southeast Asian languages. But in those, the relevant items generally function as lexicalised honorifics rather than deictic and anaphoric forms (somewhat comparable to English 'Majesty' or 'Excellency') (cf. Ho-Dac 2002; Tadmor 2004). In terms of motivations, they fall under lexical items that label culture-specific social relations, including titles and terms of address. Direct borrowing of concrete morphological forms of definite articles (as opposed to the pattern replication of articles drawing on inherited material) is rare, but Algerian Arabic makes use of the French definite article with some borrowed French nouns as a marker of plurality: Thus *risṭūra*, pl. *risṭurāt* 'restaurant(s)', *šumbra*, pl. *šnāber* 'room(s)', but *kādu*, pl. *likādu* 'present(s)', *ʔami*, pl. *lizami* 'friend(s)'.

In a number of Romani dialects, the borrowing of plural markers that also indicate plurality on pronouns coupled with the coincidental similarity between the inherited Romani third person pronouns SG. *ov* PL. *on* and those of the respective contact languages has brought about analogous formations of third person plural pronouns, as in Hungarian Romani *on-k* 'they' (Hungarian *ők*), Croatian Romani *on-i* (Croatian *oni)*, and Bulgarian (Kalburdžu and Xoraxane) Romani *on-nar* (Turkish *onlar*). By a similar analogy to Turkish, drawing on the coincidental similarity between the first and second person singular markers -*m* and -*n* respectively, some Bulgarian dialects of Romani adopt the plural formation for past-tense first and second person inflection from Turkish: 1PL -*amis* (Turkish -*VmVz*) 2PL -*enis* (Turkish -*VnVz*). In both cases, local motivations (here: formal analogy) drive the development leading to borrowing in a domain that is otherwise not prone to the re-drawing of boundaries. Pakendorf (2015) reports on the borrowing of modality paradigms (necessitative and assertive moods) from Sakha or Yakut (Turkic) to Éven (Tungusic), two Siberian languages.

Here, the drive would appear to be toward fusion of procedures of mapping modality, triggered by the load reduction pull factor. That also accounts for the adoption into Domari of Arabic auxiliary verbs and modal expressions inclusive of their Arabic person inflection, discussed above and illustrated further by the following examples:

Jerusalem Domari (Arabic derived items italicised):

(3) ama *bidd-ī* dža-m kurya-ta
 I want-1SG go-1SG house-DAT
 'I want to go home'

(4) putr-or *ḍall-o* fumn-ar-i ben-im
 son-2SG remain-3SG.M hit-3SG-PRG sister-1SG.OBL
 'Your son keeps beating my sister.'

(5) *ṣār-u* fēr-and-i *baʕḍ* *baʕd*-ē-san waṭ-an-ma
 began-3PL hit-3PL-PRG REFL REFL-PL-3PL stone-OBL.PL-LOC
 'They started to throw stones at one another'

The Arabic person-agreement markers 1SG -*ī*, 3SG.M -*o*, and 3PL -*u* accompany the nominal modal expressions *bidd-* 'want' and *ḍall-* 'keep' and the verb *ṣār-* 'to begin', respectively. Their antecedents are all part of the Domari utterance or conversation context. The wholesale borrowing of Arabic modal and auxiliary expressions also extends to the markers of continuation and habituality, demonstrated in (2), which use the inflected Arabic forms *baqē-t* 'I stayed/ continued to' and *kun-t* 'I was/ I used to' respectively.

A number of Romani dialects show alternation of finite predication grammar with lexical verbs, as borrowed verbs may retain their source language inflection. The Romani dialect of Parakalamos in Epirus in northwestern Greece shows an incipient tendency toward such compartmentalisation in the domain of lexical verbs (Matras 2015):

(6) Parakalamos Romani (Greek-derived items are italicised):
 na *bor-o* te *diavaz-o* soske *prepi* te
 NEG can-1SG COMP study-1SG because must COMP
 vojt-iz-av me daj-a
 help-LOAN-1SG my.OBL mother-OBL
 'I cannot study because I have to help my mother'

As in the above examples from Domari, modal expressions borrowed from the contact language Greek retain their source language inflection: *bor-o* 'I can', *prep-i* (impersonal 3SG) 'it is necessary'. Some Greek loan verbs are adapted and carry Romani person and tense inflection: *vojt-iz-av* 'I help'. Others however appear in their Greek inflected form: *diavaz-o* 'I study (read)'. A similar incipient tendency has been observed in Romani dialects of Russia while in some Romani dialects of the Balkans the retention of Turkish inflection with Turkish loan verbs is the norm (see Adamou, this volume; and Adamou 2010). Viewed in terms of the repertoire management strategies discussed above, example (6) shows a variety of different operations: Modal verbs undergo fusion under the load reduction pull factor and that entails their complete replication inclusive of Greek person inflection. Adapted (morphologically integrated) Greek lexical verbs serve to exhaust expressive potential, which is balanced against the accommodation factor. The replication of Greek inflection with Greek lexical verbs indicates the weakening of accommodation as an active pull factor that exerts pressure on speakers to control repertoire features by inhibiting finite predication grammar that is associated with the de-selected language (Greek); such inhibition is relaxed and is apparently not deemed an essential property of accommodation. In effect, the constraints on selection and inhibition which make accommodation possible may be said to retreat to some extent, as features of finite predication grammar are allowed to accompany lexical verbs with which they co-occur in Greek-speaking interaction contexts. The retention of Greek inflection exclusively with (some) Greek-derived verbs resembles the compartmentalisation in the verbal system exhibited by Romani dialects that carry over inflected Turkish verbs (Adamou, this volume; Adamou and Shen 2019). However, there is no evidence so far, to my knowledge, in either case, of diffusion of the borrowed inflection paradigms into inherited Romani verbs.

To summarise, while there does not seem to be any absolute constraint that categorically rules out the borrowing of nominal inflection markers, personal pronouns and demonstratives, definite articles, or finite inflection on the verb, forms belonging to these and some other categories are not frequently borrowed because the pull factors that guide repertoire management in multilingual settings do not generally give rise to a motivation to borrow them. Exceptions are the product of particular circumstances, such as analogies based on coincidental structural similarities, or accompanying by-products of other borrowing motivations such as those that apply to the adoption of cultural routines around honorific titles or to load reduction around markers of modality. When finite predication grammar is borrowed along with borrowed lexical verbs, as in the Romani examples cited, it expresses a partial retreat of the accommodation factor, yielding to the fact that the particular inflection pattern usually co-occurs with particular lexical verbs when interacting in the (non-Romani) contact language. But such feature co-occurrence irrespective of language choice in the utterance remains distinct from the processes that appear to have given rise to MLs, as we see neither diffusion of borrowed verb inflection to inherited (non-borrowed) verbs, nor a complete replacement of inherited verbs by borrowed verbs along with their borrowed inflection. In short, it is difficult to identify any evidence for a continuum between the processes that give rise to borrowing as the outcome of balancing acts of the pull factors associated with repertoire management as described above, even far-reaching ones, and the structural outcomes that characterise MLs, namely different sources for grammar and lexicon, or different sources for key inflectional paradigms (verbal and nominal), or different sources for grammatical inflection and entire pronominal paradigms. I discuss this ML 'prototype' in the next section.

3 The ML protoype

Prevailing hypotheses explain MLs as emerging abruptly through pre-determined compartmentalisation of structural material from (usually) two languages in single utterances (Bakker 1997); or alternatively as a conventionalisation of code-mixing patterns at the utterance level (see Backus 2003); or as the extreme point of a continuum between code-mixing, heavy borrowing (sometimes captured by the notion of 'fused lect'; see Auer 1999)[4] and MLs. Bakker (1997) regards Michif as evidence for the abruptness of the process, while Meakins (2011) offers Gurindji Kriol as an example of a ML formation process that is gradual and emerges across several generations. In Matras (2000b) I proposed a distinction between the processes of 'lexical re-orientation' and 'selective replication' to capture the direction of change in relation to the source of finite predication grammar. The first, 'lexical re-orientation', applies to cases where a community of speakers adopts core lexicon (possibly accompanied by grammatical features) from another language while retaining more or less intact the finite predication grammar

---

[4] Auer's (1999) term 'fused lect' has been widely cited as a transitional stage between code-mixing and MLs (see also Adamou, this volume). Auer's example of a 'fused lect', however, is Sinti Romani, which borrows heavily from German in the rather predictable domains of lexicon, conjunctions and particles, as well as some instances of negation and verb modification (aktionsart) particles, prepositions and interrogatives. Since speakers are bilingual, the full inventory of German features is constantly available in Sinti Romani for spontaneous mixing as well. Auer does not, however, set any clear threshold for what might constitute a dense inventory of structural borrowing and codemixing on the one hand, and a 'fused lect' on the other, and so it is not clear how these concepts form a continuum.

of a separate, foundation language. The second, 'selective replication', captures shift across generations in the language of finite predication grammar while other structural components are retained from an earlier ('ancestral') language. Both processes thus involve a degree of language shift or interrupted transmission across generations (see also Sasse 1992; Myers-Scotton 1998, 2003). In cases of communities with mixed households, finite predication grammar may be retained from the language of the indigenous mothers, as in Michif (Cree verb grammar), or shift to the language of male colonial settlers, as in Mednyj Aleut (Russian finite verb inflection). In cases of contact with a surrounding majority or colonial language, finite predication grammar is either retained, as in Media Lengua (Quechua predication grammar), or shifts to that of the contact language, as in Gurindji Kriol (Kriol verb formation). The distinctive speech varieties of itinerant or nomadic populations by contrast are characterised invariably by symbiosis (Smith 1995) of their finite predication grammar with that of the surrounding majority language, usually characterised primarily by group-internal or even camouflage lexicon akin to that of cryptolects (see Matras 2010: 20–26).

While the precise composition of core lexicon, non-finite and nominal inflection, and grammatical lexicon is difficult to predict, varieties that have so far been labelled MLs all show just one source language for finite predication grammar; we have no attestation of an ML that derives its past-tense inflection, say, from one language, and its present tense inflection paradigm from another, or that splits singular person inflection on the verb from plural inflection, and so on. In Matras (2003) I therefore defined the ML prototype as consisting of finite predication grammar from one language (which I abbreviated 'INFL' with reference specifically to finite verb inflection rather than grammatical inflection in general) while showing any one or more of several components from a different source language that are rarely encountered as wholesale borrowings in cases of gradual contact-induced change: core lexicon, non-finite and nominal inflection paradigms, and complete sets of (rather than the odd) personal and interrogative pronouns, demonstratives and articles. These exceptional features of MLs have been linked to the circumstances of their emergence and societal attitudes to language and identity: MLs have been described as acts of identity that symbolise community separateness (Croft 2003; O'Shannessy 2020; Mazzoli and Sippola, this volume). Yet at the same time they have also been cited by some as evidence that contact-induced language change is less predictable than one might assume and that there are few if any constraints on the borrowing of structural categories (see Thomason 2015; Seifart 2017). As I suggested above, however, there appears to be an inherent contradiction between the view that MLs show exceptional profiles due to exceptional societal circumstances, and the idea that MLs should prompt us to re-assess the predictability of contact-induced language change in conventional settings.

I take the view that MLs are fundamentally different from borrowing. For a start, lexical re-orientation typically targets, as it does in cryptolects, everyday core lexicon rather than the kind of items that typically fall under exhausting expressive potential. Angloromani is widely cited as an ML with a lexicon-grammar split; examples in the literature, however, are usually based on an idealised desktop construction of sentences (e.g. Velupillai 2015: 72, citing Hancock 1992). In fact, Angloromani speech very seldom appears in the form of entire sentences, let alone entire stretches of conversation in which all lexical words derive from Romani. Documentation of actual in-group interaction (Matras 2010) shows that what English Gypsies[5] perceive and label as 'Romany' or 'English Romany' or sometimes 'English Romanes' in fact consists of just a casual embedding into English speech of Romani-derived vocabulary. Such insertions may cover basic concepts and may be used in high density in some segments of speech, and this may render Angloromani discourse stretches unintelligible to speakers of English who have no familiarity with the Romani-derived vocabulary. Yet Angloromani does not show a consistent lexicon-grammar split, as speakers always have a choice as to when they might insert a Romani-derived lexical item. This is illustrated by the following example from recorded narration in a family context:

(7) Angloromani (Matras 2010: 6) (Romani-derived items italicised)
But anyway, and I was saying to our Jim, *kushti, dordi, dordi, dik* at the *luvva* we've *lelled* today, would'ya. How *kushti*, I'll never *sutti torati* with excitement. You know, an' all this. And me mam used to say: oh my dear, *dik* at *lesti*. *Vater*: oh how ever did that come to *lel* such a *mush*? Oh, what a *kushti chor, dik*, and it's got a *moi* like a *jukkel*.
But anyway, and I was saying to our Jim, good, dear, dear, look at the money we've taken today, would'ya. How good, I'll never sleep tonight with excitement. You know, an' all this. And me mam used to say: oh my dear, look at him. Watch: oh how ever did that come to get such a man? Oh, what a nice boy, look, and it's got a mouth like a dog.

Note that the Romani-derived elements in the example tend to include lexical items that are central to the most sensitive aspects of the content of the narrative, including taboo expressions, evaluative and judgemental attributes, and attention markers, but also a pronominal word – 'him'. Contrary to some statements (cf. Thomason 2001: 234) there is no historical evidence to support the suggestion that Angloromani ever did show a consistent split between English grammar and Romani lexicon, nor is there evidence to suggest that the present

---

5 This population uses the term 'Gypsy' as self-appellation.

structure came about through a gradual borrowing of English grammar into a variety of Romani. Instead, historical documentation of the speech of English Gypsies, which is rather plentiful, suggests that Angloromani is a product of language shift from Romani to English, with speakers holding on to a Romani-derived vocabulary for use as an 'emotive mode' of discourse (see Matras 2010).

The process that gave rise to Angloromani is clearly distinct from the one observed in Acadian French or Domari, and the structural outcome is different as well, reflecting a communicative motivation to mark out lexical content for social meaning. The choice of distinct vocabulary items for core lexicon and the pronoun 'him' in the example establishes a kind of solidarity among the participants in the interaction and prompts the listener to engage with the propositional content from the perspective of shared attitudes and experiences. I will return to the performative aspects below. Whether or not we define Angloromani as an ML depends on the extent of 'languageness' that the definition would require: I suggest that there is a continuum between varieties like Angloromani, which are stylistic choices that are reserved for particular interactions and within them to individual utterances; varieties such as Ma'a, which can be used in entire stretches of discourse but only under certain circumstances (Mous 2003); and a language like Michif (Bakker 1997), which is the all-purpose home language of a community of speakers (for a discussion of the continuum see Matras 2020: 312ff).

Some MLs contain considerable inflectional material from both their source languages and show a more consistent complementary distribution of forms by etymological source, both features that are difficult to reconcile with the repertoire management model outlined above. Consider the following examples:

(8) Michif (Adapted from Mazzoli 2019: 113) (French-derived items italicised, English derived items italicised and underlined):
Maaka   li   dariee   zhornii,   anima   la
but   DEF.M   last   day.M.INAN   that.INAN   DEF.F
maezoñ   kaa-kii-li-*rent*-ii-yaan,   ma   klee
house.F.INAN CNJ-PST-the-rent-THE.AI-CNJ.1S   POSS.F.S key
gii-doo-meek-in   kiihtwam.
1.PST-go-give.AI-IND.1S   again
'But *the last day, that house* I *rented*, I went there again to give back *my key*.'

(9) Mednyj Aleut (Golovko 1996: 65–71) (Russian-derived items italicised):
oni taanga-χ su-la-*jut*
they alcohol-SG take-MULT-3PL.PRES
'*they are* buy*ing* alcohol'

(10) Gurindji Kriol (McConvell & Meakins 2005: 11) (Gurindji-derived items italicised):
nyawa-ma wan *karu* bin plei-bat pak-*ta* *nyanuny*
this-TOP one child PAST play-CONT park-LOC 3SG.DAT
warlaku-ywaung-ma
dog-having-TOP
'*This* one *kid* was playing *at* the park *with his dog*.'

In Michif, finite predication grammar is consistently Cree while noun phrase modifiers are consistently French. In Mednyj Aleut, finite predication grammar is Russian as are subject and object pronouns, while nominal inflection (including person affixes that mark possession) derives from Aleut. Gurindji Kriol shows Kriol finite predication grammar and Gurindji-derived nominal inflection (which, as the language developed, often underwent shifts in meaning, converging with Kriol; see Meakins 2011).

To summarise, then, borrowing, as I use the term with respect to 'conventional' repertoire management in multilingual settings and the processes of historical structural change that they can set in motion, typically targets non-basic vocabulary (with a preference for lexical items denoting cultural innovations, progressively expanding to other categories in a manner that is hierarchical, as described above), grammatical items that are high on the scale of processing presuppositional gaps or other loci of potential interactional tension (the grammar of 'monitoring-and-directing'), form-meaning templates or semantic-syntactic patterns for both individual items and paradigms (for a more exhaustive discussion see Matras 2020). All these can be related to the motivations of the pull factors described above. What is crucial for our discussion is, however, what is not typically borrowed: full inflectional paradigms (both verbal and nominal), extensive core lexicon, and complete pronominal (deictic and anaphoric) paradigms. The ML prototype shows hybridity precisely in the etymological sources of those components: predication grammar from one source language, combined with one or more of nominal inflection, core vocabulary, or entire pronominal paradigms from another source language. That, I propose, is not an outcome of borrowing, but of a distinct process, which I describe in the next section.

4 Performativity and acts of identity

Drawing on a concept introduced by LePage and Tabouret-Keller (1985), Croft (2003) describes the emergence of MLs as 'acts of identity'. Let us first go back to the original use of the concept. For LePage and Tabouret-Keller (1985), languages and groups cannot be taken as given. Instead they come into being through acts of identity that individuals do and share. These are manifested by the choice of linguistic features and their association with certain extra-linguistic attributes. Linguistic items are thus the means by which individuals identify themselves and others. Linguistic behaviour constitutes a series of acts of identity through which people reveal their identity and search for social roles. Examining corpora and questionnaire-based self-assessment in the Caribbean and among young people of Caribbean background in London, LePage and Tabouret-Keller observe that the particular co-occurrence of linguistic items and non-linguistic variables is often unpredictable. Instead there are degrees of association, which are permeable, and a continuum that is multidimensional: People can share the same repertoire but differ in the extent to which they use each component. Thus, youth of Jamaican background in London use occasional Jamaican features in their English speech to assert in-group identity. They refer to this as 'Jamaican', though it is not always possible to arrange features on a linear scale from standard to non-standard. LePage and Tabouret-Keller conclude that speech acts are speakers' invitation to others to share their view of the world. Behavioural patterns allow individuals to identify groups, to get access to them, and be motivated to join them and modify their own behaviour accordingly. 'Language' therefore carries several meanings: It is in one sense the actual behaviour of people, and in another sense the perceived system that is considered to overlap with community or group membership and thus in effect the socially constructed labelling of a group's linguistic behaviour. Once linguistic behaviour is reified it becomes symbolic of group membership, often intertwined with self-ascription. Language is thus not objectively defined but rather a concept formed by individuals who project concepts onto those around them and establish networks of shared suppositions and behaviours.

Croft (2003) combines this notion of 'acts of identity' with his evolutionary model of language change (Croft 2000) which attributes change to the initiation, replication and ultimately conventionalisation of innovative linguistic templates, which he calls 'linguemes'. Croft views the formation of MLs as the spread of hybridised linguemes that draw on two source languages, the first associated with what Croft calls the heritage society, the second with the adoptive society. Referring to the concept of 'functional turnover' and the pathways of 'lexical re-orientation' and 'selective replication' described in Matras (2000b),

Croft proposes that in language contact situations positive acts of identity determine the source of basic vocabulary. Thus, in language maintenance, but also in cases of functional turnover where the ancestral language serves symbolic purposes, basic vocabulary derives from the heritage language. By contrast, in language shift and semi-shift, basic vocabulary derives from the language of the adoptive society, while mixed marriage languages adopt basic vocabulary from both. This approach regards basic vocabulary as the element that users of language most easily identify as a 'primary parent language' (Croft 2003: 68).

One might however contend that while vocabulary offers a symbolic identification with a society (in the sense of a community of cultural practices), predication grammar is an indicator of the 'primary language' (to draw on Croft's term) that users of language rely on to process utterances and therefore as the basis of communicative interaction. The point about MLs is that they tend to show a split between the language (etymologically speaking) in which utterances are anchored, and the language that is used to symbolise content. That, if we take lexicon-grammar split as the principal feature of ML formation, as Croft does. The reality is of course more complex: As we saw above, some MLs (so designated), such as Angloromani, only make occasional use of 'heritage society' vocabulary, and of minor features of heritage society grammar; others, like Michif, show, as Croft notes, mixed sources for both vocabulary and grammar, and so the notion of an identity act favouring either heritage or adoptive society is not particularly helpful as a guiding definition.

I propose that in order to account for ML formation we need to go back to the very emergence of what Croft calls the innovative 'linguemes' and hypothesise about the speech acts through which they emerge and the particular effect that their structural composition has on the interaction context. My hypothesis is that the speech acts that give rise to hybrid 'linguemes' are performative speech acts. I propose that they function as acts of identity by defying conventions on ordinary everyday language mixing or hybridity to which users in the multilingual setting are accustomed. What do I mean by 'performative' speech acts? Austin (1962) introduces the distinction between 'constatives' and 'performatives'. He describes performatives as utterances that cannot be classified as true or false, while at the same time they entail the doing of an action and so in effect they constitute actions in their own right. While constatives are assessed by their content as true or false, performatives are assessed as felicitous or infelicitous, depending on whether the conditions to execute them properly are met. That distinction is widely regarded as superseded by Austin's own taxonomy of illocutionary forces (cf. Levinson 1983: 235–236). However, for our discussion it is useful to adopt precisely that initial, rather crude distinction, as complementing its successor model. In other words, we can assume for our purposes that an utterance will have its own illocutionary force, be that an assertion, a request, a question, a directive, and so on. But in addition it can also take on a performative meaning. That performative meaning is achieved by drawing attention to the utterance through the use of a combination of structural resources that is unconventional yet still intelligible to the interlocutor. In the bilingual setting, speakers are accustomed to combining resources from within their repertoire of linguistic forms (language mixing), and so ordinary and expected code-mixing will not invariably achieve a performative effect, only through particular contextual indexing. But a composition that is unexpected even in the bilingual setting can be certain to have a performative effect. Its exceptionality will manifest itself in the defiance of common conventions on language mixing, or management of linguistic resources in the repertoire. That exceptionality sends a message to the listener and so it constitutes an action in its own right, in our case the expression of a social attitude of bonding with the listener and of resistance toward surrounding or external social values or an encroaching social order. Once it becomes a template that can be replicated by others, the 'lingueme' is formed.

At this point it is useful to refer to the further development of the concept of performativity in the social sciences. Derrida (1988 [1972]) points out that Austin's notion of 'performative' does not describe something that is outside of language, but something that produces or transforms a situation. However, given the iteration of utterances, their existence is independent of context and felicity conditions. An utterance is thus intelligible even if its referent is absent or if it is not anchored in objective reality. Derrida concludes that language structure is therefore by definition performative, because it is not possible to completely separate meaning from context, or intention from felicity conditions. This stance inspires Butler (1990, 2010) to argue that performativity refers to speech acts as a way of constituting (or de-constituting) a phenomenon. This notion of performativity counters the positivism with which we assume certain understandings of phenomena, including the presumption of certain culturally constructed categories; instead, it sets in motion processes that lead to certain realities or consequences. Butler regards identity as performative since it is manufactured through a sustained set of acts. The key to performativity is repetition (Derrida's 'iterativity') and the power through which speech acts can form and shape identity. In that sense identity is subject to 'self-making' through the means of the performative illocution that is perpetually transmitted via speech acts.

Butler (1990: 194–199) emphasises that what she calls 'signification' (the constitution of a new subject) is not a single founding act but a process of repetition; 'agency' is defined in this connection as being located within the possibility of introducing variation on repetitive processes, thereby subverting them and the identities that they produce. Of particular relevance to our discussion is what Butler describes as practices of parody: These serve a derived, phantasmatic or mimetic function that excludes something from the natural or real, subverting established norms and re-conceptualising identities as effects that are produced or generated rather then being foundational or fixed. We can apply this to our understanding of a community that is undergoing rapid transformations through shifts in cultural allegiances and practices, including such events as the coming together of parents of different backgrounds, seasonal labour migration, or rapid social changes such as the emergence of new institutions and authorities that question traditional sets of values and power relations. In many such settings, it is the young generation that assumes a new sense of agency to construe its own identity.

How can we then imagine the initial occurrence of hybrid utterances that defy conventional patterns of language mixing in a bilingual setting, in such a way as to capture the attention of an interlocutor and to construe a statement of identity and bonding? Consider example (11) from a trilingual (Hebrew-German-English) child raised in an environment where language separation (by interlocutor and groups of interlocutors) is generally maintained, even with the parents, who live in separate households. Lexical insertions and occasional code-mixing around quotations and emphasis are common as long as the interlocutors are able to understand all elements employed; there is also frequent convergence of lexical-semantic and sometimes syntactic patterns, and use of expletives and verbal gestures that crosses the boundaries of labelled languages (for a detailed description see Matras 2020: 11ff.). There is thus, despite the spatial and interlocutor-based separation of languages, a general 'license' to resort to creative combinations of elements from the wider, multilingual repertoire of linguistic resources, as long as this does not risk a breakdown in the effectiveness of communication (intelligibility). But in (11) we see a different kind of pattern, one that contrasts sharply with those general trends. The setting is the home of the Hebrew-speaking parent. There are no other participants or bystanders in the interaction. It is the evening hour and the child, aged 8 and 6 months, has been prompted by the parent to prepare for bed. As he enters the bathroom to wash he addresses the parent:

(11) Trilingual child, age 8:6 (German items italicised, Hebrew items italicised and underlined):
Aba! Where do I get a *Lappen* so I can *wisch* my *Gesicht*?
Daddy! Where do I get a *washcloth* so I can *wipe* my *face*?

While language mixing, as I explained, is common in the household and often expected in certain turns and with references to certain subjects, in (11) the child makes two choices that stand out as irregular in terms of the established interaction routines (including language mixing routines) in the home: First, while selecting the usual term of address for the parent (the Hebrew word for 'Daddy'), he chooses to address the parent in English, a language that is usually reserved in the interaction between them for quotations, idiomatic phrase replication, and otherwise lexical insertions. But here, the sentence frame, predication grammar, and illocutionary force (marking the utterance as a question) are all in English. Second, the selection of English is not consistent, but intertwined with German, which is used for all key content lexemes in the utterance. Once again, there is no such established routine in the household interaction. German, too, is drawn upon in interaction between the child and this parent for quotes, single word emphasis, or other lexical insertions, and sometimes inadvertently around discourse markers and similar expressions; but here the choice is not driven by such indexical considerations that are local to the context but instead by a wholesale aesthetic motivation. By pointing out that a key pre-requisite for the task (availability of a washcloth) is missing, the child seemingly challenges the parent's instruction and thereby the parent's authority. But that challenge is toned down through the irregular structural composition of the utterance. The utterance is performative, since it defies conventional routines of repertoire management in order to achieve a humorous effect, which might in this instance best be described as a mimicry or caricature of defiance of authority ("if you are using your authority to command me to wash and prepare for bed, then I am staging a mock rebellion by challenging you to provide the necessary pre-requisites"). At the same time, the fact that the components for the utterance are all drawn from the multilingual repertoire of structural resources that the two interlocutors share, implies a bonding, a solidarity effect, a display of loyalty and a shared pool of experiences and values that can be celebrated. What is seemingly a playful act of defiance is thus an act of shared identity construction. In reaching out to the interlocutor, the speaker is inviting an acknowledgement of such shared identity. In that respect, the utterance, in its particular composition, is an act of claiming agency.

This particular example does not represent a setting in which such utterances are likely to be replicated habitually thereby turning into what Croft (2003) calls 'linguemes'. However, we can imagine that it is precisely this kind of linguistic creativity which, in a small and tight-knit community, used among young people in search of a way to re-frame social attitudes and values, can indeed become an iterative act of identity which in time will come to represent a collective. Peng (2016) discusses the case of the adoption of the English progressive marker *-ing* in Chinese social media discourse. It involves script switching and the attachment of the marker to indicate the broad aspectual meaning of progressive action that is associated with its use in English:

(12) English –*ing* in Chinese social media texts (Peng 2016: 8–13)
 a. 福州 ING
  Fúzhōu
  'Being in Fuzhou'
 b. 有准备 ing.
  ing yǒu zhǔnbèi-ing
  'We are preparing'
 c. 复习前几天的笔记 ing
  fùxí qián jǐ tiān de bǐjì-ing
  'Reviewing the notes that were made several days ago'

As seen in the examples, -*ing* is normally placed at the end of the phrase, which can even be a place name, and it is not necessarily attached to the lexical verb as in the English source. At the same time it is often found to substitute the Chinese aspectual markers *zai* and *zhong*, which express simultaneity and proximity. Peng (2016) collected data from the popular Chinese social media outlets Weibo, Douban and Zhihu. She attributes the common use of -*ing* to a language play in defiance of normal Chinese writing conventions. The creators of this usage are described as young 'netizens' who engage in an effort to present themselves as trendy and fashionable and attract attention. They do so by identifying as members of an economic and cultural community that possesses a high level of English skills; this is taken to imply open attitudes and world experience. They thereby distinguish themselves from an older generation of non-learners or infrequent users of English.

Both examples demonstrate real-time performative use of language mixing that is not the product of a conventional balancing act of repertoire management in multilingual interaction settings. Both involve deliberate acts that expressively defy conventions of repertoire choices even in an environment that acknowledges multilingual repertoire complexity. They provide evidence for the plausibility of Thomason's (2015: 41) speculation about Copper Island (Mednyj) Aleut as involving "conscious diffusion of inflectional morphology" and an "element of deliberation". That means, however, that the intertwining of certain functional categories found in MLs such as Mednyj Aleut is not the outcome of common repertoire management routines of the kind described above, but of distinct processes.

Unfortunately, we have no substantive documentation of the conventionalisation of spontaneous performative utterances such as the one in example (11) into regular community-based styles of speech. But Peng's (2016) observations demonstrate the potential of performative language mixing to become the marker of a community. What we do have, however, is evidence from so-called 'symbiotic' MLs (Smith 1995), which essentially involve drawing on a special reservoir of lexical items for in-group communication. This kind of strategy is most commonly associated with cryptolects, a notion applied to in-group varieties ranging from youth and urban slangs such as Verlan, those of professional groups and especially itinerant traders and performers, and the in-group varieties of ethnic minorities with a tradition of peripatetic service economies.

Binchy (1993) describes how the community of Irish Travellers use Shelta (a lexicon based on sound manipulation of Irish and English words, embedded into Hiberno-English conversation) when discussing matters that are highly contextual and so require a high degree of shared background knowledge. Typical such conversation domains include making a living among non-Travellers, maintaining boundaries between Travellers and settled people and communication about intimate domains. In Matras (2010) I describe similar uses of so-called Angloromani or what the users themselves call English Romany or English Romanes. Here too the choice of the special lexical inventory that is derived from Romani (the ancestral community language, which appears to have been abandoned toward the second half of the nineteenth century) is a statement: It is a call on the listener to interpret the propositional content of the utterance in light of a specialised or exclusive presuppositional domain. In (13) a Romani man is signalling the end of a brief exchange with a friend whose conversation with a police officer he had interrupted at an open-air public event. With the police officer still being within sight though probably not within eavesdropping distance, the speaker says:

(13) Angloromani: conclusion of short interruptive exchange (Matras 2010: 135)
Right, I'll leave you to *rokker* with the *muskra*
'Right, I'll leave you to *talk* with the *policeman*'

Secrecy or deliberate camouflaging of content are not necessarily involved. Rather, the key is that of a personal message between the speaker and the addressee, concluding the brief exchange between them and expressing the speaker's withdrawal from the interaction in acknowledgment that he had interrupted an ongoing conversation with a stranger. The use of Romani here marks out the turning point in the conversation. But it also establishes an indexical hierarchy of personal loyalties, signalling recognition that although the speaker is yielding to the addressee's earlier conversation with the stranger, the bond between the speaker and the addressee is stronger than the one between the addressee and his other interlocutor, the policeman, and that the speaker is withdrawing for practical and tactical reasons, recognising the benefits of showing respect toward others' conversation.

Conversations recorded within the Romani family show a continuum of usages ranging from emphatic dramatising of states of affairs and humorous self-ridicule (14), to directives that are seemingly menacing but in reality endearing (15), to the encoding of terms around sensitive content or potential danger (16), and on to the flagging of boundaries in interaction with group outsiders (17) (data from Matras 2010: 137ff):

(14) Oh, *dik* at the state of my *bal*, oh I'll have to *jaw* somewhere to somebody could do a hairdresser to get me *bal* done, ooh *dik* at the state of it!
'Oh, *look* at the state of my *hair*, oh I'll have to *go* somewhere to somebody could do a hairdresser to get me *hair* done, ooh *look* at the state of it!'

(15) *Ol* the *obben* coz when the *raklis jels* I'm gonna *mor* yas.
'*Eat* the *food* coz when the *girls go* I'm gonna *beat* yous!'

(16) I'd tell 'em not to *chor* in the *burrika*
'I'd tell 'em not to *steal* in the *shop*.'

(17) *Mush jins* everything ya *rokkerin'* anyway.
'[The] *man knows* everything you're *sayin'* anyway.'

'Lekoudesch' was the designation used by a circle of men in the village of Rexingen in the Black Forest region of Germany for a form of speech that imitated the use of Hebrew derived vocabulary in dialectal German by Jewish cattle traders in the pre-war period. As boys, the Christian men had often been hired by Jews to help drive cattle to the markets and were thus exposed to the code. That code was accessible in principle to all members of the Jewish community; they were familiar with Hebrew vocabulary in Ashkenazic pronunciation from scriptures and prayer. However, in the vernacular it was used primarily as a way of excluding bystanders and affirming group-internal solidarity as part of the cattle trade. After World War II and the loss of the local Jewish community following emigration and the Holocaust, the boys, now adults, continued to use the principal features of the cryptolect: Hebrew-derived vocabulary and some relaxation of grammatical rules such as definite articles and the use of the present-tense existential verb. This was used as a group-internal code to comment on bystanders, and as a source of entertainment and group solidarity. As the circle of men with active knowledge of Lekoudesch declined, the style became a symbol of a tight-knit community of friends and neighbours in the village, who usually frequented one of just several local pubs and sat at a designated table for regulars ('Stammtisch'). Examples (18) and (19) are informants' replication of the original use as a language of business, while (20)–(22) record spontaneous commentaries made in the pub in respect of non-group member bystanders (data from my own recordings in 1984; Hebrew derived items are italicised):

(18) Alle *gimmel doff*.
 'All *three* are *good*'

(19) Die *båra* isch *mechätz*.
 'The *cow* is *ill*'

(20) D'r *guj veroumelt lou*.
 'The *man doesn't understand*'

(21) *Lou dibra*, d'r *guj schäfft!*
 '*Don't speak*, the *man is-there* [=a stranger is listening]'

(22) Die *goja* isch *haggel doff*, dia kennt-m'r *lekächa*.
 'The *woman* is *very pretty*, one could *take* her [=sleep with her]'

The group of men shared an inventory of narratives that were familiar to its members and appear to have been told many times for entertainment. These stories revolve around the use of Lekoudesch during the times when Jews still inhabited the village. They tend to have one of two themes: Some capture the humorous effect of a situation where an individual was excluded from a conversation through the use of Lekoudesch. Others capture the irony of a situation when somebody attempted to use the code to exclude or embarrass others, on the assumption that the code was not accessible to them, only then to learn that they were in fact immersed in it, and were able to use it to embarrass those who had tried to ridicule them in the first place. Such anecdotes gave the mixed code a new form of vitality as its function shifted to capture memories of old times while activating the shared pool of humorous stories that consolidated the group socially. Both the spontaneous use of Lekoudesch in the pub and its use in rehearsed stories amounted to a performance of a distinctive group identity among a small circle of male friends.

5 Performative functions and the formation of MLs

The discussion in the previous section demonstrated that both lexical and morphological material can be used consciously to perform acts of solidarity among individuals, family members or members of a regular circle of friends, members of a minority ethnic community with a particular socio-economic relationship to majority society, or members of an online community flagging their socio-economic position and societal attitudes. I discussed examples of spontaneous, semi-conventionalised, and highly conventionalised mixing. Common to all cases is the fact that the structural outcomes differ considerably from those that are the typical products of re-setting boundaries as part of repertoire management strategies through which speakers in a multilingual environment seek to balance three pull factors: accommodation (to the choice of features expected in the setting and context, or language choice), exhausting expressive potential (around semantic meaning), and economising processing load (primarily around interaction management and the processing of presupposition).

Discussions of MLs tend to focus on their structural profiles and do not, generally speaking, offer insights from a discourse-interaction perspective into their early stages of emergence – usually due to lack of accessible data, and in part perhaps also due to the nature of elicited data. There are, however, interpretations and analyses that suggest a performative origin of MLs, including those that involve intertwining of grammatical paradigms. Bakker (1997) views the genesis of Michif as an almost pre-determined process where the first generation of a new community born to Cree mothers and French fathers combines elements of both languages as an aesthetic representation of their independent identity. In the absence of attestation of the early stages, no exemplification can be offered of the utterances that first gave rise to the mixing pattern and their possible distinct illocutionary purpose during a period where speakers still had command of both source languages. Golovko (2003) goes further and hypothesises that the creators of MLs were generally "folk linguistic engineers" who engaged in playful mixing, manipulating components of their repertoire in forms that defy the normally attested and predicted patterns of language mixing. Mous (2003), in his description of Ma'a or Inner Mbugu, the group-internal speech variety of the Ma'a people of Tanzania, follows Sasse's (1992) suggestion that favours deliberate strategies of relexification as a way of flagging identity following the shift from the Cushitic language Gorwaa to the Bantu language Pare. As evidence Mous cites among other factors the varied composition of the special Ma'a lexicon, which includes not just Gorwaa items but also material from other sources including Maasai and manipulated Normal Mbugu (Pare). The process thus resembles the formation of cryptolects and the scenarios of lexical retention from an ancestral language, and lexical extraction from a tradition of scriptures, that characterise the emergence of Angloromani and Lekoudesch, respectively. Meakins (2011) describes the emergence of Gurindji Kriol as a form of resistance against linguistic and cultural assimilation to the pan-Aboriginal community in the north of Australia, following colonisation and the shift in most Aboriginal communities to English-based Kriol. Meakins argues that a prolonged phase of code-switching gave rise to a stable ("grammaticalised") mixed variety. Nonetheless, Meakins employs the term 'borrowing' with reference to the replication of Gurindji-derived nominal inflection in a predication that is framed and anchored by Kriol grammar. In light of the explanatory account of the ML as essentially an aesthetic act of cultural resistance, 'borrowing' must be understood in this context as something that is very different from the balancing of pull factors in everyday multilingual repertoire management. As noted above, I prefer to reserve the term borrowing to those instances and not to use it to describe the distinctive formation processes of MLs.

The essence of the performativity that is involved in ML formation can thus be understood precisely as going against speakers' intuitive and usually well-rehearsed patterns not just of where demarcation boundaries are normally construed between sets of features within the repertoire, and how repertoire components and sets of features are aligned with interaction routines, but also how such construed boundaries can be crossed and modified. The performative crossing of boundaries sets relevant utterances apart from patterns of mixing that are otherwise common and acceptable in the community of users, in order to convey an aesthetic and emotive statement. This requires us to add to the model of repertoire management an overarching dimension that allows and at times prompts users to override or interfere with the more conventional balancing acts among pull factors that serve straightforward communication, one that adds an aesthetic aspect of performativity to the range of illocutions of everyday discourse interaction.

Contributions to the present volume survey a range of structural phenomena that can be accommodated in various ways in relation to the hypothesis about the role of performativity in ML formation and help fine-tune the analytical category of MLs and its relation to (conventional) borrowing. Hannß's discussion of

Kallawaya describes what might be regarded as a classic performative function, where users choose from a contained and clearly demarcated lexical reservoir in order to perform very particular ritual acts of speech. Sippola's analysis of an Ilokano-Spanish letter gives insight into what might have been an act of bonding between writer and addressee, where Spanish lexicon, formulaic expressions such as greetings, and the occasional Tagalog loanword are inserted into what are otherwise consistently Ilokano sentences. In the absence of other similar evidence from a community of users, the letter might be regarded as a single communicative event in which the mode of combining repertoire elements takes on a performative function. Pecht's chapter on Cité Duits allows us to speculate about a possible playful language activity as the origin of an in-group variety used to flag group bonding among a circle of male speakers in a coal-mining community, marked by the use of a distinctive paradigm of personal pronouns that draws on the three source languages in the pool of shared linguistic resources. These cases show us that performativity can have a range of structural manifestations, from the use of just a single functional paradigm, through the occasional use of a special lexical reservoir.

Clements, Amaral and Garrett describe Barranquenho as a local variety that represents the distinctive identity of the inhabitants of Barrancos and their particular history of persisting cross-border contacts. Barranquenho appears to be characterised by an importation of a small number of Spanish features into Portuguese. Apart from lexical items, these include phonological features as well as convergence in the formation of the progressive aspect and the placement of clitics. All these can be accounted for as predictable products of repertoire management and the use of certain features across communication routines for which different labelled 'languages' are used (borrowing). In fact, they strongly resemble the kind of interference processes exhibited by learner varieties: persistence of an 'accent', use of selected lexicon and discourse markers, and persistence of ordering of referents in complex clauses. What appears to be emblematic and in that sense performative in Barranquenho is the permanent use of such L2 interference features and their adoption as markers of local identity, even by the younger generation that speaks Portuguese as its principal language. Thus, it appears to be the conventionalisation of linguistic interference features used by earlier generations that serves an aesthetic, identity forging function.[6]

---

[6] The case is in some aspects reminiscent of the Pacific language Rea Rapa (Walworth 2017), where speaker deliberately substitute some features of Tahitan retaining local archaisms in order to set themselves apart from the majority language of Tahiti.

I am reminded here of the formation of what has been referred to in recent literature as 'multi-ethnolects' – the slang of urban youth that is characterised by a strong impact of immigrant varieties. Evidence from some of these varieties suggests that their distinctive features involve imitation and performative adoption of the parent generation's second-language learner (interference) features by the children of immigrants. For Kiezdeutsch in Germany (Wiese 2009; Freywald et al. 2011), for instance, these include, along with the use of some lexical items and exclamations from the heritage languages, the reduction of German grammatical inflection and grammatical markers, simplification of word order rules, and a tendency to generalise listener-related connective word order patterns, as well as an over-generalisation of certain discourse marking and chaining devices. The latter two mark heavy reliance on procedures that guide listener-sided processing and reassure the speaker of interaction harmony, both typical of advanced second language learner styles (cf. Matras 2020: 63).

Bakker (this volume) refers to ML formation as an act of identity in cases of new community formation but questions its relevance to languages like Gurindji Kriol and Light Walpiri, where Aboriginal identity is retained. However, precisely that process, the mapping of group identity onto language, is described by Meakins (2011) as the act of cultural resistance that gives rise to Gurindji Kriol. It follows that 'identity' need not be understood only as the emergence of a new labelled community. Rather, it is the act of setting oneself apart that finds its manifestation in creative linguistic performativity. While it may be argued that Gurindji Aboriginals might have simply retained their ancestral language Gurindji as a way of demonstrating their ethnic identity, and that Romani Gypsies in England might have done the same with inflected Romani, the reality in both settings was the change to the repertoire management dynamics as a result of the massive impact of the surrounding languages, Kriol and English respectively. Holding on to selected structures of the ancestral language, or selective replication (Matras 2000b), is therefore precisely an act of identity. The concept of performativity allows us to link both the emergence of new communities and the maintenance of community boundaries with the patterns of utterance formation that give rise to the MLs.

Stewart and Meakins define MLs as speech varieties that are created for expressive rather than communicative purposes. Their three case studies (Media Lengua, Gurindji Kriol and Michif) appear to suggest, however, that the performative aspect of MLs is manifested by the particular combinations of morphosyntax and lexicon rather than in creative processes in phonology or phonetics, where the systems of the source languages continue more or less intact, subject to common processes of levelling. Deibel's discussion of Media Lengua word order similarly reveals that ordinary processes are in motion within the grammar of an ML irrespective of the background for its formation. The integration of French nominal stems into Cree-inflected verbal predications in Michif (Mazzoli, Bakker and DeMontigny) seemingly contradicts the template of verb-noun etymological split; but in fact it serves to show how an ML, when it becomes a full-fledged language, is subject to its own repertoire management dynamics, and the selection of features for semantic expansion is no longer guided merely by the etymology of the individual components.

Several case studies in the volume describe far-reaching structural contact phenomena that lie on the fringe of heavy borrowing and ML formation. Thus, Jopara (Dudek Herring and Clements) appears to be the conventionalisation of the principle of frequent mixing of phrases and features of Spanish and Guarani as a manifestation of a linguistically mixed identity. It may therefore best be described as a performative style rather than an ML, or the accumulation of simultaneous insertions as local expressions of repertoire management. Wutun (Sandman) is essentially a case of Sinitic morphological material that is adapted to the converging patterns of the surrounding Tibetic and Mongolic languages of the Amdo linguistic area, giving rise to Altaicised features including the loss of tones and classifiers, changes in word order, and the emergence of agglutinative suffixes drawing on Sinitic material. Apart from lexical borrowing, it also shows morphological borrowing of the incomplete aspect marker from Tibetan and of the Mongolic interrogative morpheme and terminative affix. What stands out in Wutun are the multiple sources and the combination of radical typological restructuring, along with the presence of some borrowed morphemes (in domains related to interaction management and aktionsart, which are generally prone to borrowing). These processes can be accommodated within the model of repertoire management and conventional and widely attested matter and pattern replication (see Matras 2020), and do not require a performative dimension as an explanation. In sum, Jopara does not appear to be a conventionalised ML in which new 'linguemes' have been established through replication, while Wutun does not appear to adhere to the ML prototype nor does it display a combination of structural components of different sources that cannot be accounted for within the framework of usual repertoire management or borrowing.

Discussing the usage of Turkish-derived lexical verbs that carry Turkish inflection in a dialect of Romani from Thrace, Adamou provides experimental evidence in support of the argument that Turkish-derived verbs for which speakers have no Romani-derived equivalent are processed as fast as Romani-derived verbs and that their Turkish-derived inflection does not incur additional processing cost. That differs from the processing of Turkish-derived verbs that do have Romani-derived counterparts. This would suggest that the established Turkish verbs are not part of an ongoing balancing act between pull factors, whereas those that are not established are. There is no suggestion that Turkish predicate grammar diffuses onto Romani verb stems; the synchronic picture in Thrace Romani is thus quite distinct from MLs, where there is in fact no etymological split within the predication grammar. In terms of the repertoire management model, Thrace Romani, like the incipient trend in Parakalamos Romani exemplified above, and that in several other Romani dialects, appears to show a far-reaching compromise between exhausting expressive potential, accommodation, and load reduction: Turkish lexical verbs extend expressive potential (and do not have an indigenous counterpart). They are accommodated into utterances that the setting and context define as Romani. Load reduction accompanies the process as it eliminates the need to select and inhibit features of finite verb inflection around these particular verbs. This gives rise to fusion among the two languages (Romani and Turkish) around predicate anchoring procedures for a particular class of lexical verbs. The hypothesis that Thrace Romani displays an interim stage that could lead onto the wholesale replacement of Romani-derived verbs (and their Romani inflection) by Turkish-derived verbs (and their Turkish-derived inflection) is intriguing, though no known Romani dialect in the region appears to have replaced all or even most of its Romani lexical verbs with Turkish-derived material.[7]

Where does this place Thrace Romani on the periphery between borrowing and MLs? What is exceptional here is the borrowing of a verb inflection paradigm, which, as I argued above, is not a typical outcome of borrowing (being the product of repertoire management strategies). On the other hand, in showing two distinct sources of predication grammar, and otherwise consistent transmission across generations of Romani core lexicon and grammatical features (including verb and nominal inflection, paradigms of personal and demonstrative pronouns, and so on), Thrace Romani certainly does not adhere to the ML prototype. I would therefore classify it as an exceptional case of borrowing, where, as described, pull factors interact in a unique way. My take on this uniqueness is that, rather than draw on the predication grammar of another language (here Turkish; and in the example above from Parakalamos Romani, Greek; and so on) for performative purposes, what appears to be in operation in these Romani communities is a relaxation of the pull factor which I termed

---

[7] However, it appears that Romani varieties that have lost contact with Turkish such as that of Ajia Varvara in Athens (Igla 1996) retain a smaller number of Turkish-inflected verbs than those where speakers have active knowledge of Turkish (cf. Adamou 2019, this volume). There might therefore be some evidence for a trajectory of both proportional increase and decrease of the number of Turkish verbs in Balkan Romani dialects.

above as accommodation: Adhering to the anchoring of predications in the heritage language is perceived as less of a must in displaying group membership. In that sense, we might regard Thrace Romani and similar cases as a less strict and more relaxed identity manifestation process (though thereby still a certain kind of meaningful identity act) than a positive and performative display of boundary construction.

6 Conclusion

The idea that code-mixing can have performative functions is well-established, from the conversation analytical approaches by Gumperz (1980) and Auer (1984), through to Poplack's (1980) notion of switching as a flagging of bilingual competence, Myers-Scotton's notion of marked choices in bilingual conversation, Maschler's (1994) discussion of the bonding effect of switching around meta-linguistic operators, Li Wei and Milroy's (1995) approach to language negotiation in conversation sequences, and more. While discussions of ML emergence have frequently referred to deliberate mixing and identity acts, as mentioned above, few if any have attempted to draw an explicit connection between language mixing as a performative act and the conventionalisation of mixed structures that defy predictions on conventional contact-induced change. In this chapter I have argued in favour of a performative origin of MLs. I proposed that performativity might be regarded as a super-imposed illocutionary dimension that can accompany the realisation of acts of speech and their inherent illocutions, be they assertions, directives, questions and so on. I also suggested that performativity can have an overarching effect on the management of resources within users' repertoire of linguistic features.

Users in multilingual settings are accustomed to carrying out selection and inhibition among the features that are at their disposal in a manner that is dynamic, creative and responsive to communicative contexts and situations. Such repertoire management operations are normally guided by a balancing act between three pull factors: accommodation to the expectations of the interaction context and interlocutor constellation, exhausting the expressive potential of the repertoire, and effective management of processing load. Repertoire management choices can be one-off or lead to a re-drawing of construed boundaries around sets of features within the repertoire. This results in what we perceive analytically as structural change in the profile of a labelled language. In reality that means a change in the way features from the repertoire are mapped onto communication routines. That is what we normally coin as 'borrowing', and I propose that we reserve that term for such processes. The nature of the pull factors involved, and the way they affect the inherent functional-communicative value of distinct linguistic features as triggers of mental processing operations, make the potential for re-alignment of repertoire components predictable to a considerable extent.

To be sure, other factors of a local nature play a role, and often a significant one, in prompting, or in hindering particular directions of change; such instances were named above, and other examples were recently discussed by Melissaropoulou and Ralli (2019). They tend to involve particular motivations such as formal analogies, taboos, and similar. But we can expect that unless constraining factors (such as institutional scripting) are at play, language users in multilingual settings will be inclined to re-draw construed language boundaries in particular ways, with recourse to a varied yet not unlimited set of possible pathways, such as a balance between matter and pattern replication around particular functional categories (Matras 2007, 2020). These may be among the pathways that Thomason (1995) had once described as "ordinary processes" while claiming that in the case of MLs they can lead to "extraordinary results". My argument in this chapter is that there are indeed ordinary processes, well attested empirically, but that those ordinary processes do not in fact lead to the extraordinary results that catch our attention in MLs (and therefore merit the explicit label as 'Mixed Languages'). Instead, the extraordinary results are the product of a distinct operation through which users combine features from their repertoire in a way that explicitly clashes with normal expectations of repertoire management strategies. They do so in order to achieve aesthetic, performative effects.

Performative acts stand out and thereby draw attention. They serve a rallying effect that is a demonstration of loyalty and shared norms that defy and contrast with expectations and established routines, especially those that are externally imposed. Such effects can be identified in single interactions among a pair of interlocutors, in social circles bonded by location, age, or profession, in virtual communities, in marginalised ethnic communities and in communities striving to maintain or establish a distinct cultural identity. Following LePage and Tabouret-Keller (1985) I take in this context an explicitly non-essentialist approach to 'community', regarding it as a bonding around shared practices (see also Blokland 2017; Bessant 2018; Brubaker and Cooper 2000). Multilingual performativity can become one of those practice routines around which new identities can be forged; it is a pathway toward new community formation, or in defence of an existing community that feels under threat. That is what allows performativity to be conventionalised, leading to the so-called extraordinary structures that we find in MLs. What has sometimes been referred to as the 'grammaticalisation' of casual mixing (or code-switching) giving rise to stable MLs is, in effect, the gradual neutralisation of the particular illocutionary effect of performative mixed utterances. In light of this, MLs are not counterexamples to borrowing, if we consider borrowing to be the outcomes of the ordinary processes that emerge through re-negotiation of practice routines guided by everyday pull factors. Indeed, their mere existence provides us with an insight into multilingual users' implicit awareness of the limits on language mixing in everyday communicative routines and their playful defiance of those limits for special effect or performativity.

The present volume is dedicated to what the editors identify in their introductory chapter (Mazzoli and Sippola) as core-periphery relations in the study of MLs. I take the liberty to interpret the core-periphery relationship as capturing two separate dimensions. Formally, we are dealing with a range of structural phenomena that strike us at first glance as exceptional among the pool of many cases of documented contact-induced changes. These include the high density of structural outcomes resulting from an array of different contacts in Wutun (Sandman) as well as the rare appearance of compartmentalisation in the structure of finite predication grammar in Thrace Romani (Adamou), while on the other hand phonetic and phonological processes in a number of MLs (Stewart and Meakins), word order variation in Media Lengua (Deibel), and verb derivation from nominal stems in Michif (Mazzoli, Bakker and DeMontigny) demonstrate that extraordinary outcomes, once stable, are equally subjected to ordinary processes of variation and change.

Functionally, we see a continuum of performative routines: From what may be an individual choice among a pair of interlocutors in correspondence (Sippola), though the use of a mixed casual style (Dudek Herring and Clements), onto conventionalised local preferences (Clements, Amaral and Garrett; Pecht) and ritual modes of speech (Hannß). My own examples presented above nicely match this continuum, showing one-off usage among a pair of interlocutors (child-parent interaction), a pool of lexical features used by a circle of local peers (villagers in the Black Forest), a stable lexical reservoir used by a minority community (Angloromani) and a single morphological feature marking out an online social network community (Chinese netizens). Their structural outcomes stand out as not conforming to the typical results of re-alignment of construed boundaries within the repertoire in non-performative communication routines.

The core definition of MLs might therefore be reserved for those idioms that are highly conventionalised, whose formation is best explained by taking into account the interactional perspective: MLs arise from performative acts that exploit the contrast between construed boundaries within the shared linguistic repertoire. They do so in a way that stands out, by targeting structural components and categories that are otherwise less likely to be subjected to the re-drawing of such boundaries. For that reason, they are 'extraordinary' outcomes of processes that are themselves 'extraordinary', albeit, obviously, humanly possible. But they owe their existence, in a sense, to the defiance of the processes that give rise to borrowing, and that is why they differ from ordinary borrowing.

Abbreviations

AI	animate intransitive
CNJ	conjunct order
COMP	complementiser
CONT	continuative
DAT	dative
F	feminine
IND	indicative
INDEF	indefinitie
LOAN	loan adaptation marker
LOC	locative
M	masculine
MULT	multiplicative
NEG	negation
OBL	oblique
PERF	perfective
PL	plural
POSS	possessive
PRED	predication marker
PRES	present
PRG	progressive
PST	past
REFL	reflexive
S, SG	singular
THE	theme
TOP	topic

References

Adamou Evangelia. 2010. Bilingual Speech and Language Ecology in Greek Thrace: Romani and Pomak in Contact with Turkish. *Language in Society* 39(2). 147–171.

Adamou Evangelia & Shen, Rachel X. 2019. There are no language switching costs when codeswitching is frequent. *International Journal of Bilingualism* 23(1). 53–70.

Auer, Peter. 1984. *Bilingual conversation*. Amsterdam: John Benjamins.

Auer, Peter. 1999. From Code-switching via Language Mixing to Fused Lects: Toward a dynamic typology of bilingual speech. *International Journal of Bilingualism* 3(4). 309–332.

Austin, John L. 1962. *How to do things with words*. London: Oxford University Press
Backus, Ad. 1996. *Two in one. Bilingual speech of Turkish immigrants in the Netherlands*. Tilburg: Tilburg University Press.
Backus, Ad. 2003. Can a mixed language be conventionalized alternational codeswitching? In Yaron Matras & Peter Bakker (eds.), *The mixed language debate: Theoretical and empirical advances*, 237–270. Berlin: Mouton de Gruyter.
Bakker, Peter. 1997. *A language of our own. The genesis of Michif, the mixed Cree-French language of the Canadian Métis*. Oxford: Oxford University Press.
Bessant, Kenneth C. 2018. *The relational fabric of community*. New York, NY: Palgrave Macmillan.
Bialystok, Ellen. 2015. Bilingualism and the development of executive function: The role of attention. *Child Development Perspectives* 9. 117–121.
Bialystok, Ellen, Fergus Craik, David Green & Tamar H. Gollan. 2009. Bilingual minds. *Psychological Science in the Public Interest* 10. 89–129.
Binchy, Alice. 1993. *Shelta: An historical and contemporary analysis*. Unpublished D.Phil thesis, University of Oxford.
Blokland, Talya. 2017. *Community as urban practice*. Cambridge, England: Polity Press.
Blommaert, Jan & Backus, Ad. 2013. Superdiverse repertoires and the individual. In Ingrid de Saint-Georges I. & Jean-Jacques Weber (eds.), *Multilingualism and multimodality. The future of education research*, 11–32. Rotterdam: Sense Publishers.
Brubaker, Rogers & Frederick Cooper, F. (2000). Beyond "identity". *Theory and Society* 29(1). 1–47.
Butler, Judith. 1990 [1999]. *Gender Trouble: feminism and the subversion of identity*. London: Routledge.
Butler, Judith. 2010. Performative agency. *Journal of Cultural Economy* 3:2. 147–161.
Campbell, Lyle 1993. On proposed universals of grammatical borrowing. In Henk Aertsen & R. J. Jeffers (eds.), *Historical linguistics* 1989, 91–109. Amsterdam: John Benjamins.
Croft, William. 2000. *Explaining language change: An evolutionary approach*. Harlow/Essex: Longman.
Croft, William. 2003. Mixed languages and acts of identity. An evolutionary approach. In Yaron Matras & Peter Bakker (eds.), *The mixed language debate: Theoretical and empirical advances*, 41–72. Berlin: Mouton de Gruyter.
Derrida, Jacques. 1988 [1972]. Signature, event, context. In *Limited Inc.*, translated by Samuel Weber and Jeffrey Mehlman, 1–23. Evanston: Northwestern University Press.
Elšík, Viktor & Matras, Yaron. 2006. *Markedness and language change: The Romani sample*. Berlin: Mouton de Gruyter.
Field, Frederic. W. 2002. *Linguistic borrowing in bilingual contexts*. Amsterdam: John Benjamins.
Freywald, Ulrike, Katharina Mayr, Tiner Özçelik & Heike Wiese. 2011. Kiezdeutsch as a multiethnolect. In Friederike Kern & Margret Selting (eds.), *Ethnic styles of speaking in european metropolitan areas*, 45–73. Amsterdam: John Benjamins.
Gardani, Francesco, Peter Arkadiev & Nino Amiridze. 2015. (eds.). *Borrowed morphology*. Berlin: Mouton de Gruyter.
Golovko, Evgenij V. 1996. A case of nongenetic development in the Arctic area: The contribution of Aleut and Russian to the formation of Copper Island Aleut. In Ernst H. Jahr, E. H. & Ingvild Broch (eds.), *Language contact in the Arctic: Northern pidgins and contact languages*, 63–77. Berlin: De Gruyter.

Golovko, Evgenij V. 2003. Language contact and group identity: The role of 'folk' linguistic engineering. In Yaron Matras & Peter Bakker (eds.), *The mixed language debate: Theoretical and empirical advances*, 177–207. Berlin: Mouton de Gruyter.

Green, David W. 1998. Mental control of the bilingual lexico-semantic system. *Bilingualism: Language and Cognition* 1, 67–81.

Grosjean, François. 2001. The bilingual's language modes. In: Janet L. Nicol, J. L. (ed.), *One mind, two languages. Bilingual language processing*, 1–22. Oxford: Blackwell.

Gumperz, John. 1980. *Discourse strategies*. Cambridge: Cambridge University Press.

Hancock, Ian F. 1992. The Social and Linguistic development of Scando-Romani. In Ernst H. Jahr (ed.), *Language contact: Theoretical and empirical studies*, 37–52. Berlin: Mouton de Gruyter.

Haspelmath, Martin & Tadmor, Uri (eds). 2009. *Loanwords in the world's languages. A comparative handbook*. Berlin: Mouton de Gruyter.

Heath, Jeffrey. 1984. Language contact and language change. *Annual Review of Anthropology* 13. 367–384.

Ho-Dac, Tuc. 2002. *Vietnamese-English bilingualism. Patterns of code-switching*. London: Routledge.

Igla, Birgit. 1996. *Das Romani von Ajia Varvara. Deskriptive und historisch-vergleichende Darstellung eines Zigeunerdialekts*. Wiesbaden: Harrassowitz.

Jørgensen, J. Normann. 2008. Polylingual Languaging around and among children and adolescents. *International Journal of Multilingualism* 5(3). 161–176.

LePage, Robert and Tabouret-Keller, Andrée. 1985. Acts of identity. Creole-Based Approaches to Language and Ethnicity. Cambridge: Cambridge University Press.

Levinson, Stephen C. 1983. *Pragmatics*. Cambridge: Cambridge University Press.

Li Wei 2018. Translanguaging as a practical theory of languages. *Applied Linguistics* 39(1). 9–30.

Li Wei and Milroy, Lesley. 1995. Conversational codeswitching in a Chinese community in Britain: A sequential analysis. *Journal of Pragmatics* 37. 375–389.

Maschler, Yael. 1994. Metalanguaging and discourse markers in bilingual conversation. *Language in Society* 23. 325–366.

Matras, Yaron. 1998. Utterance modifiers and universals of grammatical borrowing. *Linguistics* 36(2). 281–331.

Matras, Yaron. 2000a. Fusion and the cognitive basis for bilingual discourse markers. *International Journal of Bilingualism* 4(4). 505–528.

Matras, Yaron. 2000b. Mixed Languages. A functional-communicative approach. *Bilingualism: Language and Cognition* 3(2). 79–99.

Matras, Yaron. 2003. Mixed languages Re-examining the structural prototype. In Yaron Matras and Peter Bakker (eds.), *The mixed language debate: Theoretical and empirical advances*, 151–176. Berlin: Mouton de Gruyter.

Matras, Yaron. 2007. The borrowability of grammatical categories. In Yaron Matras & Jeanette Sakel (eds.), *Grammatical borrowing in cross-linguistic perspective*, 31–74. Berlin: Mouton de Gruyter.

Matras 2010. *Romani in Britain. The afterlife of a language*. Edinburgh: Edinburgh University Press.

Matras, Yaron. 2012. *A grammar of Domari*. Berlin: Mouton de Gruyter.

Matras, Yaron, 2015. Why is the borrowing of inflectional morphology dispreferred? In Francesco Gardani, Peter Arkadiev, & Nino Amiridze (eds.), *Borrowed morphology*, 47–80. Berlin: de Gruyter.

Matras, Yaron. 2020. *Language contact* [second edition]. Cambridge: Cambridge University Press.

Matras, Yaron & Bakker, Peter. 2003. The study of mixed languages. Yaron Matras and Peter Bakker (eds.), *The mixed language debate: Theoretical and empirical advances*, 1–20. Berlin: Mouton de Gruyter

Mazzoli, Maria. 2019. Michif loss and resistance in four Metis communities (Kahkiyaaw mashchineenaan, "All of us are disappearing as in a plague"). *Zeitschrift für Kanada-Studien* 69. 96–117.

McConvell, Patrick and Felicity Meakins. 2005 Gurindji Kriol: A mixed language emerges from code-switching. *Australian Journal of Linguistics* 25. 9–30.

Meakins, Felicity. 2011. *Case marking in contact: The development and function of case morphology in Gurindji Kriol*. Amsterdam: John Benjamins.

Melissaropoulou, Dimitra & Ralli, Angela. 2019. Revisiting the borrowability scale(s) of free grammatical elements: evidence from Modern Greek contact induced varieties. *Journal of Language Contact* 12. 707–736.

Moravcsik, Edith. 1978. Universals of language contact. In Joseph H. Greenberg (ed.), *Universals of human language*, 94–122. Stanford: Stanford University Press.

Mous, Maarten. 2003. *The making of a Mixed Language: The Case of Ma'a/Mbugu*. Amsterdam: John Benjamins.

Mufwene, S. S. 2013. The origins and the evolution of language. In Keith Allan (ed.), *The Oxford handbook of the history of linguistics*, 13–52. Oxford University Press:

Myers-Scotton, Carol 1993. *Duelling languages. Grammatical structure in codeswitching*. Oxford: Oxford University Press.

Myers-Scotton, Carol. 1998. A Way to Dusty Death: The Matrix Language Turnover hypothesis. In Lenore Grenoble & Lindsay J. Whaley (eds.), *Endangered languages: Language loss and community response*, 289–316. Cambridge: Cambridge University Press.

Myers-Scotton, Carol. 2003. What lies beneath. Split (mixed) languages as contact phenomena. In Yaron Matras & Peter Bakker (eds.), *The mixed language debate: Theoretical and empirical advances*, 73–106. Berlin: Mouton De Gruyter.

O'Shannesssy, Carmel. 2020. Mixed Languages. In Evangelia Adamou & Yaron Matras (eds.), *The Routledge handbook of language contact*, 325–348. London: Routledge.

Otsuka, Hitomi, Thomas Stolz, Aina Urdze, & Martine Vanhove (eds.). 2012. *Morphologies in contact*. Berlin: Akademie.

Pakendorf, Brigitte. 2015. *A comparison of copied morphemes in Sakha (Yakut) and Éven*. In Franceso Gardani, Peter Arkadieve & Nino Amiridze (eds.), Borrowed morphology, 157–187. Berlin: de Gruyter Mouton.

Peng, Qiu Hui 2016: Intertwining Chinese words and English –ing. Unpublished manuscript. The University of Manchester.

Pennycook, Alistair, & Otsuji, Emi. 2015. *Metrolingualism: Language in the city*. London: Routledge.

Poplack, Shana. 1980. Sometimes I'll start a sentence in Spanish y termino en español. *Linguistics* 18. 581–618.

Rasenberg, Marlou, Rommers, Joost and van Bergen, Geertje. 2020. Anticipating predictability: an ERP investigation of expectation-managing discourse markers in dialogue comprehension. *Language, Cognition and Neuroscience* 35(1). 1–16.

Sasse, Hans-Jürgen. 1992. Theory of language death. In Mathias Brenzinger (ed.) *Language death: Factual and theoretical explorations with special references to East Africa*, 7–30. Berlin: De Gruyter.

Seifart, Frank. 2017. Patterns of affix borrowing in a sample of 100 languages. *Journal of Historical Linguistics* 7:3. 389–431.

Smith, Norval. 1995. An annotated list of creoles, pidgins, and mixed languages. In: Jacques Arends, J., Pieter Muysken & Norval Smith (eds.), *Pidgins and creoles. An introduction*, 331–374. Amsterdam: John Benjamins.

Stolz, Christel & Thomas Stolz 1996. Funktionswortentlehnung in Mesoamerika. Spanisch-amerindischer Sprachkontakt Hispanoindiana II. *Sprachtypologie und Universalienforschung* 49. 86–123.

Tadmor, Uri. 2004. Function loanwords in Malay-Indonesian (and some other Southeast Asian languages). Paper presented at the Loan Word Typology Workshop, Max-Planck-Institute for Evolutionary Anthropology, Leipzig, 1–2 May 2004.

Thomason, Sarah G. 1995. Language mixture: ordinary processes, extraordinary results. In Carmen Silva-Corvalán (ed.), *Spanish in four continents: studies in language contact and bilingualism*, 15–33. Washington, DC: Georgetown University Press.

Thomason, Sarah G. 2001. *Language contact. An introduction*. Edinburgh: Edinburgh University Press.

Thomason, Sarah G. 2007. Language contact and deliberate change. *Journal of Language Contact* 1(1). 41–62.

Thomason, Sarah G. 2015. When is the diffusion of inflectional morphology not d spreferred? In Franceso Gardani, Peter Arkadieve & Nino Amiridze (eds.), *Borrowed morphology*, 27–46. Berlin: de Gruyter Mouton.

Thomason, Sarah G. & Daniel L. Everett. 2001. Pronoun borrowing. In Chang, Ch. et al. (ecs.), *Proceedings of the twenty seventh annual meeting of the Berkeley Linguistics Society*, 301–315. Berkeley: Berkeley Linguistics Society.

Thomason, Sarah G. & Terrence Kaufman. 1988. *Language contact, creolization, and genetic linguistics*. Berkeley: University of California Press.

Velupillai, Viveka. 2015. *Pidgins, creoles and mixed languages. an introduction*. Amsterdam: John Benjamins.

Wallace, S. 1983. Pronouns in contact. In Frederic B. Agard, Gerald Kelley, Adam Makkai & Valerie Becker Makkai (eds.), *Essays in honor of Charles F. Hockett*, 573–589. Berlin: Mouton de Gruyter.

Walworth, Mary. 2017. Rea Rapa: A Polynesian contact language. *Journal of Language Contact* 10. 98–141.

Whitney, W. D. 1881. On mixture in language. *Transactions of the American Philological Association (1869–1896)*, 1–26.

Wiese, Heike. 2009. Grammatical innovation in multiethnic urban Europe: New linguistic practices among adolescents. *Lingua* 119. 782–806.

Williams-Van Klinken, Catharina & John Hajek. 2018. Mixing numeral systems in Timor-Leste. In Antoinette Schapper (ed.), *Contact and substrate in the languages of Wallacea Part 2*, 65–94. NUSA.

Subject Index

act of identity 47, 382, 385, 393
Amdo Sprachbund 326

bilingualism 19, 103, 158, 248, 255, 260, 266, 290, 327, 365
borrowing 1–2, 11, 16, 111, 148, 150, 254–255, 362, 380
– constraints 10, 150, 370
– heavy 3, 9, 16, 255, 272, 369
– structural 1, 5, 8, 10, 16, 73, 362, 365, 368, 370

classification 4, 21, 28–30, 255–256
– genetic 1–2
– sociohistorical 3, 7
– structural 4, 7
code-mixing 1, 95, 229, 255–256
code-switching 4, 6, 10, 48, 58, 94, 96–97, 111, 229, 254–256, 300
cognitive factor 87, 99, 160
conventionalization 19–20, 94, 113, 289, 363, 392
convergence 9, 58, 60, 318, 372
converted language 9, 30, 60

degree of mixing 257, 267
deictic category. See personal pronoun, See demonstrative
demonstrative 12, 33, 35, 39, 51, 146, 265, 288, 310, 312, 331, 342, 372
determiner 12, 148, 232, 285, 291–292, 301

finite verb inflection 3, 11–12, 15, 32, 48, 101, 114
fused lect 93, 95, 105–106, 113

Grammar-Lexicon mixed language 4, 12, 330
Grammar-Lexicon split 4, 330
– in Angloromani 18, 29

identity 2, 228, 232, 249, 255, 318, 328, 383, 393, 397
immigrant 46, 300, 393

lack of tone 335
language maintenance 12, 20, 95, 249, 278
language shift 3, 95, 104, 256, 271, 329
lexical manipulation 5, 10, 15, 198

matrix language 11–12, 48, 94
mestizo 258, 260, 279
mixed language formation 11, 114, 393
– Barranquenho 231, 249
– Media Lengua 158
– mixing processes 10
– performativity 390
– social factors 12, 18, 255
– Wutun 327
mixed language phonology 15, 57–58, 61
mixed marriage 2, 6, 18, 230, 232, 284, 288, 327

negation 15
– in Kallawaya 205
– in Mednyj Aleut 33
– in Wutun 332
nomadic population 2, 361, 377
nomadic variety 7
nominal inflection 12, 17, 32
Noun-Verb mixed language 6, 12, 15, 27, 30, 51, 330
Noun-Verb split 5, 8

performative (speech) act 382, 397
performativity 383, 392–393
– aesthetic aspect 391, 397
personal pronoun 15, 32, 39, 51, 122, 259, 312, 319
phonemic conflict site 58, 63
phonological manipulation 208, 211, 213
processing cost 106, 110, 162

repertoire 3, 103, 268, 363
repertoire management 363, 375

secret language 7, 19, 190, 198
stability 18, 254, 299

typologically rare mixing 17–18, 99, 103, 123, 149

variation 20, 192
– in Jopara 294
– language choice 109
– pronouns 315
– word order 157, 161, 181

word order 12, 15, 100, 157
– in Media Lengua 159
– in Okrika Igbo 40
– in Romani-Turkish 100
word-internal mixing 121, 142, 149–150

Language Index

Aleut 17, 32, 60
Angloromani 4, 17, 19, 29–30, 38, 271, 378–379
Aymara 190

Barranquenho 9, 225, 231–232, 249, 392
Belgian Dutch 300, 302
Bilingual Navajo 3, 8

Callahuaya. *See* Kallawaya
Caló Català 7, 10
Chamorro 3, 9
Chindo 8
Cité Duits 18, 299–319

Domari 368–9, 371

English 7, 25, 29, 34, 36, 77, 136, 257, 260–261, 269
– Aboriginal English 34–35
– Australian English 81
– Creole English 35

Finnish 13, 102
Finnish Romani 102
French 46, 49, 60, 124, 151
– Canadian French 82–83
– Metis French 6, 122
– Nova Scotia Acadian French 367

German 24–25, 31–32, 299, 305, 388
Greek 100
Guarani 40, 277, 279–281, 286, 288
Guarani Criollo. *See* Jopara
Gurindji 6, 34, 62, 73–74
Gurindji Kriol 1, 5, 8, 16–17, 20, 29, 31, 73, 81, 95, 101
Gurindji-Kriol. *See* Gurindji Kriol

Hubner Mischsprache 31–32, 45–46

Igbo 38–40, 49
Ilokano 253, 264–267, 269–270

Javindo 8, 15
Jopara 277, 281–294, 394

Kallawaya 3, 10, 189–216
Kitchen Spanish 259
Korlai Indo-Portuguese 17, 150
Kriol 31, 33–34, 48, 77

Lekoudesch 388–389
Light Warlpiri 1, 8, 20, 34, 101

Ma'a/Ma'á 4, 17, 19, 271
Maasai 5
Modern Guarani. *See* Jopara
Mandarin 326, 331–332, 336, 339
Marathi 17, 150
Media Lengua 5, 29, 63, 67, 70, 157–158, 170, 271
Mednyj Aleut 29, 32–33, 45–46, 60, 380
Michif 6, 8, 16, 20, 29, 35, 46, 60, 81, 121–123, 149
Mongolic languages 325, 349

Navajo 8
New Tiwi 8, 35, 37

Okrika 38–39
Okrika Igbo 3, 9, 46
Okrika-Igbo. *See* Ogrika Igbo
Old Helsinki Slang 7
Oschideutsch 7

Pare 5, 17
Peranakan Chinese 8
Petjo 8
Plains Cree 6, 83, 122–123, 143
Portuguese 9, 19, 225, 227
Pukina 191, 193–194, 196–197, 200

Quechua 63, 163–164, 190, 193
– Southern Quechua 193–194

Reo Rapa 8
Romani 11, 93, 95, 102
Romani-Turkish 100–102, 104
Russian 17, 32, 102

Shelta 7, 198, 387
Spanish 5, 63, 66, 163, 225, 257–259, 277, 279
Spanish Romani 283
Sri Lanka Malay 30
Sri Lanka Portuguese 9, 60

Tagalog 255, 261, 265, 267, 269
Takia 9
Tetun Dili 9, 19
Tibetic languages 329
Tiwi 46
Turkish 100, 102

Warlpiri 34
Wutun 9, 325–355

www.ingramcontent.com/pod-product-compliance
Lightning Source LLC
Chambersburg PA
CBHW051534230426
43669CB00015B/2595